NINETEENTH-CENTURY ENGLISH LABOURING-CLASS POETS
1800–1900

VOLUME I
1800–1830

General Editor: John Goodridge
Volume Editors: Scott McEathron (1800–1830)
Kaye Kossick (1830–1860)
John Goodridge (1860–1900)

NINETEENTH-CENTURY ENGLISH LABOURING-CLASS POETS 1800–1900

VOLUME I
1800–1830

Edited by
Scott McEathron

LONDON
PICKERING & CHATTO
2006

Published by Pickering & Chatto (Publishers) Limited
21 Bloomsbury Way, London WC1A 2TH

2252 Ridge Road, Brookfield, Vermont 05036-9704, USA
www.pickeringchatto.com

BRITISH LIBRARY CATALOGUING IN PUBLICATION DATA
Nineteenth-century English labouring-class poets
    1.English poetry - 19th century
    I.Goodridge, John
    821.8'08'0920623

ISBN-10: 185196763X

This publication is printed on acid-free paper that conforms to the
American National Standard for the Permanence of Paper for Printed Library Materials

Typeset by P&C

Printed in the United Kingdom at
the University Press, Cambridge

CONTENTS OF VOLUME I

ACKNOWLEDGEMENTS

It is a great pleasure at last to be able to express my thanks and appreciation to the many individuals and institutions who have aided in the production of this volume. I am grateful, for favours large and small, to all of my colleagues on the Labouring-Class Poets project: John Goodridge, David Fairer, Simon Kövesi, William Christmas, Bridget Keegan, Tim Burke, and Kaye Kossick. Special additional thanks are owed to Bridget Keegan, for her initiation of the entire project, and for her tireless work in support of the series long after her own volume was in print. Particular thanks are also due to Katie Wales, George Collins, Matt McKinney, Sheila Hardy, Dennis Read, April London, Judy Theobald, Ruth Tinley, Veronica Wallace, and Doug Moore. The initial stages of research on this volume were greatly aided by a grant from the Office of Research Development and Administration at my home institution, Southern Illinois University Carbondale.

I received generous assistance from the staffs of many libraries, including the National Library of Scotland; the Houghton and Widener Libraries of Harvard University; the British Library; the Haddington Library, East Lothian; the Bailey-Howe Library, University of Vermont; the Shields Library, University of California, Davis; and the Washington University Library, St. Louis. Several historical societies also provided me timely assistance, including the Bradford Historical and Antiquarian Society and the Dorset Natural History and Archaeological Society. I would also like to offer deep thanks to Debbie Cordts, Tammy Winter, Loretta Koch, and David Bond of SIUC's Morris Library.

For permission to reproduce manuscript sources, I wish to thank the following: the Houghton Library, Harvard University, for George Bloomfield's 'The Poets at Odds'; and the Trustees of the National Library of Scotland, for Mary Bryan's 'The Village Maid' and 'Stanzas'. The image reproduced as the frontispiece to this volume appears with the kind permission of the Trustees of the National Library of Scotland.

This volume is dedicated to Anne Chandler, without whom it would have been perfectly impossible.

GENERAL INTRODUCTION

These three volumes make up a second series of labouring-class poets: those who published in the English language and its dialect variants during the nineteenth century. If it was a challenge to represent fairly the range of eighteenth-century labouring-class poetry in the first series, then that challenge is magnified many times here, for, as the database of labouring-class poets which we have assembled alongside these two series clearly shows, there was an enormous increase in the publication of such poetry after 1800. I would therefore begin by stating plainly that we could not have represented fully the myriad traditions and sub-traditions that developed in the labouring-class poetry of the nineteenth century. Instead we have attempted to highlight the more significant trends and topics, and some of the interesting and talented individuals who emerged in this key period, particularly those who have been neglected even by recent recovery research. Doing this has made us learn habits of thrift, as where we offer 'headnote only' entries for figures like Clare and Hogg (Vol. I), for whom excellent modern editions exist, or offer severely limited selections for figures like Ben Brierley and William McGonagall (Vol. III), who have continued to draw specialist attention or have been substantially reprinted. On the other hand, we have benefited from the far greater range of critical studies and resources that exist for labouring-class poetry of the nineteenth century, so that we are able to point to a strong selection of 'Further Reading' materials for most of the poets represented in this second series. A starting point for this series has been the work of pioneering scholars like Martha Vicinus, Brian Maidment and Florence Boos, and we hope that our collection will in turn help to pave the way for further and more detailed studies on many of these poets and their works.

The nineteenth century saw the first serious attempts to 'place' the labouring-class poets, critically and socially. Their emergence had been noted as a social phenomenon in the eighteenth century, and we have the evidence of comments, usually hostile or satirical, by individuals from Pope and Swift to Johnson and Walpole. We can also see in Joseph Spence's writings on Duck, evidence of the way in which labouring-class poetry was positively cultivated as a form of 'natural genius'. What E. P. Thompson called 'competitive patronage' is also evident in Duck's story, as the Queen and others used him to further their own political-cultural agendas. Different perspectives are offered by many of the authors themselves—from Mary Leapor imagining how a 'scribbling maid' might be perceived in the drawing room, or by other maids; from Ann Yearsley's compelling account of a raw battle with her patron over financial independence; or from many other autobiographical or quasi-autobiographical statements, often prefacing volumes of poetry, and often ritually apologising for their authors' humble backgrounds and lack of formal education.

The first systematic account of labouring-class poetry was published in 1831. Robert Southey's *Lives and Works of the Uneducated Poets* is ostensibly an extended introduction to a volume of labouring-class poetry produced under his patronage, but it develops into a more full-scale study, and certainly has a cultural agenda. It locates the emergence of the 'uneducated' tradition in the seventeenth century, and interestingly sees this tradition as being more-or-less at an end, owing to increased educational and social opportunities. Southey, by now the Poet Laureate and an establishment figure, sees the tradition as being worthy of support largely for social rather than poetical reasons. He pointedly excludes Robert Bloomfield (q.v., Vol. I) from his survey, for example, because he regarded him as a highly talented and under-regarded poet who should not be bracketed with 'deserving' but, implicitly, meagrely talented figures such as the one whose volume his disquisition prefaces (John Jones, q.v., Vol. II). To see the labouring-class poets as deserving support, however delimited this may be by the ideology of charity, is clearly an advance on the predominant eighteenth-century attitudes. It is certainly preferable to Horace Walpole's cruel allegation that Duck's success deluded numbers of honest workers into starvation; or Samuel Johnson's belief that it simply did not make sense for an uneducated worker to write poetry when they could be making shoes or carrying out some other useful task for which they were better suited; or even Joseph Spence's earnest pursuit of the rare butterfly of natural genius.

Southey, then, established the orthodox nineteenth-century view of labouring-class poets as deserving charitable rather than literary support. As the century progressed this 'deservingness' would become linked to the ideal of the 'self-made man', a figure seen as emerging from a condition of poverty or disadvantage, through his own efforts, into literary, military or political eminence. Such popular and frequently reprinted works as Samuel Smiles's *Self Help* (1859), and Edwin Paxton Hood's *The Literature of Labour* (1851, expanded as *The Peerage of Poverty*, fifth edition and final form, 1870), set the tone for public understanding of this 'deserving' figure. Some of the labouring-class poets of the nineteenth century were able to find a role for themselves within this model of laudable self-improvement, or at least to accommodate it as an element within their own self-presentations. But the frustrations felt by many at having to be presented to the world as models of humble self-improvement are also apparent, and are well represented by Ebenezer Elliott's (q.v. Vol. I) angry retort to some of the critical responses to his popular *Corn-Law Rhymes* (1831): 'Must I then conclude, that I owe the notice which has been taken of the Corn-Law Rhymes, to the supposition that they are the work of a mechanic?' (cited in Louis James, *Fiction for the Working Man* (1963), p. 174).

However, the period offered other avenues, and whilst the many volumes of poetry which are the principal sources for the present collection tend to show evidence of censorship (or more usually, self-censorship), the burgeoning print culture of newspapers and periodicals offered a less restricted forum for labouring-class poets – one, furthermore, which could bring them to a very wide audience indeed. The enormous growth in print culture had many causes and aspects, but two are particularly relevant here: the intense political activities of the nineteenth century, and the growth of municipal and regional literary cultures, the phenomena of local pride and local interest, which an astute self-taught poet could address and thus be seen to represent.

The complexities of nineteenth-century politics cannot be summarised here (the volume chronologies may be helpful in this, however). The French Revolution of 1789 heralded a period of intense worldwide radicalisation and political awakening, and one element of this in the early nineteenth century was the emergence of a distinctive proletarian literary culture. In terms of labouring-class poetry, this reached its height in the Chartist movement, which had its own newspapers, novelists, poets and dramatists, and established a literary culture whose echoes continue to reverberate today in anthologies and reprints, conferences and scholarly exegesis. (The relationship between labouring-class poetry and that other great post-French Revolutionary movement, Romanticism, is dealt with in the Editor's Introduction to the first volume, below.)

The growth of regional cultures is almost as complex a story as that of the nineteenth-century political movements, but again one can point to a general trend, which is the dramatic growth in the apparatus of local culture, particularly periodicals and newspapers. For labouring-class poets this was often vital. Newspapers and periodicals provided swift and instant connection to a potentially vast readership, locally and in some cases regionally or nationally. A poet who could find a way to tap in to topical themes from local and regional culture, like Samuel Laycock through his Lancashire Cotton Famine Lyrics of the early 1860s (q.v., Vol. III), could become enormously successful. In the industrial cities of northern England and

Scotland there was a great hunger for dialect poetry and for the poetry of location and labour. Nineteenth-century Scotland, amazingly, given its proportionally small population, actually produced *more* published labouring-class poets in the period than England, perhaps because of the consolatory sense of national pride and cultural continuity these poets seemed to offer during the terrible upheavals of land clearance and mass emigration.

I briefly discussed our use of the terms 'English' and 'Labouring-class poets' in the General Introduction to the first series. It may be appropriate to add that our aim has not been to delimit or conclusively to define these poets whom we have so enjoyed discovering, nor even to give them what someone once called the 'decent burial' of a complete scholarly edition, but rather to extend the horizons of our understanding of what was one of the most vital movements in nineteenth-century literary culture.

John Goodridge
Nottingham Trent University

INTRODUCTION

The poetry collected in this volume complicates any putatively smooth narrative of the labouring-class tradition in the early years of the nineteenth century. The most obvious literary-historical markers—the extraordinary sales of Robert Bloomfield's *The Farmer's Boy*, the emergence of James Hogg as a viable successor to the 'Heaven-taught Ploughman' Robert Burns, and the flourishing of John Clare—rightly indicate a growing pool of authors, a resilient if not quite tireless readership, and the first real softening of perceived categorical distinctions between the works of the belletristic establishment and the 'curiosities' of labouring-class writers. But this collection also reveals that, whatever the receptivity of the literary climate, the success of individual publications and indeed entire careers remained very much a hit-or-miss venture, even for energetic and distinctive writers blessed with adroit patrons. If the possibility of publishing verse was more real than it had ever been, the possibilities of financial security and critical acceptance remained highly doubtful.

Writing halfway through this period in his 1815 'Essay, Supplementary to the Preface' of *Lyrical Ballads*, William Wordsworth maintained that 'every author, as far as he is great and at the same time *original*, has...the task of *creating* the taste by which he is to be enjoyed'.[1] For the aspiring labouring-class poet, such a dictum encapsulated a real dilemma: was the better strategy actually to attempt the 'creation' of such an individuated taste, or was it wiser simply to hope that continuing public interest in 'self-taught' and 'plebeian' poets was a sufficient stand-in for the kind of originality Wordsworth envisaged? It is easy instinctively to assume that this question was moot for most labouring-class poets—that the High Romantic precepts of 'greatness' and 'originality' did not apply to their brand of verse, which generally was published by subscription, and for avowedly charitable purposes. But in fact, the successes of Burns and Bloomfield in the years between 1785 and 1800 had changed the equation considerably for the figures who came after them, raising the possibility that, just as eighteenth-century genius theorists like Hugh Blair and Edward Young had insisted, the growth of literary originality was a fundamentally organic process, perfectly suited to the conditions of the British countryside. And if, as Wordsworth said about himself, many of the poets collected in this volume 'never cared a straw about the theory' behind pastoral and rustic verse,[2] it is nonetheless true that in practice their poems reveal both a definite awareness of the literary tradition by which they were to be understood, and divergent ideas as to how and whether their demographic situations could serve the production and dissemination of their work.

Therefore, while it would be easy to conceptualize the poetry of this volume as a constellation of major themes and touchstones—patriotism and piety; anxiety over the fate of the countryside; the enticements and torments of plebeian authorship; the black cloud of the Napoleonic Wars—it is perhaps more important to underscore the collection's discontinuities. For behind conventional pastoral and historical subjects, we find here a strong drive, voiced by some poets and implied by others, to make one's own way. This is not to say that the period 1800–1830 exhibits the burgeoning diversity of voice and subject that accompanies the development of labouring-class verse in the Victorian period. But the beginnings of that diversity are clearly here. Partly this is because the writers of this period had before them an accessible and varied array of literary antecedents and potential models. James Thomson and William Cowper, the authors of *The Seasons* and *The Task*, are, as might be expected, strong presences. Their treatments of the British countryside were at once emotionally rich and politically unimpeachable; Romantic-era plebeian poets turned to them most often to set a tone of pastoral nostalgia or national pride. Wordsworth's own influence is also evident, though only Mary Bryan explicitly credits him with advancing a new poetics of low and rustic life; Ebenezer Elliott's praise for 'Wordsworth, whose thoughts acquaint us with our own'[3] is more typical, indicating a diffusion of Wordsworthian ideals in his own and others' work.

The most palpable influences on the present collection, however, are Burns, Bloomfield, and, to a lesser but still significant extent, Byron. It is a telling list, for what contemporary audiences tended to prize in these figures was not a particular style, or a theory of selfhood, but a vivid poetic enactment of personality. Burns had died in 1796, and the almost universal rapture that accompanied his verse was still very much in the air—perhaps too much so, as William Smith, 'The Haddington Cobbler', complains in his poem 'The Poet's Plea' (1821). Offering a catalogue of the various impulses that motivate authors (including moral instruction, personal vindication, and the quest for 'place', 'pension', or 'post'), Smith sees such an ocean of Burns imitators that they merit a category of their own: '[S]cribblers too, their name's my very scorn, / Ignobly bred, if not ignobly born, / Who vainly boast their songs do equal Burns' (ll. 42; 45–7). The reader will find several direct mentions of Burns in this collection, in poems or remarks by Thomas

Wilson, John Shaw, Ebenezer Elliott, and John Mitford, and many others could easily have been included. The cult of Burns was complemented by the more modest one inspired by Bloomfield, whose alter ego Giles in *The Farmer's Boy* (1800) is as reverent, thoughtful, and altogether distinct from Burns as Bloomfield himself apparently was. That people found Bloomfield's poetic company congenial is spelt out both in the runaway initial success of that debut volume, which went through fourteen British editions by 1820, and in its continued sales in Britain and America throughout the nineteenth century.[4] Because the importance of *The Farmer's Boy* was so nearly axiomatic for Bloomfield's own time, a conscious effort has been made in this volume to shed light on the network of literary figures surrounding him: his brothers Nathaniel and George, the indefatigable promoter Capel Lofft, and the admirer William Holloway. Byron's role in this literary milieu may at first glance seem bewildering, given his contemptuous references to Lofft and the Bloomfields in *English Bards and Scotch Reviewers*. Yet, perhaps partly because of his avowed hostility, he served several of these figures as a force to grapple with, to imitate, and sometimes to impersonate. Further, the aggressive self-indulgence of his verse, especially *Don Juan* but including *Childe Harold's Pilgrimage*, seems to have suggested a new avenue of artistic empowerment, and his influence is clear (and often announced) in the vein of wit, satire, and iconoclasm that runs through the present collection.

When we proceed to the subtler issue of what each poet did with these influences—if not always directly, then as diverse models of what the reading public desired—we find a fascinating realm of negotiation. Though Burns, Bloomfield, and Byron could each could be imagined as embodying a ready-made artistic type—the joyous, flawed recorder of human foibles, the earnest and dutiful Christian, the misanthropic genius—their would-be followers and colleagues resist any simple model of literary indebtedness. More than any single paradigm of artistic process, voice, or subject-matter, what labouring-class poets of the period found galvanizing in these three figures was their core commitment to self-expression—which, when successful, seemed to allow for the temporary suspension of presumptive critical strictures. To frame the matter this way is of course to suggest a paradox that we particularly associate with the Romantic era's exciting but risky premium on the public exhibition of individual subjectivity. The appeal of this kind of display is reflected in the remarks of John Shaw, a Liverpool brewer whose collection *Woolton Green* appeared twenty-five years after *The Farmer's Boy*. Introducing his own poetry by recounting the tears he shed over Bloomfield's, Shaw quickly strikes out on his own, declaring that 'There is not one in ten of the British poets, that I have ever seen, and not one in twenty that I have ever read', and adding that his work has been guided by 'the observations of a great Author, who asserts, "that if you feel your own writing, you cannot fail creating sympathy in your readers"'.[5] It is not clear what is behind Shaw's reluctance to name the 'great Author' he has in mind, and perhaps he simply mistrusted his own memory about where he had seen this Horatian adage, which had fairly wide currency in eighteenth-century fiction and rhetoric.[6] The important point, though, is that all of Shaw's linked statements move him away from particular poets, and toward the larger idea of poetic communication based on the integrity of individual utterance. So, as much as Shaw feared 'Argus-eyed, fastidious' critics,[7] they are under this model irrelevant; and in fact he is voicing a Romantic principle of self-authorization *through* originality that would change the face of literary criticism itself. Indeed, almost to a person, the poets represented in this volume seem to view literary tradition as something presently in the making, and as something that might as well include themselves.

Yet claims of pervasive artistic freedom, or of parallel opportunities for economic 'independence', must not be overstated. Caution in self-presentation was still absolutely essential, though sometimes it was delivered through gritted teeth: 'Pride in the garb of humility, is detestable', wrote Smith in his *A Collection of Original Poems* (1821), 'but I would not be doing myself justice, were I not to mention that the Manuscript was read by many persons of respectability, who, taking into view the difficulties under which the author laboured, unanimously approved of the production'.[8] More pointedly, we must also guard against the hopeful assumption that the people behind the poetry were being fed, clothed, or nurtured by it. Every poet did have a story, and more often than not it was one of considerable suffering. Readers already familiar with the harrowing life of John Clare may encounter here narratives they have not seen, such as those of Smith, Anne Candler, James Chambers, and Charlotte Richardson, all of whom were trying, with different degrees of success, simply to stay out of the workhouse. We see in their histories, as in Clare's, that the publication of original verse could be at once the best hope of material salvation, and a very flimsy buffer against the relentless demographic forces leading to destitution, ill-health, and domestic strife. Even for someone like Robert Millhouse, who through the aid of several patrons and the Royal Literary Fund was able to publish several volumes, there was never permanent financial relief. When he died at the age of fifty-one, a doctor reporting to the Royal Literary Fund was enough struck by the totality of Millhouse's hardships to report basic 'poverty' as the root cause of his continuing fevers and final illness. The memoir of Anne Candler, the only extended piece of prose contained in this volume, methodically shows every link in the chain of circumstances that entrapped her, and every moment at which some outside agent brought temporary release. Her poetry, meanwhile, reflects the dilemma undoubtedly felt by many of her colleagues, of just how far one should go in 'feel[ing] your own writing' when it came to raw personal pain. Her own tendency is to reach outward to universal human emotions, through Biblical allusion and allegory; the results are often quite moving, and yet they deliberately leave out many particulars handled in the prose account—almost as if Candler saw the two modes of writing as operating according to different rules.

It is not surprising that the figures who faced the greatest destitution tend to be the most fervent in declarations of, and reliance upon, their Christian faith. But prayers of supplication, musings upon salvation and eternity, and testimonials to divine benevolence are strong elements throughout this volume. For Candler, Millhouse, Chambers, and Charlotte Richardson, they are thematic and formal mainstays of the poetry; for others, such as Ebenezer Elliott and John Mitford, they serve more often to underscore a sense of social outrage and injustice. Essentially all of the writers here are Christians, though of different dispositions—and it should be noted that in the aggregate there are fewer religious poems in this volume than there would have been if a strict rule of proportionality had guided selection. Readers will also notice a robust showing of moral-didactic verse harking back to the mid-eighteenth century, with many apostrophes to Virtue and Wisdom, Ambition and Pride, cruel Want and dire Penury. Order itself—natural, divine, social—is still a cherished, though increasingly elusive value for many of these figures.

In the midst of such abstractions, one also finds highly specific references to the war with France and its domestic fallout: the political issue about which feelings run highest in this collection. Even William Holloway, usually studious of moderation through allegorical distance, names the war directly as the proximate cause for a welter of social problems, including hunger, human displacement, the emptying of the countryside, and the fragmentation of families. Once again, though, political allegiances are far from simple. Expressions of patriotic and nationalistic fervour often go hand-in-hand with laments over government policy, and the poetry is full of appeals to England as sanctified home, regardless of who is running the government. Indeed, the political tenor of much of the poetry seems to confirm Robert Bloomfield's late remark, made in reference to his supposed sympathies with radical thinkers: 'Fools, cannot they see that the form of Government of a Country is rather different to the administration?'[9] The poet who seeks most ostentatiously to transcend contemporary politics is Bloomfield's brother Nathaniel, though even in his case it is the violence of the Napoleonic Wars that is the prime impetus for the verse. Napoleon himself is a bogey for several of the writers here, particularly for Robert Franklin and the naval veteran John Mitford. For the agriculturalist Thomas Batchelor, the 'state of Europe…is, as it were, but a larger parish'; and thus he sees that the 'spirit of ambition actuating a Louis le Grand and a Bonaparte', reprehensible on its own terms, has also boomeranged back to rural England in the form of avarice, petty greed, and especially monopolistic enclosure. And even as Batchelor declares his advocacy of 'the cause of the lower classes of the community', he notes that the 'same encroaching and restless spirit, which regards *self* as paramount to every other consideration' is 'often as busy under a clay-built shed as in any other place'.[10]

At this point it is important to say something about selection criteria for this volume. The years 1800–1830 produced many more labouring-class poets than are represented here, and it would not have been difficult to double the number of poets included. The temptation to discuss as many writers as possible was a strong one, but ultimately it seemed more useful to strive for some depth in presentation. The labouring-class tradition has always suffered from a kind of rubber-necking on the part of critics and anthologists, who have noted the writers' dismal lives, made brief gestures toward a distinctive poem or two, and moved on. This volume can hardly be said to have righted the wrong, but it was an awareness of the problem that led me to include multiple poems wherever practicable, with the goal of conveying a reliable picture of the range and character of a given poet's work. It is also the case that I have gravitated consciously towards the obscure and difficult to obtain. Even though electronic resources are unearthing neglected texts and making them available at a dizzying rate, several of the texts excerpted here have survived in such small quantities that they are beyond the convenient reach of most readers and scholars. The vast majority of these texts were published in only a single edition and, relatedly, most have received little or no scholarly treatment. Indeed, the process of judging the work of these figures, and of locating them within literary history, has scarcely begun. Thus in the editorial introductions to these poets it has been my deliberate aim to provide some sense of how their work operates stylistically, and how the tides and phases of a given career might offer suggestions for future scholarship. On the other side of the selection ledger, it is precisely the relative availability of quality texts that led me, in the cases of the major figures Robert Bloomfield, James Hogg, John Clare, and Ebenezer Elliott, to provide bio-critical overviews only. Hogg and Clare are now available in superb scholarly editions, and a good selection of Bloomfield's verse is now in print.[11] Elliott's voluminous poetic output has not been given a modern scholarly edition, but even so his work is readily available in libraries. To print a mere handful of poems by any of these figures would be a compromising, even pointless exercise given the other resources available.

In cases where the poems were both especially interesting and especially difficult to obtain, as with William Smith, Thomas Wilson, John Shaw, and

James Chambers, the choices were easy. So too were the decisions to include Mary Bryan and George Bloomfield, because of the opportunity to present previously unpublished poems. But many of the other choices were difficult, especially when it came to exclusion; I might easily have included, to cite only a few examples, the cobbler Joseph Blacket; the Chartist thinker Allen Davenport; or Christian Milne, the wife of an Aberdeen ship-carpenter, who used the proceeds from her writing to buy a partial interest in a vessel her husband had worked on. Ultimately it became a matter of limited space, rather than of scholarly certainty about the relative importance of these figures, that led to their being omitted. Additional space would also have allowed me to include interesting sidelights like Joseph Holland's 'Appendix' to Bloomfield's *The Farmer's Boy*—written, said Holland, because in Bloomfield's portrayal of spring 'Haymaking passed over unnoticed'.[12] A more significant poet connected to the Bloomfield circle was Henry Kirke White of Nottingham, the author of *Clifton Grove* (1803) and a linguistic prodigy who died of tuberculosis in 1806, aged only twenty-one. Kirke White was excluded, finally, on the basis of his background: he was the recipient of an extensive formal education, and though he did labour for a year as a stocking-loom weaver, he was able to attend Cambridge, where he won several scholastic commendations. But though class considerations guided my decision on Kirke White, it is also true that I have tried not to be doctrinaire about the term 'labouring-class', especially since increases in social mobility were allowing for new kinds of vocational and class movement. So, for example, Thomas Wilson of Newcastle went to work in the coal mines as a young child, but by the end of his life was a financially comfortable clerk and civic leader. And at least once I have argued this point from the other end: the sailor John Mitford had family connections that were leveraged to gain him two minor naval commands, but after being dismissed from the Navy he went through a long period of decline that ended with his death in a workhouse. Even more complicated is the case of Ebenezer Elliott, who spent most of his adult life as a business manager and owner—but whose fluctuating fortunes, including a traumatic bankruptcy, contributed to his fervent advocacy of the working people of Sheffield.

Initially I assumed that this volume would necessarily track the evolution of British radicalism, and the quickening of a distinctively working-class consciousness, in the years before the great Reform Bill of 1832. Yet in the event, the collection has produced something else, for while such developments are indeed signposted in many of the lives and writings represented here, these texts together reveal the sensibilities of working people who thought hard about the socio-economic and institutional policies affecting them, and who tried to reconcile these issues with the artistic and humanistic principles that rang true to them when, in private, they read the poetry of others, or put pen to paper themselves. The individualism and essential dignity of this reflective work is described by John Clare with typically passionate directness: 'Who would not envy such a pride of place / When beauty gazes on a poets face / The common vulgar live & pass away / But poets walk with beauty every day'. Clare goes on to include the reader in that charmed circle: 'The farmers daughter loves the poets song / & reads the volume as she goes along / She reads the love that in her bosom lurks / & hides it in her apron while she works'.[13] Such exchanges of heart and mind, and of labour and leisure, have come to underwrite the present volume's quest for literary recovery.

Scott McEathron
Southern Illinois University Carbondale

NOTES

[1] William Wordsworth, *The Prose Works of William Wordsworth*, ed. W. J. B. Owen, 3 vols (Oxford: Clarendon Press, 1974), III, p. 80.

[2] Quoted in *Prose Works of William Wordsworth*, ed. Owen, I, p. 167.

[3] *The Village Patriarch*, IV.ii.16, *The Poetical Works of Ebenezer Elliott*, ed. Edwin Elliott, 2 vols (London: Henry S. King, 1876), I, p. 234.

[4] For American sales of *The Farmer's Boy*, see the essay by Bruce Graver in *Robert Bloomfield: The Forgotten Romantic*, eds Simon White, Bridget Keegan, and John Goodridge, *forthcoming*, Bucknell University Press.

[5] John Shaw, *Woolton Green* (Liverpool: Perry and Metcalfe, 1825), p. xii.

[6] I would like to thank April London for the suggestion that Shaw's source is Henry Fielding's *Tom Jones* (1749), Bk. IX, Chapter 1: 'Nor will all the qualities I have hitherto given my historian avail him, unless he have what is generally meant by a good heart, and be capable of feeling. The author who will make me weep, says Horace, must first weep himself'.

[7] Shaw, *Woolton Green*, p. xi.

[8] William Smith, *A Collection of Original Poems* (Edinburgh, 1821), p. vi.

[9] Quoted in Jonathan Lawson, *Robert Bloomfield* (Boston: Twayne, 1980), p. 46.

[10] Thomas Batchelor, 'Preface', *Village Scenes, The Progress of Agriculture, and Other Poems* (London: Vernor and Hood, 1804).

[11] *Robert Bloomfield: Selected Poems*, eds John Lucas and John Goodridge. The expanded second edition of this volume, which will include all of the poems from the volumes *Good Tidings; or, News from the Farm* (1804) and *May Day with the Muses* (1822), is due to be published in 2006 by Trent Editions.

[12] Joseph Holland, *An Appendix to the Season of Spring, in the Rural Poem 'The Farmer's Boy'* (Croyden, Surrey, 1806). Holland's 'Note to the Reader' contains the text of a letter from Bloomfield, in which he explains that 'in composing [*The Farmer's Boy*] I was determined that what I said on Farming should be Experimentally, true. There was on that small Farm no Hay to make'.

[13] This excerpt from an untitled poem is taken from John Clare, *Northborough Sonnets*, eds Eric Robinson, David Powell, and P.M.S. Dawson (Ashington, Northumberland: Mid Northumberland Arts Group and Carcanet Press, 1995), p. 59.

CHRONOLOGY, 1800–1830

1800   Act of Union unites Great Britain and Ireland. At Battle of Marengo, Italy, French forces under Napoleon defeat Austria. Robert Bloomfield, *The Farmer's Boy*. William Wordsworth, *Lyrical Ballads*, 2nd edition.

1801   James Hogg, *Scottish Pastorals*.

1802   In March, Peace of Amiens brings temporary suspension of hostilities between England and France. France invades Switzerland in October. William Holloway, *The Peasant's Fate*. Robert Bloomfield, *Rural Tales*. Walter Scott, *Minstrelsy of the Scottish Border*.

1803   War with France resumes in May. *Poetical Attempts by Ann Candler*. Nathaniel Bloomfield, *An Essay on War*. Henry Kirke White, *Clifton Grove*.

1804   Napoleon declared Emperor of France. Coleridge goes to Malta and remains for two years working as secretary to British High Commissioner. Thomas Batchelor, *Village Scenes*. Robert Bloomfield, *Good Tidings; or, News from the Farm*.

1805   Admiral Lord Nelson's naval victory over French and Spanish forces in Battle of Trafalgar, off coast of Spain. Napoleon defeats Austrian and Russian forces at Battle of Austerlitz, Austria. Scott, *The Lay of the Last Minstrel*.

1806   Charlotte Richardson, *Poems Written on Different Occasions*. Robert Bloomfield, *Wild Flowers; or Pastoral and Local Poetry*.

1807   Slave trade abolished in Great Britain, though still legal in West Indies. Hogg, *The Mountain Bard*. Wordsworth, *Poems in Two Volumes*. George Crabbe, *Poems*.

1808   Holloway, *The Minor Minstrel*.

1809   Richardson, *Poems, Chiefly Composed During the Pressure of Severe Illness*. Byron, *English Bards and Scotch Reviewers*.

1810   Crabbe, *The Borough*.

1811   King George III officially declared insane. Prince of Wales becomes Regent. Beginning of an upsurge in Ludditism, the destruction of industrial machinery viewed as threatening the traditional livelihoods of textile workers. Jane Austen, *Sense and Sensibility.*

1812   United States declares war on Great Britain. First two cantos of Byron's *Childe Harold's Pilgrimage.*

1813   Percy Shelley, *Queen Mab*. Austen, *Pride and Prejudice*. Hogg, *The Queen's Wake*.

1814   Napoleon exiled to island of Elba, off the Italian coast. Percy Shelley and Mary Wollstonecraft Godwin elope to France. Conclusion of War of 1812. Wordsworth, *The Excursion*. Byron, *The Corsair.*

1815   Napoleon escapes Elba after nine months, beginning the 'One Hundred Days'—the period between his arrival in Paris in March and his defeat by Wellington at Waterloo, Belgium, in June. Passage of postwar Corn-Law bill. France bans slave trade. Scott, *Waverly.* Mary Bryan, *Sonnets and Metrical Tales.*

1816   Meeting of the Byron and Shelley households in Switzerland, from which follows Mary Shelley's conception of *Frankenstein* (published 1818). Austen, *Emma*.

1817   Princess Charlotte, only legitimate child of the Prince Regent, dies in childbirth. Suspension of rights of Habeas Corpus. Death of Jane Austen. Coleridge, *Sibylline Leaves; Biographia Literaria.*

1818   Ebenezer Elliott, *Night*. John Mitford, *Poems of a British Sailor.* John Keats, *Endymion.*

1819   'Peterloo Massacre', the government break-up of a large outdoor rally in support of parliamentary reform at St. Peter's Field, Manchester, results in the killing of several protesters and onlookers. Passage of 'Six Acts', designed to restrict movements and gatherings of radical reformers. Cantos I & II of Byron's *Don Juan*, initially published anonymously. William Smith, 'Verses Composed on the Disgraceful Traffic at Present Carried on Of Raising and Selling the Newly Buried Dead'.

1820   Death of George III. Accession of George IV, formerly the Prince Regent. Discovery of the Cato Street Conspiracy, a plan to assassinate the ministerial leaders of the government; conspirators later executed. Keats, *Lamia, Isabella, The Eve of St. Agnes, and Other Poems*. Scott, *Ivan-*

hoe. Percy Shelley, *Prometheus Unbound*. John Clare, *Poems Descriptive of Rural Life and Scenery. The Poetical Works of James Chambers.*

1821 Death of Keats in Rome. Death of Napoleon on St. Helena. Beginning of Greek War of Independence from Turkey. Thomas De Quincey, *Confessions of an English Opium Eater.* Robert Millhouse, *Blossoms.* Clare, *The Village Minstrel.* Smith, *A Collection of Original Poems.*

1822 Drowning of Shelley off coast of Italy. First appearance, in serial form, of William Cobbett's *Rural Rides.* First appearance, in *Blackwood's Magazine,* of the series *Noctes Ambrosianae.* Hogg, *The Three Perils of Man.*

1823 Death of Robert Bloomfield. Charles Lamb, *Essays of Elia.* James Bird, *Poetical Memoirs.* Hogg, *The Three Perils of Woman.* Elliott, *Love.* William Hazlitt, *Liber Amoris.*

1824 Byron's *Don Juan* reaches sixteen cantos. Death of Byron in Greece. Hogg, *The Private Memoirs and Confessions of a Justified Sinner.* Robert Franklin, *The Miller's Muse.*

1825 Hazlitt, *The Spirit of the Age.* John Nicholson, *Airedale in Ancient Times.* John Shaw, *Woolton Green.*

1826 First part of Thomas Wilson's *The Pitman's Pay* published in *Mitchell's Newcastle Magazine.* Smith, *The Bachelor's Contest.*

1827 Nicholson, *The Lyre of Ebor.* Millhouse, *Sherwood Forest.* Clare, *The Shepherd's Calendar.*

1828 Hazlitt, *The Life of Napoleon Buonaparte.*

1829 Hogg, *The Shepherd's Calendar.* Elliott, *The Village Patriarch.*

1830 George IV dies, succeeded by William IV. Death of Hazlitt. Elliott, *Corn-Law Rhymes: The Ranter.*

NOTE ON THE TEXT

The authors in this volume are those whose first relevant publication appeared in the period 1800–1830, and they are generally arranged chronologically. The copy text in most cases is the first extant edition; deviations from this practice are recorded in the endnotes. Manuscript sources were used for three poems, George Bloomfield's 'The Poets at Odds' and Mary Bryan's 'The Village Maid' and 'Stanzas'.

The texts reproduced here follow the copy texts as far as possible, and spelling is unmodernised. Modern typographical conventions are used, however. Compositors' and other errors, included errata noted in the copy texts, are corrected.

Additional information about the poets and poems included in this volume can be found online at:

http://www.ntu.ac.uk/clare/elsie.htm

ANN[E] CANDLER (1740–1814)

Anne Candler's life story is a bleak chronicle of hardship and travail, and yet one fears her sufferings were not untypical of women of her class. Born Ann[e] Mo[o]re in the small borough of Yoxford, twenty miles north-east of Ipswich in Suffolk, and perhaps later employed in domestic service, she was married in 1763 to William Candler, a man she loved deeply but whose dishonesty, drunkenness, and irresponsibility would cause her years of grief and misery. Trouble began only a year into their marriage when William enlisted in the Army without informing Anne, even as she was in the late stages of her first pregnancy. Trudging back and forth between the towns of Sproughton and Ipswich over several days, she was able to get William enlisted in the local Militia instead, which limited him to a few weeks' service every summer. But it was an inauspicious beginning, and nearly fifteen years (and six children) later, when William again absconded, the train of ill consequences proved harder to mend, with four of the children being sent to live in the village workhouse. Two more disastrous reunions with William followed before Anne finally was able 'to renounce the idea of ever living with him again' (*Memoirs*, p. 14).

This renunciation came with great costs, however, and for twenty long years beginning in the early 1780s, Candler was forced to live at the Tattingstone workhouse with 'the dregs of human kind' ('Reflections on My Own Situation', l. 7). During this time she began to publish single poems in the *Ipswich Journal*, and finally at the turn of the century an attempt was made by a group of local women, headed by Elizabeth Cobbold, wife of the brewer John Cobbold, to gather the poems and publish them by subscription. It is possible that Mrs. Cobbold, herself a prolific poet and later the model for Mrs. Leo Hunter in Dickens's *Pickwick Papers*, edited at least some of these poems before publication. In any event, the plan bore fruit: *Poetical Attempts by Ann Candler* was published in 1803, providing her with sufficient funds to leave the workhouse. She moved to the small town of Holton St. Mary, near the residence of one of her daughters, and there lived for more than a decade until her death in 1814 at age seventy-four.

Most of our knowledge of Candler's life comes to us from her remarkable *Memoirs* (reprinted below), which she wrote at the urging of her patrons as a

1

preface to the *Poetical Attempts* volume. At once deeply personal and a vivid, even shocking piece of social history (Candler calls it 'an account of an unhappy marriage for nearly forty years', p. 15), the *Memoirs* provides a level of confessional detail rarely found in the highly conventional prefaces to labouring-class volumes; Candler's narrative reminds us that there must be equally powerful human stories behind the sketchier, less forthcoming accounts of many of her contemporaries. Most of the poems presented below have a connection with life events described in the *Memoirs*, or with individuals who, like Mrs. Cobbold or the Revd. Dr Thomas Jackson, encouraged Candler in times of need. Indeed, from the *Memoirs* we can infer that throughout her life Candler was able to cultivate and maintain meaningful friendships across class lines; her friends and supporters seem to have included the Collinson and Woodward families associated with the Sproughton Chantry estate, and even John Howe, later Lord Chedworth. The attempt to imagine the circumstances of these relationships provides much of the narrative impetus of Sheila Hardy's fictionalized account of Candler's life, *The Story of Anne Candler* (1984). Hardy also provides evidence that, despite the printed evidence of the 1803 volume and thus virtually the entire scholarly record, Candler spelt her first name 'Anne' and her maiden name 'Moore'; both spellings are clearly indicated in Hardy's reproduction of the poet's marriage certificate, which seems quite possibly to be in Candler's own hand.

FURTHER READING

Anthony Brundage, *The English Poor Laws, 1700–1930* (Basingstoke: Palgrave, 2001)
Elizabeth Cobbold, *Poems of Elizabeth Cobbold, with a Memoir of the Author* (Ipswich: J. Raw, 1825)
DNB (Elizabeth Cobbold)
Sheila M. Hardy, *The Story of Anne Candler* (S. M. Hardy in association with The Self Publishing Association, 1988)
Sheila M. Hardy, *The House on the Hill: The Samford House of Industry, 1764–1930* (Ipswich: S. M. Hardy, 2001)
Peter Higginbotham, Workhouse Website:
    <http://users.ox.ac.uk/~peter/workhouse/index.html>
Norman Longmate, *The Workhouse: A Social History*. 2nd Edn. (London: Pimlico, 2003).

From *Poetical Attempts by Ann Candler* (1803)

From *Memoirs of the Life of Ann Candler*

I am now in the sixty-first year of my age, having been born the 18th of November, 1740. I have had nine children, five sons and four daughters, three of the boys died infants, how it has pleased God to dispose of two of the remaining six I know not as I have not heard of my eldest son and daughter for many years. One of my daughters is married; I fear but indifferently, and is settled in London: my youngest son also lives in that city as a servant; he went to sea some time ago with a naval officer, but, not liking his situation, returned to London, and was in place when I last heard from his sister. My daughter Lucy is married, and lives at Copdock in this country, and is, I believe, in the true sense of the words, the *contented happy Cottager*! her husband is a sober industrious man. My youngest daughter Clara lives, in service, with Mr. John Cook, of Holton Hall, near Stratford, and blessed be God, has hitherto preserved an unblemished character. Thus of nine children two remain near me, to afford me substantial happiness and satisfaction as a parent; but my uncertainty about the others, and solicitude for their welfare, are too often painful in the extreme. It was seven years, last month, since I saw or heard from my husband; but conclude he is, if living, in the army, as he was ever fond of a military life. We had not been married above a year when he enlisted with a recruiting party of the Guards at Ipswich. A friend immediately came to Sproughton, where we then lived, and informed me of it. Though far advanced in my pregnancy I hastened to the town, and, after an infinite deal of trouble, much expense, and the inconvenience of being detained one night from home, I had, at last, the satisfaction of bringing my young warrior back again. The next day my friend sent me word, that the serjeant of the party declared he would not leave the town without him; this threat alarmed me greatly, and, regardless of fatigue, I went to Ipswich directly. My friend advised me, as the safest method I could adopt, to let my husband enter into the Militia, as they were at that time disembodied. I went home and consulted his father and mother, (for he was born at Sproughton) they approved of the plan, and, in a day or two, my old friend secured him a situation with which I had great reason to be satisfied, for, on the Sunday following some of the party came to the public house in the village, enquiring for him; but being informed that he was in the Militia, they seemed greatly disappointed. I heard not of it until the next day, but even then I trembled. My remedy you will doubtless say was a desperate one:—true, Madam, it was so, and so was the occasion; fortunately the circumstance was not attended with any bad consequence, for he only made his appearance twenty-eight days every summer, during the three years; so that affair ended without much trouble.—After the birth of my fourth child I received a small legacy bequeathed to me by a maiden aunt, which afforded me great relief, and gave me an opportunity of furnishing my family with such articles as were absolutely necessary, and had long been wanting, for my husband was ever much addicted to drinking.

Four or five years after this my ever honoured friend and benefactor, the Rev. Dr. J—n came to reside in Sproughton: at Christmas time he was pleased to distribute very liberal gifts to the poor; the generosity of the action struck me very much, and I ventured to address a few lines to him, returning thanks in a manner quite unexpected by the worthy Gentleman. The next day I heard a rap at my door; I opened it,—but my surprise and terror were indescribable on the appearance of Dr. J—n, for I dreaded a severe reprimand for my presumption. My confusion was too great to escape his observation, and the natural goodness of his heart induced him to dispel my fears, by addressing me with the greatest affability and condescension. He was pleased to take a seat, and conversed with me a considerable time. From this hour, the most fortunate of my life, I may date every act of kindness I have since experienced, for he was pleased to recommend me to his friends, and shewed them some of my writings, which, but for his endeavours to bring them into notice, would certainly have been buried in oblivion, as I wrote them merely for my own amusement. Death only can efface him from my remembrance, or cancel the obligations I am under to that best of men! Think what were my sorrows when this dear and valuable friend left the village, and I was at once deprived of his assistance, and also of his conversation, which was always affable and kind!

According to the old adage that one misfortune seldom comes alone, I found another in reserve for me which I did not expect. A younger brother of my husband, who had been enlisted in the Guards about four years, came down to see his friends. I know not how it was, but the moment that I heard that he was come, a sudden tremor seized my whole frame, and tears trickled down my cheeks. This was on the Saturday; on the Sunday he came, by my husband's invitation, to dinner, after which they walked out together, and I did not see my husband till Monday night, when he told me that his brother was gone. He seemed very thoughtful and gloomy: on the Tuesday morning he went to work, and I neither saw or heard any thing more of him till the Friday, when, by mere accident, I heard that he had enlisted with a party of the Guards then at Colchester. A neighbour offered his services to ride over to that town, and enquire into the truth of the report, and a farmer in the village kindly lent a horse for the occasion. What were my feelings, what was my agony of mind during the man's absence. I wished, yet dreaded his return. At length the awful moment came; the man had found him, and seen the cockade in his hat.—I had now six children, the eldest about fourteen, the youngest a year and half old. Good God! how did every body exclaim against him! as for me I seemed for some time in a state of stupefaction, I could not shed a tear. What a night did I pass! In the morning old Mr. W—, at the Hall, came to me, and addressed me in these very words: 'So, your husband is listed for a soldier; well, let him go, for he was always a rascal to you'. I thought at that instant, that, if I had Mr. W—'s whole fortune, I would freely give it for his discharge, but I dared not to tell him so. The report of my misfortunes brought several friends to me, and I was advised to place four of my children in this house, and kept the eldest, and the youngest with me at home; this advice I followed, but I have since repented that I did not come in with them all. That worthy man, the late I. C—n, esq. and my ever lamented friend, dear Miss F—n, agreed to pay my rent for me: thus I lived for two years, by industry and the frequent donations of kind friends protected from want. I should be guilty of the highest ingratitude were I not to remember, with veneration and respect, the late M—e R-ss-ll, esq. who almost entirely supported me, and the two children, during an illness of eleven weeks, which afflicted me in consequence of the perturbation of mind I had laboured under upon my husband's departure. During these two years I got my eldest girl out to service, and took my next daughter Catharine home: but now an event occurred which deprived me of every comfort, and gave me reason to reproach myself with imprudence and indiscretion. My husband [had a] leave of absence, and came down to Sproughton to see me. An unfortunate visit it proved to me and the children. During his stay he incessantly importuned me to go to London, and flattered me how very well we should live there, as he could throw up his pay and go to work, and how easily he could fetch the children and place them out. For some days I both chid him and absolutely rejected the proposal; but before three weeks were ended, he brought me to a compliance with his request: this was the latter end of February, and I agreed to be in town by the beginning of April. No sooner were my friends apprized of my intention, than they endeavoured to oppose it, by every argument they could employ against the absurd scheme, as some of them too justly termed it. Alas! I erred, with my eyes open. I sent the best of my goods, which were very decent, by one of the Ipswich hoys, and with my little Clara, went to town by land. As my husband knew of my going he met me, but seemed rather cool and indifferent. This reception gave me an inexpressible shock, and to add to my mortification, I had not been two hours with him before he demanded some money. I was speechless; my foolish credulity now appeared in its true colours; he had to go upon guard that very night, and I was left with my child: the state of my mind may more easily be conceived

than described! In a few days my goods came, and I was settled, as well as
my own reflections, and my husband's behaviour would permit me: for I
soon found that his propensity to drinking was as great as ever. On the sec-
ond day of June, the dreadful riots in London broke out, and he was obliged
to leave his work and return to his arms. For seven days and nights I could
not learn whether he were living or dead; and when the riots were quelled,
the Guards were all encamped in St. James' Park: thus was I once deprived
of all assistance from him, and exposed to the horrors of extreme poverty in
the midst of strangers. I omit many unpleasant circumstances, for why
should I distress you by a recital of my sufferings, when I am conscious that
they were occasioned by my own reprehensible weakness? All I can urge to
extenuate, or palliate my folly is, that he was my husband, and the father of
my children, and that my affection for him was unbounded and so at this
time were my sorrows; and, to add to their weight, I found myself in a situa-
tion that in a few months would involve me in new difficulties. I think it was
in the month of August that the camp broke up, and my husband returned
home; but he treated me in a very unpleasant manner; his language and
behaviour were intolerable! I now began seriously to consider whether I
ought not to leave him, and return home: fear, and shame, alternately took
possession of my heart; I had no house to go to, nor could I expect any fur-
ther assistance from those who had formerly been my friends. While I
continued in this painful state of suspense an incident happened which
determined me at once. An uncle of my husband's, who was mate of an Ips-
wich vessel, called to see me; I informed him of the state of our affairs, and
he, being no stranger to his nephew's manners and morals, urged me to
return to Suffolk; offering to convey me, the child, and what furniture I had,
in his vessel, free of expence: I thankfully accepted the offer, and began to
prepare for my voyage. When my husband found that I was in earnest he
seemed almost frantic; but his uncle severely reprimanded him for his con-
duct towards me; and, after much altercation, I was allowed to dispose of my
goods, as, from having been used in London, they were not fit to bring into
the country. My husband went with me to the vessel, and wept most bitterly
at parting; I was sensibly affected, but had suffered too severely to waver in
my resolution. I was almost distracted about my poor children, for whom he
never would entertain a thought; but if I attempted to propose any thing for
their welfare, was accustomed to fly into a passion: I was therefore obliged
to confine my anxiety on their account to my own bosom.

We had a pleasant passage, and my uncle set me ashore about a mile from
Ipswich: I walked over Stoke-Hills; but when I came within sight of the
Chauntry, good God! what were my sensations and emotions! I seated the
little Clara on a bank, and placing myself near her surveyed the prospect
with unutterable anguish: a torrent of repentant, but unavailing tears suc-

ceeded: I believe it was near an hour before I recovered strength and spirits
to pursue my walk. I went to Sproughton, where I staid a few days, but suf-
fered myself to been seen as little as possible; and then, without applying to
any one person, came as privately as I could into this house.

It is necessary to inform you, my dear ladies, that, before I went to Lon-
don, my beloved friend Miss F—n had commanded me to write to her
frequently. In obedience to her order I had, from time to time, given her a
faithful, though unpleasant account of my situation, and had also written to
her my determination of returning into the country again. After I had been
in the house about a month, I wrote to inform her where I was; and, to my
infinite surprise, in two or three days had the delight of seeing her! She
requested of the governess that I might be permitted to walk with her in the
garden; and soon perceiving my situation, lamented this additional misfor-
tune, and gave me the kindest assurances of the continuation of her
friendship. Not many days after she sent her servant with a letter, and a
guinea enclosed from my kind friend and benefactor J. C—n, Esq. this was
some time in October. On the 20th day of March following, about four
o'clock in the morning, I was delivered of a son, and about seven of another
son. For some days I was in imminent danger, but the goodness of God pre-
served me, and sent me unsolicited assistance. No sooner did that dear lady
Miss F— hear of my situation than she sent me an ample supply of whatever
she thought might be most useful and acceptable to me. I had likewise some
kind presents from other friends: thus did the Almighty provide for me, in
this extremity, beyond my expectations, and, I frankly acknowledge, far
beyond my deserts! I had now seven children in the house, but it pleased
God to take one of the twins at fourteen weeks old, and the other in one
short month later. When I had been in the house three years, my husband
obtained his discharge and came to see me: he proposed taking me out of
the house; but this I would by no means consent to, till we should have pro-
cured sufficient to furnish one room at least. In a few months, with a little
money which he had earned, and some that I had saved, together with a few
goods still remaining at Sproughton, I began to think that we might put our
plan in execution; I accordingly agreed to go to his lodging till we should be
able to procure and fit up a cottage. He received me with delight, and
seemed quite happy: but short lived was the pleasure to either of us; for, that
very day, he was seized by a shivering fit, which was followed by a fever of
the most alarming kind: suffice it to say that I staid with him for seven
weeks; during which time the Rev. Mr. G— procured us an allowance from
the house; but, as he still continued extremely bad, and my own money was
nearly expended, I having the youngest child with me, I was advised to go
with him into the house; this was in fact the only step I could take, and here
all my prospects of comfort ended. For several weeks my husband's recovery

was doubtful; a more pitiable object was never seen! it was better than half a year before he was able to go to his work again; he then went to seek employment at Sproughton, where, meeting with his old companions, he fell into his accustomed vice of drunkenness, to a greater degree than ever, and became so utterly degraded in appearance, manners, and morals, as determined me to renounce the idea of ever living with him again.

Thus, honored ladies, I have given you an account of an unhappy marriage for nearly forty years. I have now been upwards of twenty years secluded from the world, and have performed a severe penance for my indiscretion in leaving my comfortable cottage, and kind friends at Sproughton. You find, my dear ladies, that I have not endeavoured to exculpate myself, or to justify my proceedings: no, I stand self-convicted, self-condemned; all I can allege in my own behalf is, that I have not committed any faults of a criminal nature, and I believe I may say, without the imputation of vanity, that my conduct, during my residence in this house, has been irreproachable. I hope you will be pleased to make allowance for my many errors and bad writing; but I have been obliged to write the greater part by candle-light, as I have very little leisure by day, and the painful recollection of past scenes affected me so much in the recital, that I scarcely knew what I wrote; and as difficult a task awaits me still, that is, my dear ladies, to find words that would express my sentiments in a manner that might convince you how perfectly sensible I am of your unlimited goodness to me, in endeavouring to render the situation I am in as comfortable as possible. What have I to give in return? Alas! only a repetition of thanks, and the feelings of a heart almost breaking with a ponderous weight of grateful sensations! to a power superior to what is mutable I must the leave the cause in hand, well assured your reward will be such as is promised, 'Come, ye blessed, inherit the kingdom prepared for you'!

You will surprised at the prolixity I am guilty of: it has been by far exceeded my intention; but one circumstance was so connected with another, and one word naturally introduced others, that I could not well avoid it: I was likewise desirous to be as explicit as possible, for the satisfaction of those among your friends, who had honored me with their enquiries.

>I am, Ladies, with sincere gratitude,
>your obliged servant,
>Ann Candler.

At the time of writing the above, Mrs. Candler had not a hope of being enabled to remove out of the house of industry; but, about eight or nine months after, several of her Poems having been read and approved, in polite and literary circles, it was suggested, by the ladies to whom her letter was addressed, that, if she could publish a small volume by subscription, she might raise a sum sufficient to furnish a room, and place herself, in a state of comparative happiness, near her married daughter, where she might spend the evening of her days in peace, supported by her own industry, and occasionally assisted by those friends who know, and respect, her unobtrusive good qualities. Part of this plan is already put in execution. Her friends have procured and furnished a lodging for her at Copdock, where her daughter lives, and not far from her favourite village of Sproughton, and this little volume is published under the patronage of a most respectable list of Subscribers.

On the Birth of Twin Sons
In 1781

Hail, infant boys! and hail the dawn
    That brought your natal hour!
May no malignant planet frown
    With inauspicious pow'r.

May heav'n its kindest influence shed   5
    Around ye as ye lay,
And watchful angels guard your bed,
    And shield ye in the day.

Sweet balmy slumbers close your eyes
    Whene'er dispos'd to rest;   10
Your waking, supplicating, cries,
    With pity move each breast.

On both may truth and goodness wait
    As they advance in age,
And may they find a milder fate   15
    Than what their births presage.

O, God! behold their infant state
    Thy kind protection claim:--
For them thy mercy I entreat;
    To me extend the same.   20

Tho', poor and helpless, I am here;
    On Thee my hopes rely;
Thou canst disperse the rising tear,
    And make me smile with joy.

O! give me, while thus mean and low,   25
    An humble peaceful mind,
May love and duty guide me through,
    With fortitude combin'd.

Could these dear boys their father's love,
    Join'd with their mother's, share,   30
How vast a blessing would it prove,
    How lighten ev'ry care!

What jarring sentiments content
    And struggle, in my breast,
When I reflect they want the friend   35
    That should their youth assist!

O! peace, my soul, and be not griev'd;
    Repress each plaintive word;
And may these gifts, from heav'n receiv'd,
    Find favor with the Lord.   40

For them, for me, I humbly ask
    A portion of His grace,
And may we find, when life is past,
    With Him a resting place.

Addressed to the Inhabitants of Yoxford, in 1787

Dear Village, sweet delightful spot!
    Blest scene that gave me birth!
Though now, alas! unknown, forgot,
    I wander o'er the earth.

Yet still thy name I will repeat;   5
    A name how dear to me!

And, maugre this my wayward fate,
    Will claim my part in thee.

Say, wilt thou love me in return
    And love with pity join?   10
Not treat me with contempt or scorn,
    Or blush to say I'm thine?

Still let this pleasing hope be mine,
    Warm'd by a daily pray'r:
And fav'ring heav'n to thee and thine,   15
    Extend its guardian care.

And ye, who in this darling spot,
    Securely dwell serene,
Be ev'ry bliss in life your lot,
    And pleasure paint each scene.   20

Still unembitter'd may you taste
    The sweets of health and peace;
While plenty decks the choice repast,
    And Ceres gives increase.

May commerce flourish unrestrain'd,   25
    In social strength elate,
While neighb'ring swains admiring stand,
    To see your prosp'rous state.

May justice all her rights assert
    And bear impartial sway,   30
While truth and friendship, void of art,
    Their native charms display.

When God or man you supplicate
    May you not plead in vain;
But seek to be as good, as great,   35
    And what you ask obtain.

To the Rev. Dr. J—n
On his being appointed one of his Majesty's Chaplains

Hail, joyous tidings! soul-reviving sound!
Has Candler's friend the royal favor found?
O blest event! O, joy, to what excess!
What language can my sentiments express?
Let poets laureate shine in lofty verse,   5
And splendid stories skillfully rehearse,
Let them excel in all the pomp of rhyme,
And ransack kingdoms and the page of time;
But I, defective in the shining part,
Must write the simple language of the heart: 10
Nor will my friend esteem the off'ring less
Because array'd in nature's rustic dress.
Ah! what am I?—A stranger to the rules
Observ'd by those instructed in the schools,
Unskill'd, unpractis'd, in the art to please,   15
Not form'd, by nature, for such work as these.
From snarling critics and their censure free,
They'll not bestow a single thought on me;
No strokes of satire will they lavish here,
But let me off with one contemptuous sneer;   20
But, truce a moment,—give me leave to say,
I've not to plead the merits of a play,
Stranger alike to boxes and to pit,
And all the dazzling ornaments of wit,
The public voice will ne'er decide my fate,   25
Alike unworthy of their love and hate:
An author scarcely can their frowns survive,
While I, unnotic'd, am preserv'd alive.
Unenvied, here, my pen I may employ,
To speak thy praises J—N and my joy   30
And is it true?—art thou at length preferr'd?
In extacy the pleasing tale I heard:
O! may thy wishes still propitious be,
And may thy sov'reign still distinguish thee:
Though high thy honors, great thy present bliss,   35
Thy merits claim far greater still than this.
O! may our gracious prince his gifts dispense

To men of virtue, probity, and sense;
Then must my friend his favor still maintain,
And all the church's highest honors gain: 40
Conspicuous will each Christian virtue shine
And add new luster to the rites divine;
Thy works of mercy, and of kindness blest,
This grateful village ever will attest;
Those sacred truths we did from thee receive,   45
Thy life and manners taught us to believe.
May heav'n its choicest gifts to thee extend,
My worthy patron, and my noble friend,
May each succeeding year new bliss afford,
And peace and plenty deck thy festive board.   50

Reflections on My Own Situation
Written in T-tt-ngst-ne House of Industry,
February 1802

How many years are past and gone,
    How alter'd I appear,
How many strange events have known,
    Since first I enter'd here!

Within these dreary walls confin'd,   5
    A lone recluse, I live,
And, with the dregs of human kind,
    A niggard alms receive.

Uncultivated, void of sense,
    Unsocial, insincere,   10
Their rude behaviour gives offence,
    Their language wounds the ear.

Disgusting objects swarm around,
    Throughout confusions reign;
Where feuds and discontent abound,   15
    Remonstrance proves in vain.

No sympathising friend I find,
   Unknown is friendship here;
Not one to soothe, or calm the mind,
   When overwhelm'd with care: 20

Peace, peace, my heart, thy duty calls,
   With cautious steps proceed:
Beyond these melancholy walls,
   I've found a friend indeed!

I gaze on numbers in distress,   25
   Compare their state with mine.
Can I reflect, and not confess
   A providence divine?

And I might bend beneath the rod,
   And equal want deplore,   30
But that a good and gracious God
   Is pleas'd to give me more:

My gen'rous friends, with feeling heart,
   Remove the pondrous weight,
And those impending ills avert   35
   Which want and woes create.

Yet what am I, that I should be
   Thus honor'd and carest?
And why such favors heap'd on me,
   And with such friendship blest?   40

Absorb'd in thought I often sate
   Within my lonely cell,
And mark'd the strange mysterious fate
   That seem'd to guide me still.

When keenest sorrow urg'd her claim,   45
   When evils threaten'd dread,
Some unexpected blessing came,
   And rais'd my drooping head.

In youth strange fairy tale I've read,
   Of magic skill and pow'r,   50
And mortals, in their sleep, convey'd
   To some enchanted tow'r.

To this obscure and lone retreat,
   Conceal'd from vulgar eyes,
Two rival genii us'd to meet   55
   And counterplots devise.

The evil genius, prone to ill,
   Mischievous schemes invents,
Pursues the fated mortal still,
   And ev'ry woe augments.   60

Insulted with indignant scorn,
   Aw'd by tyrannic sway,
A prey to grief each rising morn.
   And cheerless all the day.

But fate and fortune in their scenes   65
   A pleasing change decree:
The friendly genius intervenes,
   And sets the captive free.

Content and freedom thus regain'd,
   Depriv'd of both before;   70
So great the blessing, when obtain'd,
   What can he wish for more?

The tales these eastern writers feign
   Like facts to me appear;
The fabled suff'rings they contain,   75
   I find no fictions here.

And since, in those romantic lays,
   My miseries combine,
To bless my lengthen'd wane of days,
   Their bright reverse be mine.   80

Look down, O God! in me behold
   How helpless mortals are,
Nor leave me friendless, poor, and old,
   But guide me with thy care.

On Perusing the History of Jacob
After I had left T-tt-ngst-ne House of Industry

Am I the very same, who us'd to be
Still sighing for her long lost liberty?
For twenty years and more I mourn'd the loss;
The laws were rig'rous, ev'ry task seem'd cross,
The bondage irksome, and the treatment hard,   5
From social converse and from friends debarr'd;
Excess of grief the gath'ring ills portend,
But Jacob's God has rais'd me up a friend,
Blest is that gift th' Almighty deigns to send!

Like me, for twenty years, did Jacob find   10
Men were unfeeling, selfish, and unkind,
With anxious care his fleecy charge survey'd,
And climb'd the mountains, if a lambkin stray'd
If torn by beasts, or by misfortune slain,
'Twas his the loss, or damage, to sustain,   15
From frost by night, or scorching heat by day,
He found his spirits, and his strength, decay:
Fatigued with watching and with care opprest,
His sleep departed though he wanted rest:
Ten times his wages chang'd, his hire detain'd,   20
His wealth suspected, as unjustly gain'd,
In all a strange return did Laban make,
As God had blest him for his nephew's sake;
But envy, when excited knows no peace,
As others prosper, so her pangs encrease;   25
His neighbour's wealth was great, he thought it such.
His own too little, Jacob's far too much;
But God in pity still augments his store,
His flocks and herds encrease still more and more;
A num'rous offspring plays around his tent;   30
Gold, Silver, servants, in abundance sent:
What greater blessing could he wish to see?
Alas! he sigh'd, and wish'd for liberty!—
Review'd the lone retreats where oft he'd been,
Too long frequented, and too often seen,   35
The mountain's top, the gloomy vale below,
The mazy paths so often wander'd through;

Reflects on dangers that had oft recurr'd,
The hard ungen'rous treatment long endur'd:
The scenes of early youth his thoughts employ, 40
Nor can the present yield substantial joy;
No abject fear can urge a longer stay,
Alert, he rises with returning day,
Departs in silence, and pursues his way.
Three days elaps'd e'er Laban mist his son, 45
Or knew his fav'rite household gods were gone;
Indignant then he heard that Jacob fled,
With wives and children, and with all he had!
He calls his kindred, bids his servants arm,
No good intended, though he did no harm; 50
For Jacob's God would not permit his foe
To stop his journey, or his rancour shew;
And, what may strange to divers christians seem,
The Syrian, though a heathen, told his dream,
With candor own'd the holy one appear'd, 55
Nor would conceal the dread command he heard;
Impell'd by fear, and aw'd by pow'r divine,
That pow'r which brings to nought what men design.
While Jacob urges how he oft was wrong'd,
By abject state and servitude prolong'd, 60
Deceiv'd, suspected, and his hire withheld,
No faith observ'd, promise e'er fulfill'd
Through twenty years had God increas'd his store,
Small his first stock, th' Almighty made it more:
Could Laban charge him with a breach of trust? 65
Though great his wealth, its ev'ry claim we just.
Then Pagan zeal, its idols to regain,
Ransack'd his tents: the search was all in vain,
Nor could the dumb inactive Gods complain,
What could be found among his stock or stuff 70
To merit censure or deserve reproof?
The aged sire could not the charge confute:
His heart seeks purely, and avoids dispute,
And while it, anxious, courts his children's loves,
Their want of duty and their flight reproves, 75
His purpos'd vengeance yields, his wrath subsides,
And Jacob, on his part, a feast provides;
They both a pious sacrifice ordain,
That neither should, for harm, return again;

For Jacob's God the Pagan still rever'd,   80
As thus he spake, and thus his vows were heard:
'When absent from each other we shall be,
The God of Heaven watch 'tween thee and me:
Perform thy promise when I'm gone from here
And treat my daughters with indulgent care: 85
Thy God is witness now betwixt us both;
Therefore beware, and not infringe thine oath'.
Thus Laban spake; and now prepares to go;
Clasps his dear children, and their children too;
With fond embrace the friendly mount he leaves,   90
And ling'ring looks, and a last blessing gives:
But Jacob yet was not exempt from fear;
A far more dreadful foe now claims his care;
Should Esau still retain his former hate,
Could he determine what might be his fate?   95
If gentle means could not his wrath assuage,
A simple shepherd must not brave his rage.
He [sells] his flock, and culls from thence the best,
If peradventure they may save the rest;
But when he hears of Esau's martial host,   100
He [honest] deems himself and children lost:
Yet breathes a pray'r before th' eternal throne,
And great Jehovah guides him safely on.
He meets the troop; propitious is the day,
For Esau now, his fury turn'd away,   105
With transport meets his brother's kind embrace,
And with tumultuous joy beholds his face.
On terms affectionate the brothers part,
And Jacob travels with a lighter heart;
His scene of trouble with his journey ends;   110
He meets his father and his former friends;
Each rising morn he finds his bliss increase,
He sleeps in safety, and he wakes in peace.

So may my eve of life be more serene,
More tranquil than the former part has been;   115
Thus cheering may no threatening clouds o'er cast,
That may too much resemble what is past.
O! let me spend the short remains of life
In peace and quiet, far from noise and strife,
My conduct such as best becomes my age   120

And something useful still my time engage:
Like Mary let me chuse the needful part,
But not with pious fraud or specious art.
At gloomy eve, when sol withdraws his light,
I'll beg of God to keep me through the night,   125
I'll bless his goodness each returning day,
And those who gave the bed whereon I lay.

May 24th, 1802

ROBERT BLOOMFIELD (1766–1823)

It has become something of a chestnut in accounts of Romantic-era labour-ing-class poetry to note that Robert Bloomfield's *Farmer's Boy* (1800) sold over 26,000 copies in the three years following its publication, thus vastly outselling another collection of poetry on rural themes entitled *Lyrical Ballads*. This remarkable popularity was echoed, on a smaller scale, in the testimonials of the period's labouring-class poets, who time and again cited Bloomfield as a model and source of inspiration. John Shaw (q.v.), for example, exclaimed, '[T]hat divine Poet has, with skilful hand, touched the master-chords of the human heart! whoever reads that Child of Nature, without being affected, may have other amiable qualities to recommend him in society, but I envy no one of his acquaintance' (*Woolton Green*, p. xii). Indeed, almost every poet appearing in this volume either mentioned Bloomfield directly (in poems, prefaces, or correspondence), or was compared to him by the era's literary reviewers. Stylistically, his influence is strongly felt in the works of William Holloway and Thomas Batchelor (q.q.v.), among others. Nor was his popularity short-lived, for though his later volumes never repeated the success of *The Farmer's Boy*, the steady sales of its many nineteenth-century editions made him one of the best-selling poets of the entire century. These facts of literary history, while striking in themselves, raise a surprisingly difficult question: what precisely was the nature of Bloomfield's appeal? To raise this question is implicitly to acknowledge that Bloomfield's poetry may not strike the modern reader as especially remarkable: to the contrary, much of it can appear to be a superior form of conventional verse, expressing, with a degree of grace and astuteness, the expected pastoral themes of piety, love of family, and love of country.

Bloomfield's status as a touchstone for early nineteenth-century poetic aspirants like Shaw, Holloway, and Ebenezer Elliott (q.v.) is reminiscent of Stephen Duck's legendary status for two generations of eighteenth-century labouring-class poets. The comparison to Duck is apt in other ways. Both writers earned praise and public attention for their descriptions of rustic scenery, and both not only depicted, but in some sense embodied, what Oliver Goldsmith heralded as 'a bold peasantry, their country's pride' ('The Deserted Village', l. 55). Similarly, both had spotless moral reputations, unlike Thomas Chatterton or Robert Burns, and this made them attractive to bourgeois readers and patrons. Yet such a view of Bloomfield takes us only so far. For although his patron Capel Lofft aggressively marketed him as a paragon of Christian virtue and his manifest piety was regularly mentioned by reviewers, many of Bloomfield's admirers also turned around and linked him to Burns anyway. Sometimes, of course, the yoking of the two poets was simply a matter of rhetorical convenience, aided by the pleasing alliterative balance of their surnames. But there was more to it than that; it reflected the widespread conviction that Burns and Bloomfield shared that most prized and most ineffable of literary qualities, the spark of original genius. The most concise expression of this conviction came from Ebenezer Elliott, who cast his eyes over the literary landscape in 1823 and, seeing little other than derivative verse and failed attempts at imitation, declared:

> Two coins alone are gold without alloy,
> The 'Tam o' Shanter' and 'The Farmer's Boy'.
>
> ('The Giaour', ll. 570–1)

Burns has largely maintained this reputation for singularity over the last two centuries, but while Bloomfield has not, the elements that gave rise to this view can be at least partially reconstructed.

Born in Honington, Suffolk, Bloomfield lost his father, a tailor, to smallpox while he was still an infant. (Other members of his immediate family would later fall victim to this infection; later in life Bloomfield would become acquainted with Edward Jenner, developer of the smallpox vaccine, and in 1804 would write in favour of vaccination in his poem *Good Tidings; or, News from the Farm*.) Bloomfield's mother, Elizabeth, supported her six children as a village schoolteacher. In such an environment, it is not surprising that Robert developed an early love of reading but as for most children of his class, his education was frequently interrupted by work and the demands of contributing to the family income. With the negligible addition of two to three months' attendance at the school in Ixworth, his formal education ceased completely by the time he was seven. At the age of eleven he went to serve at the farm of his uncle, William Austin, in Sapiston, Suffolk, an experience that would form the basis of *The Farmer's Boy*. When Robert was fifteen, he was sent to join his brothers, George and Nathaniel (q.q.v.) in London, going to work in George's shoemaking shop. Shoemaking had a long history as a welcoming trade for those unsuited for other, more demanding types of physical labor, and Bloomfield's association with the trade was in fact fortuitous for his development as a poet. Throughout the eighteenth and nineteenth centuries, cobbling rivalled weaving in producing artisan-poets, and George asserts in his biographical letter prefacing *The*

Farmer's Boy that his brother's literacy was encouraged by an especially accommodating workplace: thought too small and inexperienced to practice the craft when he arrived in London, Robert was employed in reading aloud to the others. It was in the London newspapers and periodicals that Robert first encountered poetry and developed a love for it. Encouraged by his co-workers, he published his first verses in *Say's Gazetter* in 1786, and claimed that he later composed the majority of the *Farmer's Boy* silently in his head while working: 'Nine tenths of it were put together as I sat at work, where there are usually six of us'. Although Bloomfield was never formally apprenticed, he set up his own shop in London in 1786, and went on to practice shoemaking for the remainder of his life. In 1790, he married Mary Anne Church, with whom he had five children.

Bloomfield might have remained in relative obscurity without the joint assistance of his brother and an ambitious patron. Capel Lofft was first approached by George Bloomfield with a manuscript of *The Farmer's Boy* in 1798, and Lofft sought out financial backers, corrected the proofs, and helped to see the poem through publication with the London firm of Vernor and Hood. (As part of his anti-Bloomfield polemic in *English Bards and Scotch Reviewers* Byron called Lofft 'the Mæcenas of shoemakers, and Preface-writer General to distressed versemen; a kind of gratis Accoucheur to those who wish to be delivered of rhyme, but do not know how to bring it forth'.) While relations between poet and patron began smoothly enough, by the time Bloomfield was publishing his second collection, *Rural Tales* (1802), they began to turn contentious, as Lofft disputed with Hood and as Bloomfield chafed both at the political additions that Lofft had made to the fourth edition of *The Farmer's Boy*, and at the explanatory notes Lofft proposed for the *Rural Tales* volume.

The Farmer's Boy, which Bloomfield began writing in 1796 and published in 1800, celebrates the intellectual and spiritual awakening through nature of the poem's speaker, the young farmhand Giles. Derived from Bloomfield's own childhood experiences, the poem endorses several values generally associated with Wordsworthian romanticism and poetic theory: the unadorned, sanctified beauty of rustic life, the importance of the innocent perspective of the child, and the merit of clear, simple poetic diction. The poem also reveals a heavy debt to eighteenth-century georgic and pastoral poetry, most obviously James Thomson's *The Seasons*, from which it borrows its four-part structure of seasonal change, as well as some elements of its diction. It also illustrates Bloomfield's awareness of the long tradition of loco-descriptive verse, and well earned him the title given to him by John Clare (q.v.): 'the English Theocritus'. Bloomfield's other influences included Milton, Pope, Goldsmith, and, in a way that has been mostly overlooked by commentators, the quiet grandeur of John Dyer's *Grongar Hill* (1726).

But these literary-historical factors do not really address the matter of the poem's attractiveness. The main bases of its appeal would seem to be its sentimental nostalgia, its evocation of a coherent social world, and its sometimes rapturous account of divine presence. It also exhibits a clear but temperate patriotism, such that readers of various political persuasions are led to feel allied with it. And throughout there is the attraction of Bloomfield's voice, at once modest, religious, unpretentious, and sweet-tempered. 'Sweetness' is indeed a watchword for the entire endeavour: the term is used by Lofft; by George Bloomfield in his biographical sketch of Robert; by Nathan Drake, the editor of the *Literary Hours* and an important early advocate of the poem; and by Robert, repeatedly, within the poem itself.

The poem begins with 'Spring', where Bloomfield seems implicitly to respond to a war-weary populace yearning for comfort and reassurance. The simple, healthy life of the boy Giles, we are told, is one of 'constant, cheerful servitude' (l. 30) in which blessings are innumerable. In this pure environment, 'the veriest clown that treads the sod, / Without one scruple gives the praise to God' ('Summer', ll. 127–8). In moving through the farmer's year—which, Bloomfield tells us, is fraught with uncertainty—the poem does occasionally offer brief treatments of the hardship Giles undergoes, but these are couched in a rhetoric of non-complaint. The harvesters in 'Summer' experience the universal rightness of their place in the universe as they gaze upon nature's bounty:

> Here, midst the boldest triumphs of her worth,
> Nature herself invites the Reapers forth;
> Dares the keen sickle from its twelvemonth's rest,
> And gives that ardour which in every breast
> From infancy to age alike appears,
> When the first sheaf its plumy top uprears. (ll. 131–6)

The volume's epigraph ('a shepherd's boy...he seeks no better name'), from Pope's 'Second Pastoral', initiates a steady strain of anti-luxurianism. Yet even as the poem tends to decry the social problems that are eroding the happy constancy of rural life, it does so in somewhat vague and circular ways. Bloomfield's depiction of the harvest-home feast in 'Summer' (ll. 287–400) appeals to the myth of an older, sturdier England, in which a once-a-year lowering of 'Distinction[']s...crest' ('The master, servant, and the merry guest, / Are [made] equal all') is deemed a true measure of social harmony. Yet Bloomfield then shifts gears abruptly and despairs that such social happiness is a thing of the past, when master and man could raise a glass together, at least on one day of the year. Now, he suggests, class distinctions have been sharpened by the rising social aspirations of the squirearchy;

'tyrant customs' and the glorification of 'Wealth' and 'Refinement' have edged the workers permanently off the guest-list, and made their daily lot inexorably worse. In such a world, 'the hope of humble industry is o'er': hard work is no longer respected or remunerated. But the lament comes without a specific call-to-arms, simply the plea to 'Let labour have its due', as Bloomfield says twice. Certainly one may desire greater argumentative clarity in such passages, but their sense of urgency is difficult to resist. So while the poem is not especially nuanced, it is sentimental without being anodyne, nostalgic without being mawkish, and offers touches of social realism and labouring-class solidarity that studiously avoid a radical agenda. Thus it is a poem people from many walks of life could admire, agree on, and in some sense make their own.

Despite the success of *The Farmer's Boy*, Bloomfield faced ongoing financial difficulties, partly because literary engagements cut into his regular business. In an act of largesse, in 1803 the Duke of Grafton found him a paid position as undersealer in the King's Bench Court. But it was a position for which Bloomfield was ill-suited, and he resigned after several months. Shoemaking continued to be his main source of income, supplemented with the building and selling of Aeolian harps. While composing the public-service piece *Good Tidings*, Bloomfield was also at work on the poems that would comprise his third collection, *Wild Flowers; or Pastoral and Local Poetry* (1806). At this same time, as he approached his fortieth birthday, his health began to suffer. In 1807 a rejuvenating journey was organized by Mr and Mrs T. J. Lloyd Baker, who took him on a tour of the River Wye. Bloomfield recorded the tour in a journal and later in his second major long poem, *The Banks of Wye*, published in 1811. It was in 1811 as well that Bloomfield's hopes for financial security met with a serious blow, due to the death of the Duke of Grafton and the failure of Bloomfield's booksellers following the death of Hood. This latter loss, in particular, hampered his efforts to gain access to his poems' copyright and thus to secure additional income from them.

Though not the financial panacea Bloomfield needed in 1811, *The Banks of Wye* displays some of the tonal and perspectival qualities that mark *The Farmer's Boy*. In a rallying prologue spoken in heroic couplets by 'the syren Pleasure' (I, l. 22), Bloomfield is exhorted to leave town and sickbed for better scenes, and the main poetic narrative, in octosyllabic verse, is suffused with the feeling of a sociable pilgrimage in high summer. With a 'cheerful group' (I, l. 35) Bloomfield treks from one literary shrine or personified locale to the next, and also back in time, as each castle ruin and sublime vista inspires reflections on nobility, history, natural grandeur, and human struggle. The explicit premise of spontaneous enjoyment is almost comically effusive but nonetheless charming; the historical allusions are accessible; the nationalism palatable. Inset ballads, imagined as the utterances of local people, extend Bloomfield's evocations of Thomson and Wordsworth (a 'Gleaner's Song' in Bloomfield's hands sounds nothing like Wordsworth, even as the ideas leading up to it share much with his theory of poetry).

In 1812 Bloomfield left London for the town of Shefford in Bedford-shire, and received the promise of a £15 annuity from the new Duke of Grafton. Even so, his financial situation was still precarious, and he traveled to London several times in the ensuing years to attend to business matters. Money was also a motive in the 1815 publication of a children's tale he had written several years before, *The History of Little Davy's New Hat*. He would also work on other poems for children, such as 'The Bird and Insect's Post Office', that appeared in his posthumous *Remains* (1824). Coupled with his physical ailments, the poet's situation eventually became so dire that there were efforts to begin a charitable subscription for him. Yet his correspond-ence in these later years continued to show abundant quantities of good-humour, resilience, and independence. He continued to write, and brought out his last collection, *May Day with the Muses*, in 1822, as well as *Hazelwood Hall*, a drama, which he would send out for publication in 1823, a few months before his death in August.

Despite the fact that Bloomfield spent the better part of his adult life liv-ing and working in London, his love of the countryside and his emphasis on rural life and values remained a constant in his work. And although he spoke to social and political concerns of his day, as in the poem to Jenner, his strongest attachments remained to the oral tradition, represented in the bal-lads and songs he frequently favored. Much of *The Banks of Wye*, for example, falls into the formal, loco-descriptive mode established for the eighteenth century by Pope in *Windsor Forest*, yet its interpolated ballads and elegies were certainly inspired by bits of local lore Bloomfield encountered on his journey. Other prime examples of this impulse are 'The Fakenham Ghost, A Ballad', from *Rural Tales*, and 'The Horkey, A Provincial Ballad', from *Wild Flowers*, the latter of which captures the dialect cadences of Suf-folk. Like Clare, Bloomfield deeply loved the natural world he described, and it seems fitting that as Clare began his own publishing career, he would look to the aging Bloomfield as a mentor—a 'brother bard and fellow labourer'. But if the poets are inevitably and rightly linked in literary history, their poetry is utterly distinct: Bloomfield's, more synthesizing, more self-con-sciously sonorous, more neoclassical in its urges toward allegory and the ideal of simplicity; Clare's, more reportorial and particularized in its depic-tion of landscape. Bloomfield's public political quietism has perhaps made the recovery of his work slower than Clare's, and slower that it ought to have been, but it now seems likely that his place as the best-selling poet of the early nineteenth century will soon lead to a thorough reexamination of his legacy.

FURTHER READING

Robert Bloomfield, *Selected Poems of Robert Bloomfield*, eds John Goodridge and John Lucas. 2nd edition. (Nottingham: Trent Editions, 2006)

DNB

Tim Fulford and Debbie Lee, 'The Beast Within: The Imperial Legacy of Vaccination in History and Literature' *Literature and History* 9, no. 1 (2000), 1–23

William Hazlitt, 'On Thompson and Cowper', *The Complete Works of William Hazlitt*, ed. P.P. Howe, 21 vols (London: Dent, 1930–4), V, pp. 85–104

Bridget Keegan, 'Cobbling Verse: Early Modern Shoemaker Poets' *Eighteenth Century Theory and Interpretation* 42.3 (2001), 195–217

Jonathan Lawson, *Robert Bloomfield* (Boston: G. K. Hall/Twayne, 1980)

John Lucas, 'Bloomfield and Clare', *The Independent Spirit: John Clare and the Self-Taught Tradition* (Helpston: The John Clare Society and the Margaret Grainger Memorial Trust, 1994), pp. 55–68

Simon White, Bridget Keegan, and John Goodridge (eds.), *Robert Bloomfield: The Forgotten Romantic* (Lewisburg: Bucknell University Press), *forthcoming.*

WILLIAM HOLLOWAY (1761–1854)

William Holloway's almost total disappearance from literary history is perplexing, given both the substance of his career and his biographical and literary affiliations with several important Romantic period writers. Like Robert Bloomfield, who would emerge as the most important influence on his mature poetry, Holloway was transplanted from country to city, leaving Dorset for London in 1798 and remaining there until his death in 1854. Having been a journeyman printer in the town of Weymouth in his early years, Holloway found work at the East India House, where he became a colleague of Romanticism's most famous belletristic clerk, Charles Lamb. Their tenures were remarkably parallel: each worked for thirty-three years (Holloway 1798–1831; Lamb 1792–1825), and each eventually received a pension from the Company. The financial terms of Holloway's employment are unknown, but if his pension approximated the $^2/_3$ salary the Company awarded Lamb (memorably described in Lamb's essay 'The Superannuated Man'), then it seems likely that Holloway's long retirement in the north London village of Hackney constituted a definitive late preference for town life, rather than a decision forced by financial need.

Though Holloway is not mentioned by name in Lamb's recollections of the East India House, V. J. Adams suggests that Lamb had him in mind in writing: 'All the morning I am pestered. I could sit and gravely cast up sums in great books....But there are a set of amateurs of the Belle Lettres—the gay science—who come to me as a sort of rendezvous, putting questions of criticism' (quoted in Adams 1982, p. 169). Indeed, though Holloway had published poems, prose sketches and apparently at least one long fictional tale while living in Weymouth, his instalment in London was undoubtedly a watershed event in his 'amateur' literary life. '[N]o sooner had he taken his seat at East India House', notes Adams, 'than his poems began to appear month by month in one of the foremost London periodicals, the *European Magazine*. Many of the poems dealt with subjects and events, some commonplace, some colourful, connected with the daily scene:—lines on a London watchman who had perished from the cold; lines occasioned by the providential rescue of a friend from suicide; extempore lines to a friend on the birth of a daughter; lines on the conduct of the populace at a late public execution' (1982, p. 169). In quoting Adams here, it should be noted that his two accounts of Holloway's life and publishing activities, which include bibliographies of the magazine writings, are far and away our most important pieces of basic scholarship on the poet; the dissemination of their information has been limited by their publication in the relatively obscure *Proceedings of the Dorset Natural History and Archaeological Society.*

The publication of Robert Bloomfield's *The Farmer's Boy* (1800) was the next decisive event in the unfolding of Holloway's career. Adams says there can be 'no doubt' (p. 170) that Holloway was the author of the joyful dialect poem, 'An Epistle from Roger Coulter of Dorsetshire to his Friend Giles Bloomfield the Suffolk Farmer's Boy', which appeared anonymously in the *Monthly Mirror* of 1802 and again in Bloomfield's *Remains* in 1824. 'When vust I heard the tuneful voice', professes the poem's speaker,

> I stood ameaz'd, an' star'd, and gap'd awoy:—
> That can't be Stephen, Ned, nor Hodge, I cried;
> When zome oone zaid—"Why, that's the Zuffolk Buoy"

Holloway's admiration for Bloomfield's poem (as well as for Goldsmith's 'The Deserted Village') helped him orient the long poem he was composing at the time, entitled *The Peasant's Fate.* Aided by Thomas Hill, a well-connected book collector and part-proprietor of the *Monthly Mirror* who had read *The Farmer's Boy* in manuscript, Holloway was able to contract with Vernor and Hood, Bloomfield's publishers, for the 1802 publication of *The Peasant's Fate.* Adams notes that the financial terms of the contract were identical to those given to Bloomfield (1982, p. 171). The volume was reviewed by *The British Critic, The Monthly Review, The Critical Review,* and others, and received generally favourable notices; a second London edition was published the same year, and two pirated American editions followed shortly thereafter. Following on the heels of this success, Holloway would publish several more volumes over the next decade, including *Scenes of Youth* (1803), *The Chimney-Sweeper's Complaint* (1806), *The Minor Minstrel* (1808), and *The Country Pastor* (1812). He also co-authored, with John Branch, the four-volume *British Museum or Elegant Repository of Natural History* (1803–4), and throughout these years his occasional poems continued to appear in the *European Magazine,* the *Monthly Mirror,* and the *Lady's Monthly Museum.* A fourth edition of *The Peasant's Fate* appeared in 1821, apparently so designated because a planned third edition had been cancelled in 1807.

In offering a general assessment of Holloway's poetry, we can say that three of the figures whose influence is most pervasive amongst the writers gathered in this collection—Wordsworth, Burns, and course Bloomfield—all leave a visible imprint on his work. Holloway's *The Peasant's Fate* and its accompanying 'Preface' contain interesting echoes of Wordsworth in 'Michael', 'The Old Cumberland Beggar', and the 'Preface' to *Lyrical Ballads*, though they lack Wordsworth's nuance. Holloway's verse also includes comic ballads and supernatural tales suggestive of Burns, but the moralizing 'application' that concludes 'Sam Sear's Three Tokens' is evidence of how his satirical impulse is kept under careful constraint. The Bloomfield connection is the most significant. Holloway's themes and subjects were influenced by his connections with the circle that included the brothers Robert, Nat, and George Bloomfield (q.q.v.); and also Henry Kirke White, Capel Lofft, and Thomas Hill. In addition to the dialect poem mentioned above, Holloway addressed several other poems to Robert, and his verse frequently recalls Bloomfield's in its piety, earnestness, anxious love of country, and intense rural nostalgia. Like Bloomfield, Holloway foregrounds a strong sense of Christian purposefulness and duty, though he is more overtly judgemental, and more willing to voice anger or disgust. Many of his poems, especially the longer narratives, work by a continual juxtaposition of an innocent rural past with a present that has been corrupted by enclosure, war, or urbanization. In these works contented rural poverty is presented as a viable worldview, though the venality of modern society makes its realization difficult.

FURTHER READING

V. J. Adams, 'William Holloway (1761–1854) and his Dorset Poems', *Proceedings of the Dorset Natural History and Archaeological Society* 60 (1982), 167–77

V. J. Adams, 'William Holloway [an addendum]', *Proceedings of the Dorset Natural History and Archaeological Society* 65 (1987), 265–6

John Barrell and John Bull (eds), *The Penguin Book of English Pastoral Verse* (Harmondsworth: Penguin, 1974), pp. 409–12

The Remains of Robert Bloomfield (London: Baldwin, Cradock, and Joy, 1824)

DNB (Thomas Hill)

James Sambrook, 'Some Heirs of Goldsmith: Poets of the Poor in the Late Eighteenth Century', *Studies in Burke and His Time* 11 (1970), 1348–61.

From *The Peasant's Fate: A Rural Poem* (1802)

From *Preface*

The changes in rural life and manners, which have taken place in this coun-
try, in the course of a few years, furnish ample matter for reflection and
regret. The spirit of avarice and monopoly has possessed almost all ranks
and degrees of people, and appears to have rendered the heart callous to the
feelings of humanity. The drift of this little attempt is principally designed,
(without adverting to political argument,) to shadow forth the evils arising to
the peasantry of this country, from the system of engrossing small farms,
and driving the hereditary occupiers to the necessity of embracing a mari-
time or military life for support, or being reduced to the most abject state of
dependence, and submitting to the galling hardship of becoming *servants* on
the spot where they once had been *masters*.

The introduction and progress of luxury, have likewise materially affected
the comforts of the lower orders of society; and though our refinements
may have advanced trade and commerce, these cannot effectually counter-
balance the injury done to husbandry and agriculture, which have been very
properly called the natural sources of the riches of every nation.

The character of this Poem is purely *English*; the good sense of the
present age having prevailed over ancient prepossession, in favour of far-
fetched subjects, of the Arcadian cast, which have to boast neither of nature
nor truth. Shepherds and shepherdesses, in a state of perfect happiness,
bowers of unfading bliss, and streams of inexhaustible pleasure, exist no
longer, but in the wild vagaries of Imagination: and the majority of mankind
has become weary of following her through long labyrinths, which resemble
'passages that lead to nothing.' A THOMSON, a GOLDSMITH, and a COWPER,
with others, of a later date, have pointed out a track, which might still be
pursued with pleasure and with interest. Rural poetry should speak the lan-
guage of Nature; and classic Criticism has, of late, learned to relax his rigid
brow, at the native wild notes of the British muse.

From *The Peasant's Fate*

'Former division of Downs...Modern changes'

The common, clad with vegetative gold,
Whose well-dried stores allay the wintry cold;
Whence ev'ry family its portion claims,
To fence the hovel, or recruit the flames
From path to path, that winds along the plain,   5
The cheerful Stephen held his rustic reign;
While, still observant of his due commands,
In act to start, the faithful *Keeper* stands.
Numbers, beside, there led their bleating charge,
Enjoy'd their pastimes gay, and rov'd at large;   10
But now no more those rural scenes invite,
Far diff'rent objects meet the aching sight;
In all the pomp of sanguinary way,
I see the military bands, afar,
Extend their glitt'ring lines, or, wheeling wide,   15
In parallel divide and sub-divide,
While, thro' the op'ning ranks, large martial strains,
Progressive, roll along the dusty plains,
Which yield no pasture to the fleecy kind,
That distant range, their juicy meal to find.   20
Scar'd from her haunts, the twitt'ring linnet flies,
The quiv'ring larks ascends the smould'ring skies,
And finches, that on downy thistles feed,
Spread their gilt wings, and seek the silent mead.

'The ancient Pastor'

The rev'rend *Pastor*, now advancing slow,
Notes with respect each salutation low:
Tho' pure his doctrines, with instruction fraught,
'His life adorn'd the doctrines which he taught.'
Far from his flock, he idled not his days,   5
Like modern teachers, lost in pleasure's ways,
Triflers! regardless of their sacred charge,
Who leave it to the enemy at large!
Good will and charity for all he bore,
And sigh'd sincerely, when he could no more.   10
But whence this change? The path with grass o'ergrown,

The mouldering tombs, the fences broken down,
While delving hogs, and toil-worn horses tread
The regions of the undistinguish'd dead,
The vicarage walls with streaks of green defil'd,   15
The windows hid with weeds and nettles wild?
The ample garden, long in deep decay,
Exhibits now no more its sun-flowers gay;
Tulips nor hollyhocks flaunt in summer pride,
Nor rasberry thickets grace its southern side.   20

'Modern Rector and Curate'

A *richer cure* the wealthy *Rector* shares,
And to an ill-paid stranger leaves his cares;
While to the distant watering-place he hies,
Or dissipations of the city tries:
Once in the year the *needful* visit pays,   25
And thro' some long-forgotten sermon strays;
While, round the yawning congregation, fly
Somnific spells, and light on ev'ry eye!
    How shall the Muse her indignation spare,
When Pride and Av'rice Merit's honours wear?   30
Fain would she plead the worthy Curate's cause,
To scanty income bound by narrow laws,
Who, while he deals th' eternal bread of life,
Hears clamorous infants and a virtuous wife
Demand, in vain, their perishable food,   35
And claim the bounty of the kind and good:
Think what the mind intelligent must feel!
How deep the wound, how difficult to heal!
    O ye! who love religion's hallow'd name,
Awake in kindred breasts a generous shame;   40
Nor longer let a blushing land forbear,
To soothe the suff'rings of those sons of Care!

'Village Smith'

    Beneath yon elders, furr'd with black'ning smoke,
The sinewy Smith, with many a labour'd stroke,
His clinking anvil plied, in shed obscure,   45
And truant schoolboys loiter'd round the door.
There would the swains, on wintry eve, retire,
To warm their limbs, and blow the rumbling fire;

While various tales their proffer'd toil repaid,
And vast improvement to the mind convey'd;   50
For much of life th' experienced sage had seen,
In peace and war, since royal Anne was queen;
And much of fights and shipwrecks sad, he told,
Of burning mountains and of Scythian cold,
Of spectre forms, that haunt the convent's gloom,   55
Or fiends that glare around the murderer's tomb!
But now the sledge, the file, no more resounds;
No more the ploughboy, from the neighb'ring grounds,
At evening, trudges with the blunted share,
Or broken traces, to receive repair.   60
Poor, stumbling *Ball* no more shall thither plod,
And dozing wait, in patience, to be shod.
The fertile lawn, of idly-pamper'd steeds,
A useless race, for false ambition, breeds.
The fallow lands, where cheerful peasants earn'd   65
Their weekly bread, to proud plantations turn'd,
Forget to yield their auburn crops of grain,
That fill'd the petty farmer's early wain,
When on his ambling nag, he took his round,
With flaggon to the tatter'd saddle bound,   70
Replenish'd well with hearty home-brew'd ale,
The toil-contending reapers to regale.
Now into one a hundred fields are thrown,
Their tenants banish'd, and their pleasures flown!
To crowded towns, the poor mechanic strays,   75
To spend the sickly evening of his days;
Or hostile fields, or boist'rous seas, he proves,
A hapless exile from the scenes he loves;
While Recollection ever to his mind
Presents those comforts he has left behind!   80

'Poor-House'

True, an unhappy *remnant* still remains,
Which grudging Pride with scanty dole sustains,
A hopeless race, that own yon bleak abode,
Of Grief and Care, beside the public road,
Propp'd are whose leaning walls, whose hanging door   85
Drags heavy, jarring on the earthen floor;
Keen thro' the shatter'd casements cold winds blow,

The half-stripp'd roof admits the whirling snow;
Scarce, on the gloomy hearth, one lingering spark
The cricket cheers, or gilds his cavern dark;   90
While, shivering round, the wretched inmates stand,
A ragged, meagre, pale, dejected band!
Here is the man who wealthy days has seen;
Here is the widow, once the village queen;
Here too, the damsel, who, in guardless hour,   95
Fell a sad victim to Seduction's pow'r!
Curst be the villain, whose insidious art
Tainted her virgin purity of heart,
Then left her, thus, to shame, reproach, and grief,
Sure only in the grave to find relief: 100
Here orphans bend to Poverty's hard laws,
Whose fathers perish'd in their Country's cause!
Wives, anxious wives! for distant husbands mourn,
In vain anticipating their return!
Mothers, of their last duteous sons bereft,   105
Without one hope, or consolation left;
With numbers more, whose tale but to disclose,
Would swell 'the catalogue of human woes.'
    In genial climes, where softer seasons reign,
Amid the bosom of the placid main,   110
Where never Commerce nor the Arts deign'd smile
On the rude natives of some lonely isle,
Well might the wood, the cave, or cliff afford
Sufficient shelter to the wand'ring hoard;
But in this land of elegance and ease,   115
Where all that sweetens life conspires to please,
Can polish'd man, behold his fellows pine,
In scenes like these, and every joy resign?
Beneath the torturing passions' cruel strife,
To languish out the poor remains of life?   120

'England compared with the most fruitful Countries'

    Oh, happy land! ere Luxury learnt to roam,
In quest of pleasures, better sought at home,
Where Heav'n, impartial, spreads her blessings wide,
Nor, captious, sets her meanest sons aside;
Say, do the purple borders of the Rhine,   125
Or Arno's sides with brighter fruitage shine,

Than thine own vales? Hesperian vineyards fair
Boast fresher streams, or breathe a purer air?
What, tho' the Ganges' hallow'd tide be roll'd
O'er rocks of diamond, and o'er sands of gold,   130
Tho' ancient Nile, with fructifying waves,
An earthly paradise unfailing laves;
Behold *our* fields, with glorious harvests crown'd;
Voluptuous meads, where fat'ning herds abound;
Those plains, where Pan his fleecy charge attends,   135
The countless stores that rich Pomona sends:
Then say, shall ALBION envy other climes,
Or mourn, inglorious, here degenerate times?
Yes, *mourn* she must! For, lo! a venal band
On Nature's bounty lay the gripping hand,   140
Wrest from the poor the patrimonial cot,
His paddock add to their superfluous lot,
Meanly dependent, bid him seek his bread,
While, Timur-like, their vassal down they tread,
Frustrate the scheme wise Providence has plann'd,   145
And half depopulate their native land!
    Have you no bowels, you, who claim the name
Of *Man*? Or different is your mental frame,
Whose ears, unmov'd, can hear the voice of woe,
Whose eyes behold the streams of sorrow flow?   150
How shall *you* lift those hands to MERCY's throne,
Which ne'er to deal her liberal gifts were known?

From *The Minor Minstrel* (1808)

To Robert Bloomfield, on the Abolition of the Slave Trade

Have feats of arms, and deeds of blood
    Found many a harp of living fire,
To spread their triumphs far abroad,
    And Emulation's soul inspire;

And are the Bards of Britain mute,   5
    That should have pour'd the loudest lay,
To celebrate, at Afric's suit,
    The dawn of Freedom's glorious day?

O! had fair Olney's Poet liv'd
    To see Britannia burst the bands,   10
O'er which his feeling bosom griev'd,
    From sad Angola's sable hands;

Who can now tell what numbers dear
    From his delighted heart had flow'd!
What tides of transport strong and clear,   15
    Had borne his praise to Britain's GOD!

Then, ROBERT! say, shall we refuse—
    In sympathy—akin to wake
The warblings of the rural muse,
    For Britain's—and for Afric's sake?   20

Not e'en the poor enfranchis'd slave
    Should higher raise his grateful voice;
Or louder, o'er the western wave,
    Exulting shout—'Rejoice! Rejoice!'

The Common;
Or, The Soil of Liberty

Why do I love this lonely haunt,
    With straggling furze and fern o'er run;
With slopes, and banks, of verdure scant,
    Parch'd by the fervid summer sun?
        O! ever was it dear to me;   5
        For 'tis the soil of Liberty!

I envy not Circassian groves,
    Whose roses boast perennial bloom;
Nor Persian bow'rs, where Fancy loves,

In silent ecstacy, to roam,   10
  While thus, from Tyrant-terrors free,
  I trace this tract of Liberty.

Here, by the sandy, deep-worn ways,
  Where grinding wheels but seldom pass,
The poor their clod-wall'd hovels raise,   15
  And thatch their roofs with broom and grass,—
  And fathers, children's children, see,
  Sport on this soil of Liberty.

What though fair Cultivation hies
  From hence, to seek a happier seat,   20
Where mounds, and proud enclosures rise,
  To guard its walks from vagrant feet?—
  No Lordling here, of fortune vain,
  Claims undisputed right to reign.

Beneath the furze-bush, dress'd in gold,   25
  The crow-foot and the daisy spring:
Above the fox-glove bells unfold;
  And round the brake sweet woodbines cling;
  Dear is this walk, all walks above,
  To village Amity and Love!   30

The labourer cuts his fuel here,
  His faggot binds, and feeds his beast;
And, tired, beneath the hawthorn near,
  Outstretch'd, enjoys unbroken rest.
  With envy well may Grandeur see   35
  How he enjoys his Liberty!

Happy the boy who keeps those sheep!
  Who hunts the hornet o'er the down,
Plucks early violets where they peep;
  Or with the wild thyme weaves a crown: 40
  I'd rather share his joys with him,
  Than wear a despot's diadem!

Yes! let the souls of niggard taste
  Call it a desert, and a wild;
I love the solitary waste: 45
  I lov'd it from a cottage-child;
  And joy'd to range, uncheck'd and free,
  Along this soil of Liberty.

O! I could spend the longest day,
   On dale, or down, a lonely wight!— 50
Charm'd with some wild, romantic lay,—
   From peep of dawn, till close of night;
      And short would seem that day, to me,
      Spent on this soil of Liberty.

And, Hampstead! hence thy heath delights, 55
   Beyond proud London's neighb'ring tow'rs;
For there the MINSTREL'S FRIEND invites
   To academic walks and bow'rs,
      Where Love, and Peace, and Poësy,
      Endear the soil of Liberty. 60

Amidst a world of wars, and wrongs,
   What true-born Briton's heart but glows,
That still to his dear Land belongs
   One spot, where Freedom may repose?
      For this my praises rise to thee, 65
      Thou GOD of Briton's Liberty!

Sam Sear's Three Tokens;
Or, John Hurdler's Tale

I never pass that mill below the wear,
But, as I pass, I think poor SAM SEAR:
For there he liv'd, as easy as could be,
An honest, plodding, simple soul was he,
Well known to all the villagers around, 5
For many a mile, and still their corn he ground:
As punctual as the morn, with sacks a store,
The constant miller call'd at ev'ry door;
The children ran familiar when he came,
Patted his horse, and called him by his name, 10
And hail'd the grist—welcome to all who bake—
Forerunner of nice tart, and hot plum-cake.

Now SAM had mighty faith in signs and dreams,
Tokens, and ghosts, and tattling gossips' themes:
He could expound the mewing of a cat,   15
Howl of a dog, or scratching of a rat:
A death-watch ticking at his own bed-side,
Always fore-doom'd a neighbour ere he died;
Nor could a screech-owl scream, or raven croak,
But its portent was told to cottage-folk!   20
Once, on a long dark night, of hail and rain,
Sam restless woke, and slept, and woke again.
He waited long to hear the striking clock,
Or the first crowing of the early cock;
For past the hour of twelve it was, he guess'd—   25
Then sought he to compose himself to rest:
But the bleak wind howl'd hollow o'er the moor,
And three low knocks assail'd the bolted door—
And hark! a voice that might the boldest scare,
Distinctly calls—'SAM SEAR! SAM SEAR! SAM SEAR!'   30
Down in his bed he shrunk, and pull'd the rug,
In agitation, o'er his burning *lug*.
So morning worms, disturb'd by early tread,
Shrink back into their holes, and hide the head.
He lay and held his breath, for very fear,   35
Nor durst his nose above the pillow rear:
At length he feels his courage half renew'd,
And strives to chase the terrors that intrude;
By slow degrees they leave his vapour'd brain,
And sleep returns, to close his eyes again.   40
Not long he slept—and only woke to hear
The self-same sounds—'SAM SEAR! SAM SEAR! SAM SEAR!'
His rushing hair (to Fancy's feeling) rose,
And with a bristly tumult rais'd the clothes,
Beneath whose weight he groan'd, and buried lay,   45
Like delving hog beneath a stack of hay:
A cold, cold dew, ran trickling o'er his frame,
And fast his fainting spirits went and came.

The tedious hour lagg'd on, with heavy pace,
At length he ventures to unveil his face,   50
To take one peep, if yet he may descry
A streak of dawn, along the eastern sky:
When, hark! the dreadful voice salutes his ear,

Three times again—'SAM SEAR! SAM SEAR! SAM SEAR!'
Oh! who can tell what pangs this daring cost?   55
Without a doubt he gave himself for lost!
He felt his heart within him dying fast—
'Ay! Ay!' thought he, 'my time is come at last!
Not only thrice it call'd, but three times three—
Nine days, perhaps, are all allotted me!'   60
Then he bethought himself of many a sin,
While ev'ry bone was quaking in his skin,
But div'd so deep, and stopp'd his ears so hard,
That future sounds were utterly debarr'd.

Imagine, you that can, how long the night   65
To him appear'd—how welcome the morning light;
With trembling haste, he huddles on his clothes,
Unbars the door, and to the stable goes.
A snore, or groan, first startled him, I ween;
But soon he pluck'd up courage, and peep'd in,   70
There, underneath the manger, coil'd, he saw
His friend, *John Woodrow*, grov'ling in the straw.
That night poor *John*, by *Jack o' Lantern* led,
Had been entice'd an endless maze to tread—
Losing his way, from town returning late—   75
Somewhat with fumes of ale confus'd his pate—
Had flounder'd thro' the mire, and thro' the flood,
'Till half exhausted grown, and cas'd with mud:
Had bawl'd till tir'd, at SAM'S unopen'd door,
Then sought this place to rest, and bawl no more.   80

'So! so!' the Miller cried, with valour stout,
'Now I perceive the cause of all this rout;
I verily believ'd, as I have breath,
Your call on me, last night, betoken'd *death*!'
'*Fegs*, and 'twas nearly true', poor *Woodrow* cried,   85
'For had you staid much longer I had died;
I am so wet and cold, that I require
A breakfast, and a comfortable fire.'
'That thou shalt have', cried SAM, 'with all my heart,
I'll tap the cider—come and take a part: 90
I warrant, *John*, and don't you think me right,
We both shall remember this sad night?'

Application

Such idle fears and terrors still they see,
Who fain would look into futurity:
Rest we contented with the little known, 95
And leave conceal'd events to God alone!

Roke Down
A Descriptive Sketch

The Down was blue with scented thyme;
 The sky-lark soar'd and sung;
Kine low'd; and, from the Farm of Roke,
 The voice of Labour rung.
'Mother, our journey let us take; 5
 There's no excuse to day'—
Cries little Will—His mother yields,
 And lo! they trudge away.

Full light of heart, and light of foot,
 He bounds along before; 10
Now, stopping, curious questions asks;—
 And asks them o'er and o'er.
The well, that in the bottom lies,
 Round which the cattle throng
At parching noon; the bramble-bush, 15
 Where linnets trill their song:—

The distant heath; the distant wood,
 With winding walks about;
The flocks; the shadows of the clouds,
 That pass in airy route— 20
All these, in turn, attract his eye,
 Till on the hill's green brow
He sees the swelling barrow rise
 And runs, to wonder, now:

For there with pick-axe, crow, and spade,   25
    The swains explore their way;
And human bones, and mould'ring urns,
    Lie all expos'd to day.
They say, a battle here was fought
    In England's mournful times,   30
When pour'd o'er all the western coast
    The foe, from foreign climes;

And here, in one vast mingled heap,
    Promiscuously, the brave,
Strangers and friends, unnam'd, unknown,   35
    Possess one common grave!
'Twas love of fame, and thirst of pow'r,
    Caus'd all this waste of life;
And oh! how long did thousands mourn
    The fierce, unnat'ral strife?   40

And thus the matron moraliz'd,
    And felt her bosom sad,
To think mankind should be so vain,
    So sinful, and so mad;
The little rustic ponder'd too,   45
    Or tattled, as he ran—
'Since men so wicked are, no more
    I'll wish to be a man!'

Charity

Occasioned by a sight of the Anniversary Meeting of the Parochial Charity-Schools at St. Paul's

Fairest of all the guardian Seraph train,
Sweet CHARITY! auspicious is thy reign
In Britain's capital; while tyrants pour
The tide of war o'er many a ravag'd shore,
Behold thy num'rous family with smiles,—   5
The rising offspring of the British Isles!

Handmaid of Providence! to thee they turn,
Thou friend and comforter of those that mourn!
And cheerful to this consecrated dome,
To offer the first-fruits of Praise they come: 10
Now let the tributary anthem rise
To Heav'n, an acceptable sacrifice.
Now let the heart, that feels for human kind,
Enjoy the transports to the Good assign'd!
Imperial Rome, at subject nations' cost,   15
Her stately amphitheatres might boast,
Triumphal arches rear'd for men of blood,
And fane of many a fabled Demi-God;
But could she boast a spectacle like this—
Ten thousand infant candidates for bliss?   20
Snatch'd from the jaws of want and infamy,
And train'd for hope and immortality!
These shall sustain our parts another day,—
When this declining race is pass'd away;—
And scatter'd o'er the world combine the fame   25
Of British Charity with Britain's name.
Those hearts shall kindle in their country's cause,
Partake her triumphs, and defend her laws,
To deeds of pure benevolence aspire,
Adorn the arts, or rouse the patriot fire.   30
Still, Xerces-like, I feel one bosom-truth,
'Midst all this range of beauty, health, and youth;
These numbers, tier o'er tier, that charm mine eye,
Ere yet a hundred in dust must lie!
But from their ashes a new race shall spring,   35
And equal honours to their nation bring;
Improv'd mankind shall mark their virtuous course,
And trace its influence to this hallow'd source.

NATHANIEL BLOOMFIELD
(1759–AFTER 1822)

The trajectory, and relative failure, of Nathaniel Bloomfield's literary career is an interesting case study in the prickly dynamics of the reception of labouring-class poetry. The brother of Robert Bloomfield (q.v.), whose *The Farmer's Boy* (1800) was perhaps the foundational text for Romantic-era labouring-class poetry, Nat was a tailor by trade who produced a single volume of poems, *An Essay on War, Honington Green, and Other Poems* (1803). It earned a mixed critical response and a second edition, and its title poem generated some pointed controversy. But despite his evident skill and the potential selling-power of the Bloomfield name, Nat never published any additional verse, even as Robert went on to publish new volumes in 1802, 1804, 1806, 1811, and 1822 (with a posthumous *Remains* appearing in 1824). In the two centuries since *An Essay on War* appeared, it has provoked virtually no scholarly commentary.

In the marketing of *An Essay on War*, every attempt was made to capitalize on Nat's sibling connection. As with his brother's volume, the Preface was written by the political reformer and bellettrist Capel Lofft (1751–1824) and was based on biographical details supplied by a third brother, George (q.v.). Lofft's introduction stressed the brothers' closeness, and was suffused with the kind of dripping grandiloquence that had characterized his introduction to *The Farmer's Boy*. Describing, for example, how Nat's youthful interest in church music was ended when his voice changed to a bass 'of extremely narrow compass [...] *weak* and *tremulous*', Lofft mused, 'This latter defect of voice was observ'd in THOMSON: and perhaps it may arise sometimes not from a fault in the natural quality of the voice, but from exceeding sensibility to *Poetry* and *Music*' (pp. vii–viii). Similarly, in correcting Nat's date of birth to 23 February 1759, Lofft paused for a gratuitous footnote:

> I had said, and certainly upon full authority, 23d *April*, which the Author his-self believ'd to be the Day: and had remark'd accordingly it was a Day distinguish'd by the *Birth* and *Death* of SHAKESPEARE. But Mr N. BLOOM-FIELD discover'd and immediately communicated the mistake as to the

Day. Thus we lose an interesting coincidence: but we gain what is of greater value; a just and prompt sacrifice to truth and candor (p. vi).

In retrospect it appears that this strategy of marketing Nat as another earnest and virtuous Bloomfield was, if perfectly understandable, nonetheless ill-advised. There may have been some market over-saturation, of a kind that provoked Byron snidely to ask, 'if Phoebus smiled on you / BLOOMFIELD! Why not on brother NATHAN too? / Him too the Mania, not the Muse has seized; / Not inspiration but a mind diseased' ('English Bards and Scotch Reviewers', ll. 781–4).

But it is probably less the case that the Bloomfieldian glow had worn off, than that Nat and his poetry needed a fundamentally different kind of advocacy. For the fact is that the major poems of *An Essay on War* reject sentimentality in favor of an independent-minded, sometimes dark assessment of human motives and behaviour, and the volume's overall sensibility is quite different from that of *The Farmer's Boy*. In the 'Elegy on the Enclosure of Honington Green', Nat deplores the social and environmental destruction caused by enclosure, but then concludes the poem on an entirely different note, arguing that the children of future generations will never miss the unenclosed landscape:

> Tho' the pressure of Wealth's lordly hand
> Shall give Emulation no scope,
> And tho' all the' appropriate Land
> Shall leave Indigence nothing to hope.
> So happily flexile Man's make,
> So pliantly docile his mind,
> Surrounding impressions we take,
> And bliss in each circumstance find (ll. 165–72)

If such sentiments reveal his independence, significantly more startling are the assertions he makes in the volume's title poem. The 'Essay on War' aims at a disinterested anthropological perspective on human conflict, arguing that war is a sad but 'necessary' consequence of humanity's inevitable tendency to overpopulate:

> [I]n proportion as Mankind increase,
> So evils multiply: till Nature's self,
> (The native passions of the human mind)
> Engender War; which thins, and segregates,
> And rectifies the balance of the world:
> As thick-sown plants in the vegetable world,
> With stretching branches wage continual War (ll. 84–90).

Enlightenment ideals, however attractive, are ultimately powerless: 'Advanc'd
Society's prudential Laws, / The moral virtues of the enlighten'd mind, /
And all the ties of Interest and of Love, / In vain conspire to nurse their
favourite Peace, / And banish dire Immanity and War' (ll. 62–6). Bloomfield
also includes a remarkable digression on gunpowder, a substance he admires
because it allows combatants to kill at a distance, and thus be spared the guilt
and psychic trauma that would accompany hand-to-hand conflict. Lofft was
clearly hesitant about several aspects of the poem:

> The PRINCIPLE of the ESSAY ON WAR appears to me, I shall own, more
> paradoxical than I should I think, to judge, from their conduct, it can
> appear to the ruling part at least of Mankind in general. I indulge the hope
> and expectation that WAR shall one day be universally and finally extin-
> guish'd. But I will confess also, that appearances would tempt us to
> apprehend that day is far distant. And while we make War for Sport on
> useful, generous, inoffensive Animals, it is not easy to imagine that we
> shall cease to make War on one another. But whether the Principle of the
> Poem be well or ill-founded, I can hardly imagine any abstract proposition
> to be more poetically, more forcibly, or comprehensively maintain'd. (pp.
> xvii–xviii)

Contemporary reviewers shared Lofft's reservations, and with the added evi-
dence of George Bloomfield's poem 'The Poets at Odds' (q.v.), we can now
speculate that the reception accorded the title poem caused Nat a great deal
of distress. George's description of critics who 'Cruelly hunted down' Nat
may seem overblown, almost hysterical. In fact the reviews were, in the
aggregate, reasonably balanced if grudging, and virtually every review com-
mended some aspect of Nat's craft. But it is evident that he had invested
much of his artistic and intellectual capital in 'An Essay on War', and the crit-
ical impulse to condemn it—or, even more dishearteningly, to ignore its
argument entirely—evidently caused him to despair of the whole enterprise.
Indeed, it is important to say that the 'Essay on War', as much as any single
poem collected in this volume, carried with it the implicit claim that the
labouring-class poet had a right to real and substantive ideas. It is evidently
the case that for Nat, the experience of having these ideas greeted with
scorn or witty condescension led him to conclude that his public aspirations
would always be thwarted, and his dignity assailed in the process.

We do not fully understand the process by which Nat came to the views
articulated in 'An Essay on War', but we can assume that he was influenced
both by his own experience and his awareness of what, in 'More Bread and
Cheese' he calls 'the news from Versailles or the Hague' (l. 12). Bloomfield,
like his brothers, was a participant in the major late-eighteenth-century pop-
ulation migration from country to city, having moved to London from the
Norwich town of Harling after the completion of his apprenticeship as a

tailor. Though economic considerations drove him, he made frequent visits to the countryside, and clearly came to lament what Wordsworth famously described, in his 'Preface' to *Lyrical Ballads*, as the 'increasing accumulation of men in cities'. Nat first settled in the area of Woolwich, where he met Charlotte Noble, whom he married in 1787. Woolwich was the site of a major British naval yard (where Robert Bloomfield's father-in-law worked as a shipbuilder), and Nat would have had an especially close view of the frenzied military activity of the post-Revolutionary period—not only France's declaration of war on Britain in 1793, but the war's horrifying spread across Europe during the 1790s. Nat's attempt to understand crises of war, population, and death may also have been influenced by his terrible experience of the smallpox, which claimed the lives of three of his five children, one of whom died even as Lofft was preparing the Preface to *An Essay on War*. But despite these many trials and the occasionally hard-edged tone of the poems, Nat always maintained the intensely devotional religious impulse that George describes as having emerged in his late teens.

In a brief comment in a facsimile edition of *The Farmer's Boy* and *An Essay on War*, Donald Reiman remarks, 'Certainly Nathaniel possesses little of Robert's naturalness and innocent charm, and Lofft's puffing of the less talented elder brother undercuts his earlier praise of young Robert' (p. ix). Though the basic elements of this observation seem true—that is, the fact of Lofft's puffing, and Nat's apparent determination to be controversial in ways that clash with the 'naturalness' of his brother—the conclusion seems unfair. In the selections contained here is ample evidence of what makes Nathaniel Bloomfield an interesting poet, and a truly, if perhaps self-consciously, daring one.

FURTHER READING

British Critic 22 (July 1803), 81–2

Critical Review ser. 2 v. 37 (April 1803), 406–15

DNB (Capel Lofft)

Tim Fulford and Debbie Lee, 'The Jenneration of Disease: Vaccination, Romanticism, and Revolution', *Studies in Romanticism* 39 (2000), 139–63

Literary Journal, A Review 1 (Feb 24, 1803), 149–50

Monthly Epitome 2 (March 1803), 158–61

Monthly Mirror 16 (Nov 1803), 315–7

Monthly Review 42 (Dec 1803), 378–81

Monthly Visitor n.s. 3 (March 1803), 223–7; n.s. 3 (April 1803), 331–6

Poetical Register 2 (1802), 428–9

Donald H. Reiman, 'Introduction', Robert and Nathaniel Bloomfield, *The Farmer's Boy; Rural Tales; Good Tidings; with An Essay on War* (New York: Garland, 1977)

Henry Kirke White, 'Melancholy Hours VI', *The Poetical and Prose Works of Henry Kirke White*, ed. Robert Southey (Edinburgh: Gall and Inglis, 1840).

From *An Essay on War* (1803)

An Essay on War

Man's sad necessity, destructive War,
Sweeps to the grave the surplus of his sons,
Where'er the kindly clime and soil invite
To Love; and multiply the Human Race.
   Around the World, in every happier spot   5
Where Earth spontaneous gives nutritious fruits,
Her softest verdure courting human feet,
And mossy grots, beneath protecting shades,
The Stranger's envy, the Possessor's pride;
There, as increasing numbers throng each bower,   10
Frequent and fatal rivalships arise;
And ruthless War erects his hideous crest.
   Soon as Appropriation's iron hand
Assays to grasp the Produce of the Earth;
And youths assert hereditary power,   15
Propriety exclusive, and in arms
League to defend their patrimonial rights,
Indisputable claim of Fruits and Fields
Contending, oft their massive clubs they raise
Against each other's life: often, alas,   20
The needy cravings of the unportion'd poor
Provoke their jealous wrath; relentlessly
Tenacious of their store, they shut him out,
'Midst desert Famine, and ferocious Beasts,
To guard his life and till the steril soil;   25
And thus extend the range of human feet.
   Still as Experience, in her tardy school,
Instructs the Shepherd and the Husbandman
To great increase their flocks and herds to rear,

To till the ground, and plant the fruitful tree   30
In slow progression rising into use,
Nurtur'd by Her the infant Arts appear.
While sage Experience thus teaches Man
The useful and the pleasant Arts of Life,
She in harsh lectures, in the frequent broil,   35
Enjoins her Pupil still to cultivate
The fatal, necessary Art of War.
    The Artizan, who from metallic ores
Forms the sharp implements to dress the glebe,
And prune the wild luxuriance of the tree;...   40
By him is made the sword, the spear, the shaft,
By Man worn to defend him against Man.
    Most bless'd the country where kind Nature's face
In unsophisticated Freedom smiles:
Happy the tenants of primeval days   45
When young society is in its spring:
Where there is room and food for millions more,
Love knows no check, the votaries of Love,
The happy votaries of Wedded Love,
Know not the curse of peopled, polish'd, times: 50
The curse to wish their children may be few.
    Sweet converse binds the cords of social love;
When the rude noise and gestures that ere while
Imperfectly express'd the labouring thought;
By social concourse are improv'd to Speech: 55
Speech, reasoning Man's distinguishing perfection;
Speech, the inestimable vehicle
Of mental light, and intellectual bliss;
Whence the fair fruits of Holy Friendship grow,
Presenting to fond Hope's enamour'd fight   60
The fairy prospect of perpetual Peace.
    Advanc'd Society's prudential Laws,
The moral virtues of the enlighten'd mind,
And all the ties of Interest and of Love,
In vain conspire to nurse their favourite Peace,   65
And banish dire Immanity and War.
Strong Nature's bent, continual increase,
Still counteracts Humanity's fond wish,
The perpetuity of Peace, and Love;
Alas! progressive Increase cannot last.   70

Soon mourns the encumber'd land its human load:
Too soon arrives the inauspicious hour;
The Natal Hour of the unhappy Man,
Who all his life goes mourning up and down
That there is neither bough, nor mud, nor straw   75
That he may take to make himself a hut;
No, not in all his native land a twig
That he may take, nor spot of green grass turf,
Where without trespass he may set his foot.
Now Want and Poverty wage War with Love;   80
And hard the conflict: horrible the thought,
That Love, who boasts of his all-conquering impulse,
Should have to mourn abortive energies …
But in proportion as Mankind increase,
So evils multiply: till Nature's self,   85
(The native passions of the human mind)
Engender War; which thins, and segregates,
And rectifies the balance of the world:
As thick-sown plants in the vegetable world,
With stretching branches wage continual War;   90
Each tender bud shrinks from the foreign touch
With a degree of sensitive perception;
Till one deforms, o'er-tops, and kills the other.
    Like Summer swarms, that quit their native hives,
The offspring of increasing families,   95
Who find no room beneath their father's roofs,
No patrimony nor employ at home,
Colleagu'd in bands explore the desart wilds,
To seek adventures; or to seek their food:
If chance they meet with rovers (like themselves)   100
Whose home is far away in distant vales,
Behind the mountains, or beyond the lake;
Instinctively they war where'er they meet;
The friendly parley cannot intervene;
The unknown tongue does but create alarm: 105
With jealous fears, stern looks, and brandish'd arms,
They stand aloof: as birds of distant groves
At the strange note prepare for instant War.
    At first they skirmishing dispute the right
Of hunting in the unappropriate waste: 110
But every onset aggravates their hate;
Till each increasing force, whetting their swords,

With purpos'd malice seeking out the foe,
Alternate by reprisal and revenge,
Doubly compensate each discomfiture.   115
Yet seek not to attack each-other's home,
Where Age, and Infancy, in safety dwell:
They war but with freebooters: private Peace
And Female Covert, Valour scorns to assail.
But when in evil hour some female hand,   120
Whether by force of Love, or force of Arms,
Is led across the desart by the Foe;
The jealous fury kindles to a flame:
No longer sacred the domestic hearth:
Fire, Death, and Devastation, mark their way,   125
And all the horrid crimes of savage War.
     Now War becomes the business of the State:
The most humane, the most pacific men,
Must arm for War, or lose all they hold dear:
The sorrows of the Aged, Infant cries,   130
And Female Tears, resistlessly prevail:
Can gentlest natures be in love with Peace,
When Love, most tender Love, excites to War?
No...When some lov'd and honour'd youth distress'd,
Raising his head amongst his arm'd compeers,   135
Tells that the well-known honourable Maid,
The Virgin Mistress of his dearest hopes,
Is ravish'd from him, borne by force away;
Though pierc'd with grief, yet nobly he exclaims,
'Think not I wish to embroil you in my fate: 140
For though not one of you espouse my cause,
I singly will attempt the desperate deed.
Farewell: I go to find my Love, or die!'
     Silent and motionless the legions stand,
By looks examining each-other's heart: 145
But soon a murmur through the ranks proceeds,
Swelling as quickly a terrific roar;
Like heavy waters breaking from their mounds,
A long, and loud, and inarticulate shout,
While every weapon vibrates in the air,   150
And hisses its fierce vengeance at the foe.
     The righteous cause admits of no delay;
No tardy foot impedes the immediate march:

The Enemy, not taken by surprise,
Wak'd by the watchful fears of conscious guilt,   155
On their frontiers await the coming foe.
   Now at the near approach of threatening Death,
Full many a thinking, sighing, aching heart,
Indulges secretly the hopeless wish
For Life, and Peace ... Alas! it cannot be: 160
To advance is to encounter dreadful danger;
But to recede, inevitable death;
His own associates would deal the blow:
   Thus led by Fate, behold upon the plain,
The adverse bands in view, and in advance.   165
Now Fear, Self-pity, and affected Courage,
Speak in their hideous shouts with voice scarce human;
Like that which issues from his hollow throat
Who sleeping bellows in a frightful dream.
More near their glaring eye-balls flashing meet;   170
Terror and Rage distorting every face,
Inflame each-other into trembling fury.
   Soft-ey'd Humanity, oh! veil thy fight!
'Tis not in Rationality to view
(Even in thought) the dire ensuing scene;   175
For Madness, Madness reigns, and urges men
To deeds that Rationality disowns.
   Now here and there about the horrid Field,
Striding across the dying and the dead,
Stalks up a man by strength superior,   180
Or skill and prowess in the arduous fight,
Preserv'd alive: fainting he looks around;
Fearing pursuit, nor caring to pursue.
The supplicating voice of bitterest moans,
Contortions of excruciating pain,   185
The shriek of torture and the groan of death,
Surround him; and as Night her mantle spreads,
To veil the horrors of the mourning Field,
With cautious step shaping his devious way,
He seeks a covert where to hide and rest: 190
At every leaf that rustles in the breeze
Starting, he grasps his sword; and every nerve
Is ready strain'd, for combat or for flight.
   Thus list'ning to ward off approaching foes,
A distant whispering, sighing, murmuring sound   195

Salutes his ear, and to his throbbing heart
Soft tidings tells of tenderness and love.
For on that fatal day of vengeful ire,
At fearful distance following the host,
From either country came a female throng;   200
And now beneath the covert of the night
Advancing, guided by the voice of woe,
Where on the earth the wounded mourners lay,
With trembling steps and fearful whispering voice,
Each seeks, and calls him who she came to seek: 205
And many a fugitive, whom force or fear
Had driven from the Field, steals softly back,
Anxious to know the fate of some lov'd friend.
Mutual fears appal the mingled group,
Starting alternate at the unknown tongue: 210
They fear a foe in each uncertain form
That through the gloom imperfectly appears.
The mournful horrors of the doleful night
Melt every heart:...and when the morning's beam
Shews the sad scene, and gives an interview,   215
Resentment, that worst torment of the mind,
Resentment ceases, satiate wrath subsides.
Woman is present: and so strong the charm
Of weeping Woman's fascinating tears,
That though surviving Heroes' unwash'd hands   220
Still grasp the falchion of horrid hue,
And though their fallen brethren from the ground
May seem to call for Vengeance from their hands,
The impulse of Revenge is felt no more;
No more the strange attire, the foreign tongue   225
Creates alarm: for Nature's-self has writ
In every face; where every eye can read
Repentant Sorrow, and forgiving Love.
Their mingled tears wash the lamented dead:
On every wound they pour soft Pity's balm: 230
Ere Sorrow's tears are dried, they feel the spring
Of new-born joys, and each expanding heart
Contemplates future scenes of Peace and Love.
    Long, even as long as room and food abound,
They interchange their friendly offices   235
For mutual good; reciprocally kind:

And much they wonder that they e'er were foes.
Still War's terrific name is kept alive:
Tradition, pointing to the rusty arms
That hang on high, informs each list'ning youth   240
How erst in fatal fields their Grandsires fell;
Childhood attentive hears the tragic tale;
And learns to shudder at the name of War.
    GUNPOWDER! let the Soldier's Pean rise,
Where e'er thy name or thundering voice is heard: 245
Let him who, fated to the needful trade,
Deals out the adventitious shafts of Death,
Rejoice in thee; and hail with loudest shouts
The auspicious era when deep-searching Art
From out the hidden things in Nature's store   250
Cull'd thy tremendous powers, and tutor'd Man
To chain the unruly element of Fire
At his controul, to wait his potent touch:
To urge his missile bolts of sudden Death,
And thunder terribly his vengeful wrath.   255
Thy mighty engines and gigantic towers
With frowning aspect awe the trembling World.
Destruction, bursting from thy sudden blaze
Hath taught the Birds to tremble at the sound;
And Man himself, thy terror's boasted lord,   260
Within the blacken'd hollow of thy tube,
Affrighted sees the darksome shades of Death.
Not only mourning groves, but human tears,
The weeping Widow's tears, the Orphan's cries,
Sadly deplore that e'er thy powers were known.   265
Yet let thy Advent be the Soldier's song,
No longer doom'd to grapple with the Foe
With Teeth and Nails…When close in view, and in
Each-other's grasp, to grin, and hack, and stab;
Then tug his horrid weapon from one breast   270
To hide it in another:—with clear hands
He now expertly poizing thy bright tube,
At distance kills, unknowing and unknown;
Sees not the wound he gives, nor hears the shriek
Of him whose breast he pierces….GUNPOWDER!   275
(O! let Humanity rejoice) how much
The Soldier's fearful work is humaniz'd,
Since thy momentous birth—stupendous power.

In Britain, where the hills and fertile plains,
Like her historic page, are overspread   280
With vestiges of War, the Shepherd Boy
Climbs the green hillock to survey his flock;
Then sweetly sleeps upon his favourite hill,
Not conscious that his bed's a Warrior's Tomb.
 The ancient Mansions, deeply moated round,   285
Where, in the iron Age of Chivalry,
Redoubted Barons wag'd their little Wars;
The strong Entrenchments and enormous Mounds,
Rais'd to oppose the fierce, perfidious Danes;
And still more ancient traces that remain   290
Of Dykes and Camps, from the far distant date
When minstrel Druids wak'd the soul of War,
And rous'd to arms old Albion's hardy sons,
To stem the tide of Roman Tyranny:...
War's footsteps, thus imprinted on the ground,   295
Shew that in Britain he, from age to age,
Has rear'd his horrid head, and raging reign'd.
 Long on the margins of the silver Tweed
Opposing Ensigns wav'd; War's clarion
Dreadfully echo'd down the winding stream,   300
Where now sweet Peace and Unity reside:
The happy peasant of Tweed's smiling dale,
Whene'er his spade disturbs a Soldier's bones,
With shudd'ring horror ruminates on War;
Then deeper hides the awful spectacle,   305
Blessing the peaceful days in which he lives.
 Since Peace has bless'd the villages on Tweed,
And War has ceas'd to drive his iron car
On Britain's shore, what myriads of men
Over the Eastern and the Western Seas   310
Have follow'd War, and found untimely graves.
Where'er the jarring interests of States
Excite the brave to advance their native land
By deeds of arms, Britons are foremost found.
The sprightly bands, hast'ning from place to place,   315
Gayly carousing in their gay attire,
Invite, not force the train of heedless youths,
Who crowd to share their jollity and joy:
To martial music dancing into death,

They fell their Freedom for a holiday; 320
And with the Rich and Great 'tis Glory charms,
And Beauty's favour that rewards the Brave.
   All the historic Records of the World
Are little more than histories of Wars;
Shewing how many thousands War destroy'd, 325
The time, the place, and some few great ones' names.
The mournful remnants of demolish'd States,
The Greeks, the Roman, and long-exil'd Jew;
Are living monuments of wasting War's
Annihilating power: and while they mourn 330
Their Grandeur faded, and their Power extinct,
To every State *memento mori* sounds.
From age to age the habitable World
Has been a constant theatre of War:
In every land with Nature's gifts most blest, 335
Frequent and fatal War's destructive rage.
So bland is fair Britannia's genial clime,
So liberal her all-protecting Laws,
So generous the spirit of her Sons,
So fond, so chaste, her Daughters' virtuous love, 340
That human offspring still redundant grows,
And free-born Britons must contend for life.
   O! envy not the lands where Slaves reside,
Though their proud Tyrants boast of *peaceful* reign,
Where hard Oppression, freezing genial love, 345
Performs the work of War in embryo:
Let not mistaken fondness dote on Peace,
Preserv'd by arts more horrid far than War!...
Let the dull languor of the pale Chinese
Desert their Infants, and their *Peace* enjoy! 350
But, O! let Britons still in Love and War
Exert the generous ardour of the soul;
Protect the Fair, and softer Infancy.
   By strenuous enterprize, and arduous toils,
Is public safety purchas'd and secur'd. 355
Negative merit, 'I have done no harm,'
Is an inglorious boast: shall he who sits
Secure, enjoying Plenty in the lap
Of Ease, vaunt his recumbent Virtues?...He
Brand with harsh epithets the Warrior's toils? 360
While 'tis to them he owes sincerest thanks

For Peace and Safety, that are earn'd in War…
As well might he who eats the flesh of Lambs,
And smacks the ichor in a savoury dish,
Boast his humanity, and say 'My hand   365
Ne'er slew a Lamb;' and censure as a crime,
The Butcher's cruel, necessary trade.
   In Battle, the chance-medley game of Death,
Where every one still hopes 'till he expires,
Less horror shocks the mind contemplative,   370
Than where, in slow procession's solemn pace,
Doom'd wretches meet their destin'd fate in bonds,
Who know the moment to expect the blow,
And count the moments 'till that moment comes:
Or where Oppression wages War, in Peace,   375
On the defenceless: on the hapless man
Who holds his breath but by another's will:
Whose Life is only one long cruel Death!…
Hardly he fares, and hopelessly he toils;
And when his driver's anger, or caprice,   380
Or wanton cruelty, inflicts a blow,
Not daring to look angry at the whip,
Oh! see him meekly clasp his hands and bow
To every stroke: no lurid deathful scene
In Battle's rage, so racks the feeling heart;   385
Not all the thunders of infuriate War,
Disploding mines, and crashing, bursting bombs,
Are half so horrid as the sounding lash
That echoes through the Carribean groves.
   Incessant is the War of Human Wit,   390
Oppos'd to bestial strength; and variously
Successful: in these happy fertile climes,
Man still maintains his surreptitious power;
Reigns o'er the Brutes, and, with the voice of Fate,
Says 'This to-day, and that to-morrow dies.'   395
Though here our Shambles blazon the Renown,
The Victory, and Rule, and lordly Man;
Far wider tracts within the Torrid Zone
Own no such Lord: where Sol's intenser rays
Create in bestial hearts more fervid fires,   400
And deadlier poisons arm the Serpent's tooth;
In gloomy shades, impassable to Man,

Where matted foliage exclude the Sun,
The torpid Birds that crawl from bough to bough
Utter their notes of terror: while beneath   405
Fury and Venom, couch'd in murky dens,
Hissing and yelling, guard the hideous gloom.
O'er dreary wastes, untrod by human feet,
Without controul the lordly Lion reigns;
And every creature trembles at his voice: 410
When risen from his den, he prances forth,
Extends his talons, shakes his flaky mane,
Then whurrs his tufted tail, and stooping low
His wide mouth near the ground, his dreadful roar
Makes all the desert tremble: he proclaims   415
His ire—proclaims his strong necessity;
And that surprise or artifice he scorns.
    Unskill'd, alas! in philosophic lore,
Unbless'd with scientific erudition;
How can I sing of elemental War,   420
Or the contending powers of opposite
Attractions, that impel, and poize, and guide,
The ever-rolling Spheres: Animal War,
The flux of Life, devouring and devour'd,
Ceaseless in every tribe, through Earth, and Air,   425
And Ocean, transcends my utmost ken.

    From obvious truths my Song has aim'd to shew
That War is an inevitable Ill;
An Ill through Nature's various Realms diffus'd;
An Ill subservient to the General Good.   430
    With sympathetic sense of human woes
Deeply impress'd, the melancholy Muse
With modesty asserts this mournful Truth:
'Tis not in human wisdom to avert,
Though every feeling heart must sure lament,   435
The SAD NECESSITY OF FATAL WAR.

Elegy on the Enclosure of Honington Green

1

Improvement extends its domain;
    The Shepherds of Britain deplore
That the Coulter has furrow'd each plain,
    And their calling is needful no more.
'Enclosing Land doubles its use;   5
    When cultur'd, the heath and the moor
Will the Riches of Ceres produce,
    Yet feed as large flocks as before.'

2

Such a lucrative maxim as this
    The Lords of the Land all pursue,   10
For who such advantage wou'd miss?
    Self-int'rest we all keep in view.
By it, they still more wealth amass,
    Who possess'd great abundance before;
It gives pow'r to the Great, but alas!   15
    Still poorer it renders the Poor.

3

Taste spreads her refinements around,
    Enriching her favourite Land
With prospects of beautified ground,
    Where, cinctur'd, the spruce Villas stand;   20
On the causeways, that never are foul,
    Marshal'd bands may with measur'd pace tread;
The soft Car of Voluptuousness roll,
    And the proud Steed of Greatness parade.

4

Those fenc'd ways that so even are made,   25
    The pedestrian trav'ller bemoans;
He no more the green carpet may tread,
    But plod on, 'midst the gravel and stones:
And if he would rest with his load,
    No green hillock presents him a seat,   30
But long, hard, tiresome sameness of road
    Fatigues both the eye and the feet.

5

Sighs speak the poor Labourers' pain,
   While the new mounds and fences they rear,
Intersecting their dear native plain,   35
   To divide to each rich Man his share;
It cannot but grieve them to see,
   Where so freely they rambled before,
What a bare narrow track is left free
   To the foot of the unportion'd Poor.   40

6

The proud City's gay wealthy train,
   Who nought but refinements adore,
May wonder to hear me complain
   That Honington Green is no more;
But if to the Church you e'er went,   45
   If you knew what the village has been,
You will sympathize, while I lament
   The Enclosure of Honington Green.

7

That no more upon Honington Green
   Dwells the Matron whom most I revere,   50
If by pert observation unseen,
   I e'en now could indulge a fond tear.
E'er her bright Morn of Life was o'ercast,
   When my senses first woke to the scene,
Some short happy hours she had past   55
   On the margin of Honington Green.

8

Her Parents with Plenty were blest,
   And nume'rous her Children, and young,
Youth's Blossoms her cheek yet possest,
   And Melody woke when she sung: 60
A Widow so youthful to leave,
   (Early clos'd the blest days he had seen)
My Father was laid in his grave,
   In the Church-yard on Honington Green.

9

I faintly remember the Man,   65
    Who died when I was but a Child;
But far as my young mind could scan,
    His manners were gentle and mild:
He won infant ears with his lore,
    Nor let young ideas run wild,   70
Tho' his hand the severe rod of pow'r
    Never sway'd o'er a trembling Child.

10

Not anxiously careful for pelf,
    Melancholic and thoughtful, his mind
Look'd inward and dwelt on itself,   75
    Still pensive, pathetic, and kind;
Yet oft in despondency drown'd,
    He from friends, and from converse would fly,
In weeping a luxury found,
    And reliev'd others' woes with a sigh.   80

11

In solitude long would he stay,
    And long lock'd in silence his tongue;
Then he humm'd an elegiac lay,
    Or a Psalm penitential he sung:
But if with his Friends he regal'd,   85
    His Mirth, as his Griefs, knew no bounds;
In no Tale of Mark Sargent he fail'd,
    Nor in all Robin Hood's Derry-downs.

12

Thro' the poor Widow's long lonely years,
    Her Father supported us all: 90
Yet sure she was loaded with cares,
    Being left with six Children so small.
Meagre Want never lifted her latch;
    Her cottage was still tight and clean;
And the casement beneath its low thatch   95
    Commanded a view o'er the Green.

13

O'er the Green, where so often she blest
   The return of a Husband or Son,
Coming happily home to their rest,
   At night, when their labour was done: 100
Where so oft in her earlier years,
   She, with transport maternal, has seen
(While plying her housewifely cares)
   Her Children all safe on the Green.

14

The Green was our pride through the year,   105
   For in Spring, when the wild flow'rets blew,
Tho' many rich pastures were near,
   Where Cowslips and Daffodils grew;
And tho' such gallant flow'rs were our choice,
   It was bliss interrupted by Fear—   110
The Fear of their Owner's dread voice,
   Harshly bawling, 'You've no business here.'

15

While the Green, tho' but Daisies its boast,
   Was free as the Flow'rs to the Bee;
In all seasons the Green we lov'd most,   115
   Because on the Green we were free;
'Twas the prospect that first met my eyes,
   And Memory still blesses the scene;
For early my heart learnt to prize
   The Freedom of Honington Green.   120

16

No Peasant had pin'd at his lot,
   Tho' new fences the lone Heath enclose:
For, alas! the blest days are forgot,
   When poor Men had their Sheep and their Cows.
Still had Labour been blest with Content,   125
   Still Competence happy had been,
Nor Indigence utter'd a plaint,
   Had Avarice spar'd but the Green.

17

Not Avarice itself could be mov'd
    By desire of a morsel so small: 130
It could not be lucre he lov'd;
    But to rob the poor folk of their all.
He in wantonness ope'd his wide jaws,
    As a Shark may disport with the Fry;
Or a Lion, when licking his paws,   135
    May wantonly snap at a Fly.

18

Could there live such an envious Man,
    Who endur'd not the halcyon scene?
When the infantine Peasantry ran,
    And roll'd on the daisy-deck'd Green: 140
Ah! sure 'twas fell Envy's despite,
    Lest Indigence tasted of Bliss,
That sternly decreed they've no right
    To innocent pleasure like this.

19

Tho' the Youth of to-day must deplore   145
    The rough mounds that now sadden the scene,
The vain stretch of Misanthropy's Power,
    The Enclosure of Honington Green.
Yet when not a green turf is left free,
    When not one odd nook is left wild,   150
Will the Children of Honington be
    Less blest than when I was a Child?

20

No!...Childhood shall find the scene fair,
    Then here let me cease my complaint;
Still shall Health be inhal'd with the Air,   155
    Which at Honington cannot be taint:
And tho' Age may still talk of the Green,
    Of the Heath, and free Commons of yore,
Youth shall joy in the new-fangled scene,
    And boast of *that* change we deplore.   160

21

Dear to me was the wild-thorny Hill,
    And dear the brown Heath's sober scene;
And Youth shall find Happiness still,
    Tho' he roves not on Common or Green:
Tho' the pressure of Wealth's lordly hand   165
    Shall give Emulation no scope,
And tho' all the appropriate Land
    Shall leave Indigence nothing to hope.

22

So happily flexile Man's make,
    So pliantly docile his mind,   170
Surrounding impressions we take,
    And bliss in each circumstance find.
The Youths of a more polish'd Age
    Shall not with these rude Commons to see;
To the Bird that's inur'd to the Cage,   175
    It would not be Bliss to be free.

More Bread and Cheese
A New Song, Writtten in the Beginning of the Year 1793

To the Tune of 'Nottingham Ale'

1

My Brothers of this world, of ev'ry Nation,
Some maxims of prudence the Muse would inspire.
Now restlessness reigns throughout every station;
The low would be high, and the high would be higher;
    Now Freedom's the word,   5
    That unsheaths ev'ry sword,
But don't be deceiv'd by such pretexts as these:
    'Tis not Freedom, nor Slavery,
    That calls for your Bravery;
'Tis only a scramble for more Bread and Cheese.   10

2

When others some party are venting their rage on,
Inflam'd by the news from Versailles or the Hague,
Let Mum be your maxim…beware of contagion…
For Anger is catching as Fever or Plague:
    Now Victuals is scanty,   15
    And Eaters are plenty,
The former must rise, or the latter decrease;
    If in War they're employ'd,
    Till one half are destroy'd,
The few that are left will have more Bread and Cheese.   20

3

Think not that Employment's the grand requisition;
That if men had work it would make the times good:
No man would want work if he lack'd not provision;
The cry for Employ is the cry for more Food.
    Now every Trade,   25
    From the Gown to the Spade,
Oppress'd by its numbers feels Scarcity's squeeze;
    From the Prince to the Peasant,
    'Tis true, tho' unpleasant,
There must be fewer mouths, or else more Bread and Cheese. 30

4

Now our Hive is so pinch'd, both for room and for honey,
The industrious Bees would fain kick out the Drones:
But expose not your Life, for victuals nor money;
'Tis better you supperless sleep with whole bones.
    Then shuffle, and hustle,   35
    Keep clear of the bustle,
Step out of the way when they kick up a breeze:
    Preserve your own Life,
    Till the end of the strife:
Then the few that are left will have more Bread and Cheese. 40

5

Think not Hell is let loose with a terrible mission,
To punish a world for incor'gible Sin.
Not from angry Gods, nor from deep Politicians,
War nat'rally springs from the Passions of Men:
    'Tis for room and for food,   45

That Men fight and shed blood;
When sufficiently thinn'd the inducement will cease:
   There'll be room for us all,
   When our numbers are small:
And the few that are left will have more Bread and Cheese.   50

Lyric Address to Dr Jenner

1

Rejoice, rejoice, Humanity!
   The fell, destructive, sore Disease,
The pest of ages, now can be,
   Repell'd with safety and with ease.

2

He well deserves his Country's Meed,   5
   By whom the peerless blessing came;
And thousands from destruction freed,
   Shall raptur'd speak of JENNER's name.

3

Yes, JENNER's vigilance is crown'd;
   A sovereign antidote is given: 10
The Blessing flows the Nations round;
   Free he diffus'd the gift of Heaven.

4

So well approv'd its sure effect,
   To turn aside the impending harm;
And shall parental Love neglect   15
   To minister the precious balm?

5

Oh! no; beware of dire Delay,
   Ye, who caress your Infants dear:
Defer it not from day to day,
   From month to month, from year to year: 20

6

Lest you, like me, too late lament,
   Your Life bereft of all its joy;
Clasp now the Gift so kindly sent,
   Lest you behold your dying Boy!

7

Lest you see with trembling Fear,   25
   With inexpressible Distress;
The purple spots of Death appear,
   To blast your Hopes and Happiness:

8

Lest your keenest grief to wake,
   Like mine your suffering prattler say,   30
'Go, bid my Father come and take
   These frightful Spots and Sores away.'

9

Quickly from such fears be free:
   Oh! there is Danger in Delay!
Say not to-morrow it shall be:...   35
   To-morrow! no; to-day, to-day.

10

Embrace the Blessing Heaven hath sent;
   So shall you ne'er such pangs endure:
Oh! give a Trifle to prevent,
   What you would give a World to cure.   40

THOMAS BA(T)CHELOR (*fl.* 1804–1809)

Probably born in 1775, Thomas Batchelor was raised in the small village of Lidlington, Bedfordshire, forty miles north of London, and there he developed a deep interest in the region's agriculture, geology, and social history. After working as a tenant farmer under the Duke of Bedford, he published a series of works focussing on this locale: in 1804 a volume of poetry, *Village Scenes*; in 1808 the *General view of the agriculture of the county of Bedford*; and finally, in 1809, *An orthoëpical analysis of the English language; and, An orthoëpical analysis of the dialect of Bedfordshire*. A facsimile edition of this last work, edited by Arne Zettersten, was published in 1974. Together these works suggest that Batchelor's affinity for his native landscape had a strong practical inflection.

Contemporary reviews of Batchelor's poetry were favourable if not extensive. The *Literary Journal* employed cautious double negatives, calling *Village Scenes* 'not below mediocrity' and 'not unworthy of attention' (pp. 90–1). The *Eclectic Review* said the 'cultivated taste, true feeling, and harmony, which generally appear throughout the volume, are far beyond the customary attainments of uneducated poets' (p. 664), and concluded that 'if [Batchelor's] performances do not equal those of a Burns or a Bloomfield in genius, we do not hesitate to express our opinion, that they discover a superior knowledge and taste, and are less exceptionable on a moral principle' (p. 668). The *Annual Review* was more guarded in making a similar comparison, calling the poems 'unquestionably far inferior in merit to the productions of Robert Bloomfield', but still applauding their 'correct and flowing versification, unaffected sentiments, and minute and accurate delineation of natural objects' (p. 596). There has been little recent critical discussion of Batchelor; a promising area of inquiry is suggested by Juan Christian Pellicer, who locates Batchelor's *The Progress of Agriculture* among other formal georgic poems of the era. The economist Robert C. Allen discusses Batchelor as an agriculturalist, seeing him as an especially reliable analyst of 'the costs of farm operations' ('Labour', p. 1) and using the accounting data from the *General view...of Bedford* as the basis for models of labour productivity in large English farms *circa* 1800. There has been some suggestion that even as Batchelor the poet was largely dismayed at the effects of enclosure, Batchelor the agriculturalist embraced the greater efficiency it promised. More work remains to be done on this topic; John Barrell, in a passing reference, intimates that Batchelor saw aesthetic beauty in well-ordered fields.

As the excerpt below from *The Progress of Agriculture* indicates, Batchelor's work—in tone, theme, diction, and patriotic sentimentality—is remarkably similar to that of William Holloway's *The Peasant's Fate* (q.v.). Although Batchelor is much more firmly invested in 'progress', he does interpose throughout the poem the considered doubts of a farmer who, like many rural villagers, has been impoverished by the widespread conversion of arable land to pasture (ll. 386 ff). This latter part of the poem provides a thoughtful counterpoint to the opening 'survey', which tends to disparage traditional farming practices as wasteful. As a formal georgic poem, *The Progress of Agriculture* is a direct descendant of Virgil's *Georgics*, trans. John Dryden (1697), and is also influenced by eighteenth-century works including John Phillips's *Cyder* (1708; on the growing of apples) and John Dyer's *The Fleece* (1757; on sheep-raising and the manufacture of wool). Dyer's general confidence regarding economic efficiency and improvement—he believes increased distribution of British wool will 'fold the world with harmony' (*The Fleece* IV.664)—resonates strongly with Batchelor's tenacious belief in progress. More particularly, Batchelor follows Dyer in praising the fen-drainage program instigated by the Fourth Duke of Bedford.

FURTHER READING

Robert C. Allen, *Enclosure and the Yeoman: the agricultural development of the South Midlands, 1450–1850* (Oxford: Clarendon Press, 1992)

Robert C. Allen, 'Labour Productivity in English Agriculture, c.1800'. http://www.eh.net/XIIICongress/cd/papers/85Allen248.pdf

Annual Review 3 (1804), 596–7

John Barrell, *The Idea of Landscape and the Sense of Place* (Cambridge: Cambridge University Press, 1972), pp. 32; 75

Eclectic Review 1 (1805), 664–8

Imperial Review 5 (August 1805), 201–2

Literary Journal, A Review 4 (July 1804), 90–1

Monthly Mirror 18 (Sep 1804), 181

Juan Christian Pellicer, 'The Georgic at Mid-Eighteenth Century and the Case of Dodsley's "Agriculture"', *Review of English Studies* n.s. 54, no. 213 (2003), 67–93

Poetical Register 4 (1804), 495

James Sambrook, 'Some Heirs of Goldsmith', *Studies in Burke and his Time* 11 (1970), 1348–61.

From *Village Scenes, The Progress of Agriculture, and Other Poems* (1804)

From *The Progress of Agriculture; Or, The Rural Survey*

Gay Spring, adieu! sweet emblem of that age
When thy fair scenes the opening mind engage;
Fled are thy odorous gems of various hue,
Thy young-ey'd graces vanish'd from my view,
And Summer, hast'ning on with train sublime,   5
Waves his bright scepter o'er each northern clime.
   Behold! while Phoebus, golden prince of day,
Refulgent speeds his high etherial way,
How pant the herds beneath his burning beam,
How glow the fields, how glitters ev'ry stream: 10
Wak'd to new life, by his concoctive power,
The pulpy fruit succeeds the painted flower;
Through vegetable veins rich nectar flows,
With sun-dy'd tints the blushing fruit-tree glows;
Rich, mealy corn extends the swelling ear,   15
Exub'rant plenty smiles, and crowns th' exulting year.
O, blest Britannia! on thy favour'd isle,
The mildest suns, the softest seasons smile;
Not long the breath of winter chills thy plains,
Or fervid summer melts thy toiling swains,   20
Ere genial Spring the mellow'd soil unbinds,
Ere lib'ral Autumn glads thy lab'ring hinds.
   Calm are thy seasons, fruitful is thy soil,
Yet much to art is due and manual toil.
What woody wastes and vast savannahs spread,   25
Colombia, where thy artless Indians tread
Extensive, fertile scenes, that never bore
The harness's team, nor smil'd with Ceres' store;
And still, O Albion! favourite of the skies,
On thy fair bosom many a desert lies.   30
   But lovelier scenes th' extensive prospect fill,
That spreads, O *****! round thy fir-crown'd hill,
To yon blue hills, that bound my wide survey,

Nature and art their mingled pride display.
Ah, come! ye powers, that shun the noisy throng,   35
To pour your graces o'er the rural song:
Come, thou fair Muse, that tun'd the Mantuan lyre,
With tuneful notes my pastoral reed inspire;
And Ceres, patron of the Georgic train,
Let thy great name exalt my artless strain;   40
For, as the radiant gems of night decay,
Absorb'd and lost amid the blaze of day,
All arts retire, eclips'd in thy fair fame,
And commerce shrinks from thy imperial name.
    Pure source of wealth, from whose auspicious smile   45
Flows all the wealth, the glory of the isle;
Thy herds and flocks a thousand meads adorn,
Oaks clothe thy hills, thy valleys golden corn:
Adown thy dales meand'ring currents glide,
Whose silvery waves reflect thy various pride;   50
And farms and cottages, on ev'ry hand,
Pour forth their rural groups to dress the fertile land.
    Yet have I seen, nor long elaps'd the day,
When yon rich vale in rude disorder lay;
Each scanty farm dispread o'er many a mile,   55
The fences few, ill-cultur'd half the soil;
Seen rushy slips contiguous roods divide,
Mid worthless commons boundless stretching wide,
Where ev'ry owner sought his proper land,
By rude initials in the grass-grown sand.   60
    In vain the culturer, in this anarch state,
Employs his skill, all share a common fate.
Oft on his soil th' encroaching plough-share glows,
Nor bound by art, but custom's laws he sows.
He dooms the thistly race to death, in vain!   65
They flow'r secure o'er all th' adjacent plain:
While o'er his soil the downy nuisance sails,
Borne on the wing of summer's gentlest gales;
And e'en, when autumn's gifts his labours crown,
He reaps a *tenth* he must not call his own.   70
    Seest thou yon rising ground, that far extends,
Till heaven's blue concave on its verge descends:
A formless waste, through many a year it lay,
Unfenc'd, untill'd, in nature's rude array;

Pierc'd with the mellowing frost, the vernal rain,   75
And fann'd with summer's rip'ning breath in vain;
There wand'ring flocks, by lonely shepherd led,
On russet ling, or dwarfish verdure fed;
Scarce known to them the sweet return of spring,
No flow'r to blush, nor plumy choir to sing.   80
Lo! still the ruins of their humble shed,
Half sunk in earth, with heathy sods o'erspread,
Destin'd a safe retreat from drenching show'rs,
The boreal snows, and summer's burning hours.
    Arabia! thus thy torrid tracts appear   85
O'er many a barren league of deserts drear;
But, ah! far happier the wild scenes I view,
Whose naked sands no bloody frays imbrue:
O'er bless'd Britannia strays no savage horde,
No arm'd banditti lift the lawless sword.   90
    Oft as I walk'd, when ev'ry breath was still,
O'er the rough convex of yon russet hill,
Around my feet the timorous, light-heel'd race,
By night embolden'd, left their hiding place;
Cropp'd the young herbs, and frequent tripp'd away,   95
Sportive and bold in Cynthia's dubious ray.
Unknowing they what dark, insidious snares,
T' arrest their steps, the art of man prepares.
Inur'd to blood, 'tis thus the savage chace
Invites the houseless, vagrant, Scythian race: 100
Amidst the woods the furry ermines hide,
Elks, rein-deer, foxes, o'er the valleys glide;
And these to hunt, along th' eternal snows,
Is all the joy the shiv'ring native knows.
    Where is that swamp that oft has met my eyes,   105
While morn's first blush suffus'd the orient skies?
Dull scene! where Nature, with herself at strife,
Teem'd but with useless vegetable life.
The soil, with rains and secret streamlets fed,
Unstable grew, and quak'd beneath the tread.   110
Foul, stagnant pools rose o'er the dark morass,
With rushes fring'd, and chok'd with sedgy grass;
And frequent thence mephitic vapours sprung,
Which all the peasants' brawny nerves unstrung;
And oft, when Night's dark mantle cloth'd the sky,   115
Phosphoric glimmerings met the traveller's eye;

Delusive lights o'er the faithless pools that play,
And tempt th' unwary to a dangerous way.
    Though firm the soil of yon irriguous plain,
Where Ouse meandering leads his Naiad train;   120
Yet oft, when summer bade his showers extend,
And rushing torrents from the heavens descend,
Swift down the hills the tumbling waters pour,
Glide o'er the vales, and whiten round the shore.
The river now, by confluent currents fed,   125
Amidst his willows lifts his reed-crown'd head,
Rolls o'er the banks, and unresisted spreads
A shining deluge o'er th' adjacent meads.
Driven from his home, the ruin'd peasant flies,
While all his farm a watry mirror lies;   130
And drops, perhaps, an unavailing tear
O'er the lost hopes that charm'd th' auspicious year.
    Where classic Cam, with Ouse's placid tide,
In confluence to the eastern ocean glide,
Whole vales, that long had slept beneath the stream,   135
Now wave their corn in summer's rip'ning beam.
Drawn from the bosom of each liquid vale
By mills, whose vanes obey the whistling gale,
The vagrant waters seek their parent flood,
And teeming Nature clothes th' unsightly mud.   140
The soil to guard, when wintry torrents pour,
High-swelling mounds extend on ev'ry shore;
Whose giant strength defies th' impetuous surge,
While floods and storms their mightiest efforts urge.
    Thus, long Batavia lay a swampy waste,   145
Supine, in ocean's watry arms embrac'd,
Till art and agriculture's genial reign,
Subdu'd th' amphibious empire of the main.
    And thus, around my natal soil I see
The bless'd effects of peaceful industry.   150
And thine, fair Freedom! thine the gen'rous hand
That guards, improves, and dignifies the land:
If thou but smile, fair Ceres' jocund train
Spread, o'er the trembling swamp th' unfertile plain;
Or spread on wilds, or frowning heaths, the day,   155
While seasons rise, and gradual roll away.
At length subdu'd and tam'd th' obdurate soil,

Abundant harvests crown their various toil:
Pomona decks their trees with flow'ry gems,
With gold and rubies loads the burden'd stems;   160
Or vegetation's humbler powers expand
A painted carpet o'er the smiling land.
Hence population, in the arms of peace
Reclining, sees the social train increase;
Sees farms and cottages innumerous rise,   165
With recent churches pointing to the skies;
And Commerce proudly bids her gay canals
Pierce through the hills and shine along the dales;
While o'er her streams the waving pennants fly,
And wealthy cities meet th' astonish'd eye.   170
    Lo! the wild heath, where starv'ling flocks have stray'd
Mid scatter'd fern to seek a shrivel'd blade;
Where, hid in many a subterranean den,
The furry people shunn'd the view of men;
Lost are its fleet inhabitants, its flocks   175
No longer pine o'er ling and arid rocks.
There oft the plough has turn'd the glowing sand,
The spade, the pickaxe, smooth'd the rugged land;
Harrows sharp-tooth'd, and rolls, with pond'rous toil,
Have pulveriz'd and cleans'd the weedy soil;   180
Manures and argil o'er the surface spread,
Fix'd the loose sands consistent to their bed.
Hence, many a year has seen their harvests glow
In emulous rivalry of fertile vales below;
And, e'en where steep the rocky heights arose,   185
The verdant fir, the larch aspiring grows;
Array'd in gold, here broom adorns the scene,
Or humbler gorse, deck'd in eternal green.
Thus, Caledonia sees her hills array'd,
When keen-edg'd frost and fleecy snows invade: 190
Thus verdant pines Norwegian mountains grace,
When Nature sleeps in Winter's cold embrace.
    Whose are yon roofs that rise beside the hill?
Whose humble names those decent mansions fill?
What, though nor stone, nor brick the walls sustain,   195
Nor slate, nor tile, avert the falling rain,
Content and happiness may there reside,
Nor breathe one sigh for seats of costly pride.
His *little field* th' industrious peasant plants,

Richly supplying all domestic wants;   200
And oft retir'd, at noon-day's burning hour,
Where arching woodbines weave a fragrant bow'r,
Bless'd with all joys, that *ever bless'd the poor,*
He views the *cyper* figur'd o'er his door,
And breathes, when slaves and bigot minds defame,   205
A grateful sigh to gen'rous *Russel's* name.
      How firm the surface of yon ancient moor
Where sedgy swamps, unknown to Ceres' store,
Long ages lay a fibrous, spungy mass,
Unsafe for beast, or human foot to pass.   210
Deep, through the soft consistence of the soil,
The delving lab'rers urg'd incessant toil;
Behind them, yawning fissures mark their way,
Sunk to the bed of gravel, sand, or clay.
The earth return'd; through hidden tracks, below,   215
Incessant streams still, gently oozing, flow;
Till gradual harden'd, in the solar beam,
The arid glebe invites the harness'd team.——
The verdure fades in summer's fervid air,
And lab'ring hinds consuming fires prepare.   220
Swift, from the heap'd-up sedgy clods arise,
Blue curling volumes dark'ning half the skies,
With mould'ring flames the glowing hillocks burn,
Till all dissolv'd to fertile ashes turn.
      Happy the man who thus employs his toil,   225
With scorching fires to fertilize the soil!
While sons of blood, with fell demoniac hand,
O'er trembling nations lift the flaming brand;
He rests secure, nor views th' ensanguin'd car,
Nor hears the hoarse, tremendous voice of War.   230
      Lo, where the ameliorating flames were tried,
A fairer aspect beams on every side.
No longer now the cattle walk with dread,
Nor sink, ingulph'd, as o'er the mire they tread;
No noxious fumes from stagnant pools arise,   235
Nor lights nocturnal, cheat the trav'ller's eyes;
But there the oat its quiv'ring bells displays,
The barley whitens in the tropic blaze;
The wheat, fair crest in Nature's diadem,
Unripe, yet trembles on its yellow stem;   240

And scented zephyrs court the new-mown hay,
White-blossom'd beans, and pease with crimson gay.
    And hence convey'd, the subterranean rills,
By springs replenish'd from contiguous hills,
Roll on to reservoirs beside the mead,   245
A watery store reserv'd till times of need.
If chance the year its genial showers deny,
When Sol o'er nature darts his piercing eye,
The gates unbarr'd, th' imprison'd waters flow
Diffusive o'er the thirsty plains below;   250
Round the parch'd roots, the soft'ning drops pervade,
Distend the stem, expand the shrivel'd blade;
From op'ning pores aërial streams exude,
And Vegetation feels her powers renew'd.
    Thus, Ethiopia! o'er thy arid plains,   255
When burning skies deny th' accustom'd rains,
And parch'd with hopeless drought the pilgrims stray,
Lost and bewilder'd in their trackless way;
If chance some riv'let meets their anxious view,
Or one dark cloud obscures th' etherial blue,   260
Through every nerve returning spirits fly,
Glow in each breast, and shine in every eye.
    Near yon gay plain, the huntman's early horn
Oft woke the slumb'ring echoes of the morn;
While, o'er the wide champaign, no thicket rose,   265
To shelter Reynard from his mortal foes,
Spread o'er the fallow clods, the rushy sward,
Promiscuous flocks the scanty herbage shar'd,
Ploughs, harrows, rolls, subdued the stubborn soil,
From distant hamlets mingling in their toil;   270
But, Industry, thy unremitting hand
Has chang'd the formless aspect of the land.
To distant fields no more the peasants roam,
Their cottage-lands and farms surround their home;
And hawthorn fences, stretch'd from side to side,   275
Contiguous pastures, meadows, fields divide.
    Seest thou afar, near Ouse's placid stream,
Yon casements glitt'ring in the evening beam:
Of late, the lapwing built her nest alone,
In those dull scenes, unheeded, and unknown: 280
But now, see! stables, granaries, barns extend,
White fences shine, and household smokes ascend;

Carts toll their pon'drous loads, and flails resound,
And oxen low, and horses neigh around.
   Whate'er of fragrance woos the passing gale,   285
Now scents the bosom of the flowery vale;
Whate'er of fruits the British islands know,
There bloom in spring, in fervid summer glow;
And though, Britannia, climates mild as thine,
Not India's spices boast, nor Gallic wine;   290
Though here no fig, nor priz'd anana grows;
Nor golden orange in thy vineyards glows;
Nor that sweet cane—the curse of many an isle,
Nor gold, nor diamonds sleep beneath thy soil;
Yet thy own wealth attracts the richest stores   295
With power magnetic to thy favour'd shores.
And chief thy flocks, that crown each mountain's brow,
And deck each vale, from these thy riches flow;
These meet my view, innumerous grazing wide,
Their unshorn lambs yet sporting by their side.   300
Some destin'd soon, by unrelenting fate,
To smoke on tables of the rich and great;
But those of finest shape, and noblest size,
Again must view the vernal year arise,
Spread their young progeny around the land,   305
And yield their fleeces to the shearer's hand.
These eyes have seen when ant-hills cloth'd yon fields,
And gorse where clover now its fragrance yields,
And swells its cluster'd flowers: behold how tall
The stems uprise, and waving wait their fall!   310
Reserv'd till vegetation shrinks and dies;
Till yon fair spotted tribes, that range the dale,
And frequent wait the ruddy milkmaid's pail,
View the gay plains where verdure wont to glow,
Incas'd in ice, or buried deep in snow.   315
   Benignant clime! here autumn's choicest store
Fails not, while winter's latest tempests roar!
Far other scenes proclaim his tyrant-reign,
Where chill Siberia bounds the northern main,
All powers of life and vegetation fled,   320
The fields repose as Nature's self lay dead,
The earth to rock, the sea to crystal turns,
Till the bright sun with tropic splendor burns.

Yet sure yon patient, woolly tribes demand
The generous care of man's providing hand;   325
Unless for them his shivering limbs must vear
Th' enfeebling rigours of th' inclement year.
Or, wrapt in skins, the human form debase,
To a vile semblance of the savage race;
And Ceres still thy fostering care supplies   330
Abundant food when wintry glooms arise;
For them, o'er many a fruitful acre spread,
Th' aspiring colewort lifts its verdant head;
For them the turnip swells its juicy form,
And stands unharm'd through many a piercing storm.   335
But chief, when Phoebus' vivifying ray
Glows on the painted scenes of rosy May,
Where'er thy hand its plastic power applies,
Herbs, flowers, and fruits in rich profusion rise;
Vanish the glooms that mark the steril soil,   340
The rocks relent, the wildest deserts smile.
Blest hour! when Art and Luxury are poor,
And Grandeur's golden scenes delight no more!
'Tis Nature calls: and, lo, the rich and gay,
Princes, and sceptered kings, the call obey,   345
And bid their chariots haste in splendid train,
Amidst the sweets of Flora's vernal reign.
    The purest pleasures still attend his toil,
Who spends his days on his paternal soil;
Too low to listen to the syren's tale,   350
He never bids Ambition's dreams prevail;
And, blest with health and calm domestic joy,
No fears of poverty his breast annoy.
On him if liberal Science deigns to shine,
To banish errors, and the art refine,   355
Ill-shapen tools, of weak, uncertain pow'r,
Fall to decay, and are renew'd no more.
To them effective instruments succeed,
His herds and flocks display a nobler breed,
No rampant weeds devour the rising corn,   360
But well-cleans'd vig'rous rows his fields adorn;
When fav'ring seasons on his labours smile,
Nor thistle, rush, nor gorse deforms his soil,
But all the gifts that nature lends to crown
The brow of art—he proudly calls his own.   365

Oft from his gates, see many a pond'rous load,
Of harvest spoils oppress the burden'd road;
These, weekly to some destin'd spot convey'd,
Await the mandates of the sons of Trade;
—If near some river's navigable tide,   370
Pil'd in a deep capacious barge they ride,
To where proud cities shine along the strand,
Or commerce beckons with a golden wand.
     Great queen of arts! when shall thy blissful sway,
From every heart, command the grateful lay?   375
For, hark!—methinks far other notes I hear,
Which, sad and solemn, strike my wounded ear;
Beneath yon willow sits a minstrel swain,
Nor Wealth nor Grandeur hearken to his strain;
While lonely there, his plaintive notes arise,   380
The drops of anguish glisten in his eyes.
—'Sweet-smiling vale! that nurs'd my infant years,
Whose scenes enchanted, and whose name endears!
Still glow thy fields in summer's fruitful ray,
Thy harvests flourish, all thy meads are gay;   385
But not for me fair Nature spreads her store,
Life's smiling prospects must be mine no more!
     Ye blissful hours! which once this breast has known,
When half the village sow'd and reap'd their own;
When social feelings glow'd in ev'ry breast,   390
Each master gen'rous, and each servant blest;
When competence, and peace, and rural joy,
Smil'd in each cottage, cheer'd each day's employ;
Alas! your beams are vanish'd from the plain,
As with'ring flow'rets fade in winter's iron reign.   395
     Friends of my youth, who bade my fortunes rise,
Death's ruthless hand for ever seals your eyes,
Where yonder high tow'r lifts its ivy'd head,
Ye rest, reposing on your clay-cold bed:
Envied retreat!—while your surviving heirs   400
Inherit life with its ten thousand cares!
     Fled is your long-accumulating store,
Your houses, meadows, fields, are theirs no more;
Where long your race manur'd and till'd the soil,
With easy competence and healthful toil,   405
Monopoly has rear'd her gorgon head,

To strike the source of rural comforts dead!
    I ask not Science to withdraw her hand,
Nor hoary Custom still to rule the land;
Prais'd be the scene when ev'ry hill and plain   410
Exulting owns fair Cultivation's reign;
When verdant fences o'er each field extend,
Limits define, and property defend:
Ye noble few, whose patriot-bosoms glow
In this fair cause, may glory gild your brow!   415
—But say, ye great! who bid, o'er all this isle,
Green pastures spread where harvests wont to smile,
Who change, for herds, the life-supporting grain,
With *woolly tribes* displace the reaper train,
Who build a *palace* for the wealthier few,   420
But drive to squallid huts the *ruin'd* crew;
Shall not those wretched sons of Want repine?
Yes—helpless myriads mix their sighs with mine!'

CHARLOTTE RICHARDSON (1775–?1825)

Charlotte Richardson, née Smith, was born in York in 1775, and received some basic education at a charity school that provided training in domestic service. Though she began working as a cook-maid, a series of calamities left her first widowed and then unable to run the school she opened after her husband's death. Her plight came to the attention of the philanthropist Catharine Cappe (1744–1821), widow of the prominent dissenting minister Newcome Cappe, who wrote to the *Gentleman's Magazine* in order to secure subscribers for a volume of Richardson's poetry, and also produced a memoir detailing Richardson's literary talents, personal misfortunes, and good Christian character. This campaign was extremely successful: *Poems Written on Different Occasions* (1806) attracted nearly eight hundred subscribers (including Robert Bloomfield and Anna Barbauld), and 'six hundred more copies than the number subscribed for were sold' (*DNB*). Four of Cappe's own publications, all religiously oriented, were advertised in the volume's back matter.

The fund-raising impetus behind Richardson's publishing career is further evidenced in her second volume, *Poems, Chiefly Composed During…Severe Illness* (1809), which Cappe opens with the confession that 'The Editor of Charlotte Richardson's former little volume of Poems had no intention of again introducing her humble Muse to the notice of her friends or the public, had not repeated attacks of the same distressing disease, an abscess in the side, obliged her to relinquish a school, in which she had every prospect of success' (p. iii). Cappe goes on to say, with some equivocation, 'It is not then solely as an act of charity, nor merely on account of the merit of the poetry, whatever that may be, that the Editor has again presumed to solicit the patronage of the Author's friends and the public' (pp. iv–v). There is perhaps more hedging in this statement than was necessary. For while it is true, as Elizabeth Lee noted in the *DNB*, that Richardson's poetry is not especially distinctive, frequently featuring 'paraphrases of passages from the New Testament and addresses to relatives and friends', Richardson does show real facility with these formats, as well as a sure command of rhythm. Cappe's tentative comments probably reflect the fact that she had edited Richardson's poems from manuscript, and perhaps engaged in some fairly extensive revision of the originals.

The shape of Richardson's career after 1809 is a matter of great uncertainty. The *DNB*, the British Library catalogue, and most other bibliographic sources credit Richardson with short new volumes in 1815 and 1817, and a much longer one, *Harvest*, in 1818, dedicated to the English mathematician Charles Hutton (1737–1823). ('I tremblingly invok'd the infant Muse', Richardson writes, 'You blest her earliest efforts'.) These sources also credit her with a novel, *The Soldier's Child* (1821), and a final volume of poetry, *Ludolph, or the Light of Nature* (1823). But there is recent evidence to suggest that these later works are by an altogether different writer, Charlotte Caroline Richardson. A direct comparison between the York volumes of 1806 and 1809, and the various post-1815 volumes, suggests strongly that they are the work of different hands. And an obituary recently unearthed by Roger Sales suggests that Charlotte Richardson of York died in 1825, even though most indexes apply to her both the name (Charlotte Caroline Richardson) and death-date (?1850) of the second writer. The problem is compounded still further because bibliographies often confuse these two figures with yet a third writer, Caroline E. Richardson, who published a novel and several volumes of poems between 1800 and 1835. The relative obscurity of all three of these writers has no doubt contributed to the state of scholarly confusion.

FURTHER READING

British Critic 31 (1808), 347–8

Catharine Cappe, *Memoirs of the Life of the Late Mrs. Catharine Cappe: Written by Herself* (London: Longman, 1822)

DNB

Gentleman's Magazine 75, part ii (1805), 813–14; 78, part ii (1808), 697–8

J. R. de. J. Jackson, *Romantic Poetry by Women* (Oxford: Clarendon Press, 1993)

Monthly Repository 1 (1806), 380–2

Helen Plant, *Unitarianism, philanthrophy and feminism in York, 1782–1821: the career of Catharine Cappe*, Borthwick paper 103 (York: Borthwick Institute of Historical Research, University of York, 2003)

Roger Sales, 'The Maid and the Minister's Wife: Literary Philanthropy in Regency York', *Women's Poetry in the Enlightenment: The Making of a Canon, 1730–1820*, eds Isobel Armstrong and Virginia Blain (Basingstoke: Macmillan, 1999), pp. 127–41.

From *Poems Written on Different Occasions* (1806)

Written Under Great Doubt, and Anxiety of Mind, 1801

O Thou whose piercing eye surveys
The inmost secrets of my soul,
O guide me in thy sacred ways,
    And all my actions, Lord, controul.

Wisely to choose is my desire,   5
    But O do thou that choice direct,
And let thy grace my soul inspire,
    The false pretender to detect.

My future happiness or woe,
    Upon my present choice depend,   10
Show me the way I ought to go
    And be my Father, and my Friend!

Let not this treach'rous heart of mine
    To inclination yield the sway,
But unto thee my fate resign,   15
    And wait, till thou shalt point the way.

He Sleeps 1805

Oft as I wander round the spot,
    To Sorrow sacred made,
Beneath whose consecrated turf,
    My RICHARDSON is laid;
My bleeding heart again recalls   5
    Past hours of heart-felt bliss,
Whilst mem'ry only serves to make
    My sorrows flow afresh!

But soft! methinks I hear a voice
   Descending from above   10
Which cries, 'my chast'ning hand I lay
   On those I dearly love;
To try their faith, their love to me,
   I bid their joys decrease,
But all who on my word rely,   15
   In me find perfect peace.'

My God! I hear thine awful voice,
   And dare no more repine,
Humbled beneath thy mighty arm,
   I own the stroke divine!   20
I'll strive to overcome this grief;
   Assist me with thy grace,
And let me in affliction's hour,
   Possess my soul in peace!

For ah! why should this wayward heart   25
   In fruitless sorrow mourn,
Since pain and sorrow are the lot,
   Of all of woman born;
My RICHARDSON from every woe
   Has found a sweet release,   30
And in the mansions of the tomb,
   He sleeps, and is at peace!

No more can Envy's secret sting
   Its pois'nous canker spread,
Malice and Calumny no more   35
   Their baneful venom shed,
Vain are their efforts now to wound,
   Their idle rage may cease,
For safe within the silent tomb,
   He sleeps, and is at peace!   40

But chief, no more the tyrant Sin,
   Can e'er his soul enslave,
The captive's loosen'd from his chains,
   Through Jesu's pow'r to save;
His warfare now is at an end,   45
   And all his conflicts cease,

For ever freed, he now enjoys,
   Uninterrupted peace!

But, when th' Archangel's voice is heard,
   Resounding through the skies,   50
(That voice which cleaves the pond'rous tombs,
   And bids the dead arise)
The graves obedient hear the call,
   Their prisoners release,
And all who sleep in Jesus now,   55
   Shall reign with him in peace.

May I, at that tremendous hour,
   With holy joy awake,
And, with the ransom'd of the Lord,
   In endless bliss partake;   60
My RICHARDSON I then shall join,
   Where pain and parting cease,
And spend a sweet eternity,
   In harmony and peace.

From *Poems, Chiefly Composed During the Pressure of Severe Illness* (1809)

After Reading Clarkson's Narrative

Hail, gen'rous friend of Afric's injur'd race,
   Who dar'd to plead the hapless Negro's cause;
Could'st truth amidst the mass of error trace,
   And vindicate Jehovah's sacred laws.

O ever blest, who in life's early prime,   5
   When science held the glittering prize to view,
Freely devoted talents, fortune, time,
   The power of stern Oppression to subdue!

What keen emotions shook thy pious mind,
    When the dark picture to thine eyes arose,   10
Thy heart, where all the virtues were combin'd,
    With horror shrunk from viewing Afric's woes.

But no cold unavailing grief was thine;
    Thy persevering ardour pierc'd the shade,
And with an energy almost divine,   15
    To Britain's eyes the dreadful scene display'd.

Each virtuous bosom felt the kindling flame,
    Indignant spurning at Oppression's yoke;
And dear the Muse shall hold each honour'd name,
    Through whom at length the galling chain was broke.   20

Though sordid Interest marshall'd all her powers,
    And shunn'd the light of Truth's refulgent beams,
At length the glorious victory is yours,
    And Freedom's sun once more on Afric gleams.

O CLARKSON! when at length the voice divine   25
    Shall bid thy spirit to its God ascend,
A crown of radiant glory shall be thine,
    While angels hail with joy the Negro's friend.

The Washerwoman's Reply to E. Waring
July, 1808

Presumptuous youth, whose daring muse
Could such a theme for satire choose,
The day of washing to abuse,
        So slightly.

As champion of my sex, I rise,   5
With indignation in my eyes,
That thou our labours should despise
        So lightly:

Because on that eventful day
The rooms in some disorder lay,   10
And round the fire in close array,
   Displeasing;

When wint'ry clouds o'ercast the sky,
Wet linen hangs in rows to dry,
Or when the raging storn beats high   15
   Unceasing.

To rise before the morning light,
And toil incessantly till night;
To make, hard task, both clean and white,
   The linen.   20

Our labour great, but not our gains,
Save weary limits and aching pains;
While thoughtless youth our toil disdains,
   Poor women!

Suppose, upon the British ground,   25
Nay more, in all the world around,
No females willing should be found,
   For washing;

I wonder then what thou would'st do,
The miry streets when pacing through,   30
Where rain, despite of boot or shoe,
   Comes dashing:

Thy hose, well soak'd and splash'd all o'er,
With dirty linen, evil sore,
Thy muse, methinks, would be no more   35
   So daring.

JAMES HOGG (1770–1835)

Early nineteenth-century labouring-class poetry sometimes seems describable as an overt competition to claim the mantle—or fulfill the thwarted destiny—of the 'Heaven-taught Ploughman', Robert Burns. If any one poet can be said to have 'won' this competition in his day, it is James Hogg, whose immersion in Scottish folk and ballad culture, sharp satirical instinct, sparkling personality, frequent insolvency, aura of sexual knowingness, failures at farming, and truly remarkable autodidacticism fit nicely with the Burns of truth and legend. Ironically, though, to pay Hogg the great compliment of being Burns's rightful heir is to misrepresent and perhaps even to diminish his actual achievement. Hogg was a vastly prolific and versatile writer for whom the Scottish ballad tradition yielded numerous outgrowths in novels, stories, and sketches, as well as in lyric and narrative poems. Yet for a whole series of reasons, including the range and variety of his work, the complexity of his poetry's use of folk sources, and, most significantly, the longstanding, almost incomprehensible lack of available editions of his work, Hogg has been poorly served by critical narratives of Romantic or nineteenth-century literature. Even as he was as genuine an autodidact and as singular an original genius as any mythology of labouring-class or Romantic poetry could require, Hogg until very recently has been relegated to the sub-fields of literary history dealing with 'regional' and 'dialect' writers.

Hogg lived and worked for most of his life in Ettrick Forest in the Scottish Borders, an extremely isolated region in which shepherding was essentially the only gainful occupation. If Hogg's account of his life in his *Memoir* is to be believed, then Nelson Smith is right in calling him 'almost uncontaminated by contact with the traditions of English literature' (p. 16). His father's financial ruin forced Hogg to leave school, and to begin working, at the age of six. 'Thus terminated my education', he remembered, and he was hired by a farmer to herd 'a few cows', with his year's wages being 'a ewe lamb and a pair of new shoes' (*Memoir*, pp. 5–6). Hogg kept cows ('the worst and lowest known [employment] in our country') until, in his early teens, he moved on to sheep-herding, in which he would be engaged until the age of thirty. At twenty he took his employment at the house of James Laidlaw of Blackhouse, under whose encouragement he began his adult acquaintance with books and learning. There is some indication, in fact, that Hogg was more or less functionally illiterate until beginning with Laidlaw. Yet within a few years he had formed an informal literary society with his brother and several other shepherd friends, earning a reputation in his district as a slightly crazed, entertaining versifier and a boon companion. A poem of his appeared in the *Scots Magazine* of 1794, and in 1797 he heard Burns's poem 'Tam O'Shanter', from then on his declared favourite.

With the turn of the century the first stage of Hogg's literary career began. In 1800 his rousing war poem 'Donald Macdonald' (promising resistance to Napoleon) was a popular success in the *Scots Magazine*, and he followed it the next year with a short first volume of poems, *Scottish Pastorals*. Soon he made the acquaintance of Walter Scott, with whom he would have a long but troubled friendship, later described in his volume *The Domestic Manners and Private Life of Sir Walter Scott* (1834). A second volume of poems, *The Mountain Bard*, appeared in 1807, and reflected his growing conviction that he could follow Scott and others in producing successful modern imitations of ancient ballads. A third collection, *The Forest Minstrel*, a volume of 'amorous phantasies' based on traditional songs and airs (and described by the *Scots Magazine* as an attempt to 'outdo even the vulgarity of the lowest vulgar'), was published in 1810. His profits from these publications were lost in unsuccessful farming ventures, however, and in 1810, broke and admittedly desperate—but still exhibiting the immense reservoir of self-confidence that drew so many people to him—Hogg moved to Edinburgh. For a year he almost single-handedly produced a journal called *The Spy*, packed with sardonic sketches of life in the city. Though he had received much-needed financial support from old and new acquaintances in Edinburgh, *The Spy* also failed for lack of money. But then came his major breakthrough—the book-length poem *The Queen's Wake* (1813), organized around the conceit of a poetical competition in honour of Mary, Queen of Scots. The work, featuring two especially popular poems, 'The Witch of Fife' and 'Kilmeny', was widely hailed. Hogg seized the moment. An 1815 volume, *Pilgrims of the Son*, featured imitations of older English writers, and he then planned a volume that would feature contributions from the great living poets of Britain. When potential contributors, most especially Scott, backed out or otherwise declined to participate, Hogg turned the venture into a collection of imitations and parodies, including the brilliant Wordsworthian send-ups 'James Rigg' and 'The Flying Tailor'.

In 1815 Hogg was given Altrive Farm at a permanent nominal rent by the Duke of Buccleuch, and in 1820 he married the much younger Margaret Phillips, with whom he eventually had five children. But soon his financial situation was again desperate, mainly because he was pouring resources into a large additional farm called Mount Benger. Acutely conscious of the need for money, he produced three novels between 1822 and 1824: *Three Perils of Man* (which he names as War, Women, Witchcraft*)*; *Three Perils of Woman* (Love, Leasing, Jealousy); and *The Private Memoirs and Confessions of a Justified Sinner*, his most famous work in any genre. In 1825 he published his comic epic of Scottish myth, *Queen Hynde*. While none of these publications was particularly successful, he was nevertheless becoming famous for his role as 'The Ettrick Shepherd' in the popular dialogues called 'Noctes Ambrosianae', which appeared in *Blackwood's Edinburgh Magazine* beginning in the early 1820s. These comic exchanges, purporting to be conversations in Ambrose's Tavern amongst several of the magazine's leading writers, were crucial in consolidating Hogg's public persona. As Douglas S. Mack notes, 'Much of the success of *Blackwood's* depended on the "Noctes"; and much of the popularity of the "Noctes" derived from the character of the Shepherd, a rural philosopher-clown' (Mack, *The Shepherd's Calendar*, p. xiii). The Shepherd's pungent and witty observations on life provided Hogg with a durable alter ego and continuous public presence (the pieces ran until 1835, the year of his death) that was distinctly unusual for a plebeian poet. But the 'Noctes' were mostly written by John Wilson, not Hogg himself, and if the image they presented of 'The Shepherd' was generally affectionate, it was also caricatured and foolish. In seeking something like the authentic 'wit and wisdom' of James Hogg, one might better take up his whimsical and reflective late volume *Lay Sermons* (1834). Several of the other works printed near the end of Hogg's life, like *The Shepherd's Calendar* (1829) and *A Queer Book* (1832), were collections of material published previously in journals. An expensive edition of his prose entitled *Altrive Tales* was planned, but the bankruptcy of the publisher after the first volume (1832) derailed the project. When Hogg died at Altrive Farm in 1835, he was a well-known and admired figure, though the public perception of him as an amiable Falstaffian rustic underestimated both his intelligence and the frequent darkness of his vision. That darkness is most easily seen in remarkable stories like 'The Brownie of the Black Haggs', 'Tibby Hyslop's Dream', and 'Marion's Jock', in which desire, lust, and aggression, once tapped, cascade and eventually engulf the characters. But as with so many of Hogg's stories and tales, the pathways of destruction charted by these works are unpredictable and strangely unhurried. All conclude with shockingly graphic scenes of violence, but at any point their narratives are susceptible of comic interruption, usually in the form of a peasant speaker whose authority is signalled by the thickness of the Scots dialect.

Even in Hogg's lifetime his work was frequently bowdlerized; and Victorian editions, especially those published by Blackie and Son of Glasgow in the 1830s and 1860s, further suppressed Hogg's recurring thematics of

sexuality and power, in both comic and tragic settings. The result of this san-
itization, it is generally agreed, is that the idiosyncratic energy of Hogg's
writing was almost totally forgotten: what remained in view was not the
man's individual genius, but his groundings in tradition and his propensities
as a folklorist. It was not until André Gide's admiring 1947 introduction to
an edition of the *Memoirs and Confessions of a Justified Sinner* that Hogg was
rediscovered by the twentieth century. This novel's masterful reworking of
Romantic-era Gothicism, achieved through a satirical indictment of hard-
line Scots Presbyterianism, has lately been receiving a measure of the critical
appreciation it deserves. Even so, Hogg's copious and varied *corpus* remained
almost totally unavailable until the 1990s, when the Edinburgh University
Press published the first of a projected thirty-one volume collection of his
complete works. Appearing under the general editorship of Douglas Mack
and usually referred to as the Stirling/South Carolina edition, this monu-
mental project promises to transform our understanding of Hogg and to
restore him to his place as one of the great writers of nineteenth-century
Britain. Several of the volumes include the first-ever unexpurgated publica-
tions of individual Hogg texts. (See 'Further Reading' for reviews of the
Stirling/South Carolina edition's initial volumes.)

As scholars begin what promises to be a long period of reassessment, one
key issue is that of Hogg's style. The tendency of his prose to engage in
shifts of voice and emphasis has long been assumed to be a sign of his lack
of polish and artistic control. Even his admirers have tended to characterize
his writing as uneven and internally inconsistent. Increasingly, however, crit-
ics are noting the confidence and authorial conviction that pervades Hogg's
writing, and are suggesting that his gaps and shifts reflect both a virtuosic
capacity to adopt the mindsets of diverse characters—especially characters
from different social classes—and something like a Keatsian 'negative capa-
bility', seen in Hogg's willingness to inhabit mysterious mental states
involving the co-mingling of superstition, religious mania, and religious
belief. It is this latter quality, especially in its compassionate aspects, that
most clearly separates him from Burns. Though many of Hogg's works,
including *Confessions of a Justified Sinner*, are protests against strict Calvinism,
and though Hogg follows Burns in advocating leniency, fellow-feeling, and
humour in the face of human failings, he nonetheless recognizes both the
basic power of religious feeling and its function as a psychological life-line
for the poor of rural Scotland. Something of this can be seen in the follow-
ing passage, from the essay called 'Storms' in *The Shepherd's Calendar*:

> The daily sense so naturally impressed on the shepherd's mind that all his
> comforts are so entirely in the hand of him that rules the elements, con-
> tributes not a little to that firm spirit of devotion for which the Scotish

shepherd is so distinguished. I know of no scene so impressive as that of a family sequestered in a lone glen during the time of a Winter storm; and where is the glen in the kingdom that wants such a habitation? There they are left to the protection of heaven, and they know and feel it. Throughout all the wild vicissitudes of nature they have no hope of assistance from man, but are conversant with the Almighty alone. Before retiring to rest, the shepherd uniformly goes out to examine the state of the weather, and make his report to the little dependant group within—nothing is to be seen but the conflict of the elements, nor heard but the ravings of the storm—then they all kneel around him, while he recommends them to the protection of heaven, and though their little hymn of praise can scarcely be heard even by themselves as it mixes with the roar of the tempest, they never fail to rise from their devotions with their spirits cheered, and their confidence renewed, and go to sleep with an exaltation of mind of which kings and conquerors have no share. Often have I been a sharer in such scenes and never, even in my youngest years, without having my heart deeply impressed by the circumstances. There is a sublimity in the very idea. There we lived as it were inmates of the cloud and the storm, but we stood in a relationship to the ruler of these that neither Time nor Eternity could ever cancel. Wo[e] to him that would weaken the bonds with which true Christianity connects us with Heaven and with each other. (pp. 3–4)

This voice is not the one we have come to expect from the buffoonish character known as the Ettrick Shepherd, nor from the writer whose novels featured 'speculations about promiscuity and prostitution, and [...] prayers so chattily informal that reviewers found them blasphemous' (Barrell, p. 14). Instead, the sympathetic and eloquent anthropology seen here is but one of many other facets of Hogg's astonishing talent. With the continuing republication of his work in fine scholarly editions, our expectations will assuredly continue to be enlarged.

FURTHER READING

John Barrell, 'Putting Down the Rising', *London Review of Books* (22 February 1996), 14–15

Edith C. Batho, *The Ettrick Shepherd* (Cambridge: Cambridge University Press, 1927)

Douglas Gifford, *James Hogg: A Reassessment* (Edinburgh: Ramsey Head, 1976)

David Groves, *James Hogg. The Growth of a Writer* (Edinburgh: Scottish Academic Press, 1988)

James Hogg, *Memoirs of the Author's Life and Familiar Anecdotes of Sir Walter Scott*, ed. Douglas S. Mack (Edinburgh: Scottish Academic Press, 1972)

James Hogg, *Selected Poems of James Hogg*, ed. Douglas S. Mack (Oxford: Clarendon Press, 1970)

James Hogg, *The Shepherd's Calendar*, ed. Douglas S. Mack (Edinburgh: Edinburgh University Press, 1995)

'John Clare and James Hogg: A Special Issue', *John Clare Society Journal* 22 (2003)

Douglas S. Mack (ed.), *The Stirling / South Carolina Research Edition of The Collected Works of James Hogg* (Edinburgh: Edinburgh University Press, 1995–)

Karl Miller, 'The Cannibal King', TLS (29 December 1995), 4

Karl Miller, *The Electric Shepherd: A Likeness of James Hogg* (London: Faber and Faber, 2003)

Edwin Morgan, 'The Stirling / South Carolina Edition of James Hogg', *Scottish Literary Journal*, Supplement 44 (Spring 1996), 1–2

Louis Simpson, *James Hogg: A Critical Study* (Edinburgh: Oliver and Boyd, 1962)

Nelson C. Smith, *James Hogg* (Boston: Twayne Publishers, 1980)

Fiona Stafford, 'Review Article: The Stirling / South Carolina Research Edition of The Collected Works of James Hogg', *Review of English Studies*, n.s. 50 (1999), 66–8

Alan Lang Strout, *The life and letters of James Hogg, the Ettrick Shepherd* (Lubbock, Texas: Texas Tech Press, 1946).

GEORGE BLOOMFIELD (1757–1831)

Manuscript evidence reveals that George Bloomfield, known within the labouring-class tradition as the main source of biographical information on his brothers Robert and Nathaniel (q.q.v.), was also an aspiring poet. While his total poetic output and level of ambition remain matters of conjecture, papers held at the British Library suggest the provisional outlines of a volume with the working title *Verses on Several Occasions*. The poem printed below, entitled 'The Poets at Odds', is from another important collection of Bloomfield family materials at Harvard's Houghton Library, and it has been chosen for inclusion here because it touches on several issues related to the three brothers' professional contacts and literary fortunes. Evidence surrounding 'The Poets at Odds' shows that George had some aspirations toward a public literary life, since the poem was sent to Thomas Hill of the *Mirror Monthly* magazine with the specific request that it be included in a future issue. Even so, the piece had its genesis less in George's public ambitions than in his brother Nat's public difficulties, since it was conceived specifically as a response to the harsh critical treatment given to Nat's 1803 volume, *An Essay on War*.

'The Poets at Odds' comes to us as a sort of labouring-class 'Kubla Khan', a report of a fragmentary vision in a dream. In his cover letter to Hill—which was copied to William Holloway (q.v.) and confusingly addressed to both men—George describes how he read Holloway's 1808 volume *The Minor Minstrel*, and, before falling asleep, became upset with the volume's transition from poems of pastoral nostalgia to poems of war and misery: 'I found that sort of pleasure I have so often found in roaming about the flower-deck & meadows at Honingt[o]n with my Brothers—but all at once I found you gon[e] over the stile! [L]eft the pleasant meadows and peaceful Towns for WAR. [T]his bestir'd the water in my brain, and after the agitation cea[s]ed I fell into a rhyme-atical Sleep and dream'd of a Brother I dearly love, and of an unknown friend, they were conversing' (George Bloomfield to Thomas Hill, fMS Eng 391). George's self-deprecating coinage 'rhyme-atical Sleep' seems an attempt to downplay the seriousness of his compositional intent, but after presenting the poem he includes a note that reveals the true depth of his feelings. Now addressing Holloway, he writes,

I have beg[']d of Mr Hill to give these Lines a place in his *Mirror*. I wish I could have Done them better. I know Nat would be the last man to defend his opinion, though no one is more Capable. [H]e is to[o] much a Christian to return a blow. [H]e was Cruelly hunted Down by the Critics and may be considered as a *dead* man and I am jealous of any one who Disturb his Ghost. Poor Henry Kirk[e] White did him justice. But Henry is dead to[o]—Oh for a Scrap of *Latin* or *Greek* to tagg this with but Allass I am no Scholar. (fMS Eng 391)

What is startling here is not only George's assertion that Nat 'may be considered as a dead man', but that he views this death in such literal terms that he can go on to remark, with no apparent irony, on the fate of their acquaintance, the poet Henry Kirke White, who had died of tuberculosis in 1806. As is indicated in my Introduction to Nathaniel's work (q.v.), George's commentary on the cruelty of critics provides an implicit answer to the question of why Nat chose not to publish after 1803, and it is significant that 'The Poets at Odds' is designed to allow Nat to speak again: the poem is structured as a dialogue in which Nat and an 'unknown friend' named Will (not, evidently, Holloway himself) revisit the Malthusian precepts of 'An Essay on War'. Through all of this, the reader senses the intense fraternal feeling that George evinces, and the pain of Nat's wounds fully six years later. We should also note George's diffidence about entering the poetic arena himself, as he both defends his brother's literary skill and frets over his own lack of 'a Scrap of *Latin* or *Greek*'.

Because the manuscript copy of 'The Poets at Odds' contains many confusing irregularities of spelling and punctuation, the version printed below has been heavily edited, employing modern typographical conventions. I have addressed some of the details of these silent corrections in the notes. The version of the poem printed below should be considered a reading text.

FURTHER READING

The Earl of Cranbrook (ed.), *Parnassian molehill: an anthology of Suffolk verse written between 1327 and 1864*. 1953. Reprint edition (Aldeburgh: The Aldeburgh Bookshop, 2001)

DNB (Robert Bloomfield)

E. J. Hobsbawm and Joan Wallach Scott, 'Political Shoemakers', *Past and Present* 89 (1980), pp. 86–114.

The Poets at Odds

NAT

'Observe,' cries Nat, 'and learn the cause,
Of all those fatal cruel wars,
Men like the Bees in swarms combined,
In hopes each social joy to find,
As they increase their food grows scant,   5
They rather choose to fight then want,
Too soon they're formed in Martial bands,
Intent to pillage foreign lands,
War's scythe produces swift [decrease]
The cause remov'd men wish for peace.'   10

WILL

'Was man a social creature made,
To thin his race with Murder's blade,
Ah tell us not at Honor's call,
That Myriads every age must fall,
That thus th' encumber'd world has need   15
Its victims oft should fight and bleed,
I hear the God of truth reply,
"—Twas Hell's arch-fiend devis'd the Lie—"'

NAT

'Softly dear Will, I pray be civil,
Perhaps thy zeal belie the Devil,   20
If the satanic King declare,
That mankind still are thin'd by war
Whoever reads the historic page,
Of ev'ry clime, of ev'ry age,
This obvious truth needs must find   25
(Unless by prejudice they're blind)
All historians display it,
Truth, is Truth, let who will say it.'

WILL

'Think on God's Word,—   30
His Gospel bids our bick'rings cease,
And only whispers—love and peace,
Could not the Power who life supplied

For all his creatures wants provide
Accommodate th' increasing race   35
With food, convenience, health and space,
And in the course of nature give,
Sufficiency for all that live,
Let truth oppose the Sophist band,
Lo Sin and Death go hand, in hand.'   40

                        NAT
'I made the search of scripture truth,
The study of my early youth,
Tis said to mankind great and small,
Resist not, injuries at all
Resist not, says the Law of Love,   45
Yet you defensive war approve!
No doubt but God the great first cause,
Could *force* obedience to his laws,
Bid national distinction cease
The [schemes] of patriots Efface,   50
Self interest drown in the great sea,
Of general philanthropy
That *peace* and *love* the world might crown,
The soldier and his trade unknown,
And for room, should men be scanted,   55
Could make another world and plant it.'

                       WILL
'Ungrateful it were to rob the brave,
Whom Heaven ordained to shield and save,
Of laurels Worthy to be worn,
From fierce ambitions trophies torn   60
When tyrants rouse the world to arms,
And deck Destruction's form with charms,
But would the proud and mighty hear,
And listen with impartial ear,
Whatever system they defend,   65
How'er successfully contend,
Beyond the rule of self defence,
Unjust is every vague pretence.'

NAT

'Give me your hand for I protest
My sentiments you have express'd   70
Nor can there be twixt any two
More concord then twixt me and you.'

WILL

'Hold Hold friend Nat,
Commissioned War is but the rod,
And scourge of an offended God!'   75

NAT

'As each contending state declare,
Theirs the just cause for waging war,
Each [warft] their prayers to the Skies,
For aid to crush their enemies,
Then how shall any mortal white   80
Dare to decide *whose* cause is right,
And arrogate the place of God
[O'er] fellow sinners shake the rod
Abstract perfection leads us far,
From what mere mortals really are,   85
Promiscuous, man's Lot may seem,
As good, and bad, swim down Life's stream
But yet there is a chosen race,
Who follow after *Love* and *peace*
Nor do the storms of war destroy,   90
Their hopes of solid lasting joy,
We Deplore what can't be mended
Tis fickle Man, Not God offended,—
Yet I know.—'

Here I awoke and Lo it was a Dream!!—

MARY BRYAN (*fl.* 1815–1829)

The poems of Mary Bryan are at once immensely communicative and shrouded in mystery, and in this sense they reflect our current understanding of Bryan herself. Until very recently, she was known to us entirely through her sole volume, *Sonnets and Metrical Tales* (1815), and the critical work that had been done on her—Jonathan Wordsworth's introduction to the 1815 volume in a 1996 Woodstock Books facsimile edition, and an essay by Stuart Curran in the *Wordsworth Circle*—sought in part to unravel the biographical puzzles that the volume seems aggressively to foreground. Bryan's preface hints at the dire economic circumstances that prompted her, as a widowed mother of six, to try and publish her poetry, and the poems themselves are deeply autobiographical, chronicling with some intimacy the emotional crises of a small family unit. But even as the poems construct a mosaic of psychic travails—especially those involving her husband and possibly her sisters—she refuses us crucial information. What were the circumstances of her marriage, which, though evidently passionate, apparently included her husband's 'total' (*SMT*, p. xiii) prohibition of her writing? Who are the intended recipients of the many poems titled or subtitled 'To—'? And what precisely motivates Bryan's dual impulses toward disclosure and concealment, assertion and withdrawal?

Recently the biographical record has been greatly enhanced by the work of Sharon Ragaz, who has discovered ten letters written by Bryan to Walter Scott between 1818 and 1827. Revealing both Bryan's proud self-determination and her abject attempts at ingratiation, these letters describe debt, illness, and other obstacles to Bryan's goals of writerly productivity and profit, and open a fascinating window on the dynamics of patronage and labouring-class poetry. Ragaz also offers us several major discoveries: that Bryan's deceased husband had run a printing business in Bristol; that Bryan inherited the debt-ridden business after his death and published *Sonnets and Metrical Tales* through its offices; that she eventually married her patron, the dedicatee of *Sonnets and Metrical Tales*, Dr. James Bedingfield; that, under the name of Mary Bedingfield, she published a novel, *Longhollow: A Country Tale*, in 1829; and that over the years she contemplated several other publishing ventures, seeking advice and assistance not only from Scott, but also from

Wordsworth, Hazlitt, and Samuel Rogers. (No existing correspondence with any of these latter three writers has yet been discovered.) Her possible connection with Wordsworth is especially tantalising since, as Curran has said, 'it could be forcefully argued that no poet writing in [the wake of *Lyrical Ballads*] had so true an understanding of their impelling principles of overlaid association and psychological shading, nor was there anyone who so insightfully recreate[d] their ethos in an original manner and for a later time' (p. 115).

Wordsworth is honoured as the addressee of the first poem in Bryan's collection, and echoes of his verse, especially the Lucy poems, sound unmistakably throughout, as in 'Anna' and 'Julia' below. There are other influences and modes clearly at work as well: 'The Dream' brings gothic conventions under the sway of domestic realism, while 'Anna' is one of several pieces that convey the danger and allure of sensibility. The poems repeatedly express two opposed but inextricably linked feelings. One is the suffocating fear of being alone, abandoned, or unloved; the other is the desire to transcend (or totally submit to) this fear by escaping into death. In reading Bryan, one thinks of the Brontë sisters, not simply because the poems suggest the hothouse atmosphere of an isolated rural family, but—both more vaguely and more evocatively—because of the texture of their emotional concentration. Again and again we sense that the speaker's intelligence and very subjectivity are being narrowed and squeezed into feverish derangement, with poetic expression itself serving as the speaker's last, best hold on rationality. The massive psychological strain Bryan feels is expressed in the early lines of 'Mary', where neither day nor night offers any hope for rest: 'Unwelcome shades of the unwelcom'd day, / Now told the tir'd one th' approach of tedious / Night' (ll. 6–8). Though Bryan's meters are frequently irregular, it is her sure sense of cadence and rhythm that allows her poems to trade so fully in the language of strong feeling, without becoming mawkish or self-indulgent. Their success derives from her keen sense of how the careful withholding of information or explanation can, as in Wordsworth's Lucy poems, create a sense of intimacy and expressive power; and this remains true even as our understanding of Bryan's life has become so helpfully enlarged.

Two poems by Bryan are published here for the first time, edited from archival material housed at the National Library of Scotland. 'The Village Maid', a narrative of seduction which dates roughly from the era of *Sonnets and Metrical Tales*, has qualities reminiscent of the poems of that volume: what begins as a conventional pastoral veers into the wilds of sensibility, desire, and fear. Though the poem has a familiar moralistic conclusion, the depiction of real desire—on both sides—is more urgent, and less euphemistic, than convention would favour. In its ability to evoke authentic emotion within a traditional generic context, 'The Village Maid' is a prime example of what makes Bryan a compelling poet. The second poem, 'Stanzas' ('Return my Muse'), dates from nearly a decade later and speaks directly of Bryan's struggle with an apparently degenerative eye problem that threatened her with permanent blindness. Bryan repeatedly states that she is 'cut off' from former scenes and modes of happiness, but her plaintive cry ('Return my humble muse, return to me') indicates that the poet in her is not dead, and she reveals that during this period she was composing other poems 'with a sort of fevered avidity' (NLS MS 3905, fol. 8). Indeed, 'Stanzas' suggests that although her sight is lost, her acceptance of the finality of the disaster may actually be a source of inspiration:

> Return my muse—for now the conflict's o'er,
> For now these sightless eyes have ceased to flow:
> Return and solace with thy yet loved lore
> The long unbroken night that shrouds me now. (ll. 5–8)

FURTHER READING

Critical Review 2 (1815), 519–23

Stuart Curran, 'Isabella Lickbarrow and Mary Bryan: Two Wordsworthian Poets', *The Wordsworth Circle* 27 (1996), 113–18

Sharon A. Ragaz, 'Writing to Sir Walter: The Letters of Mary Bryan Bedingfield', *Cardiff Corvey: Reading the Romantic Text* 7 (Dec 2001). Online: Internet (15 December 2002): http://www.cf.ac.uk/ncap/corvey/articles/cc07_n02.html.

From *Sonnets and Metrical Tales* (1815)

To W. W—h, Esq.

> Thou! who dost well reprove the sordid fear,
>   That spoils the springs of bliss—wasting life's powers,
> O wilt thou *mourn* th' ungenial influence here,
>   One moment pausing o'er these wither'd flowers?
>
> Like thee thro' many a darling haunt I stray'd;   5
>   And if to thee sublimer views were given,

Dear were the scenes my ling'ring steps delayed—
    As dear the silent grove—the starry Heav'n.

Far in the shelter'd vale, I never knew
    To mark great nature in her wonders drest;   10
Around her child her tend'rest charms she threw,
    And smiling, hid me in her tranquil breast.

No sordid wishes drew me from her bowers—
    Not such the passion that these strains reveal;
No sordid cares consume my wasting powers—   15
    My infant spoilers wear the bloom they steal.

—O, happiest of Poets, as of men,
    Who dost delight to shew his feelings true,
The maiden, dearest in her native glen,
    Spontaneous graces blending with her view—   20

Hast thou ne'er watch'd her cheek's decaying bloom?
    Hide—hide it ever from thy cheerful ken—
The faded mourner should not ask a tomb,
    To chill thy breast—O, happiest of men!

Poet of Nature's—Reason's—Beauty's light—   25
    Who nobly scorn'd the Muse by custom drest:
If too long dazzled, the bewilder'd sight
    Mark not her glories in her simpler vest;

The futile glare at length will cease to charm,
    At length awakening truth delight to find   30
A Muse with genuine hopes, and passions warm;
    Too warm for form—'Too pure to be refin'd'.

Anna
To — —

Sweet maid thy cheek's soft roses peer
    With those of rarest hue,

While on that cheek the pitying tear
    Outvies the rose's dew.

But once there was a cheek as fair   5
    As any rose that blew—
Alas! if tears of early care
    Should blanch my Carline's too!

Young ANNA was a lovely maid,
    And I remember well,   10
Where shelter'd by the elm-grove shade,
    Did gentle ANNA dwell.

For then a little vagrant foot
    Sought ANNA's garden bowers;
And there a playful prattler's suit,   15
    Won ANNA's fairest flowers.

And I remember ANNA's smile,
    That oft I flew to meet,—
If it disguis'd a tear the while,
    I saw the smile so sweet.   20

But ANNA grew a pensive maid,
    And then she lov'd to rove,
Beneath the silent, sullen shade,
    Of L***'s deserted grove.

A time-reft tree of baneful yew,   25
    A mould'ring mansion near;
Appall'd whoe'er their legend knew,
    'Twas such a tale of fear.

Yet, soon, she left her peaceful cot,
    Her gardens flow'ry bound,   30
And sought the desolated spot
    When night-birds scream'd around.

Unheard her solitary sigh,
    Unmark'd her frequent tear,
Still smiling to each smiling eye,   35
    She only sorrow'd here.

None, save the pensive ANNA, nigh
    Approach'd the dreary scene,

Unlovely weeks rose wild and high,
 Where sweetest flowers had been;   40

So base to sight, yet bold, to brave
 Reflection's sick'ning view,
O spoilers proud o'er virtue's grave—
 They look'd, methought, like you.

Still ANNA sought the blighted yew,   45
 In L***'s deserted shade;
And there from every eye withdrew
 The sad mysterious maid.

And very pale grew ANNA's cheek,
 But none knew ANNA's care: 50
They said the wintry blast so bleak,
 Had chill'd the roses there;

And spring would come, and ANNA bloom
 When other flowers were gay:
The spring-flow'rs deck'd her humble tomb,   55
 Once fairer far than they.

Young ANNA mourn'd no treach'rous vow,
 Nor unrequited flame;
The tears that laid the mourner low,
 Embalm'd a spotless fame.   60

Still lives in every tender breast,
 How early ANNA fell
By strange untimely cares opprest,
 And still, as fond, they tell,

How much the village maidens find   65
 Their artless wonder move,
That one so fair and gentle, pined
 And died—but not for love!

The Dream
C—H

The Winds around my cottage rudely blowing
  Bear on the midnight hour a fearful tone,
Near and more near—loud and still louder growing;
    Terrors shrill scream—
      And now—a feeble, dying moan:—   5
Awaking from a fever'd dream—
  I listen to the howling storm!
Slow from the dark and haunted stream,
    Her shadowy arms uprise,
'Till all, appear'd a phantom maid;   10
  Ah not in beauty's wonted form,
As fair, and fond, but much betray'd,
  And weary of her ceaseless woe,
    She sought a sleep
    So still and deep,   15
Where dark the waters flow.—
Blue vapours round her play'd
  She cannot rest in deep and night,
  And ever gleams a ghastly light
That haunts the unquiet shade.   20
Abhorring! from that light her eyes
  Still turn, but turn in vain;—
Methought on me a look they cast
  No eye might look again.
    And then, methought a fatal claim!   25
    'Come victim of as false a flame!'—
A murmur on the blast—
    So indistinct the tone
    That to the heart alone,
Spake, fearfully, and pass'd.   30
  Then, then, she sunk the deep below:
Yet, still a shadowy arm did wave;
To her unblest, unhallow'd grave
  Where dark the waters flow.

On Reading Lines to Tranquility

O, MAIDEN, is the Poet's breast,
Where thou so coy, so calm wilt rest.
   I long have sought thee ev'ry where;
   And if thou quiet shelterest there
   From noisy joy and busy care   5
I would I were that bosom's guest—
I would not break its peaceful rest.

I come not like some Lady gay,
With such I know thou wouldst not stay;
   I bring a pensive tear-dimm'd eye;   10
   A cheek without the rosy die,
   The wreck of sensibility,
And early sorrow's with'ring day,
And much I weary of the way,

And now I would I were with thee,   15
Where'er thou art—Tranquility.
   But is a Poet's breast thy seat?
   I had not thought such guest to greet
   Where all the haughtier feelings meet:
Thou art some proud—Tranquility   20
I fear—not what that maid should be.

And now that I reflect awhile,
Thou hast no tear, thou wear'st no smile—
   Thou canst not be that timid maid,
   Of summer's glowing suns afraid,   25
   That leads him to the mossy shade:
And how the wintry gloom beguile—
Such chilling gloom—without a smile!

At least awhile withdraw thy claim,
And leave him to a humbler dame;   30
   Now Poet would that I might be,
   That simple little maid to thee;
   And thou a sheltering rest to me.
A little feeble mortal frame
Has known to soothe the sons of fame,   35

When other Power's invoked in vain
Have shun'd th' intruders grief and pain,
  From such, as Poets are not free;
  P'rhaps not the best of Poets—thee,
  O then I would that I might be,   40
Thy nurse—to try some soothing strain;
To close thy eyes on grief and pain,

And watch thy rest, and think the while
How I might wake thee with a wile
  That should the cruel ills disarm,   45
  Of more than half their power to harm,
  For grief and pain there is a charm;
And e'en the breast that knows no guile,
Might harmless think of such a wile.

If vain conceit and low-born pride,   50
Affect to judge and dare deride;
  O would I might be near thee now,
  And gently smoothe thy ruffled brow,
  And tell—I could not tell thee—*how*
Revered thy talents, nor how wide,   55
That now by ignorance decried,

A host of feeling hearts approve:
I would not have such folly move,
  Thy generous heart—thy ample mind
  For mightier purposes design'd;   60
  But bid thee turn from these and find
What Poet's breast should ever prove,
The boundless bliss of—'boundless love'.

To — —

Sonnet

Wilt thou e'er find a love like mine?
Look on those eyes that gaze on thine:—
Those eyes would weep thy slightest pain,

And canst thou let them plead in vain?
And will thy lips pronounce my doom?   5
Yet not the dark and silent tomb
I fear—but long, long days unblest—
But nights of cruel agony!
What nights will bring my night of rest,
To think where thou wilt be!—   10
Perhaps when worn with wasting woe
I find a quiet grave,
To thee 'twill be a bitter throe,
To think thou wouldst not save!

To — —

Yet—yet forbear the cruel theme
    The fatal truth forbear,
Nor chase the fond delusive dream
    That leaves me to despair.

Disturb not yet this treacherous rest   5
    Awhile thy victim spare,
Nor mock while hanging on thy breast
    The dream thou canst not share.

Deck'd all the scene with gayest flow'rs.
    Thy fancy loves to stray,   10
But poisonous weeds and baneful bow'rs
    There meet my wandering way.

'Twas in its dreary maze beguil'd
    Involv'd in night and storm,
I sought thee in my terrors wild.   15
    And clasped a fearful form!

Thy life, my death—thy weal, my woe,—
    Thy love—no—not my hate—
But whom thou lov'st my bitt'rest foe,
    My sad and certain fate!   20

Yet sorrow now were shewn too soon,
　　Too soon, for one so bless'd—
And then it were too late a boon,
　　To grieve for one at rest.—

O thou art all my world of bliss,　　　　　　　　25
　　And while thou yet art mine,
To hold thee to my heart like this!
　　I would not once repine.

Not once, too vast the joy I deem
　　With aught of pain to share,　　　　　　　　30
And tho' 'tis all a treacherous dream
　　That leaves me to despair,

Yet proudly will thy ELLEN scorn
　　To weep such transient woes,—
That day will have a fearful morn—　　　　　　35
　　But night and death will close!

Mary

'Twas a lone hut, where, sick as she journey'd
A poor wand'rer lay—ah, long from all of
Peace and good—long had she stray'd and grievous
'Twere, abandon'd and alone, unaided
And uncheer'd, to bear the accumulated ills.　　　5
—Unwelcome shades of the unwelcom'd day,
Now told the tir'd one th' approach of tedious
Night—long days and nights—pain early taught
How slow its watchful hours: in childhood oft
Had I press'd the couch of ling'ring sickness;　　10
And when health, and joy, smil'd on my young cheek
As fond to bless with all their dearest gifts
Their long neglected child—I ne'er forgot
The past—how, still, o'er all my pain, Pity
Unwearied hung, and she requires that boon　　15
From Sorrow's victims which she kindly gives.

—Obscur'd by wild flow'rs of unheeded growth,
Autumnal twilight's last sick glimm'rings, beam'd
Thro' the patch'd window, faint fantastic shapes;
And all the scene, and the pale hour so still,   20
Blending with meekest sympathies, attuned,
To tenderness and love, the thinking mind.
I sought with cautious step the Suff'rer's bed
Lest sleep perhaps, and dreams most precious
To the wretch, dreams of innocence, and health,   25
Might charm her wounded mind with transient peace.
And she did sleep;—so quietly I pass'd,
And sitting on the rude bench watch'd the night
Closing around.—Methought unusual gloom
Hung on the dark'ning scene, and oft I turned   30
List'ning, with breath suppress'd, her waking sigh.—
To the sick sense of returning anguish
Unwatch'd to wake, to thee, poor outcast, must
Alas! most grievous be.—How still—how chill—
This lonely place—I almost fear to wait   35
Thy waking, Mary.—Good Spirits! guard
Thy sleep—'tis long and peaceful.—Restore her,
Gracious Heaven! and as I have gain'd, I hope
With Thy bless'd aid I may amend, her heart!—
Sleep, sleep, poor suff'rer! I will not leave thee.—   40
Darkness envelop'd all—grim mock'ries fill'd
The undistinguished void when the last hour
Broke on the solemn silence, fearfully!
Awaking from a trance of thought I rose.
MARY!—I whispered low—MARY!—no voice   45
Replied—no sigh. I said the fever hath
Lethargic pow'r—poor burning, throbbing brow!—
I bend—my hand extend—and gently touch—
Aghast I stood!—death! death, unfelt before,
Yet instant known, froze my young heart with fear   50
And dread amaze!—How sudden! and, Oh GOD!
How unprepar'd!—Departed! where art thou?—
I clasp'd my hands in agonizing thought.—
Then rush'd the mightiest tide of kindred love!
My soul pursued her guilty sister's flight,   55
I pour'd, in terror wild, the phrensied prayer—
Vain!—I heard th' eternal doom.—Tumultuous

And presumptful thoughts arose, that Vengeance
Was not Justice.—Rebellion, new and strange—
Grief quell'd the tumult and I sunk o'ercome.   60
Oh—I shall never hail the sun, nor more
Shall hail the face of vernal beauty, fair—
Nor smile to see the smile of infant love—
Nor bless my GOD in thankfulness and joy,
But loath the life HE gave!—O desp'rate woe!—   65
Religion—canst thou offer hope to me,
While to eternal misery, condemn'd
Millions of human kind?—go, poor! poor!
Comfort.—O Thou, ALMIGHTY GOD! art THOU
Indeed our FATHER?—are we THY children?—   70
THY crimeless children once—and what is life?—
Frail creatures of a few unhappy years.
Oh, wilt THOU doom to everlasting woe!

    Whence was that calm—and whence the cheering hope—
Whence the still voice which told that punishment   75
Was mercy—Love, infinite and changeless—
In its course, mysterious yet certain,
True to its glorious purpose still to bless,
Having created all, would all restore.

The Spinning-Wheel

Oft has thy simple humming soothed my ear,
Musing on some rude bench where woodbines wove
Around the cottage window—hours so dear,
That more than skillful airs, thy changeless tones I love.
And there I heard a plaintive strain the while—   5
Some ancient ballad's warning history
Of banish'd youth, by cruel stepdame's wile,
Of fairest lady's fall, man's wicked perjury.
I thought, alas! of love and constancy,
While tears and smiles told all my bosom then,   10
O, falsest *****! I gave the smiles to thee—

The tears to damsels wrong'd by wicked men!
For, ah! what maid that heard thy winning tale,
Could dream that e'er such tears, should thy deceit bewail.

Julia

I was the loneliest thing on earth
    When sorrows press'd me sore—
I thought of ev'ry living friend
    But most of her, no more!

I wander'd to that dearest place,   5
    My parent's peaceful dome;
My sister, brother happy seem'd
    As when I left my home.

They bless'd their lost one with a smile,
    I trembled then with fear—   10
Lest my full bosom's rising throb
    Might change it to a tear.

I sought my young companions then
    And all were dear to see;
But mirth danced light in every eye,   15
    My tears would check their glee.

—My spirit sought my JULIA's grave
    I had no earthly spot of rest—
Nor other spot where I might weep,
    And not disturb some happy breast.   20

From Unpublished Manuscripts

The Village Maid

From the ways and wiles of men,—
Stranger;—comest thou to this glen?
The blessings of a quiet heart
With thee go—in peace depart—
Turn not on thy path again;—   5
Her timid greeting, quick & shy,
Embarassed look and changing cheek,
And blushing—shrinking form bespeak
A village maiden—pass her by.—
—Nay; if thou art some gentle youth   10
Of ardent mind—untainted truth,
Thou yet mayest linger nigh:
Unseen pursue that reckless speed
O'er hill and dale away;
Pursue where e'er the [roses] lead   15
And watch where she will stay:
And now she flits from flower to flower
To wreath her garlands gay,—
Are these to deck her faëry bower,
For moonlight [roundelay]?   20
Still on she takes her pathless flight
In eager—aimless—wild delight—
A wood nymph in her glee.—
She stops;—what voice hath reached her ear?
She turns;—nor sight—nor sound is near—   25
Amazed—and yet she hath no fear:—
But thought hath seized the trifler now.
Her fingers press her chastened brow,
And she will seek the thickest shade,
And 'neath the entwining umbrage laid—   30
The Lady of the lonely glade. —

And that hath pass'd—and she hath caught
Some distant vision sadly fraught;
Visions remote, for now her gaze
Is far, and fixed on other days.   35
In that recess so lonely sweet

The stream glides silent at her feet;
And now the musing maid might seem
The naiad of that stealing stream,
For she hath loosened from her brow,   40
As something press'd or pained it now,
The fillets of her hair:
O'er all her form her tresses stray,
That slender form, and round it play
Stirr'd by the [mated] breeze,—   45
Her [rest] is in the upper air
And in the leafy trees:—
From all around a balmy rest
Breathes on the maiden's yielding breast
A gracious power—a weight so sweet—   50
Her bosom sinks,—then swells to meet.—
But dreams have troubled that repose;
Like visitings of parted woes;
Beneath the lid of that closed eye,
Breaks slowly the unheeded tear;   55
Where are those cheeks' young roses fled?
That glowing hand, that even now
Flung its wild [wreaths] on every bough,
That hand, so pale and motionless,
Might freeze the bosom it doth press—   60
What strange untimely grief might be
To blanch such cheek—and chill such glee?

—Unconscious words her lips have spoken;
Strange words of love and fear,—
And lo;—the maiden's trance hath broken   65
And blushes on her cheek appear
And o'er her form have spread;—
She blushes at her extacy,
And, springing from her grassy bed,
She gathers up her long, dark hair,   70
And binds the tresses on her head;
In the clear stream she laves her brow;—
Then pauses, calling to her mien
Those scattered thoughts that gently spread
In pensive smile and quiet care;—   75
But now no village maid is seen,
No [sprightly] faëry of the green,—

Sedate [her] step, her eye serene:—
An [she] who climbs the tall cliff's height
To [view] the closing scene.—   80
Rising from the misty ground,
A [pain] oblivious gathers round,—
A [moment] o'er the maiden's soul—
Nature prevails—and fears confound—
Dubious—darkling—dim—profound:—   85
Her spirit strives—, her piercing eye
Would claim her lost—but native sky,—
And earth is gone,—but heaven is found,
While proud, ineffable desire,
Touches, and raises, and inspires:—   90
Mute—fervid—motionless she stands
With forehead raised and clasped hands.—

—Lost in yon vale her cottage lies;
And now she sees its grey smoke rise:
Above,—beneath,—one look is cast—   95
One lingering look;—and that is pass'd.
Down the dark glen she glides along,
Swift as some timid dove,
Far from its cote that fears some wrong,—
But life is now so fair,   100
The maiden trusteth in her love,
Her love is everywhere.
    —'Too late our Ellen stays to night:—'
But Ellen's step is near;—
For now the even's deepening glooms   105
Half hath hid the social room:
She steals upon the circle dear,
Startles each listening, anxious ear,
And Ellen;—Ellen;—she is here!
They clasp the truant, round and round,   110
And by her own dear hearth so bright
Again the village maid is found.—

Stanzas

Return my Muse! since I am so bereft;
Not in this sad estate do thou forsake:
Return, my Muse, that many a day hath left
My soul to languish, and my heart to ache.

Return my muse—for now the conflict's o'er,   5
For now these sightless eyes have ceased to flow:
Return and solace with thy yet loved lore
The long unbroken night that shrouds me now.

Alas my mornless night! doth not the Sun
Pursue his glorious course along the skies?   10
Alas for me! since I am so undone,
The fair green Earth forlorn and fearful lies.

Forbear my faltering step—my trembling feet,
Since dread and darkness are where e'er I go:
From morn till night, I keep my mournful seat,   15
Leaning, upon my hand, my pensive brow.

What voice is that which calls me, that doth seem
As from some wandering phantom of the night?
Whence is this darkness?—is it but a dream?
Alas, my friends! why are you out of sight?   20

Fain would my friends console me—but alas!
Friends are not now to me what they have been:
Like one cut off, to them I cannot pass,
Nor they to me—a dark gulf lies between.

Not that my heart is yet so cold and sear   25
But I can love, though every joy be fled
But oft, in some kind voice, I seem to hear
A mournful requiem for the living dead.

I am cut off alas—I feel full sore
How drear, how dark, how desolate my doom: 30
I shall behold nor child nor husband more;
But one long, lonely night shall lead me to my tomb

I am cut off—alas how dark and drear
Is all around me—every hope is gone:

The doom that I have dreaded many a year,   35
Is sealed at last—my heart is chilled to stone.

Is there no way? am I cut off from all?
Is there no little spot where I might be?
The poor blind bird still singeth in its thrall
Return my humble muse, return to me.   40

Oh come my humble muse, & take me where
Thou didst beguile me in my childhood's dreams;
Far in my vale, where greenest pastures are,
And lawny glades, and sweetly sheltered streams.

Ah me—my western Vale! for ne'er again   45
Shall my feet wander though thy flowery ways:
But still my muse shall mitigate my pain,
And bring me back to thee, and happier days.

Yes—through thy peaceful haunts again I'll roam,
And linger pensive on thy moonlight hills,   50
And turn again unto my cottage home,
And meet again the smile that through my bosom thrills.

JOHN MITFORD (1782–1831)

For the sailor John Mitford, a series of promising family and professional connections were dissolved variously by his own alcoholism and grandiosity, and by political circumstances beyond his control. His connection to the Mitfords of Mitford Castle, Northumberland, though distant, furnished him with a midshipman's berth in 1795 through the sponsorship of John Free-man-Mitford, Lord Redesdale, and he would later tout his pedigree (not always accurately) in his writings. Having seen action in the battles of Tou-lon, Santa Cruz, and the Nile (1795–8), and despite having deserted in 1800, he was eventually given low-level commands of a revenue cutter and a brig in Italy and the Mediterranean. The patronage of Viscountess Perceval, a rel-ative of Redesdale, proved less fortunate. She retained Mitford in 1811 as a hired pen in defence of the embattled Princess of Wales, but then eventually sued Mitford for perjury, fearing that the writings would be traced to her. The fact that Mitford had been committed to Whitmore House, a lunatic asylum at Hoxton, for some nine months in 1812–13, and had been released at the Viscountess's behest, may have given her a sense of safety in this betrayal; but because Mitford was able to produce correspondence proving the original arrangement, he was acquitted in February 1814.

Following this acquittal he was discharged from the Navy owing to insan-ity and, as John Knox Laughton memorably puts it in the *DNB*, 'took to journalism and strong drink'. For the rest of his life he worked hand-to-mouth, producing three known volumes of poetry and writing for several minor periodicals. Laughton describes Mitford's being sheltered by benevo-lent publishers, and given daily rations of food and gin money in exchange for daily parcels of written work. Such lore attests partly to the addictive, self-sabotaging tendencies in Mitford that may have stemmed from mental illness (he evidently estranged himself from his wife and children, who con-tinued to receive support from Redesdale), but also to a stylistic copiousness that publishers rightly saw as marketable. Mitford himself, sadly, was unable to capitalize on these talents, and after a decade or more of decline, died in St Giles's workhouse on Christmas Eve, 1831.

Mitford's main publications reflect an instinct for literary opportunism. His *Adventures of Johnny Newcome in the Navy* (1818), a socio-political satire in four cantos that he first published under the pseudonym Alfred Burton (but whose second edition appears in his own name), is clearly a crib of an earlier work, *The Military Adventures of Johnny Newcome* (1815), usually attributed to David Roberts. Yet, while retaining the original text's concerns with political jobbery and the bloated bureaucracy of warfare, Mitford overhauls the poetry itself, discarding his predecessor's heroic couplets in favour of a vigorous octosyllabic verse that is at least fleetingly reminiscent of Byron's *Don Juan*. Unfortunately its sprawling, 7,000-line narrative makes *Johnny Newcome in the Navy* poorly suited for excerption here. The same is true of a follow-up poem, *My Cousin in the Army, or, Johnny Newcome on the peace establishment* (1822), which though ascribed on the title page to 'a staff officer', is almost certainly Mitford's. Mitford's most 'reputable' publication, in Laughton's words, is the 1818 collection *Poems of a British Sailor*. Bearing a list of over 500 subscribers, the volume shows Mitford busily interweaving popular-balladic and heroic-elegiac storylines suggested by the Napoleonic Wars. This is not to say that the individual poems are very subtle, though they succeed, for the most part, as a mélange of elegiac, patriotic, and sentimental lyricism in a populist key. Most are suffixed with a dateline that is clearly meant to authenticate their contents, and several include lengthy explanatory footnotes (a technique used extensively in both tales of *Johnny Newcome*). The poems collectively stage several interesting tensions of which Mitford must have been aware: his shifting degrees of identification with 'sea-boys' on one hand and Admiral Horatio Nelson on the other hints at his unusually convoluted experience of class relations, and his poetic interest in bloody land-battles is matched by his first-hand knowledge of disease, loneliness, and penury as the more mundane threats to the 'British sailor'.

FURTHER READING

DNB

John Mitford, *The Important Trial of John Mitford on the prosecution of Viscountess Perceval for perjury* (London: T.A. Phipps, 1814)

John Mitford, *A Peep into W——r Castle, after the lost mutton. A poem.* (London: 1820)

Sketches of Obscure Poets (London: Cochrane and McCrone, 1833), pp. 91–101

John Wade, *British history, chronologically arranged*, 'Annual Obituary, 1831', 3rd Edn. (London: Henry G. Bohn, 1844).

From *Poems of a British Sailor* (1818)

Mary; or The Suicide

Where down the vale blithe Wansbeck pours
    Its slowly winding tranquil stream,
And over Mitford's mouldering towers
    The pale moon darts her glancing beam.

Where trembling aspens lightly wave,   5
    And Alde church rears its spire on high,
Fond memory points to Mary's grave,
    And calls forth many a mournful sigh.

Oh, Mary, thou wast dear to all,
    For wit, for worth, and youthful bloom;   10
Yet, who upheld thy solemn pall?
    What hallow'd strains breath'd o'er thy tomb?

No pious preacher rais'd his hand
    To bless thy much-lov'd form so low;
But impious tongues the memory brand,   15
    Of her who shorten'd life and woe.

Dire was the act—may Heaven forgive—
    'Twas frenzy urg'd thee to the deed;
May he who caus'd the crime long live,
    And misery make his heart-strings bleed.   20

Curs'd be, through life, the miscreant vile
    That peace and virtue could betray;
May mankind on his sufferings smile,
    When dead, Heaven's portals bar his way.

Oh, may the prayer for misery's child   25
    Ascend to Him whose power can save;
And Heaven's dread sentence pass as mild
    As sweeps the night-wind o'er her grave.

Oft shall the minstrel mourn thy doom,
    In pray'r by Wansbeck's murmuring stream,   30
At midnight hour, when o'er thy tomb
    The pale moon darts her glancing beam.

Mitford Hill, September, 1800

The Maniac's Song; or The Coat of Blue

Young stranger! turn, oh, turn to me—
   I love thee for that coat of blue;
Methinks my love again I see,
   My Henry! loyal, brave, and true.

That coat—aye, such my Henry wore—   5
   Didst thou attend him to the grave—
Saw'st thou him fall on Egypt's shore,
   And couldst not thou my Henry save?

What, weeps thou? dry those tears of thine,
   For deeper woes reserve that tear: 10
Wait till the morning's sun doth shine,
   And drop it on my mother's bier.

She died of grief when Henry fell—
   My senses fled beside her grave—
She lov'd my Henry, lov'd him well,   15
   For none ere died more good and brave.

But Henry can return no more!
   Feel, feel, good friend, my burning brain;
'Twill burn till Henry comes on shore,
   Or till, in Heaven, we meet again.   20

'Tis time to pray—the hour wears late—
   This kiss!—a maniac's last adieu!
Say, when thou speaks of Mary's fate,
   She lov'd thee for that coat of blue.

Dalintober, Argyleshire, 1806

Elegiac Stanzas,
To the Memory of
Robert Burns

Why seeks the muse the shelter'd glade,
   Why hangs the poet's lyre unstrung?
The bard of nature low is laid,
   And silent is his tuneful tongue.

No more his 'native wood-notes wild',   5
   Shall sweetly hail the rising day;
Nor more shall Scotia's darling child
   On Ayr's green banks enraptur'd stray.

The rising hill—the lowly dale—
   The hawthorn hedge, or gliding stream,   10
From which he form'd the varied tale—
   No more shall be the poet's theme.

No more upon the mountain's brow,
   While raves the tempest, shall he roam;
And soaring o'er the expanse below,   15
   In thought ascend his Heavenly home,

That heart, which beat with love to all,
   Which own'd a just and righteous GOD,
Now heaves no more at nature's call,
   But silent rests beneath the sod.   20

Remembrance oft shall musing tread
   The turf which hides him from her eyes;
And there, upon his clay-cold bed,
   Shall burst his widow's heart-felt sighs.

The traveler, too, shall thither come   25
   In search of him—for ever fled;
The 'voice of COILA' now is dumb,
   The breast inspir'd amongst the dead.

But as thy soul-lamented bard,
   Immortal lives near GOD on high;   30
So shall thy fame on earth meet just reward—
   Thy matchless works can never die.

Sorrow; to Bertha

Oh, Bertha, look not thus with scorn,
  For I can bear that look no more;
My soul, dejected and forlorn,
  For ever will this change deplore.

Relax that frown—unbend that brow,   5
  Thou canst not joy to give me pain,
And ill forget each broken vow,
  And never dream of love again.

Nor will I think how dear we lov'd,
  When o'er the heath-clad hills we stray'd   10
Down Mecklinn stream delighted rov'd,
  To rest beneath the jessmine's shade.

Where I have watch'd thy sun-bright eyes,
  With melting softness on me turn—
The mantling cheeks—the half-check'd sighs,   15
  And life streams in the lips that burn.

'Twas then thy panting bosom fair
  I kiss'd with more than mortal pleasure,
And saw, through locks of flowing hair,
  Rise blushing from the lips warm pressure.   20

The looks demure, and downcast eye,
  Can I forget these scenes? ah, never;
But Bertha's chang'd, those visions die,
  And love and joy are fled for ever.

Death of the Sailor-Boy

Swift flew the scud along the wave,
  Repeated thunders roll'd on high;
All hands on deck the storm to brave,
  At midnight was the boatswain's cry:

Aloft sprung every soul apace, 5
   But one bereft of human joy,
Within a hammock's narrow space,
   Lay stretch'd this hapless sailor-boy.

Once, when the boatswain's pipe would hail,
   The first he was of all the crew 10
On deck to run, to trim the sail,
   To steer, to reef, to furl, or clew;—
Now fell disease had seiz'd his form,
   Which nature cast in happiest mold:
The bell struck midnight through the storm— 15
   His last—his funeral dirge it toll'd.

Oh, GOD, he pray'd,—oh, SAVIOUR, dear!
   Before my spirit seeks the skies,
Is there no friend, or messmate near,
   To close in death my weary eyes. 20
All hands on high! loud blows the wind!
   And loud surrounding billows roar!
He rais'd his head,—he bow'd,—resign'd,
   And backward sunk to rise no more!

The morning sun in splendour rose, 25
   The gale was hush'd, and still'd the wave;
The sea-boy found his last repose,
   In ocean's deep and boundless grave.
But HE who guards the humblest head—
   HE who can save, or can destroy, 30
Caught the pure spirit as it fled,
   And rais'd to Heaven the sailor-boy.

On board the Zealous, on the coast of Egypt,
near Alexandria, October 4th, 1798

The Island Fiend

To Elba's green island a demon has flown,
   The horror and scourge of mankind;

As hard as the iron, and cold as the stone,
Which in Elba's dark manes and her quarries are known,
   Is his heart to all evil inclin'd.   5

The agent of mischief to torture the world
   His brows with a diadem bound;
But the genius of virtue her standard unfurl'd,
And his sons thronging round, from his pinnacle hurl'd,
   And struck the foul fiend to the ground.   10

Condemn'd in this island, imprison'd to sigh,
   His passion for mischief prevails:
When the wind whistles loud, and the wave rises high,
His lists to the sound of the mariner's cry,
   And smiles at the storm-shatter'd sails.   15

Though the race of mankind are no longer his prey,
   Still cruelty pleasures supply:
The generous dog must the tyrant obey,
He plucks from the dove her soft plumage away,
   And, DOMITIAN like, tortures the fly.   20

But he suffers at intervals horror and fright;
   For the demon must tremble and fear,
When the shadows of PICHEGRU, PALM, D'ENGHEIN, WRIGHT,
Appear in the darkness and stillness of night—
   Then his eye sheds the cowardly tear.   25

Hope, the wretch's last friend, from his bosom has fled,
   And despair dark encircles him round;
Wherever he lies, or wherever he treads,
Plants noxious to life rear their venomous heads,
   And venomous reptiles are found.   30

Here, unpitied, unwept, till the final decree,
   Let the blood-sated demon remain;
In vain from himself still attempting to flee;
That he tastes not of death let his punishment be,
   And his conscience his torturing pain.   35

Donald and Mary,
A Tale of the Isle

On Arran's cliffs the wild waves roar,
    And winter's howling tempests fly;
Dark clouds on Goat-fells' summit lou'r,
    Clos'd is day's weary languid eye.

All free from care lay lock'd in rest,   5
    And night reign'd empress of the vale,
When MARY rose with woe opprest,
    Unbarr'd the door, and brav'd the gale.

Where rocks o'erhang the western flood,
    And mock the boiling surge below,   10
High on their summit MARY stood,
    And thus the widow's sorrows flow:–

LAMENT

O'er the white-bosom'd ocean I cast mine eyes sadly,
    When nightly I wend to this summit to mourn:
How great once my transports, my heart beat how gladly,   15
    When from Erin's green isle I saw DONALD return.

Though small was his bark, yet, alas! 'twas our all,
    And though trifling its cargo, 'twas riches to me;
Of my child's hungry cries it soon silenc'd the call,
    And brought DONALD with happiness safe o'er the sea.   20

Ten guineas he'd got, hardly earn'd from the world,
    These he barter'd for goods upon Erin's green isle.
That done, his low sail he with rapture unfurl'd,
    And in fancy beheld of his MARY the smile.

The hills of dear Arran his eyes now are greeting,   25
    Before me he soon hopes to spread his small store;
Ah! DONALD, the visions of fancy are fleeting,
    Thy wife and thy babe thou didst never see more.

Like an eagle, that darts on the dove as his prey,
    A tender appear'd, and made DONALD the prize;   30
To the dark-bosom'd hulk they have borne him away,
    Where they teaz'd him to anguish, and scoff'd at his sighs.

His poor humble bark was both plunder'd and wreck'd;
   He pleaded his wife, and they laugh'd at the name:
His pride rose in silence, his feelings he check'd,   35
   For oppression is dead to love, pity, and shame.

White and few were the locks on the temples of age,
   And furrow'd the cheeks where tears flow'd for a child;
Accurst be his name in true honour's bright page,
   Who look'd down on a father and scornfully smil'd.   40

'Twas the parent of DONALD, whose prayers were in vain,
   A short, a last look was denied of his son,
He was spurn'd from the ship where a monster held reign,
   And Despair clos'd the work which Oppression begun.

In silence he came:—yes, his lips clos'd for ever,   45
   My child round his knees a fond father desired;
The tears of the aged said, 'never, ah! never—
   Thy father's a slave'—he look'd up, and expir'd.

To the climes of fell India my DONALD was hurried,
   Where pestilence kills both the coward and brave,   50
Beyond the Atlantic my DONALD is buried,
   Where the tears of a wife cannot water his grave.

Oh, Ruthless Destroyer of all my heart cherished,
   The curse of the widow and orphan be thine;
May lasting remorse in thy bosom be nourish'd,   55
   And thy sufferings, if possible, greater than mine!

Rich wast thou, a tyrant, abusive of power,
   But the great and all-powerful looks down on thee now,
His mercy will fly thee at life's latest hour,
   And horrent despair settle dark on thy brow.   60

   On Arran's cliffs the wild waves roar,
      And winter-howling tempests fly;
   No MARY treads the sounding shore,
      With tearful, supplicating, eye.

   All free from care are lock'd in rest,   65
      And night reigns empress of the vale;
   The cold earth hides the poor distrest—
      O'er MARY's bosom sweeps the gale.

On Arran's cliffs, whilst waves beat high,
Or wild heath on her mountains bloom, 70
For her the tear shall gem each eye,
Who sank in misery's deepest gloom.

The wand'ring bard thy tomb shall view,
All lonely near the western wave,
And strike his harp, to feeling true, 75
In sadness o'er thy humble grave.

Written at Belfast, in Ireland, on board the Wickham cutter, in 1807

War Song

Rouse, sons of BRITANNIA! and fly to your arms,
'Tis Napoleon threatens your coast,
On your shores he already has spread war's alarms,
And the conquest of England's his boast.

United and free, in defence of your laws, 5
To the standard of victory spring;
Raise high the right hand in a truly great cause,
For your country, religion, and king.

French gold and French freedom we equally hate,
Gold plunder'd from nations once brave; 10
Let prostrate Helvetia arise and relate,
What freedom the conqueror gave.

In chains the fond father a captive is borne,
Conscription the son tears away,
His lost wife and daughters abandon'd, forlorn, 15
To the vilest of mortals a prey.

Stand off, horrid fiend! 'tis a mother that pleads
For a daughter! and she is undone;
Then raise thy curst dagger, add death to thy deeds,
For that crime only death can atone. 20

She falls! from her breast streams the last blood of life,
    And she smiles on the opening grave;
Hark! a husband expires in defence of his wife—
    I have heard the last groans of the brave.

The murderer of Jaffa looks sternly around,   25
    On the car of destruction he springs;
Blood-dy'd are his garments, and hark to that sound!
    Breathing vengeance to Freedom and Kings.

To bravery death, and meek virtue despair,
    He deals 'mid the battle's loud roar;   30
And the banners of Anarchy, rais'd in the air,
    Are the signal that Freedom's no more.

And is happy BRITANNIA reserved for this end,
    The fairest isle under the sky?
No! we swear our lov'd country to keep and defend,   35
    Or entomb'd in its ruins to lie.

Hand to hand, foot to foot, on our sea-beaten shore,
    To receive our proud foe will we stand;
Surrounding blue waves shall be purpled with gore,
    Ere his feet shall pollute our dear land.   40

Then rouse, Sons of Freedom, defending just laws,
    To the standard of Victory spring,
Raise high the right hand in a truly great cause,
    For your Country, Religion, and King.

Dublin Castle

The Glories of Britannia; or The Records of Fame

The war dream of sorrow, of anguish, and sighing
    Is fled, and bright peace now illumines the ball,
The watch-word no longer is conquering or dying,
    But, live and be free, is the theme 'one and all!'

To bless thee, BRITANNIA, all nature combining,   5
   Sends Truth thy great deeds to the world to proclaim;
Ever green be the laurels thy temples entwining,
   Immortal thy works in the Records of Fame.

Silver Isle of the Ocean! with mild lustre shining,
   Rock of Freedom! unshaken, and never to fall!   10
To thy prince, Father NEPTUNE, his trident resigning,
   Exalts thee a bulwark and safeguard to all.
Where man sunk debas'd with vile tyrants around him,
   Thy WELLINGTON flew and releas'd him from shame:
Sublime be the glories his actions surrounding,   15
   And first be their place in the Records of Fame.

He who grasp'd in his fancy the thunder of Heaven,
   By whose caprice expir'd both the virtuous and brave,
To disgrace, by thy NELSONS and WELLINGTONS driven
   Exists, by permission, a fugitive slave.   20
Ah, NELSON! the hero who liv'd in commotion,
   That peace which thou died for our cannons proclaim;
Exalted on high is the Hero of Ocean,
   And deathless his acts in the Records of Fame.

Oh, blest be the heroes who Glory's bed died on,   25
   And soft be their slumber in Honour's proud grave,
Due praise and reward to the living we pride in,
   Who fought the good fight, and who conquer'd to save.
Ah, happy BRITANNIA! where beauty residing,
   Smooths joyous love's pillow, each warrior's claim,   30
Ever green be the laurels thy daughters confide in,
   Ever first stand thy sons on the Records of Fame.

JAMES CHAMBERS (1740–182?)

Even within a verse tradition that often views art as a last hedge against privation, the autobiographical narratives of the 'Itinerant Poet' James Chambers are remarkable for their emphasis on the sustaining power of poetry. This emphasis is all the more notable for its iconoclastic strain, as the often-destitute Chambers seems to scorn others who, like the workhouse residents he describes as 'Belial's sons of contention and strife' ('The Poor Poetaster', l. 160), share his poverty but not his tenacious belief in God's abiding power. A vagrant, peddler, and herbalist who for some years supported himself mainly by selling handmade nets, Chambers began to market his verses to local gentry sometime in the late eighteenth century. It is not clear whether these early productions were printed or merely recited, for the few contemporary accounts of his activities suggest that he had a limited ability to write and at least sometimes employed an amanuensis. The need to commit his verses to memory may well have contributed to his interest in verse acrostics, in which the initial (and sometimes subsequent) letters of each line spelt a name or phrase. Three of these acrostics, including the one that was evidently Chambers's first poem, are included here, and though we may consider the form as little more than doggerel, Chambers seemed to understand it as allowing for the encapsulation and preservation of individual identity, as in the poem entitled, 'James Chambers, Itinerent [sic] Poet, despised by Man'.

The first contemporary references to Chambers date from a decade before the 1820 publication of his sole volume, *The Poetical Works of James Chambers*, and suggest that he was a familiar figure in and around Suffolk. He was first referenced in the loco-descriptive poem 'Haverhill' (1810), by the weaver poet John Webb, who described him as:

> A lonely wand'rer he, whose squalid form
> Bore the rude peltings of the wintry storm:
> An hapless outcast, on whose natal day
> No star propitious beam'd a kindly ray (ll. 159–62)

Subsequent mentions of Chambers appeared in the *Ipswich Journal* of 1810 and the *Suffolk Garland*, both of which are included in what still stands as our best account of his life, C. Ragan's preface to the 1820 volume. There Ragan presents what may well be the single most dismal picture of any poet from the labouring-class tradition: 'a more wretched appearance and combination of rags and filth, words are not capable of describing—his visage nearly excluded from the public eye, by the uncouth manner of wearing a tattered hat, his feet exposed to the rough greetings of stones, gravel, and wet' (p. viii); Chambers is said to sleep 'on a couch of dried herbs' in a rude hut, 'surrounded by the impure stench of the interior, and a mass of filth which forms a mound at the door' (p. xi). Yet, says Ragan, Chambers transcends this physical wretchedness through his honesty, kindness, and moral rectitude: 'Cruelty (a stain upon rationality) he holds in detestation, and was never known to commit any action that could be justly challenged as such' (p. ix).

For all the desperation of his situation, Chambers was a highly pragmatic author. He understood poetry as a commodity that could be bartered (as in 'The Author's Second Day at Helmingham') and ruefully acknowledged in the autobiographical 'Poor Poetaster' that personal disaster was helpful for poetic invention. Yet even as he learned the strange utility of his suffering, the poems themselves strive to convey delicacy and personal dignity. Stylistically this translates to a sometimes overwrought neo-classicism ('Fulgent luster Sol displaying, / Brighten'd all the azure sky', 'Morning Winter Piece', ll. 73–4), but the artifice of his diction does not efface the genuine narrative interest of the poems, which emerge from often traumatic experience. Similarly, though the poems frequently return to the conventional themes of providential design and goodness, Chambers's religious beliefs are clearly hard-won. For the author who wakes up covered in snow, or is repeatedly beaten and robbed, or has his only scrap of meat stolen by a dog, life's material difficulties represent a daily challenge to religious faith, and the poems often trace such sudden shifts of fortune. These shifts are also played out on the larger stage of divine creation, and Chambers frequently depicts the changing seasons as evidence of spiritual presence—with the summer bounty made to represent God's eternal goodness, and the dire wintertime an impressive warning as to the despair and misery that await the unrepentant sinner.

FURTHER READING

J.R. de J. Jackson, *Annals of English Verse 1770–1835. A preliminary survey of the volumes published* (New York & London: Garland Publishing, 1985), p. 461

C. R. Johnson, *Provincial Poetry 1789–1839: British Verse Printed in the Provinces: The Romantic Background* (London: Jed Press, 1992)

John Webb, *Haverhill, A Descriptive Poem, and Other Poems* (London: J. Nunn, 1810).

From *The Poetical Works of James Chambers* (1820)

Acrostic on the Author's Name
The First He Ever Composed

James Chambers is my name,
And I am scorn'd by rich and poor,
Many a weary step I came,
Enduring hardships very sore;
So I design to take a wife,   5
Can I but have one to my mind,
Henceforth to live a better life,
And then we may true solace find;
May I but have the lass I love,
Both to each other constant prove,   10
Endeavour thus to live in peace,
Renewing love in every case,
So to remain till life does cease.

Morning Winter Piece
Written one Morning in a Cart-shed, on the Author finding
his Limbs covered with Snow, blown through the Crevices

What a striking scene's displayed,
    Winter with his freezing train,
Verd'rous fields in white arrayed,
    Snow-drop whiteness decks the plain.

See the wond'rous pow'r of heav'n,   5
    Operating here below,
While, by boist'rous winds are driv'n,
    Tow'ring piles of glist'ning snow.

Peasants by the rich employed,
    Cut out paths for public good,   10

Lest man's precious life's destroyed,
    Lost 'midst snow or spreading flood.

Poor men view rich friends suspicious
    Who, their drooping hearts to cheer,
Spread the board with food delicious,   15
    And with choice domestic beer.

May kind gentry, bliss enjoying,
    Blest with virtues dwell secure,
Free from direful foes annoying,
    Free from hardships I endure.   20

Sure thought I, when wak'd this morning,
    I'm with trials quite replete,
Ere Aurora's light is dawning,
    Snow-hills rising chill my feet.

Snow-flakes round my eyes are flying,   25
    Sprinkling o'er my rural bed;
Soon I'll rise—'tis dang'rous lying—
    No close curtains screen my head.

Straw's my couch, no sheets nor bedding,
    Pond'rous snow dissolving lies,   30
When I wake no carpet treading,
    Fleecy snow its place supplies.

No grand tap'stry decorating
    These drear walls now moist with snow,
Nought my spirits exhilarating,   35
    Doom'd alas to pungent woe.

In aerial regions hovering,
    Keenly chill'd in exigence,
Plumed tribes retire for cov'ring,
    No shrill matins here commence.   40

I forsake my snow-deck'd pillow,
    Traverse snow-enamel'd vales,
Zephyrs whisp'ring o'er the willows,
    Soon advance to flatuous gales.

Limpid dews, with gelid feature,   45
    Silver o'er the glist'ning scene,

'Tis not tinsell'd art,—but nature
    Speaks heaven's power in climes terrene.

Pierc'd by hunger's dart I wander,
    Trackless knee-deep snow pervade,   50
Cheer'd not by the rill's meander,
    View no florid sylvan shade.

Snow which Boreal blasts are whirling
    Rapid through the ambient air,
'Gainst my sordid vestment hurling,   55
    Dim my eyes and chill my hair.

This vile raiment hangs in tatters—
    No warm garment to defend,
O'er my flesh the chill snow scatters—
    No snug hut, nor social friend.   60

Though by cold severe I perish,
    No warm viands friends impart,
No rich cordial wine to cherish,
    Or revive my languid heart.

Here in vernal hours I strayed,   65
    Fields and limpid torrents view'd,
Splendid prospects here surveyed,
    Cheering solace then insue'd.

Plumed choirs were sweetly singing
    Anthems of celestial praise,   70
Soaring larks their flight were winging,
    Pleas'd melodious notes to raise.

Fulgent luster Sol displaying,
    Brighten'd all the azure sky,
With his glorious light conveying   75
    Glowing lustre from on high.

Cheering all this gay creation,
    Fields and fertile vales below,
Fertilizing vegetation,
    Which does pleasing presence show.   80

Fain I'd gain a situation
    Quite retire, near rural shades,

There imbibe, for recreation,
    Vernal air, 'mid op'ning glades,

Florets pluck, or crop rich foliage,   85
    Some for drink and some to smoke,
There, when tir'd by arduous toilage,
    I'd the sylvan muse invoke.

There, assisted by Urania,
    Friends t' oblige, I'd verse compose,   90
Verse that might be priz'd by many
    Who adopt the theme I chose.

Heaven's rich bounty celebrating,
    I'd extol our Highest Friend,
Lenient cordials animating,   95
    Who t' impart does condescend.

Power supreme was erst exerted,
    Flaming bolts in Ether roll'd,
Minds terrene with fear then started—
    Now recoil at winter's cold.   100

Bursts terrific, vivid flashes,
    At heaven's fiat sound or shine,
Ice-like morsels, rime like ashes,
    Scatter'd forth by power divine.

Flakes of snow like wool descending   105
    From dense clouds yon lawn o'erspread,
With nocturnal hoar-frost blending,
    Grain's preserv'd, well covered.

Friends who wish in peaceful station
    Herbs t' amass, much good to do,   110
Patient wait for vegetation,
    While conceal'd beneath the snow.

Soon yon luminary shining
    Snow will melt on orient hills,
To its radiant warmth resigning,   115
    Praise resounds from tuneful rills.

Soon yon landscapes, groves, and bowers,
    Will a brighter verdure wear,

Rich parterres, expanding flowers,
   All in lovely hue appear.   120

Drinks salubrious then preparing,
   Seek a neighbour's joy and health,
Kind supernal favors sharing,
   Far transcending India's wealth.

Let's attend to truth and reason,   125
   While we snow-form'd mounds pervade,
Our Great Donor, in their season,
   All things beautiful has made.

Winter, Summer, still returning,
   Order'd are by sov'reign power,   130
Grief's sad sighs, and tears of mourning,
   Cease, and bring the joyful hour.

There serenely acquiescing,
   On rich Providence depend,
May our hearts, true grace possessing,   135
   With most grateful praise ascend.

Rest in solid peace and pleasure,
   Aided by celestial love,
Still aspire when brighter treasure
   Shines in blissful courts above.   140

There no gelid thrillings enter,
   There's a rich exhaustless store,
There, aspiring to their centre,
   Saints the great Supreme adore.

Light supernal all pervading,   145
   They to bright perfection come,
Vital coronets unfading,
   Flourish in eternal bloom.

Lines on a Little Black Dog
Stealing the Author's Meat

In the spring of the year eighteen hundred and one,
These thoughts struck my mind while musing alone,
How bright and serene is the sunshiny day,
The birds sweetly whistle, the lambs sport and play,
The nightingale's accents resound through the grove,   5
All seem to aspire to bright regions above,
The whole gay creation most beauteous appears,
And each vernal scene a bright aspect wears,
All nature declares the Creator is good,
Yet I pine with distress, and languish for food;   10
My thoughts could I muster, and form them in rhymes,
Of half my sharp sufferings in these trying times,
The rich who regale in their luxury and pride,
Would exert ev'ry nerve that my wants might subside,
Yet if no sympathetic compassion they shew,   15
I have still some kind friends that will pity my woe,
I'll to Providence trust, though I've nothing to eat,
Then a kind lady gave me a piece of good meat,
And seeing me languid, my spirits to cheer,
She drew me a mug of her good home-brew'd beer;   20
Being bravely refresh'd, and 'twas late in the day,
I put up my meat, and I hasten'd away;
How bright was the prospect, the trees in full bloom,
The cowslips and violets sent forth their perfume,
I gather'd them into my bag so complete,   25
Thought I, now I'm furnish'd with med'cine and meat,
I'll purchase three pennyworth of 'tatoes tonight,
To eat with my meat, it will give me delight.
How vain are our sanguinest projects below,
What losses await us, no mortal does know;   30
A tradesman I met coming out of an Inn,
A short friendly intercourse soon did begin,
In this social converse I told him some rhymes,
He said he'd some hopes we should have better times;
Says he you must suffer, provision's so dear,   35
Will you stop and take share of a mug of good beer?
I set myself down on the stepping-block stairs,

Of the robber's approach I'd no foreboding fears,
With a morsel of bread and a draught of fine ale
Before my fresh journey myself to regale;   40
I took from my bag an ancient good book,
And shew'd to the tradesman, he in it did look,
The book was concerning the door of salvation,
Unlock'd by the key of regeneration;
While we with attention fresh objects pursue,   45
A little black dog just appeared in view,
Snatch'd the pork from my bag and soon slipt away,
Crept in a sly corner to feast on its prey;
The dog being hungry, in that starving time
To search for another piece thought it no crime,   50
But quickly return'd, and carried away
Four ounces of suet I bought yesterday:
The maid cried out, Jimmy, you'll have nothing to eat,
A little black dog has run away with your meat;
Said I, the dire cur seeing me off my guard,   55
My pork has devour'd, and stole my hog's lard;
The dog when pursu'd did the suet resign,
And now for the future it is my design
To be more circumspect wherever I go,
Or my friends will compare me to poor patient Joe;   60
'Tis a similar case, and we sure must grow thinner,
I'm depriv'd of my supper, and he of his dinner;
My pig's suet is safe, yet one loss I've sustain'd,
My pork is quite lost, and can ne'er be regain'd,
Yet no more I'll repine, or grieve at my cross,   65
Some kind recent friend will compensate my loss.

On a Brindled Greyhound
Carrying a Piece of Meat to the Author

In the Summer one thousand eight hundred and eight,
I travers'd gay fields, but had no food to eat,
And having no cash, no provision could buy,

Sure ne'er was poor bard so distressed as I;
Once near the Buck's Horns I was robb'd of meat,   5
Depriv'd of my supper, severe was my fate,
'Twas in the Spring time, eighteen hundred and one,
Seven years are expir'd, yet I eat bread alone,
On hard mouldy crusts and cold water live,
Yet hope I these mercies shall grateful receive;   10
An excellent Prophet had nothing to eat,
'Till ravens supplied him with bread and with meat,
I've heard of a good man, 'twas poor master Dodd,
Had nothing for dinner, but trusted in God!
Rich gentry choice viands prepar'd for grand guest,   15
A nice joint of mutton for dinner was drest,
A vigilant dog with rapidity enter'd,
To steal the choice meat he most daringly ventur'd,
He quickly convey'd it to poor master Dodd,
Domestics all feasted, and blessed their God!   20
Kind mercy supernal my wants will supply,
Inspire me with gratitude, solace, and joy,
I'll suffer with patience, and cease to complain,
In exigence I but short time may remain,
Rising sighs I'll suppress, and bid fears subside,   25
Sustain'd by this motto, 'kind heaven will provide':
I enter'd a farm-house, told gentry some rhymes,
They sympathetiz'd with me in these trying times,
With good bread and meat I my vitals did cheer,
Refresh'd languid spirits with good home-brew'd beer;   30
But though for the present well sated with meat,
That I the next evening might have more to eat,
Kind Providence order'd a brindled greyhound
To filch me a piece, then recline on the ground,
The young cur most tacit resign'd it to me;   35
Soon ev'ry domestic did kindly agree
That I should reserve it to eat the next day,
Thus Providence surely will fodder our way;
We should not trust in man, but in aid most divine
'Tis best in all seasons our wills to resign,   40
For though by one dog I sustained a cross,
Another relieves and compenses my loss:
If ever poor Fly should be drove to distress,
If 'tis in my power, his wants I'll redress,

If he should be hungry and have nothing to eat,   45
I'll give him a bone when I've stript off the meat.

The Author's Second Day at Helmingham

On Tuesday morn, I rise and dress,
    My mind seems more at ease,
Think I, as I'd success last night,
    I still will strive to please.

Among the booths no more I'll rove,   5
    But study near the Hall,
Whose inmates are replete with love,
    And I'll oblige them all.

The does are sporting full of glee,
    While bright the Sun does shine;   10
I write beneath the spreading tree,
    Where servants milk their kine.

And whilst I write my friends to please
    I view the lovely fair
Walk out with elegance and ease,   15
    To taste the vernal air.

As through the spacious park they walk,
    Or o'er the meadows rove,
Of nature's works they seem to talk,
    Or muse on virtuous love.   20

Some ladies fair and gentlemen
    Enter the gliding boat,
To move for pleasure all begin
    Round the capacious moat.

The gentlemen the ladies row,   25
    The spacious Hall around,
While limpid streamlets gently flow,
    And bells harmonious sound.

They cry'd 'you view each lovely scene,
    On this you'll rhyme a verse',   30
'I'll them' said I, 'howe'er so mean,
    The pleasing tale rehearse'.

Beneath the spreading shady tree
    For study I recline,
View bucks and does in sportive glee,   35
    While solar rays do shine.

If gentry most benign permit,
    I'll hail reviving Spring,
Beneath these leafy branches sit,
    And hear the long peal ring.   40

The cheerful ringers still obey
    The Noble Donor's will;
In ringing changes every day,
    They shew their strength and skill.

But now comes on the close of day,   45
    Bells cease awhile to ring,
In lovely strains the music play,
    Some chaunt 'God save the King'.

Two special ringers I espy'd,
    A farmer and his son,   50
Who kindly me with cash supply'd,
    The junior thus began:—

'My Sister dear, who erst was kind,
    While verses you compos'd,
Lately her vital breath resign'd—   55
    And death her eyelids clos'd.

I wish you, in these vernal days,
    An Elegy to write';
'I'll strive, kind Sir, your mind to please,
    And wish you both good night'.   60

Now courteous friends, I've told the tale,
    Of walking in the Spring,
To hear the cheering tuneful peal
    Of bells melodious ring.

Verses on Grundisburgh Fair

On Whitsun-Monday was a Fair,
Gay Ladies bright assembled there,
'Twas on a pleasant rural green,
Where gentlemen to walk were seen,
While nature bloom'd in gaudy pride,   5
To deck the scene at Whitsuntide.

Bright Sol emits a lucid ray,
'Tis a serene and pleasant day;
Some did the verdant meads pervade,
And to their friends a visit paid,   10
Young females walk for vernal air,
Their sweethearts meet at Whitsun Fair.

Most courteous they young ladies treat,
And buy them luscious fruit to eat,
Then at the Dog, or Half Moon drink,   15
The reck'ning pay in ready chink;
The Yeoman, with his much-lov'd bride,
Walks to the Fair at Whitsuntide.

The peasant's wife her cottage leaves,
A penny for her offspring saves,   20
Does for each child a fairling buy,
With nuts and cakes does them supply,
While beaux for rural sports provide,
The Fair to adorn at Whitsuntide.

Rude boys, whose hands were fast'ned tight,   25
Strove hard some treacled rolls to bite;
A Jingling Match did then begin,
That one a genteel Hat might win,
Several to catch the Jingler try'd,
But one prevail'd at Whitsuntide.   30

A Donkey-race too there was seen,
Two asses run on yonder green,
Rustics then for sweet lumps did run,
While gazing lowns laugh'd at the fun,
The winners thus were well supply'd,   35
With dulcet cates at Whitsuntide.

The lads who lucky were to win,
Might social meet at yonder Inn,
There, as the beverage was sweet,
With porter, wine, or good old beer,   40
At Whitsuntide, their hearts to cheer.

Methinks I hear these words resound
From pious Christians dwelling round,
I vain amusement do not love,
Of sacred writings I approve,   45
With choice provisions I'm supplied,
I'll feast at home at Whitsuntide.

To visit Fairs I'm not inclin'd,
The noise and bustle hurt my mind,
There fleering lowns, who without cause,   50
Will break the peace and wholesome laws,
While worthies grand in chariots ride,
And peace enjoy at Whitsuntide.

I feel no real pure delight,
To riot in excess all night,   55
It me enerves, it gives me cold,
'Tis neither good for young or old;
Should heaven a peaceful home provide,
I'd there repose at Whitsuntide.

Not long I'd tarry at a Fair,   60
Unless I'd special business there,
Or with a friend to stop and dine,
And cheer my languid heart with wine,
At home then supper to provide,
I'd leave gay scenes at Whitsuntide.   65

Some Christians shun a nightly Fair,
And say there works of darkness are,
Ebriety and fornication
Abound in this our Christian nation,
Blasphemy, luxury, and pride,   70
Disgrace the Fairs at Whitsuntide.

I hope, my friends each vice will cease,
And Fairs and Markets not disgrace,
That virtues in their stead may reign,
And discord ne'er our bosoms pain,   75

With plenty may we be supplied,
And peace enjoy at Whitsuntide.

The Poor Poetaster

I, the poor Poetaster, bewail my hard fate,
Sad losses and cares have depress'd me of late,
My cash is dispers'd, friends seem to turn foes,
I've walk'd till I'm weary, and worn out my clothes.
My stockings are torn as I walk in the dirt, 5
And some months I've existed without any shirt
My feet they go wet, and my neck takes much cold,
And rustics despise me because mean and old;
As to pay for a bed I've of late not been able,
By permission I've slept on some straw in a stable; 10
Friends lent me a cloth to preserve me from harm,
In sharp freezing weather I sometimes lie warm;
I lodg'd in a calf's-crib by leave of a friend,
Gelid snow and short straw did promiscuously blend;
The boys did insult me, they filched my store, 15
They my property spoil—'tis my fate to be poor:
From place then to place I was harass'd about,
Ston'd, robb'd, and insulted by every base lout;
While I was at Church they play'd a sad joke,
They stole all my nets, and my pitcher they broke; 20
I mov'd to a whin-shed, 'twas worse still indeed,
They filch'd my good books, now I've not one to read;
Into a cold pig-stye I sometimes did creep,
Undress'd me, and there on the damp floor did sleep,
Stones came in the day, and snow in the night, 25
Which hurt me and chill'd me, forbidding delight,
Dire foes to insult me exerted their spite;
When under a corn-hole I often reclin'd,
There with a low ceiling was nightly confin'd,
A bed in the straw-stack I make down below, 30
The rain pour'd upon me—I'm sprinkled with snow:

Ye gentry, who on a soft down bed repose,
Consider poor bards who in gelid air does;
On Sunday when I to sacred courts went,
Louts and morts, to filch from me, the precious hours spent;   35
Again in the hog's cote I slept among strife,
Was mobb'd out of town, and escap'd for my life;
In barns I'm surrounded too oft by the mob,
And slyly they enter, they spoil and they rob.
A farmer of late was to me very kind,   40
For in his new building by leave I reclin'd;
I, by a dire scold, was chas'd out with all speed,
As they wanted the place the turkies to feed;
By hurry and bustle my money I lost,
I'm cashless and starving—how poor bards are cross'd;   45
My writings I lately had dropp'd near the yard,
Of them I've not heard—sure my fate it is hard;
In a large open shed I reclin'd day and night,
The muse to invoke, to rhyme verses, and write;
In a waggon I take my nocturnal repose,   50
No covering alas! but my old tatter'd clothes,
No blanket nor rug, me to screen from the storm,
Keen pinching air breathes—how can one lay warm;
My sufferings are grievous in these trying times,
Though noted for making and speaking of rhymes,   55
And tho' some friends in Suffolk still kindly behave,
Yet I'm so reduced, I this country must leave,
Yet favours I'd prize, and most grateful would be
To gentry benign, who shew kindness to me;
If life should permit, soon to Ipswich I'll go,   60
In search of new friends, and to Colchester too:
Good Christians, no doubt, of compassionate heart,
Will sympathize with me—choice favours impart;
Should schemes prove abortive, to Cambridge I'll go,
Relate my sad tale of ineffable woe,   65
Perhaps I a weekly collection may find,
My frame to sustain, and to sooth my sad mind:
If Providence kind, recent friends does not raise,
I in a dread workhouse must finish my days,
Must cease turning verses, and noding choice twine,   70
While some fellow-mortals in these branches shine.
'Tis true workhouse rulers plain viands prepare,

And paupers industrious in wholesome food share,
A hot dinner three times a week they provide,
Good pudding and meat, and some butter beside,   75
Each one that's mature has a pint of small beer,
Of ale each a pint, three or four times a year;
Half a bed on a garret, with covering warm,
Would there be my lot, to defend me from harm,
By day I must dwell where there's many a wheel,   80
And a female's employ'd to sit down and reel,
A post with two ringles is fix'd in the wall,
Where orphans when lash'd, loud for mercy do call;
Depriv'd of fresh air, I must there commence spinner,
If I fail of my task, I lose a hot dinner;   85
Perhaps at the whipping-post then shall be flogg'd,
And least I escape my leg must be clogg'd,
While tyrants oppress I must still be their slave,
And cruelly used, though well I behave:
'Midst swearing and brawling my days I must spend,   90
In sorrow and anguish my life I must end:
Of this cruelty I've had experience before,
And wish, their keen lash to come under no more;
The young, they encouraged the old to abuse,
They both youth and age do inhumanely use,   95
Friendless orphans they beat, while for mercy they cry'd,
The blood it gush'd forth—they in agony dy'd,
Dropp'd down on the floor, no more did they rise,
Which struck timid minds with a sudden surprise;
I too was abus'd, 'twill again be the case,   100
If a great happy change has not taken place:
For numbers of years I have verses compos'd,
In hopes to find solace, ere life shall be clos'd,
A baleful requital for all labours past
'Twill be, if in prison I breathe out my last;   105
If I must submit, then farewell blooming trees,
Farewell gliding streamlets, and zephyr's soft breeze,
I now bid adieu to the cool sylvan shades,
Adieu! tuneful muses, and fine florid glades,
Farewell all connections in country and town!   110
Farewell worthy gentry, of fame and renown!
Kind neighbors farewell! you no more will me see,
If those direful mansions reserv'd are for me;
But sure wealthy friends, when they see I look old,

And view my bare limbs thus expos'd to the cold,   115
Replete with philanthropy soon will be kind,
Impart some relief to compose my sad mind,
Procure me a dwelling-place and a good fire,
With all needful blessings, this life can desire,
I then would not envy the rich nor the great,   120
But strive to prepare for a more blissful state.
I wish for a garden, fruit trees, and a vine,
And though on coarse viands and herbage I dine,
Secure in my dwelling none dare me molest,
A hymn I'd compose, in tranquillity rest;   125
The Scriptures I'd search, which are worthy esteem,
And moments most precious I'd strive to redeem;
Rich grace and free mercy should then be my theme,
In bright vernal hours—when by power divine,
Sol's clear fulgid rays most pellucid shall shine;   130
When gay florid scenes decorate fertile fields,
Meads beauties display—each bright scene solace yields,
When cheer'd plumed choirists their dulcet notes raise,
In accents melodious chant heaven's high praise,
I'd walk for fresh air in the fine open glades,   135
And crop precious herbs in the cool sylvan shades,
To plant in my garden, selecting the best
For chemists of art, to distil or digest;
Or anodynes form, which will give present ease,
I'd exert every nerve, the kind gentry to please.   140
Yet tho' worthy friends I've express'd my desire,
All hope still declines this my wish to acquire,
I'm incessantly troubled, while foes me oppress—
From gentry benign, I'd solicit redress;
From this wretched station, kind friends, me release,   145
Sarcasms and insults obtrude on my peace;
Confine me in prison, recluse from man's sight,
That I, like JOHN BUNYAN, experience may write,
Or study Acrostics, of various kinds,
Fair Ladies to please, and sooth gentlemen's minds;   150
Plain verses and sonnets in gaol I might rhyme,
The lone muse assisting, I'd thus spend my time,
Or like one in Newgate, replenish'd by Lore,
Who took a survey of America's shore,
Surmounted dire foes, and increased his store;   155

Or let me exist in a drear exile state,
I'd either prefer to my sufferings of late;
But rather than pass through more drear scenes of woe,
Or into Soham mansions of industry go,
'Mongst Belial's sons of contention and strife,   160
To breathe out the transient remains of my life;
In a neat market town I'll reside for awhile,
There friends t' oblige, fleeting moments beguile,
A chamber or garret I'll cease to refuse,
Like a mean Grub-street bard there in solitude muse.   165

Treble Acrostic
(James Chambers, Itinerent Poet, despised by Man)

Joy sometimes visits one	In sordid	Dress,
And he does cordial	Thanks to heaven	Express,
Most cruel foes	Infest to filch his	Store,
Elate with pride they	New contempt will	Pour;
Sarcastic speech vain tongues	Emit	Indeed;
Comfort, and peace of mind	Retire with	Speed.
Here I, who powers	Exert in verse t'	Excel,
Am oft advis'd	Near Cambridge town to	Dwell;
May worthy Gentry	There a cottage	Build
By limpid streams, 'twill	Peace, and solace	Yield;
Erected on the verge	Of Soham's bright	Mere,
Residing there,	Each prospect will	Appear
Still brighter, if	True Christian friends live	Near.

Treble Acrostic
(Acrostic for Robert Roe,
Printer in Copperplate, and Engraver, Cambridge)

Adorn'd superb,	Pellucid rays	Appear,
Creation shines	Refulgent, far and	Near,
Resplendent scenes	In Autumn yield	Delight,
Omnifick power may	New applause	Excite;
Spring will revive,	The grand parterre look	Neat,
Those florid scenes will	Entertain the	Great;
In Spring the blushing	Rose sheds beauties	Rare,
Carnations breathe perfume	In vernal	Air;
Frail man must sure, when	Nature's works he's	View'd,
Obey celestial	Calls, each vice	Elude,
Resent all thoughts	Obscene, and converse	Rude;
Rich gentry, void of	Pride, dear babes	Caress,
Obedient children	Prize, of meek	Address,
Blessings attend, no	Enemies	Molest,
Enamell'd scenes	Revive the languid	Breast:
Rich neat engravings	Polish'd, and	Refin'd,
To please true friends to	Love who are	Inclin'd,
Relations at his	Absence seem	Distrest,
Old Ipswich friends	Treat a welcome	Guest,
Each hour on Christmas	Eve much joy will be	Exprest.

JOHN CLARE (1793–1864)

John Clare is unquestionably the best-known poet included in this volume. Of all the British poets generally categorized as labouring-class, moreover, he has undergone the most extensive, as well as the most contentious, modern republication. The sure rise in Clare's status is perhaps most easily seen in the fact that his 2003 biography by Jonathan Bate received the sort of mainstream reviews, in outlets such as the *Times Literary Supplement*, *The New Yorker*, and *The New York Times Book Review*, traditionally accorded to literary lives of major figures like Shelley or Keats. As appreciative as these review essays have been, however, they also serve to show how difficult it is for any brief overview of Clare's tumultuous life to engage deeply with, or even really to convey, the substance and scope of his *oeuvre*, which includes several thousand poems and prose pieces beyond the four volumes of poetry he published during his lifetime. As scholarly interest in Clare has burgeoned in the last three decades—his career in many ways crystallizes arguments in favour of re-configuring the Romantic canon—so too has his poetry been making its way steadily into university courses on British Romanticism, and into the anthologies used in such courses. Still, much work remains to be done before the critical interpretation of Clare is fully backed by widespread familiarity with the extraordinary range of his work.

Fascinating anecdotes about Clare's life abound. One may cite, for example, his careful plan of action in acquiring his own copy of Thomson's *Seasons*, when he was just thirteen; his later bedevilment at being forced, through economic necessity, to participate in the enclosing of the common land around his native village; or, even more poignantly, any number of apparently delusional episodes from the nearly three decades he spent in mental institutions, including his confused attestation that he had been sentenced to prison for bigamy, and his occasional insistence that he was the champion prize fighter Jack Randall. That Clare wrote as much as he did, and that he wrote as well as he did, is astonishing given the challenges he faced: punishing poverty, frequent bouts of severe physical and mental ill-health, the constraints imposed by condescending patrons, and a capricious literary market that first encouraged and then abandoned him. Within the poetry itself, however, we find Clare dwelling as much on the joys of his life as on its sorrows. As Bate has noted, one of the most frequently repeated phrases in Clare's poetry is the declarative, 'I love', used to introduce a description of a scene or natural object. Clare's plangent 'love of every simple weed' and his meticulous awareness of nature have made him a central figure in recent eco-critical approaches to Romantic literature.

Clare's home was Helpstone, a Northamptonshire village about five miles to the south-east of the market town of Stamford. His father, Parker, worked as a farm labourer and thresher, and passed on his own love of ballads and folklore to his only son. Clare's mother, Ann, was the daughter of a shepherd, and illiterate. Clare was born with a twin sister, who died after several weeks; he would have two more sisters, but only one, Sophy, lived to adulthood. Clare began attending a local dame school at the age of five and later moved to the village school at Glinton, though his attendance there was irregular owing to the family's inability to meet the necessary fees (Bate, p. 22) and the need for Clare to assist his father with seasonal field-work. He left school permanently at the age of thirteen, but continued his studies on his own in mathematics, geography, botany, and other subjects, using second-hand and borrowed textbooks as he could get them. Despite his erratic formal education, Clare's passion for learning accelerated through his early adulthood. He seized every opportunity to pursue that passion, fully aware of the social sanctions against it: he recalled in 1821 that 'as it is common in villages to pass judgment on a lover of books as a sure indication of laziness, I was drove to the narrow nessesity of stinted oppertunitys to hide in woods and dingles of thorns in the fields on Sundays to read' (*By Himself*, p. 6). Clare's pursuit of knowledge under duress is, of course, comparable to the struggles of many labouring-class intellectuals in the period of the Industrial Revolution; the difference is that the magnitude of his achievement, in both qualitative and quantitative terms, far surpasses that of any other poet of similar background, with the possible exception of James Hogg (q.v.), during the nineteenth century. His productivity is all the more noteworthy for having occurred in a climate of perpetual distractions, above and beyond the material exigencies we might assume. Amidst a series of short-lived apprenticeships and temporary jobs, numerous flirtations and liaisons (at least by his own account), and the constant draw of tavern conviviality, Clare found time for the solitary wanderings that, for him, nourished a serious life of the mind. Bate observes that if Clare had any steady occupational identity, it was probably as a gardener—a fortuitous circumstance among so many unhappy ones, since it complemented his own fascination with local flora.

During his teen years, Clare kept his writing largely a secret. The cost of paper forced him to use any available scrap for his early efforts, and he recalled that it was some time before he could bring himself to tell his mother that he did not wish the written fragments he had stored in a hole in the wall to be used as kindling. Clare's parents, however, were a discerning first audience for his poetry; he took care, initially, to present his own verses to them as the work of another, but later worked up the courage to ask and receive their opinions on his own behalf. In 1814, at 21, Clare purchased a blank notebook from J.B. Henson, a printer and bookseller in the nearby town of Market Deeping. Four years later, Clare revealed to Henson his ambitions to publish, and Henson advised him to do so by subscription, promising to print a collection for him when he had secured 300 subscribers—though he later reduced the requirement to 100 (Bate, pp. 110–15). Clare composed a prospectus which included his first printed poem, the sonnet 'The Setting Sun', and this caught the attention of Edward Drury, a Stamford bookseller who proposed more favourable terms to Clare for publishing the volume, and who also helped to him to publish some poems in local newspapers. Most important at the time, Drury assisted Clare and his family with much-needed cash advances.

Ultimately it was Drury's cousin John Taylor, the London publisher of John Keats, who brought into print Clare's first collection, *Poems Descriptive of Rural Life and Scenery* (1820). Clare's relationship to Taylor has itself been a matter of scholarly debate for some years: it was at all events a complex alliance in which mutual self-interest became entangled with paternalism and genuine personal regard. On the one hand, Taylor's corrections to Clare's manuscripts have been condemned, by such modern editors as Eric Robinson, as symptomatic of class-based oppression; on the other, there is ample evidence from Clare's own letters to show that at least some of the time he welcomed Taylor's editorial interventions and indeed assumed from the outset that Taylor would be correcting his work. Recent research indicates that Clare was more irritated by the ideological interventions of his subsequent patrons Eliza Emmerson and Admiral Lord Radstock, who sniffed out any lines suggesting political radicalism and demanded that he remove them. Here was one of many respects in which Taylor's role was a mixed one: he shared Clare's outrage at such demands, rebuffing them with assertions of editorial privilege, but was also capable of yielding selectively to these and similar requests as his own reckoning of public taste dictated.

Poems Descriptive of Rural Life and Scenery was the best-received and best-selling of the four volumes that appeared in Clare's lifetime. Early reviewers saw him as exemplifying the ideal of 'natural genius', the received explanation for how 'peasant poets' could surmount their educational disadvantages. Almost inevitably, these critics compared Clare with his predecessors Stephen Duck, Robert Burns, and Robert Bloomfield—and, befitting the notion of plebeian artistry as a flash in the pan, were hesitant about encouraging any future efforts. Clare, however, quickly set to work on his second collection, *The Village Minstrel* (1821), the long title-poem of which offered a more sustained autobiographical glimpse of the poet in the figure of Lubin, the work's pensive protagonist. His third collection *The Shepherd's Calendar* (1827) and final volume *The Rural Muse* (1835) each received dimmer notice from the reviewers than had the first two volumes; yet the modern critical consensus is that these 'middle years', marred though they were by terrible sufferings, represent Clare's richest period of artistic growth. In fact, Clare had hoped that a completed collection called *The Midsummer Cushion* would appear in 1832, and the four published volumes deliver only a fraction of what he actually wrote. The full extent of his productivity has only become clear during the past twenty years through the publication of Oxford English Text editions of his complete works, edited by Eric Robinson, David Powell and P.M.S. Dawson.

Although Clare did meet with a degree of success after his first volumes appeared, he never enjoyed the financial freedom to devote himself solely to poetry. Clare married Martha 'Patty' Turner in 1820, and the couple had nine children (two of whom died in infancy). He worked irregularly, and his poor health meant that the family was often faced with dire hardship and debt, even as he also supported his parents on his small income. In 1832, in an effort to alleviate the family's troubles, several of Clare's supporters, including Eliza Emmerson, assisted the family in relocating three miles from Helpstone to Northborough, and to a new home with a small parcel of land for a garden and orchard. Clare was extraordinarily sensitive to the smallest details in his immediate environment, and this move proved not to be as salutary as his friends had hoped. His emotional and physical state, never robust, began sharply to decline. 'O poesy is on the wane', he wrote in 'Decay: A Ballad':

> For fancys visions all unfitting
> I hardly know her face again
> Nature herself seems on the flitting
> The fields grow old & common things
> The grass the sky the winds a blowing
> Are sighing 'going all a going'
> O poesy is on the wane
> I hardly know her face again (ll. 1–8)

He suffered severe depression and began to experience delusions. In 1837 he was admitted to High Beech Asylum, a private facility near Waltham Abbey, on the northern outskirts of what is now greater London. In 1841, Clare decided to leave High Beech, and, starving and delirious, walked 80 miles back to his home in Northborough. The journey was a failed attempt to see his childhood sweetheart, Mary Joyce, who actually had died in 1838 but who continued to function in Clare's imagination as an all-purpose muse and object of romantic desire. Clare's brief memoir of this 'escape', written in its immediate aftermath, shows with distressing directness how his mind interleaved rationality and utter confusion.

A few months after leaving High Beech, he was committed again, this time to the Northampton General Lunatic Asylum, where he would remain for the last twenty-three years of his life. Though the rate of Clare's poetic output declined somewhat over these decades, he nonetheless continued to write, often in feverish bursts, with much of this later poetry transcribed by the asylum's steward, W. F. Knight. He was also given roaming privileges, permitted to wander the grounds and experience the beauty of trees, sky, and wind. Yet in these late years, the landscapes of Clare's poetry became increasingly internal. As his wavering sense about the actuality of his own identity became a primary subject of his verse, he wrote the poems that have emerged as the core of his canon. A group of short poems composed between 1844 and 1861, especially 'I Am', 'A Vision', and 'An Invite to Eternity', have become staples of nineteenth-century anthologies, and offer a concise, harrowing picture of a man who feels shrunken and unrecognizable, a kind of revenant who has become lost to his family, to himself, and even to the natural world. In these poems, and in the letters that survive from this period, Clare's love of paradox reaches a tortuous, nonsensical apex, in which 'the path has lost its way' and 'the sun forgets the day' ('Invite to Eternity', ll. 5–6). But, useful as these poems are in revealing the mental labyrinths in which Clare dwelt, they do not give the entire picture of the late poetry. Clare's powerful assertions and retractions of his own existence were accompanied by intense delusional identifications with celebrated poets, and led him to compose 'additional' cantos of Byron's *Don Juan* and *Childe Harold*. 'I'm the same man', he was reported to have said, 'but sometimes they call me Shakespeare and sometimes Byron and sometimes Clare' (Blunden, pp. 39–40). Also emerging in this period are harsher, more apocalyptic poems of good and evil, sin and redemption, and, especially in the *Don Juan* additions, misogyny and female betrayal.

As noted earlier, our understanding of the entirety of Clare's career has been immeasurably advanced by the recent completion of the Oxford English Texts edition of Clare's poetry. At the same time, the editorial issues surrounding it have been accompanied by controversy. Eric Robinson, chief editor of the OET editions since work on the project began almost forty years ago, claims ownership of the copyright on all of Clare's unpublished manuscripts, based upon a 1965 transaction with Whitaker's publishing house in which he purchased 'all rights whatsoever possessed by the company in the published and unpublished works of John Clare'. (The process

by which Whitaker acquired copyright is discussed by Bate, pp. 536–42.)
Alongside Robinson's copyright claim is his advocacy of a set of editorial
principles that can be described as 'textual primitivism', in which Clare's
poems are presented in forms approximating the manuscript originals as
closely as possible, thus reproducing Clare's highly irregular grammar and
orthography. Opinions about the appropriateness of this approach vary
widely. Some critics view the 'primitive' form of the texts—featuring little or
no punctuation, and rampant inconsistencies in spelling, often within a sin-
gle poem or line—as effectively enforcing a view of Clare as ignorant,
unintelligent, and unsuited to serious academic study. Others view any
impulse to modern editorial intrusion as merely another form of the conde-
scension that has always typified the literary establishment's approach to the
poet. Several proponents of Clare have suggested a middle ground, in which
the texts are subject to light editorial alterations—such as the insertion of
traditional capitalizations and obvious possessives—in order to facilitate
basic comprehension and eliminate the most confusing of Clare's graphic
and syntactic anomalies. The whole issue has been further complicated by a
particular strain of academic self-consciousness, in which the mandate of
properly 'respecting' the lower-class artist becomes not only an argumenta-
tive weapon against one's opponents, but also a source of personal hand-
wringing and ideological angst. Certainly it is a sharp irony that Clare, whose
poems repeatedly describe his ramblings over free, unenclosed landscapes as
his greatest happiness, should appear to have come under a form of editorial
ownership more than a century after his death. Yet there is much to be said
for at least a partially 'primitive' presentation of Clare's poems, including the
enlivening mixture of accessibility and urgency that student readers tend to
find in them, once the initial strangeness of their appearance has been over-
come. Indeed, one of the reasons that Clare's poetry is being increasingly
and successfully taught is that it is so clearly the work of a real person with
an immediately discernible voice. Aside from the practical ramifications of
such textual 'primitivism', however, the controversy surrounding the copy-
right claim has created an aura of uncertainty regarding future editions.

Both Clare's poetry and his broader sense of self were inextricably bound
up with the changing landscape of Helpstone and its surrounding fields and
streams. Indeed, the nominal boundaries dividing himself from others,
thought from feeling, and nature from art, were blurred and even erased by
Clare in moments of spontaneous rapture:

> [P]oesy is a language meet
> & fields are every ones employ
> The wild flower neath the shepherds feet
> Looks up and gives him joy

A language that is ever green
That feelings unto all impart
As awthorn blossoms soon as seen
Give may to every heart ('Pastoral Poesy', ll. 9–16).

Clare responded to the world around him as both a local and a natural histo-
rian, and it is in this poetic guise that he is best known and most readily
accessible. Hundreds of Clare's poems, many of them sonnets like the fol-
lowing, take the form of observational catalogues, recording, one line at a
time, the ordinary objects of nature and rural life as they fall within his field
of vision:

> The stepping stones that stride the meadows streams
> Look picturesque amid springs golden gleams
> Where steps the traveler with a warey pace
> & boy with laughing leisure in his face
> Sits on the midmost stone in very whim
> To catch the struttles that beneath him swim
> While those across the hollow lakes are bare
> & winter floods no more rave dangers there
> But mid the scum left where it roard & fell
> The schoolboy hunts to find the pooty shell
> Yet there the boisterous geese with golden broods
> Hiss fierce & daring in their summer moods
> The boys pull off their hats while passing bye
> In vain to fright—themselves being forced to fly

While far from the most dramatic exhibit of Clare's creativity, 'Stepping
Stones' usefully demonstrates many of his poetic habits and impulses. In
matter-of-fact fashion, the poem shifts repeatedly from one aesthetic model
to another, offering, in effect, a viewer's narrative running parallel to that of
the action-packed stream. It begins by redirecting our blueprint of the 'pic-
turesque' away from the obvious meadow stream to the less obvious shapes
within it. From there, the scene reveals to Clare's eye, in a kind of integrated
jumble, a series of natural and social phenomena that resist tonal unity: the
decidedly unromantic attitude of the boys, the simultaneous beauty and
aggression of the geese, and the summer stream's continuing registry of vio-
lent winter floods. Dialect words (struttles, pooty shell) are used
unselfconsciously, as the first and best terms for the occasion; here and else-
where, Clare is quite purposefully of one voice with the people he writes
about. Furthermore, the final couplet does not strive for a grand or
emphatic sense of closure, but instead employs a kind of wistful, meditative

shift in tone—a shift that, as in many of his sonnets, is also accompanied by an implied physical movement away from, or out of, the poem's visual field.

'Stepping Stones' is atypical in presenting the boys as being antagonized by the geese; Clare more commonly decries the daily dangers faced by animals, especially at the hands of humans. He often speaks for the neglected wildlife of his native region, as it witnessed the devastating effects of agricultural 'improvement' and parliamentary enclosure. John Barrell's *The Idea of Landscape and the Sense of Place* (1972), the first major modern treatment of Clare's poetry, continues to provide the best discussion of Clare's political and aesthetic response to environmental change. The immediacy of Clare's engagement with his own milieu, involving for example a recurrent sub-theme of insect and bird life, clearly anticipates the ecological ethic voiced by such modern nature poets as Gary Snyder and Seamus Heaney. But while Clare often makes nature an object of scientific study, he also presents it as the incarnation of God, and at other times as a psychological or emotional entity: a site of refuge, fancy, or nostalgia. Sometimes it is all of these things within a single poem.

Clare is also more than simply a 'poet of nature'. His voracious reading is evident in the intertextual allusiveness of his work, which reaches back to the sixteenth and seventeenth centuries (where key influences include Shakespeare, Milton, and Izaak Walton) even while depending firmly upon the oral tradition within which he grew up (and whose ballads and stories Clare, an accomplished fiddle-player, spent much of his time collecting). As Barrell notes, Clare's representations of nature are related not only to his first-hand study of the Northamptonshire fields and fens, but to his reading of James Thomson. Belying his limited education, Clare read the work of other English poets, including his contemporaries Wordsworth and Keats, with probity and enthusiasm. His conversation with the English poetic tradition, as well as his implicit bid to join it, is reflected in the variety of forms and themes he used throughout his career—and also in his numerous broodings about the temptations and dangers of poetic fame. Clare was a skilled writer of sonnets, songs, and ballads, as well as of longer loco-descriptive poems, and his experiments with voice and perspective in these modes are among the most daringly original to be found in early-nineteenth century literature. Clare eschews the elevated vantage-point of earlier picturesque poets like Goldsmith and Crabbe, and writes instead as an earthbound participant in the 'seasons', both literal and figurative, of rural communities. Even as many poems express a desire to abandon human society in exchange for 'eternal nature', many others exhibit a strong impulse to chronicle the traditions, practices, and personalities of village life, with pointed emphasis on the rituals of courtship and kinship (and, often, on the elderly raconteurs who preserve these folkways).

In some sense, it is the very range of Clare's work—or, more accurately, the way in which his corpus is characterized at once by thematic coherence, internal variety, and sheer, almost unmanageable size—that has contributed to its relatively slow rate of dissemination in undergraduate classrooms and among prospective readers generally. Yet an examination of the superb on-line bibliography of Clare scholarship maintained by Simon Kövesi and John Goodridge (www.johnclare.info) reveals a remarkable quantity of critical work on the poet, especially over the last twenty-five years. Much of this work is that of specialists with detailed knowledge of Clare's manuscripts. But the bibliography also indicates a disparity between the narrow 'public canon' of Clare and the far wider universe of his work that scholars have been discussing in recent years. And with the recent publication of a number of inexpensive editions of Clare's poems, there is reason to believe that scores of heretofore non-canonical poems will soon be competing for the love and attention of readers both within and outside the universities. It can also be predicted that this movement will galvanize—and broaden—the continuing debates as to what territory should be encompassed by the terms 'Labouring-Class Poet', 'Nature poet', 'Romantic poet', and, indeed, 'Romanticism'.

FURTHER READING

John Barrell, *The Idea of Landscape and the Sense of Place, 1730–1840* (Cambridge: Cambridge University Press, 1972)

Jonathan Bate, *John Clare: A Biography* (New York: Farrar, Straus and Giroux, 2003)

Edmund Blunden (ed.), *Sketches in the Life of John Clare, by Himself* (London: Cobden-Sanderson, 1931)

John Clare, *John Clare By Himself*, eds Eric Robinson and David Powell (Ashington: Mid Northumberland Arts Group, and Manchester: Carcanet, 1996)

Johanne Clare, *John Clare and the Bounds of Circumstance* (Kingston and Montreal: McGill-Queens University Press, 1987)

George Deacon, *John Clare and the Folk Tradition* (London: Francis Boutle, new edition, 2002)

John Goodridge (ed.), *The Independent Spirit: John Clare and the Self-Taught Tradition* (Helpston: The John Clare Society and the Margaret Grainger Memorial Trust, 1994)

John Goodridge and Simon Kovesi (eds.), *John Clare: New Approaches* (Helpston: The John Clare Society, 2000)

Hugh Haughton, Adam Phillips, and Geoffrey Summerfield (eds.), *John Clare in Context* (Cambridge: Cambridge University Press, 1993)

The John Clare Society Journal (1982–)

James C. McKusick, *Green Writing: Romanticism and Ecology* (New York: St. Martin's Press, 2000)

Eric Robinson, David Powell, and P. M. S. Dawson (eds.), *John Clare: Poems of the Middle Period*, 5 vols (Oxford: Clarendon Press, 1996–2003)

Roger Sales, *John Clare: A Literary Life* (New York: Palgrave, 2002)

Mark Storey (ed.), *Clare: The Critical Heritage* (London: Routledge & Kegan Paul, 1973)

Mark Storey (ed.), *John Clare: Selected Letters* (Oxford: Clarendon Press, 1988)

Alan Vardy, *John Clare: Poetry and Politics* (New York: Palgrave, 2003).

ROBERT MILLHOUSE (1788–1839)

Robert Millhouse of Nottingham was one of ten children, and before reaching his teens was sent to work as a stocking-loom weaver. In 1810 he joined the Nottinghamshire Militia (later 'The Royal Sherwood Foresters'), and began writing poems shortly thereafter. Although some of these early efforts were published in the *Nottingham Review,* for most of the remainder of the decade he was primarily occupied with weaving and his regiment, in which he eventually rose to the rank of corporal. After marrying in 1818 he began, according to his brother John, 'seriously to consider his future prospects in life; and perceiv[ed] that he had no other chance of bettering his position than by a publication' (quoted in *Blossoms,* p. 17). Efficiently packaging new writing with various combinations and recombinations of earlier material, Millhouse produced a series of slim volumes over the coming years, including *Vicissitude* (1821); *Blossoms* (1823); *The Song of the Patriot* (1826); *Sherwood Forest* (1827); *The Destinies of Man* (1832); and *The Destinies of Man, Part II* (1834). The promise of his early work and the vigorous lobbying of his patron, The Revd. Dr Luke Booker, Vicar of Dudley, helped earn him a grant from the Royal Literary Fund in 1822, and his subsequent volumes were steadily reviewed in the periodical press. (An abridged list of these reviews is contained below within 'Further Reading'.) But despite the outward appearances of a successful publishing career and the support of several other patrons and friends, including Thomas Wakefield, Spencer T. Hall, and, later, Ebenezer Elliott (q.v.), Millhouse was frequently beset with financial and health-related difficulties. He was forced to continue working as a weaver until 1832, when he secured a position at a savings bank. The following year brought the death of his wife. Millhouse remarried in 1836, but took seriously ill two years later and died in 1839.

A posthumous collection of Millhouse's *Sonnets and Songs,* including previously unpublished material and a fairly detailed biographical sketch, was published in Nottingham in 1881; its editor John Potter Briscoe followed Millhouse's earlier patrons in urging his connection to the pantheon of rustic and labouring-class poets. 'Millhouse was a brilliant example', Briscoe intones, 'of the might of that genius which has welled up from the ranks of the toil-worn and penury-stricken crowd. Some of his productions rank with

those of Bloomfield, Clare, and even the great Wordsworth [...] Millhouse
has been designated "the Burns of Sherwood Forest'" (p. v). Regarding this
last, it is hard to conceive a more misleading appellation—Millhouse's most
consistent voice being one of earnest and impassioned rectitude—but in
naming Clare and Bloomfield, Briscoe was merely echoing the more favour-
able of the early reviews. In fact Millhouse's poetry evinces a sometimes
peculiar mixture of elitism and radical populism. His diction is formal, ele-
vated, and frequently stilted, and Gerald Le Grys Norgate noted in the *DNB*
that 'in his later life he looked upon any but literary work as derogatory to
his talent'. Millhouse generally assumes the voice of the scold, the school-
marm, or the last honest man; for a measure of his un-Burnsian sense of
decorum, one has only to imagine his 'Address for a Society of Odd Fellows'
(q.v.) in Burns's hands. Nonetheless the sentiments of Millhouse's verse are
frequently radical, or at least demotic. In 'The Proud Man's Contumely' he
identifies as a pervasive, widely repeated lie the charge that the poor are sim-
ply inferior. He consistently inveighs against greed, hypocrisy, and the
corruption of the rich, and these condemnations are given an overtly reli-
gious context, in which all will be equal before God. Millhouse's essential
position regarding his art can be summarized in lines from the sonnet 'The
Bard': the poet is blest, he says, 'if he teach (on Truth's eternal plan) / That
Virtue only dignifies the Man' (ll. 13–14). Repeatedly he advocates storing
up one's treasures in heaven, but the angry tone of many of his poems indi-
cates that these future prospects often provide only cold comfort in the face
of the inequities of daily life.

Millhouse is at his strongest in his sonnets, and with only one exception,
it is sonnets that are included here; his narrative, historical, and minor epics,
which comprise a substantial portion of his work, are hyberbolic but unin-
teresting, though they were frequently praised by early reviewers for their
patriotism, piety, and correct feeling.

FURTHER READING

British Critic n.s. 15 (June 1821), 660–6

DNB

Eclectic Review n.s. 19 (March 1823), 258–61; 3rd ser. 8 (Oct 1832), 349– 57

Evangelical Magazine (1823)

Gentleman's Magazine 93 (1823), 101–2; n.s. 11 (1839), 662–3

Literary Gazette (9 Sep 1826), 562–3

Robert Millhouse, *Sonnets and Songs*, ed. John Potter Briscoe (Nottingham and Lon-
don, 1881)

Monthly Magazine 55 (April 1823), 252

Monthly Review 96 (Sep 1821), 98–9; 99 (April 1823), 433–4

New Monthly Magazine (Sep 1826)

Sketches of Obscure Poets (London: Cochrane and McCrone, 1833), pp. 32–45

Alfred Stapleton, *In the Footsteps of Robert Millhouse* (Nottingham: Nottinghamshire Guardian, 1908)

<http://jillsfamilyancestry.co.uk/Part_1_Millhou/Research__Robe.html>

From *Blossoms* (1823)

To Gold

Fee for the knave, in every age and clime!
Thou shield to gilded Ideots! slave to Kings!
Pander to War and other horrid things
That stain with blood the chronicles of Time;
When, shining Mischief! shall the Poet's rhyme   5
Tell of thy virtues in the good man's hand,
Chasing away grim hunger from the land,
And proving true thy alchymy sublime?
If Evil spring from thy deceitful wand,
Nor good nor ill thou bring'st to such as I: 10
For here gaunt Poverty stands shivering by
To snatch the scanty portion from my hand—
Give my thy power, thou thing of Good or Guile!
And I will teach sad Poverty to smile.

The Proud Man's Contumely

Imperious Mortal! can thy pigmy soul
Treat thus the poor man for a good design?
Know, that thy ill-judg'd mandate of controul
Moves but the censure of the Power Divine.
In Heav'n's esteem my blood is pure as thine,   5

And the creation to my sight as fair:
Yea, haply may my humble frame combine
Seeds, could they once a genial culture share,
Might lift me far beyond thy misty sphere.
And shall not Poverty the licence have,   10
With Merit and with conscious Truth, to dare
To climb one fathom on this side the grave?
The howling wintry blasts may take their fling;
But, in due time, comes on the blushing Spring.

Written in the Country

Oh! there's a wild-rose in yon rugged dell,
Fragrant as that which blooms the garden's pride;
And there's a sympathy no tongue can tell,
Breath'd from the Robin chanting by its side:
And there is musick in that whispering rill,   5
Far more delightsome than the raging main;
And more of beauty in yon verdant hill,
Than to the grandest palace can 'pertain:
For there is nought so lovely and serene
Throughout the chambers of the mightiest King,   10
As the pure calm that rests upon this scene,
'Mid sporting lambkins and the songs of spring:
Yet, oft attracted by some dazzling show,
Man flies from Peace, pursuing gilded woe.

To Antiquity

Thou solitary waste of former days!
Gone are all they who sojourn'd on thy plain—

The imperial Monarch and the simple Swain;
Philosophers, and Bards of heaven-wrought lays—
With them, near some base Miser, lies reclin'd   5
A wretch now freed from sorrow and despair,
Who ceaseless strove in vain, by toilsome care
To cast grim Penury and Want behind.—
The Good, the Vile, the Coward, and the Brave,
The Foolish and the Wise, in common rest—   10
And, if a floret spring on Cæsar's breast,
That flower would bloom as sweetly o'er a Slave.—
Nor Great, nor Small shall pass the deathful gloom,
Till the last Trumpet summon to the Doom.

The Bard

Blest be the Bard with glorious length of Fame,
Who meditates on Sun, and Moon, and Skies,—
The pensive Twilight, and the various dyes
Of beam-ting'd Rainbows,—and the rapid flame
Of forked Lightnings, and the Thunder's sound,—   5
The never-ceasing murmurings of the Rill,—
The awful summit of the snow-clad Hill,
The Green-wood shades, and Ocean's dread profound;—
The song of Birds, and flowery pride of Spring;—
The beauteous Summer, and the saddening glooms   10
Of Autumn, fatal to the myriad blooms,
And icy Winter's tempest-bearing wing—
Blest—if he teach (on Truth's eternal plan)
That Virtue only dignifies the Man.

From *Sherwood Forest and Other Poems* (1827)

The Lot of Genius

To feel a conscious dignity within,
And be despised amidst a crowd of fools;
Too proud by slavish purposes to win
The paltry favours of Oppression's tools:
Born to no heritage but that of mind—   5
To waste in penury the sand of life;
To look on wounds without the power to bind;
To lift a cobweb-shield to baffle strife;
To labour with a patriotic zeal,
And meet with calumny from thankless man;   10
And trust to after ages to repeal
A nation's apathy, and critic's ban;
Ages—which rear base piles to mock the dead,
And shame the sons whose sires denied them bread.

To the Herb Chickweed

Chickweed! will no one sing thee? Like thy bard
Lowly, and little noted though thou art,
Creeping o'er fallows with thy pallid sward,
Thou in my humble strains shalt claim a part.
When summer flowers to churlish autumn yield,   5
And gaunt December bends the leafless groves,
Thou, to the small birds trooping o'er the field,
Art food—the stimulus to future loves.
Henceforth let none despise thee for thy birth,
For powers medicinal in thee are found;   10
And haughty man shall own thy sterling worth,
And crave thine aid to cool the anguished wound:
The lordly oak may lift his head on high,
Thou still wilt creep beneath the self-same sky.

Address
For a Society of Odd Fellows

Brothers in fellowship! this night we call
To action sympathies esteemed by all.
Need it to your enlightened minds be told
What noble aims are in our bonds enrolled?
Aims, that require no advocate to tell   5
That they originate in meaning well;
Self-evident the seeds of worth expand,
Nor shame the wisdom of their planter's hand.

Still be it ours, removed from petty strife,
To gild with smiles the rugged front of life;   10
To pass in mutual joy the social hour,
And seize each harmless bliss within our power;
The friendly ties of brotherhood to prove,
Unswayed by all but dictates from above;
Ours be unwarped the Patriot's steady zeal,   15
And ours that friendship which delights to heal;
Sincerity, with her benignant form,
And Perseverance, struggling with the storm,
Firm as the rock, whose jutting crags defy
The warring tempests of the wintry sky.   20

But what is that which man to man endears,
Whose accents catch the music of the spheres,
Whose deeds no trivial rules or objects scan,
Expansive in its vital good to man?
What though unseen its secret current flow,   25
And all its good the world should never know,
And though it seem as it had never been,—
In its effects its living power is seen.
This is Benevolence! whose deeds confest,
Make the receiver and the giver blest.   30

Then not in vain be our assemblage now
To shed glad rays upon the darkened brow;
And to the weak and cheerless heart dispense
The spring-tide fullness of its influence;
And as high heaven the cleaving ploughshare speeds,   35
And fits the soil for its allotted seeds,

Thus, what ye spread with liberal hand, no less
Guided by Him, shall meet with like success;
Proceed we ever in the task avowed,
Of man's best aims and interests only proud.   40

EBENEZER ELLIOTT (1781–1849)

Ebenezer Elliott, the 'Corn-Law Rhymer', was born in Rotherham, Yorkshire, one of eleven children. His father, a stringently Calvinist iron-worker nicknamed 'Devil Elliott', was known for his hot temper, but the young Ebenezer was notably shy, perhaps owing in part to facial scars left from a nearly fatal case of smallpox. He evolved a love for solitary countryside rambling in the manner of John Clare (q.v.), a practice which led to his first poem, 'The Vernal Walk' (1801), written when he was seventeen and heavily reliant, as he later admitted, on ideas 'stolen from Ossian and Thomson' (*Works*, 1840, p. 9). At around this same time Elliott began working at his father's foundry in Masbrough. After earning negligible wages for several years, he married into a substantial fortune in 1806, and became partner and proprietor of the business. But the foundry was never successful, and after a decade of struggle, Elliott went bankrupt. Wholly dependent for a time on his wife's relatives for financial support, Elliott moved to Sheffield in 1819, where he eventually established a profitable business as an ironmonger.

The poetry written in this first stage of Elliott's career, essentially the two decades between 'The Vernal Walk' and the move to Sheffield, was clearly connected to both loco-descriptive and gothic-dramatic strains of Romanticism, yet he had difficulty finding publishers. Frustrated, Elliott wrote to Robert Southey in 1808, beginning what would become a fifteen-year correspondence. Southey's advice was ruthlessly pragmatic: he told Elliott to refine his craftsmanship, to submit poems to newspapers, to avoid using his real name until he was established, and to resist rushing his verse into print. (It was perhaps this advice that led Elliott to publish the 1810 volume *The Soldier; and Other Poems* under the pseudonym 'Britannicus'.) Southey also called Elliott's early style 'too exuberant in ornament' (22 Nov 1809), a criticism he would repeat fully a decade later after the publication of Elliott's *Night* (1818). Describing contemporary poets who 'over-labou[r] their productions, and overloa[d] them with ornament, so that all parts are equally prominent, everywhere glare and glitter', Southey commented that in Elliott's volume 'some of the most uncouth stories imaginable are told in a strain of continued tip-toe effort; [...] you are vexed to see such uncommon talents so oddly applied, and such Herculean strength wasted in preposterous exertions' (Letter to Walter Scott, 11 March 1819). One could argue that the verbose Southey was the last person to urge such a point credibly, but he was not alone; the few reviews of *Night* and of Elliott's subsequent volume, *Love* (1823), tended toward similar observations, with the *Monthly Review* calling 'Night' (or 'the Legend of Warncliffe') the '*Ne plus ultra* of German horror and bombast'. Indeed, Elliot's early poems are interesting mainly for their excesses. His gifts for natural description and tragic feeling often seem misplaced within sensational, pseudo-epic elaborations of history and legend. Somewhat more promisingly, the title poem of *Love* is an overwrought but expressly modern progress-of-poesy which insists on the possibility of inspiration within poverty, as in the case of John Clare.

Elliott's sense of portent in recent literary history takes a different turn in 'The Giaour', a satirical denunciation of Byron included in the *Love* volume of 1823. This poem's biting tone is an early indication of Elliott's homing-instinct for the moral outrage of class oppression. Here, in a prefatory address to his target, Elliott savagely imitates and inverts Byron's own critical posturing:

> The language in which I purpose to address you will be somewhat less adulatory than that to which you have been too much accustomed. If I say anything improper, my Satire is a 'lampoon,' and therefore blameless—or I misunderstand your Lordship [...] whether I am or am not envious, petulance, egotism, arrogance, and cruelty, are, I presume, legitimate objects of satire [...] in examining some of your declared opinions, I may possibly condescend to imitate the Byronian snarl. *(Love, p. 135)*

By 'some of your declared opinions', Elliott refers to Byron's poem *English Bards and Scotch Reviewers* (1809), which had derided Robert and Nathaniel Bloomfield (q.q.v.), the cobbler-poet Joseph Blacket, and indeed the whole phenomenon of labouring-class poetry. In turn, Elliott invokes Robert Bloomfield on three separate occasions in his attack on Byron, here claiming that only Bloomfield and Burns have produced purely original literary gold and imputing, by contrast, that the title-character of Byron's 'The Giaour' (1813) owes too much to the villain of Ann Radcliffe's gothic novel *The Italian* (1797):

> See one—whose Alma-Mater was the grove,
> Whose ablest teacher was the lip of love—?
> See Bloomfield bend, 'the tenant of a stall',
> See Want's poor Minstrel soar beyond them all.
> While, College-taught, each self-deceiving cheat
> Passes from fool to fool his counterfeit,
> Two coins alone are gold without alloy,
> The 'Tam o' Shanter' and 'The Farmer's Boy'.

But should some Lord—his head with learning fraught,
And yet in soul 'unteachable, untaught',—
Mock shamed Instruction with his heart of earth,
Deride the noble poverty of worth,
At naked genius lift his golden heel,
'And, without feeling, torture all who feel';
Or, filch from Radcliffe's pages hour by hour,
Kidnap Schedoni, and yclepe him Giaour (ll. 564–79)

Elliott's hostility to Byron would later diminish significantly, though his appetite for *ad hominem* argument would not. The larger point to be taken from this satiric exercise is that Byron's critical snobbism was linked, for Elliott, with all of the social and economic forces arrayed against 'Want's poor Minstrel'—and that Elliott's positive interest in seeing this heroic archetype 'soar beyond them all' was even stronger than his animus against 'them'.

This broader vision is evinced in Elliott's book-length poem *The Village Patriarch* (1829), which treats the disturbing social changes witnessed by a centenarian stonemason, Enoch Wray. In Book IV of the poem, Elliott actually proposes Byron as the voice of the present era, much as Pope presided over an earlier age. Revaluating Byron some five years after his death, Elliott now sees his brand of impassioned genius as more likely to reach an Enoch Wray than the tamer, though perhaps nobler works of Burns, Joanna Baillie, Cowper, Wordsworth, Coleridge, and even Shelley (IV.ii). The semi-apologetic interlude fits smoothly into the main conceit of the poem, whereby the now-sightless Enoch—clearly an abler descendant, both as muse and bard, of Thomas Gray's 'mute inglorious Milton'—feels his way about familiar landscapes and remembers what irresponsible capitalism has done to his family and friends. Despite some powerfully apocalyptic images of belching smokestacks and the embattled masses (reminiscent of Blake as well as Shelley, and predictive of Dickens), the poem condemns neither industry nor capitalism as such, but rather political perversions of each. These include the 'Avarice' (IX.x.2) of the Tory oligarchy and local squires, especially as connected to the prosecution of the Napoleonic Wars; the Peterloo massacre of 1819; and, most of all, the passage in 1815 of a newly protectionist Corn Law. This measure guaranteed a stable grain market for British farmers by taxing foreign imports, but Elliott and many others believed that it led to artificially inflated prices, such that it was difficult for many wage-earners to buy bread. Controversy over the legislation persisted throughout the 1820s and 1830s, as the government's economic policies became entangled with questions of universal suffrage and factory workers' rights. Elliott's poem repeatedly portrays the inherent nobility of skilled workers, and their refusal to succumb to governmental authority and 'paupery', even unto death. As

Enoch fingers the inscriptions on his loved ones' gravestones, Elliott slips in a sardonic reference to the generic 'Sir Cornlaw' (X.xi.4) who rests nearby, and then fondly memorializes Enoch's ascension into heaven. If the central character is ultimately less arresting than the supporting cast, *The Village Patriarch* is nevertheless a highly assured, original work, rechanneling Elliott's earlier poetic tendencies into an eloquent social history.

Interestingly, the development of Elliot's anti-Corn Law polemic took place alongside the steady improvement of his iron business in Sheffield. But this parallel is less odd than it may initially appear. In some ways, Elliott was now becoming the very sort of enlightened citizen-entrepreneur to whom he dedicated a number of his poems. At the same time, he retained his sense of identification with working-class people, not least because his earlier bankruptcy gave him a lifelong fear of financial ruin. Betrayal, exile, and bereavement (with the promise of reunion in the hereafter) had been staples of his early verse romances; he was now honing these elements to a political point. Thus 'Steam at Sheffield,' dedicated 'To Charles Hindley, Esq., M.P., one of our creators of national wealth', celebrates 'Watt! and his million-feeding enginery!' (l. 66), and steam itself as a sublime force—yet also addresses the ambivalence of Andrew Turner, a blind (again) blacksmith torn between admiration and a sense of loss. Besides pitting 'the thoughtful engineer' (l. 182) against 'Grip', an archetype of Tory provincialism, Elliott is also at pains in the poem to say that a noble humanity resides in the town labourer, as surely as it does in his rustic counterpart.

Such commingled beliefs and anxieties, including Elliott's nearly obsessive attribution of his family's financial woes to protectionist legislation, inform *Corn-Law Rhymes: The Ranter* (1830), the first of several volumes bearing the rubric. Where *The Village Patriarch* gains its power from episodic variety, the brief and unified narrative of *The Ranter* is a rhetorical *tour de force*. In presenting the nonsectarian preacher Miles Gordon, an 'artisan' six days of the week (l. 4), as the supporter of his widowed landlady and her five children, Elliott makes very free with phrases such as 'bread-tax'd labour', 'bread-tax-eating thief', and 'bread-tax'd toil and grief' (ll. 41; 44; 45)—but he then recedes, to let the thin and wasting 'prophet' (l. 85) do the talking, in what Miles himself knows will be his final sermon. That Miles speaks in the open air, 'on the mountain's brow' (l. 84), buttresses his condemnation of the 'scribes and pharisees' (l. 106) behind the Corn Laws. It also tempers what might otherwise seem a bombastic celebration of 'world-reforming Commerce'—that is, free trade—as the great liberator of working men (ll. 342–58). And, his burial not in the crowded churchyard, but 'where the rude heath hears the plover cry' (l. 416), allows Elliott to reintroduce the idea of himself, or someone very like himself, as the vigilant 'patriot bard' (l. 405)—a title he resumes in 'A Poet's Prayer', found in the second installment of *Corn-Law Rhymes* (1831).

Unlike *The Ranter*, which stood alone in its volume, most of the 1831 *Rhymes* are short verses in ballad or song meters (some assigned a particular folk tune). Yet they do retain Miles Gordon's oratorical momentum through sharp, pithy first- and second-person addresses, favoring imagery over narration. Some are homely elegies to relatives who have died of overwork, malnutrition, or disease; others pay tribute to the heroes of the Reform movement, with which Elliott was sporadically involved (the 1831 collection is dedicated 'To all who revere the Memory of Jeremy Bentham, our second Locke'); still others excoriate Tyranny in its various guises. Subsequent volumes offered an expanding series of poems under the 'Corn-Law Rhymes' heading, eventually totaling over forty; Elliott also produced twenty poems designated 'Corn-Law Hymns'. These later editions included extensive footnotes denouncing governmental policies and individuals, and promoting free trade as his abiding principle. The long poem *The Splendid Village* appeared in 1833, followed by new editions of the *Corn-Law Rhymes* that included reprintings of some of his early poems. In 1840 William Tait of Edinburgh published a collected edition of Elliott's works; after his death, Elliott's son Edwin edited a revised compilation in two volumes, *The Poetical Works of Ebenezer Elliott* (London, 1876). Two biographies were published in 1850, one by John Watkins, Elliott's son-in-law. For a bibliography of Elliott's work, including the many short occasional essays he produced in the 1830s and 1840s, see the entry below under Arthur A. Eaglestone; note that this 'commemorative brochure' is often indexed under the name 'Roger Dataller', a pseudonym employed by Eaglestone.

The 'Corn-Law Rhymes' marked an epoch in Elliott's career, and though they were not instantaneously popular, they soon became so, earning the praise of Wordsworth, James Montgomery and, most famously, Thomas Carlyle, who cast Elliott as a hands-on labourer ('a quite unmonied, russet-coated speaker [...] a Sheffield worker in brass and iron') who produced poetry as another of his wares. Carlyle placed Elliott's rise within a mythical setting of 'deep Cyclopean forges',

> where Labour, in real soot and sweat, beats with his thousand hammers, 'the red son of the furnace;' doing personal battle with Necessity, and her dark brute Powers, to make them reasonable and serviceable; an intelligible voice from the hitherto Mute and Irrational[.] (pp. 339–40)

If the language here is as overheated as the imagined workshop, it does in fact correspond fairly well to the relentless harangue of the Corn-Law Rhymes, as exemplified in the following poem:

Caged Rats

Ye coop us up, and tax our bread,
   And wonder why we pine;
But ye are fat, and round, and red,
   And filled with tax-bought wine.
Thus twelve rats starve while three rats thrive,
   (Like you on mine and me,)
When fifteen rats are caged alive,
   With food for nine and three.

Haste! Havoc's torch begins to glow—
   The ending is begun;
Make haste! Destruction thinks ye slow;
   Make haste to be undone!
Why are ye call'd 'my Lord' and 'Squire',
   While fed by mine and me,
And wringing food, and clothes, and fire,
   From bread-tax's misery?

Make haste, slow rogues! *prohibit* trade,
   Prohibit honest gain;
Turn all the good that God hath made
   To fear, and hate, and pain;
Till beggars all, assassins all,
   All cannibals we be,
And death shall have no funeral
   From shipless sea to sea.

Here and throughout his writings, Elliott's claims about the destructive power of the Corn Laws, and the redemptive power of the working man's voice, were remarkably direct, unmitigated by doubt or apology. The following passage, which begins with a reference to his *Village Patriarch*, is worth quoting at length for its fury of tone, its advocacy of labouring-class poetry, and the particulars of its free-market platform:

My poem may be a weed, but it has sprung, unforced, out of existing things. It may not suit the circulating libraries for adult babies; but it is the earnest product of experience, a retrospect of the past, and an evidence of the present, a sign of the times, a symptom, terrible, or otherwise, which our state doctors will do well to observe with the profoundest shake of the head; for it affords a prognostic, if not a proof, that Smith and M'Culloch must soon be as familiar as Dilworth to schoolboys. And is it of no importance what a man of the middle class—hardly raised above the lowest— thinks, when the lowest are beginning to think? To Sir Thomas Bread-Tax

Pauper, Lady Betty Pension, and all the great and small vulgar, my opinions may be the *ne plus ultra* of impropriety; but, believing, as I do, that the Corn-Laws have a direct and rapid tendency to ruin my ten children and their country, with all its venerable and venerated institutions, where is the wonder if I hate the perpetrators of such insane atrocities? Their ancestors, I believe, were good men. The Savilles and the Rockinghams, were not palaced almoners, nor are their successors like the Shelleys and the Landerdales. But when suicidal anti-profit laws speak to my heart from my children's trenchers—when statutes for restricting the industry of a population, which is only superabundant because it is oppressed, threaten to send me to the treadmill, for the crime of inflicted want—when, in a word, my feelings are *hammered* till they are 'cold-short'—habit can no longer bend them to courtesy; they snap—and fly off in sarcasm. Is it strange that my language is fervent as a welding heat, when my thoughts are *passions*, that rush burning from my mind, like the white-hot bolts of steel? You do not seem to be sufficiently aware of the importance of *these low matters of trade*; you do not seem to suspect, that, if the Corn-Laws continue much longer, the *death-struggle* of competition will terminate *suddenly!*
(*Works*, 1840, p.101)

It may have been Elliott himself, then, who inspired Carlyle's application of metal-working tropes to the jeremiadic fervour of his verse.

It is tempting to extend such metaphors to Elliott's unsubtle manipulation of the bread-tax issue. Consciously or not, he shared the vested interest of many middle-class businessmen in resisting the industrial wage increases necessitated by the farm subsidy. (He decries 'the crime of inflicted want'; yet the question of whether his verses appealed most to charitable, activist, or paternalist impulses must remain open.) And his warnings of revolution, along with his sense that all issues of Reform boiled down to the issue of free trade, are belied by a complex, three-decade history of legislative wrangling—a history that included two significant rollbacks of the corn tariff before its repeal in 1846.

Putting aside for the moment Elliott's 'white-hot' feelings, we should note his defense of the common man's opinion ('is it of no importance what a man of the middle class—hardly raised above the lowest—thinks, when the lowest are beginning to think?') as both nakedly earnest and cannily crafted. It points to a subtext of intellectual advocacy that pervades Elliott's mature verse, for Enoch Wray and Miles Gordon are explicitly painted as sharp thinkers, and there is nothing naïve or childlike in the working-class speakers of the Corn-Law Rhymes. And it points further to a concern with thought as the essence of human value. It is '*Mind*', named in italics as an entity, that *The Splendid Village* twice identifies as the ultimate victim of class oppression (V.xi.66, VI.ii.19), and in the roughly contemporary 'What Art Thou, Mind?'

Elliott distills his theme of reunion after death into a reflection bearing unexpected marks of Coleridge and Shelley:

> What art thou, Mind, that mirror'st things unseen,
> Giv'st to the dead the smiles which erst they wore,
> And lift'st the veil which fate hath cast between
> Thee and the forms which are not, but have been?
> What art thou, conscious power, that hear'st the mute,
> And feel'st the impalpable? Thy magic brings
> Back to our hearts the warblings of the lute,
> Which long had slept with unexisting things!
> And shall we stand, doubting immortal wings,
> In presence of the angels? Ask the worm,
> And she will bid thee doubt; yet she is meek,
> And wise—for when earth shakes, she shuns thy form,
> But never saw the morning on thy cheek,
> The blue heav'n in thine eye, the lightning break
> In laughter from thy lips. (ll. 22–36)

> Yet doth she err; our limbless sister errs;
> For on thy cheek, O Man! the morning glows,
> And fair is heaven's bright bow. The wayside furze
> Discredits her; the humblest weed that stirs
> Its small green leaves, can undemonstrate all
> Her proofs triumphant, that celestial light
> Shines not at noon. (ll. 42–8)

It seems right to expect that, even as closer examination of Elliott's polemic enriches our ideas of late Romanticism at the height of the Industrial Revolution, there will also be a renewed attentiveness to the philosophical and aesthetic commitments that, over the course of a long career, served as the outer frame of reference for the *Corn-Law Rhymes*.

FURTHER READING

Arthur A. Eaglestone, *Ebenezer Elliott: a commemorative brochure* (Sheffield City Library and Rotherham Public Library, 1949)

Simon Brown, *Ebenezer Elliott: the Corn Law Rhymer : a bibliography & list of Letters. Victorian Studies Handlist* 3 (Leicester: University of Leicester Victorian Studies Centre, 1971)

Simon Brown, 'Ebenezer Elliott and Robert Southey: Southey's Break with *The Quarterly Review*', *Review of English Studies* n.s. 22:87 (1971) 307–11

Thomas Carlyle, 'Corn-Law Rhymes', *Edinburgh Review* 55 (July 1832)

Keith Morris and Ray Hearne, *Ebenezer Elliott: Corn Law Rhymer and Poet of the Poor* (Rotherwood: Rotherwood Press, 2002)

William Odom, *Two Sheffield Poets: James Montgomery and Ebenezer Elliott* (Sheffield: W. C. Leng, 1929)

George L. Phillips, 'Elliott's "The Giaour"', *Review of English Studies* 15:60 (1939), 422–31

G. S. Phillips, *The Life, Character, and Genius of Ebenezer Elliott, the Corn Law Rhymer* (London: Huddersfield, 1850)

G. S. Phillips, *Memoirs of Ebenezer Elliott, the Corn Law Rhymer* (London, 1852)

E. A. Seary, 'Robert Southey and Ebenezer Elliott: Some New Southey Letters', *Review of English Studies* 15: 60 (1939), 412–21.

Michael J. Turner, 'Radical Opinion in an Age of Reform: Thomas Perronet Thompson and the *Westminster Review*,' *History* 86 (2001), 18–40

John Watkins, *Life, Poetry, and Letters of Ebenezer Elliott* (London: Mortimer, 1850)

Samuel Wellington, 'Ebenezer Elliott and the story of the corn laws', *Westminster Review* 162 (1904), 477–95.

WILLIAM SMITH (*fl.* 1819–1826)

Although there are several aspects of the poetry of William Smith, the 'Haddington Cobbler', which make him a figure of special interest within the labouring-class tradition, what initially distinguishes him is his identification with a subject far removed from the tradition's usual concerns: the trade in grave-robbing for the purpose of providing bodies for medical dissection. Smith's 'Verses Composed on the Disgraceful Traffic at Present Carried on Of Raising and Selling the Newly Buried Dead' (1819), one of his first published poems, is a heated denunciation of a secretive but widespread black-market trade that would explode into the public's consciousness ten years later with the case of Burke and Hare in the nearby city of Edinburgh (see Notes). Smith's poem appeared the same year as an important speech by the surgeon John Abernathy before the Royal College of Surgeons advocating passage of the Anatomy Act, which proposed expanding the pool of corpses legally eligible for dissection. As Ruth Richardson notes in *Death, Dissection, and the Destitute*, her study of the Anatomy Act, 'Since Henry VIII's time, the sole legal source for corpses for dissection had been the gallows—bodies of murderers handed over to the anatomists as a *post-mortem* punishment' (p. xv). Proponents of the Act, a version of which eventually passed in 1832, favoured making the corpses of paupers and the indigent eligible for dissection, and both the trade itself and the proposals regarding its regulation stimulated a violent series of religious, ethical, social, and scientific debates. Though Smith does not argue, as some did, that disinterring and dismemberment might prevent the eternal union of body and soul, he refers to the 'Resurrection Men' as 'demons' and 'monsters' who 'rob the grave to please the devil'. In his first full volume, *A Collection of Original Poems* (1821), Smith includes three additional poems on the subject; each depicts an active organization of local citizens assembled to guard the Haddington cemetery at night. The first of these, 'The Mansions of the Dead, or the Grave Watcher's Soliloquy', seems to be written in Smith's own voice, and if so it would indicate that he himself took part in these guarding activities.

Several other fragmentary details about Smith's life and his writing can be gleaned from *A Collection of Original Poems*. He began to publish poetry because physical ailments were threatening his livelihood as a cobbler:

> These three long years for work I've not been fit.
> Yet anxious still, my trade I've carried on,
> Whilst many weeks scarce two days work's been done[.]
>
> ('The Poet's Plea', ll. 88–90)

Yet even as the volume nakedly declares itself a for-profit venture—beginning with some doggerel in the preface which rhymes 'eighteen pence' (the volume's price) with 'good sense'—Smith is extraordinarily defensive about his decision to take up the pen. Indeed, authorship for Smith is at the water's edge of legitimate employment, especially for those who already have trades:

> I freely grant the name of lazy lubber
> To those in health who leave their wonted labour,
> And turn rhyme-mad, or borrow prose, and scamper,
> To tell their tale, and back and belly pamper.
>
> ('The Poet's Plea', ll. 61–4)

While the closing vignette from 'The House of Mourning' has Smith forcefully repudiating begging, he fears his writing will be viewed as begging's near cousin, and in the excerpt below from 'A Summer Evening Walk Improved', he imagines his neighbours whispering that he is both lazy and fraudulent. Finally, though, the potential catastrophe of economic 'dependence' overrides all reservations about the legitimacy of the poet's trade.

Another area of special interest is Smith's conception of, and imaginative identification with, the black slave. The frontispiece to *A Collection of Original Poems* features a remarkable engraving of a black man seated under a tree, a book at his side and paper in his hand, with a white man standing over him. Each man points at the other with his forefinger, and each wears a beneficent, gentle expression. Further, while both men are well-dressed, the white man is clothed entirely in black, and the black man entirely in white. The overall impression conveyed by this design is one of reciprocity and mutual esteem, though this impression is partly undermined by the white man's standing position, which suggests some degree of dominance. In the aggregate, the seated black man seems conceptually aligned with Smith himself, the aspiring cobbler poet, an identification that is strengthened by the epigraph from Cowper on the facing page, which begins, 'The Nightingale may claim the topmost bough, / While the poor Grasshopper must chirp below: / Like him, unnotic'd, I, and such as I, / Spread little wings, and rather skip than fly'.

That Smith himself was partly of African descent seems an extraordinary possibility, and one for which there is no material evidence. Yet the main alternative is hardly less extraordinary: that Smith conceived of the status of the labouring-class poet as being so socially and culturally difficult that he would assert an analogy between his situation and the plight of slaves and former slaves. The key to such an identification might be found in his intense self-consciousness about having abandoned his trade and 'proper' station in life. Repeatedly in his poems Smith's real or imagined critics charge him with hubris, idleness, and other subversions of the social order. These concerns are linked to the travails of slaves and former slaves in 'The Effects of Nature and Cultivation Contrasted'; but the key poem in this regard is 'Ye are Idle', based on an episode from the fifth chapter of Exodus in which Pharaoh increases the requisite daily labour of the enslaved Hebrews. Drawing an explicit analogy between the biblical Hebrews and contemporary negro slaves who are accused of laziness, Smith suggests that the tyranny of the masters is manifest as much in their repeated, taunting accusation 'Ye are idle' as it is in the actual physical punishment they inflict on the enslaved. Victimized by this accusation himself—or at least morbidly fearful of it—Smith locates himself in this brotherhood of the oppressed. While he does not claim a comprehensive equivalency between his situation and theirs, it is clear that he feels no unease about drawing the parallel in the first place. I do not know of any assertion of vocational and existential alienation in the labouring-class tradition that is stronger than this one.

A final word should be said regarding Smith's style. Though the poems mentioned above might seem to imply that Smith was a relentlessly serious poet, in fact his verse contains considerable varieties of tone and voice. So, alongside works on the threat of grave-robbing, the beauties of Haddington, the glories of the Creator, and his psycho-vocational struggles, *A Collection of Original Poems* contains a series of comic poems in Scots, written in variations of the 'Standard Habbie' verse form and strongly influenced by Burns. This strain of work is represented here by the vigorous 'Turbot's Head Dissected'. Smith's comic impulse is given extended play in his second and apparently final volume, *The Bachelor's Contest* (1826), most of which is comprised of the title piece, an extended satire comparing the situations of the bachelor and the married man. *The Bachelor's Contest* also contains a few short poems that Smith indicates had been published individually sometime before 1826. We know nothing of Smith after that year, and he is not mentioned in the available histories of Haddington. The Haddington burial register does, however, list a William Smith who died, at age 59, on 11 February 1831.

FURTHER READING

Tim Marshall, *Murdering to Dissect: Grave-robbing, Frankenstein and the anatomy literature* (Manchester: Manchester University Press, 1995)

Ruth Richardson, *Death, Dissection and the Destitute.* 2nd Edn. (Chicago: University of Chicago Press, 2000)

J.G. Wallace-James, 'A Forgotten Haddington Poet', *The Haddingtonshire Advertiser* (4 March 1910).

Verses
Composed on the Disgraceful Traffic at Present Carried on
of
Raising and Selling the Newly Buried Dead

Of all the traffics yet invented
    By monsters, or by men of skill;
Of all the baits by hell presented,
    This appears the foremost still!
This that I'm about to mention;—   5
    I shudder at the very thought!
Such crimes demand a *quick* prevention—
    The dead by living men are bought!
Vile Brutal wretches, basely hired,
    Drag their bodies from the grave;   10
By demons merciless inspired,
    Risk their souls for what they crave!
Love of money—root of evil:
    'Tis this they crave, this their desire;
They rob the grave to please the devil—   15
    Inhuman monsters! hence retire!
Dead to every human feeling:
    Abhorred, detested, is your name:
Enrich yourselves the dead by stealing!—
    They shall perish like your fame.   20
Nothing got by means unlawful,
    Prosper with the gainers shall;
No, not on earth; but still more awful
    When the last trump the dead shall call!
Think, ye monsters! iron-hearted!   25
    If thought your breasts does e'er possess;
Think on the grief for friends departed,
    Felt by survivors, more or less.
Bound by the strongest ties of nature,
    Here they live in mutual love;   30
As in a glass you view each feature,
    So they on earth, till death remove.
Sharers in each other's sorrows,
    Joyful in the day of health,
Elated not with long to-morrows,   35

Craving not unlawful wealth.
With a scanty share contented,
   Of what this world calleth good;
If by grace from sin prevented,
   They fear not for their daily food.   40
By all the ties that are endearing,
   Father, Mother, Husband, Wife,
Son, or Daughter, all are cheering,
   When affection rules their life.
As in life they're undivided,   45
   So at death they still are more;
A better mansion is provided,
   Survivors wait their time to soar.
At the dread summons nature shudders,
   Yet submit the highest must;   50
None can bribe the kind of terrors;
   He is faithful to his trust.
View his tender mother weeping
   For a dear and only son;
View a widow comfort seeking   55
   For her husband lately gone.
No expence by them was spared,
   Their bodies decent to inter;
As they in life each comfort shared,
   More strong at death, we may infer.   60
To the narrow house appointed,
   Silent mourners them attend;
Dust to dust is then consigned,
   Slow and gentle they descend.
Friends and neighbours all attending,   65
   Bid a long and last adieu;
Respected dust is worth defending,
   As well as worth a tear or two.
Yes, it is, and shall be watched,
   Both by true and faithful men;   70
Daring tigers! if ye're catched,
   Justly dread their vengeance then!
How can ye, ye monsters callous!
   Worse than wolves and tigers prove;
Deaf to the widow's moan, alas!   75
   Dare her dead for to remove!
What below her humble ceiling

Has she not already felt?
And will you lacerate her feeling?
   Steal her dead, her eyes will melt.   80
Think, ye monsters! how they're used!
   To pieces by dissection brought!
And, if after, boil'd or burned!
   Who can stand the dreadful thought!
Love of gain's your leading feature,   85
   What can you expect from such?
Price of the dead in human creature!
   This will not avail you much.
Hast thou a neat well furnished dwelling,
   Purchased with the price of dead—   90
By their flesh and bones a-selling?
   Admire with horror and with dread!
The very bread you eat is cursed,
   Between your teeth is human flesh;
Your cash, your clothes, all are infused   95
   With the tincture, 'I'm not fresh'.
Worse than those poor blinded wretches,
   Cannibals by name we call,
Rejoicing over human screeches,
   Slay, and then devour them all!   100
Worse than robbers the most daring,
   With them we may our own part take;
Worse than brutes! your crime is glaring;
   The dead can no resistance make.
Were it so, ye cowardly traitors,   105
   Lurking at the dead of night;
Could the dead lay you in fetters,
   Soon your deeds would come to light,
Were some pale and ghastly figure,
   By permission, you to grip,   110
How soon would then your daring vigour
   Lose its power, and backward slip!
You may on earth thus pass unpunish'd,
   Yet the time may come about;
But then your wicked course is finished,   115
   'Be sure your sins will find you out'.
To suppress these daring robbers,
   Let us join both heart and hand;

Fir'd with the spirit of true brothers,
Soon we'll scatter this vile band.   120

From *A Collection of Original Poems* (1821)

The Mansions of the Dead,
or The Grave Watcher's Soliloquy

Within these lone and sacred walls,
My cheerful lot to watch it falls,
And to protect, my duty calls,
  The mansions of the dead.
The sparkling eye, the rosy cheek,   5
That once bloom'd fair with lustre meek,
Beneath these turfs a shelter seek,
  And find a resting bed.

The honoured father's hoary hairs,
Worn out with toil and worldly cares,   10
To his long home, in peace repairs,
  The mansions of the dead.
The once lov'd wife, and tender child,
Their dear remembrance kind and mild,
That weary hours, and time beguil'd,   15
  Here find a resting bed.

From this repose, no chain can bind,
Though doubled thrice, affection kind:
Yet still there is a hope behind
  The mansions of the dead.   20
No piercing cry Death's ear can reach,
No favour, bribe, nor soothing speech,
This humbling truth, each tomb doth teach,
  None shun this resting bed.

In the cold grave our dust shall rest,   25
The crown'd, the fam'd, the poor opprest,

Then who so bold as to molest
    The mansions of the dead?
The strongest ties by friendship knit,
Refined taste, and polish'd wit,   30
Love strong as death, here must submit;
    This is their resting bed.

Those we in life did value much,
Our love at death, known it is such,
We dare the worthless then to touch   35
    The mansions of the dead.
Tho' strange it is, yet it is true,
That of such wretches there's not few,
That from these graves the dead they drew,
    And rob'd their resting bed.   40

Respected dust! to us so dear,
We mourn thy fate, and drop a tear,
Thee to protect we'll nothing fear
    'Mongst mansions of the dead.
The worm's protectors we are named,   45
By those whose character's defamed.
If they escape, let us be blamed
    If at this resting bed.

Affection strong rewards our pains,
Respect alone to dear remains,   50
We scorn the name of worldly gains
    From mansions of the dead.
The mem'ry of our bosom friend
Calls loud that we assistance lend
From worse than worms to them defend,   55
    And watch their resting bed.

How soon our fate, there's none can tell;
We with our kindred dust shall dwell,
When dull shall sound the passing knell
    To mansions of the dead.   60
One anxious thought does fill each breast,
That here our bones in peace may rest:
Intruders base! we'll do our best
    To guard this resting bed.

Brave Haddington deserves respect,   65
'Twould be to blame, this to neglect,
That brought this plan into effect
  For mansions of the dead.
With pleasure here I frankly own,
The most respected in this town,   70
I've seen forsake their mid-night gown
  To guard this resting bed.

Here one verse more I humbly crave,
(Tho' dull my rhyme) the dead to save;
Let us all seeming dangers brave   75
  For mansions of the dead.
Let not our first, best hopes be lost,
By darksome night, nor nipping frost,
Nor time efface our man-like boast,
  To guard this resting bed.   80

A Call to the Watchmen

Let mirth and folly from this place be banish'd,
 Let no excess with duty interfere,
Let every breast with courage be replenish'd,
 And know, and feel, the cause that brought them here.
As soon as mounted, let the watch go round,   5
 We know not when the artful thief may come;
And let each quarter echo back the sound
 Our footsteps make, as we the Church-yard roam.

Let not this book, this house, these sacred walls,
 Bear some foul mark, to tell we were remiss;   10
Let us each other vie, when duty calls,
 Who shall mount first, and who shall last dismiss,
For why? the time is short and quickly flies,
 That shall us number with the silent dead;
And as the watchman pass, say, 'Here he lies,   15
 That oft with us these sacred haunts did tread.'

Haddington Resolution

Hail, happy town! no task to thee seems hard,
Thy worthy deeds shall meet a due reward;
For if thine arm but only aim the blow,
Confus'd, confounded, falls the daring foe.
Thy noble sons in peace and safety dwell,   5
Born to be free, aspiring to excel,
And to protest unsullied and unstained,
Thy property and rights, by virtue gain'd.

Even where thy dead entomb'd in silence rest,
There, even there, thy sons the foe arrest,   10
And fearless, smiling, matchless courage show,
Nor dread the storm, nor yet deep-drifted snow.
Some people say, and venture to affirm,
That Metal-Safes are both secure and firm;
But Haddington says to her faithful watch,   15
'Go put to silence, or the Ruffians catch.'

The Poet's Plea;
or the Author's Candid Reason for Publishing

Behold yon vessel on the ocean tossed,
By adverse winds and foaming billows crossed,
Her spreading sails in weather fair may serve,
But in a storm they're only a reserve.

Behold the crew, a helpless, hopeless group,   5
Cling to the mast, or tottering deckward stoop;
First this, then that, a grasp at all they make,
Yet nought avails, the whole becomes a wreck.

The last resource, with speed the boats let down,
Yet still rude Boreas, with a vengeful frown   10
And fatal blast, with raging foaming waves,
Upsets the whole, engulphed in wat'ry graves.

All lives are lost, and as they said, they wept!
All might been safe, had they the vessel kept.
What madness this! (exclaim'd the Wise on shore,)   15
To risk the boat! was e'er the like before?

Yes, oft it has; despair and hope between,
Many fair wreck, and frantic trials been;
And many well-meant efforts too have fail'd,
And fortune's blasts o'er fortune's sails prevail'd.   20

And many, too, the world has counted mad,
Who to some honest shift recourse have had,
Unmindful of the struggles Hope has made,
Yet after baffled and unpitied paid.

How many on life's ocean softly slide,   25
Enjoy a calm, and safe at anchor ride,
Whilst others, toss'd and driv'n from place to place,
Steer where they will, the wind blows in their face!

I envy not, O no! the lot of those
Who have the power to ease another's woes,   30
Nor yet do I at my own fate repine,
Nor idly wish to lead a life supine;

But plainly here, to state the reason why
I write to publish, nor give truth the lie;
Nor vainly boast my works such merit claim,   35
To rank 'mong men of worth my humble name.

Few authors write without some end in view,
To clear the old, or bring forth something new,
To virtue guide, or where destroyers go
To strew wild tares, or useful seeds to sow.   40

For place or pension, or for post, some crave,
And some compose, a ruin'd name to save;
Whilst others, scorning fee, such light display
As with bright knowledge gilds the radiant day.

Some scribblers too, their name's my very scorn,   45
Ignobly bred, if not ignobly born,
Who vainly boast their songs do equal Burns:
Stop! froward Muse, my rhyme satiric turns!

Few, few such wits upon the stage have been,
I leave a blank his wit, and worth between;   50
But shall a scribbler mimic wit so rare,
Or with the kernel, once the shell compare?

Let lesser wits on lower boughs stand by,
Nor with cropp'd wings attempt a flight so high;
Few works like theirs enrich the public treasure,   55
And may be valued at the public's pleasure.

Some friends advise me not to write at all,
If right they judge, a waste of time it call;
I differ much, if not to an extreme,
And in my case, sick time improv'd it deem.   60

I freely grant the name of lazy lubber,
To those in health who leave their wonted labour,
And turn rhyme-mad, or borrow prose, and scamper,
To tell their tale, and back and belly pamper.

I never wrote for love of worldly gain,   65
But to beguile a long, long hour of pain;
And if in health a verse I do compose,
Brisk as my awl, my rhyming mem'ry goes.

Nor yet would I in borrow'd feathers shine,
Just like the jack-daw 'mongst the peacocks fine;   70
For, stript of these, my colour would appear,
And my rough caw be noxious to the ear.

If health refuse that hands employment find,
Can reason once object to employ the mind?
Or literature refuse the natural spark,   75
Or greatness scorn the poor yet just remark?

I trust that nothing from my pen shall drop
To truth pervert, or give to vice a prop;
Nor give offence, where none I'm sure's intended:
The cause is bad that cannot be defended.   80

I publish then because I can't do better;
The stone is good that helps to step the water;
And if dependent many may me deem,
Let independence blush to scornful seem.

That I'm affliction's son, those best can tell   85
Who knew me from the first, and still know well;
And if my friends my own word will admit,
These three long years for work I've not been fit.

Yet anxious still, my trade I've carried on,
Whilst many weeks scarce two days' work's been done,   90
And if my friends can my experience judge,
From lingering pain, they'll feel without a grudge.

I'd spill my ink, and cast my pen away,
To find employment in some better way;
Sometimes I dream some patron kind is near,   95
But when I wake, my hope turns frantic fear.

O independence! whither hast thou fled?
Shall I by thee no more be joyful made?
That man who has his health, and work to do,
Can boast thy freedom, and be grateful too.   100

So now my friends, your patronage I crave,
(This I have had before,) my cause to save:
'If I risk the boat', and if it should upset,
There's many wiser shar'd as hard a fate.

The Effects of Nature and Cultivation Contrasted

Fir'd with no ambitious project,
    No sanguine hopes my breast inspire;
Nature's fruits my highest object,
    To dress in Nature's plain attire.

The primrose and the mountain daisy,   5
    Nature's beauties well may boast;
But the rose, transcendant nosegay,
    Compar'd with it their lustre's lost.

Each in their spheres are fair and comely,
    Fulfilling Nature's grand design,   10

The rose is nurs'd, the others homely,
    No cultivation to refine.

Full many spots that lie neglected,
    Nature decks with nicest plan;
While many others high respected,   15
    Greatly owe their taste to man.

Leave them but only for a little,
    Let their roots grow rank with weeds;
Then say, ye florists, say how brittle,
    Are your choicest flowers and seeds.   20

With all your care to nurse and foster,
    Oft your choicest roots misgive;
Nature says, Stop, vain imposter,
    I cease to aid, roots cease to live.

View yon meadow, oxen grazing,   25
    Cows and sheep at pasture free,
Round its borders, 'tis amazing,
    Richly deck'd with flow'rs you see.

Although by many not respected,
    Many do admire them much;   30
What wonders Nature hath effected,
    Nature's lovers tell can such.

Delicious fruits and fragrant flowers,
    Spring from Nature's fost'ring hand,
Health to the sick, refreshing showers: 35
    Be grateful, man, and shout, O land!

The great, the gay, for pleasure ramble,
    Who daily taste juice from the vine,
If in their way lies a ripe bramble,
    They eat its fruit, and call it fine.   40

From Nature what hath science learned?
    Let literati answer make;
The finer arts, and all concerned,
    From Nature views and landscapes take.

Literature to Nature joined,   45
    Happy pair when well improved,

Rough Nature shines best when refined,
 And oft she weeps 'cause they're remov'd.

Concealed beneath yon humble ceiling,
 Where learning's mystic streams ne'er flow'd,   50
There lives a wight, oppress'd with feeling,
 To tell what Nature hath bestow'd.

Full of thought, and deep reflection,
 Yet how to utter cannot find,
Want of lear brings pale dejection,   55
 And racks his full expressive mind.

High as heaven's orbs resplendent,
 Elevation lifts his soul;
Low as hell where demons pendent,
 Roams his mind without controul.   60

Afric's coast, the seat of slavery,
 Cannot bound his feeling heart;
Gains got by oppressive knavery,
 Oft a source of grief impart.

Love to the human race unbounded,   65
 Colour, whether black or white;
On solid principles well founded,
 Feels love flow, and drops his mite.

From Nature's produce often gleaning
 Blades of grass, or grains of sand,   70
Nought to him seems void of meaning,
 That's in the sea or on the land.

The work of grace, all works surpassing,
 Wonderful! to glory join'd,
This theme his inmost thoughts compassing,   75
 Leaves all other themes behind.

Whether virtue, grace, or Nature,
 High his thoughts and bosom swell,
Conformity in every feature;
 And fain their sweets would others tell.   80

But yet alas! tho' full intended,
 What he feels to write, dispute;

For want of words his hopes suspended,
   The want of school keeps Nature mute.

And so it should without disputing,   85
   Though rich the soil, it culture wants,
Literature without refuting,
   Graces Nature's richest plants.

Yet literature in all its glory
   Cannot gain the wish'd for mark,   90
Those heads can best confirm my story
   Who want intrinsic Nature's spark.

Learning's fruits are more delicious,
   Yet a surfeit proves a snare;
Nature's fruits are oft pernicious,   95
   If not selected with great care.

May science, art, and Nature flourish,
   Useful knowledge all their theme;
Let learning Nature's weakness nourish
   By every well-concerted scheme.   100

Let us, whilst on life's ocean ploughing
   Or traversing solid land,
Whether we be reaping, sowing,
   Own the God of Nature's hand.

The Country Wright;
or the Sameness of Genius

A country wright, of genius bright,
Thought in the world appear he might;
Or at the least, just by the bye,
Resolved his utmost skill to try.

To work he goes, concerts his plan,   5
But first resolves to tell no man;

And if it chanc'd to raise his fame,
None but himself the praise should claim.

He ne'er had seen, nor heard it said,
Bed castors were in use, or made;   10
Yet these it seems he had in view,
And hop'd to furnish something new.

He at the first made progress fast;
Too hasty steps stop short at last;
So he with all his skill and notion,   15
Fell short to give his castor motion.

Or make it wheel about at pleasure:
His study fail'd, and so did leisure;
So finding all his efforts vain,
He dropt the point he could not gain.   20

Yet, counting on the time he'd lost,
And how much study it had cost,
Blasted hopes, and unpaid labour,
Submits at last to tell a neighbour.

So to an artist eminent,   25
That lived in town, one day he went,
And shew'd to him his new production,
The same to finish, begg'd instruction.

The artist look'd, and smiling said,
Though you're an honour to your trade,   30
This is not new what you produce,
For castors have been years in use.

The wright, amaz'd at this disaster,
Soft in his pocket slips his castor;
Soon as convenient bade good day,   35
And, disappointed, sneak'd away.

So like wright mayn't authors too
Produce a work, and call it new,
Yet their ideas, words and logic,
Be deemed a borrow'd, same thing subject.   40

And, like him too, may ne'er have seen,
Nor heard it said such works have been,

Which tends to prove, although with lameness,
Likeness of genius, and the sameness.

Yet he that borrows from a neighbour,   45
Does justice when he owns the favour;
If word or sentence merit claim,
Place underneath the author's name.

From *A Summer Evening Walk Improved*

[The Author overhears his neighbours]

The older people at their doors,
Open their budgets of news stores;
Some put their neighbour's wrongs to right,
But keep their own quite out of sight.

Some are of a more gen'rous cast,   5
Place their faults first, their neighbour's last;
As could I but my failings see,
But his appears so plain to me.

To hear their strange disputes, debates,
The first inquires, the second hates,   10
The third approves, and strongly pleads,
His neighbour's wounded cause that bleeds.

'What think ye, nei'bour, o' the times,
Whan common fo'k are makin' r'ymes,
And printin' bukes like men o' lear,   15
I think wi' some far less might sair?'

And sae do I, but what'le ye say,
There's mony ae scheme now a-day;
There's unco little doin' at hame,
Or lazy turn'd, and say they're lame.   20

Or henna health, and mony a thing,
To screen themsel's on bo'rd they bring,

And scour the country far and near,
Their bukes to sell and gather gear.

I's no be sae ill-tongu'd as some,   25
Wha say they lie, o'er far they come,
Nae dou't they'll gang as near's they can,
But tell a lie, it's awfu', man.

But tell us, you that has some skill,
What think ye o' our nei'bour Will,   30
And his braw poem, Man's fa' and a';
He's gaen far round our backs to claw.

And sic ado about the bairns,
Better he'd mind his own concerns;
If samples ay are like the stocks,   35
His weans will be like ither fo'ks'.

Out spoke a third, heard all that past:
'Neighbours, I think, ye're rather fast,
I've read Will's poem frae en' to en',
And think it just, as far's I ken.   40

As for his bairns, or for his sel',
He's mak's no brag, the truth to tell;
He shortly tells your state and mine,
At present day, and auld lang syne.

I wiss his little buke great speed,   45
There's few will dou't that he has need
That it may sell; an ailin' man,
Wi sic a group, needs parritche pan.

I dinna think his health weel bodes,
Though some do say they ken nae odds;   50
Nae dou't to bed he's no confin'd,
Yet gaen trouble's lang unkind.

What pleasure to a man o' health,
For to impose and live by stealth;
Nae man possest o' sense or mense,   55
Wad slur his name wi' this pretence.

Sae far as through it I can see,
He means his buke to usefu' be;

He neither brags, nor vainly says,
That it deserves the sma'est praise.   60

Maist men like him, o' lear' but scant,
Their r'ymes to grace feel much the want;
Without a patron, or a frien',
Their verse looks blunt, by poortith mean.

The mean that we Reviewers ca',   65
Of them nae notice tak' at a';
And darin' critics like themsel',
Pick aften holes whare claith is hale.'

From *The House of Mourning*

[The Mourner tells his story]

'When first in freedom's lap my head was laid,
And from one bondage scarce escape had made,
Then Cupid with his dart my heart did wound,
And in love's fetters strongly I was bound.
The object of my choice to me appeared,   5
By Beauty nurs'd, and by true Virtue reared,
Her graceful mien, likewise her modest look,
My bosom warm'd, and youthful fancy took.

My gentle scruples she would oft reprove
My ardent passion and my too fond love;   10
Yet nothing seem'd a barrier in my way,
Love urg'd the conflict, and love won the day.
What fancy whisper'd when I first her loved,
Now by experience, thrice the bliss has proved,
The joy, the comfort, and the prop of life,   15
The tender mother, and the loving wife.

We little had, but fortune's wheel did kick,
And like the crows we gather'd stick by stick;
By dint of labour we increas'd our store,
Content with little and o'erjoy'd with more.   20

Time wing'd its flight, in peace our lot was cast,
Enjoy'd the present and review'd the past;
For future comforts hop'd beyond the skies,
And daily offer'd grateful sacrifice.

Scarce had twelve months fulfill'd their wonted round,   25
Than I myself a happy father found,
With joy beheld a living child and mother,
And prais'd the kindness of their elder Brother.
Each other year a smiling child was given,
Till time increas'd our number unto seven;   30
Whilst health, content, and labour, want remov'd,
And groundless fears for future days reprov'd.

Strife was a stranger, nor gave way to sorrow,
If pinch'd to day, we hop'd for more tomorrow;
And if we could not boast of money saved,   35
One comfort had, we were but seldom craved.
Thus pass'd the sunshine of our early days,
With scarce a cloud to intercept its rays,
To wealth unknown, nor obligation's debtor,
Close lock'd in friendship's and in love's blest fetter.   40

But ah! my friend, those happy days are fled,
And dire disease a woful change has made;
For one whole year scarce hath one smile been seen,
But sickness pale where cheerful health had been.
Three of my children, blooming fresh and fair,   45
Have victims fall'n to death and to despair;
Two in one grave in silent sorrow laid,
Which on my mind a deep impression made!

I own'd the rod, yet felt the stripes severe,
Yet sharper still remains for me to bear,   50
The partner of my grief, my hope, and stay,
Six weeks has linger'd in a faint decay.
No hope remains, life seems to ebb apace;
This is a trying and a hopeless case:
With her I hop'd for to surmount my woes,   55
With her to live, with her my life to close.

For her, could I a healing cordial find,
To ease her trouble, and relieve my mind,
I'd happy be; ah! must I here complain?

Support that's needful I cannot obtain.   60
On former days my earnings well supplied
The day's demands, and craving want defied:
The day of health requires but common cheer,
But ah! a sick bed', here he dropt a tear.

'I never knew to cringe, nor bounty crave,   65
Yet know not how my present case to brave;
But shall I fret, whose sorrows are but new,
Receive the good and not the evil too.'
Here utterance fail'd, the Mourner heav'd a sigh,
I felt its force, in silence made reply;   70
I left the Mourner here and bade adieu,
And said, this is the House of Mourning true.

As homewards thus I thoughtful did return,
And sigh'd the cause that made this suff'rer mourn,
A living contrast full appear'd in view,   75
Bold, insolent, yet crav'd the Mourner's due:
A sturdy beggar, with a heavy load
Of alms procured, came briskly on the road;
He crav'd my mite, the same I did refuse,
For which the pauper did me hard abuse.   80

With oaths and wishes, horrid in their kind,
He curs'd my narrow and contracted mind;
And with a daring look of discontent
Revengeful mutt'ring on his way he went.
The bashful Mourner modestly conceals   85
The anguish he in mind and body feels,
And if one effort, or one hope remain,
Pinch'd Independence blushes to complain.

Ye are Idle—Exod. v.17

Harsh the sound the Hebrews heard,
By oppressors hard prepared,
'Ye are idle', pull away,

There's no straw for you to-day.
Yet your task you must fulfil,   5
Get you straw just where you will;
Nought from your works shall you diminish,
Still your tale of bricks shall finish.

'Haste ye', why, as heretofore,
Bring ye not your daily score?   10
Do your work, your wonted task,
Nor for straw presume to ask.
So it is with many such,
Who oppress inferiors much,
Neither means nor health consult,   15
'Ye are idle's' the result.

He is lazy, is the cry,
If not work, why, let him die;
Nought from me shall he receive,
He is lazy, I believe.   20
Harsh to him appears this sound
That's in servile fetters bound,
And to him that's ailing too,
Nor his wonted task can do.

Thus felt a poor Negro slave,   25
Tott'ring on the very grave;
Whilst well favour'd he appear'd,
Yet disease a bulwark rear'd.
Long made he a heavy moan,
Yet to pity there was none;   30
This his master oft would say,
'Ye are idle', pull away.

With a friend he went one day,
His poor slaves for to survey;
Found this poor man faint and slow,   35
Dragging out a life of woe.
Says the friend, 'were this man mine,
I'd to work his heart incline—
I would cure him of his sloth—
He is lazy', said they both.   40

His master, then, unfeeling wretch!
Did his cruel arm outstretch;

And as he lash'd, was heard to say,
'Ye are idle', pull away.
Thus they left their victim faint: 45
Reader, can you anguish paint?
With his stripes he breath'd his last.
And by death forgot the past.

Shall not He, that pray'r regards,
Give oppressors their rewards?   50
Shall not words and actions too
Bring their users justice due?
Yet for all that I have said,
I have no impression made;
Still, methinks, I hear you say,   55
'Ye are idle', pull away!

The Turbot's Head Dissected

Ye wha are vers'd in politics,
An' ken the quirks o' faction's tricks,
An' aiblins hae come through the pricks
        O' bribery,
Your sage advice I kindly crave,   5
Experience best the dupe can save,
Wha to his frien' turns out a knave,
        Base glibery.

I'm fear'd that I'm catch'd in a snare,
An' gin it's sae, O neibours spare,   10
An' o' sic bribes let a' tak' care,
        An' turn wi' speed.
O' gi'en o' bribes there is a knack,
An' some at takin' them no slack,
Yet after a' can turn their back   15
        In time o' need.

There's some, they say, tak' bribes aff hand,
Yet some mair dou'tfu' mak' a stand,

An' sell their cow, or piece o' land,
      At sic a price;   20
An' some afore their mark they'll miss,
Allow their wife to sell a kiss;
Syne in her cheek Squire slips the bliss,
      Some guineas nice.

An' some get posts, and some get pensions,   25
An' bribes there are of a' dimensions;
Some for a gutsfu' sell their conscience,
      Ah! needfu' tool:
We hang an' head a' wha are traitors,
An' punish ither depredators;   30
An shamefac'd sits a' fornicators,
      On cutty stool.

But what's for them that trust betrays?
Or what's for those the bribe that pays?
A' honest men in fury says,   35
      Gae hang an' burn 'em.
Fo'k aye shou'd speak just as they think,
Nor promise first, syne sneer an' wink,
An' whan they're wanted rin and jink,
      Rin shame an' turn 'em.   40

But least that I your patience tire,
Or blaw the spark into a fire,
Or drive the swine back to the mire
      In dirt to wallow,
I'll tell you now, an' that wi' speed,   45
A story 'bout a Turbot head;
I'm fond o' fish, but aye takes heed
      Nae banes to swallow.

The ither day, wha wad hae thought it?
A Turbot head, a callan brought it,   50
An' says, 'For you John B----------n bought it,
      An' sent me wi't.'
Says I, 'My man, ye're surely wrang,
Is Johnny aff or on the fang?'
'Atween the twa, an' by my sang
      He bade me gie't;   55

'The Nor'-East Port, an' up a stair,
An' to Will Smith ye'll gie't wi' care;
It's just for you, so say nae mair,
   But just e'en tak' it.'
Says I, 'My man, gin ye're mista'en,   60
Ye'll ken whare to come for't again,
The law ca's gifts as free's fok's ain,
   Sae I'se no break it.'

Some hours ran roun', nae word about it;
That it was mine I didna dou't it,   65
'Twas cheap enough nane can dispute it,
   A dainty lump.
Jean made it clean, an' had it cloven,
Syne sent it to Rob M-------y's oven,
An' weel had Rob the birkie stoven,   70
   The skin was crump.

Ye needna dou't we had a mess,
An' gin it relish'd ye may guess,
For ilka bane o't, mair an' less,
   Was just like marrow;   75
The weans gat a' the banes to pick,
An' clean baith dish an' banes did lick,
Scarce what was left, though on a stick,
   Wad feed a sparrow.

Now, Johnny lad, the head's disseckit,   80
And a' the brains o't weel inspeckit;
But yet there's ae thing I've negleckit,
   To thank ye for't;
Thanks t'ye, than, that's easy said,
Ware ither debts as easy paid   85
Ane might hae soon a fortune made,
   Or live but short.

To mak' amends, my honest Johnny,
I tak' a smoke, as sae does mony,
Your penny worth's as guide as ony,   90
   An' sometimes better:
Sae at your shop ye shall me see,
Ane at the least may gratefu' be,

Although I'm sure ye want nae fee
  For sic a matter.   95

Whan till a feast a chiel's invitit,
An' by anither kindly treatit,
An' gets his skin wi' whisky heatit,
  What ca' ye that?
I ca't a bribe, tho' in disguise,   100
An' under thum' a favour lies,
An' Faction frae her curtain cries
  Put on your hat.

I dinna mean a strife to breed,
But may not Johnny, gin he need,   105
Say, Willie, mind the torbit head,
  Or some sic story?
This is the snare that I sae dread,
An gin I'm wrang, advise wi' speed;
Ye wha hae never sham'd the breed 110
  O' turn-coat glory.

Shou'd Johnny turn out politician,
Instead o' 'bacco, pipes, an' saishin',
Wha' kens but he may me petition
  Just for my vote;   115
What cou'd I say? but I'm your debtor,
But aiblins ye may ken some better,
Ye wha can boldly scorn the fetter,
  AN HONEST SCOT.

JOHN SHAW (*fl.* 1824–1836)

Virtually everything we know about John Shaw derives from the preface to his only full-length volume, *Woolton Green* (1825), where he sketches his struggles to find a fit profession. Having first been a farmer in 'stubborn and unprofitable soil' (p. ix), he was 'At fifteen [...] transplanted to more polished society'—possibly as a domestic servant, though he is silent as to details. Whatever the experience, it convinced him 'what a weed I was', and after his employer became 'unfortunate', he again looked elsewhere. After a brief period as a seaman, Shaw unexpectedly found work and success as an actor, and he claims to have gained 'the warm plaudits of a generous Public'. (The title page of the volume describes him as 'Late of the Theatres Royal, York, Hull, Newcastle-upon-Tyne, &c'.) Praising 'that much neglected profession', he describes his fellow actors as 'a generous, open-hearted crew—willing to share their last six-pence, with a brother in distress! and to them I owe the little talent I possess, for I there found that information, and instruction, my soul so much thirsted after!' (p. x). Regardless of these successes, Shaw eventually left the theatre for a new enterprise, which, though unnamed, was evidently the operation of a small brewery.

Of his sentimental title poem, Shaw remarks, 'I am not ashamed of acknowledging [writing] it cost me more tears than any other Author I ever read, except Bloomfield, and that divine Poet has, with skilful hand, touched the master-chords of the human heart! whoever reads that Child of Nature, without being affected, may have other amiable qualities to recommend him in society, but I envy no one of his acquaintance'(p. xii). It is true enough that the rural-domestic setting and general stylistic contours of 'Woolton Green' are reminiscent of Bloomfield, but the overall effect of its long, maudlin narrative is one of tedium. Several other poems, like 'The Selling of Grayface, An Old Favorite Cow', indulge in a similar pathos, something like a poetic equivalent of the genre paintings of Shaw's contemporary, William Collins. But Shaw's work is not limited to sentimental nostalgia: he is also by turns introspective, comic, angry, and partisan, and the selections printed here reflect this variety of moods. In 'The Bard's Plaint', with its ambivalent account of filial affection and alienation, we find surprising echoes of John Clare (q.v.), while 'To My Mare Gip' leavens its sentimentality with humour.

More humorous—and more partisan—is Shaw's paean to the Tory minister and longtime Liverpool M.P. George Canning, whom Shaw in the volume's dedication calls 'the ablest representative, the steadiest advocate, and the truest friend that Liverpool ever had, or perhaps ever will have'. In his 'Lucubratory Lines' to Canning, Shaw denounces William Cobbett, Henry Hunt, and other radical reformers with vitriol and real playfulness, as when the rustic brewer advises Thomas Wooler, editor of the radical journal *Black Dwarf*: 'I'm but a bumpkin, and 'tis fit thou know it, / A sort of driveling, whining, small beer poet, / Who tells thee as a friend, thy Dwarf's not read, / The Whigs are turn'd—the Radicals are dead' (ll. 105–8).

Liverpool, as a city and a collection of personalities, is an abiding subject for Shaw. Indeed he could be said to conceive of himself primarily as a local poet, though he does not comment upon that most highly charged and repercussive of local issues, the central role that Liverpool had played in the Atlantic slave trade. (Canning had been an abolitionist, despite his party affiliation.) Shaw's sprightly chattiness regarding local gossip and the city's political imbroglios tantalizes and frustrates historical reading; in two poems not included here, the breezy 'Liverpool Laureate' and the darkly comic 'Poor Jem's Lament for the Loss of his Dog Quhay', Shaw's rapid-fire references to the city's governance, bureaucracy, and geography resist satisfying explication. In light of this topicality and the dearth of information on Shaw himself, the list of further reading below is directed towards historical context.

FURTHER READING

John Belchem, *'Orator' Hunt: Henry Hunt and English Working-Class Radicalism* (Oxford: Clarendon Press, 1985)

Tim Burke, '"Humanity is Now the Pop'lar Cry": Labouring-Class Poets and the Liverpool Slave Trade, 1787–1789', *The Eighteenth Century: Theory and Interpretation* 42 (2001), 245–63

Wendy Hinde, *George Canning* (New York: St. Martin's, 1973)

C. R. Johnson, *Provincial Poetry 1789–1839: British Verse Printed in the Provinces: The Romantic Background* (London: Jed Press, 1992), 816–18

Michael Scrivener, *Poetry and Reform: Periodical Verse from the English Democratic Press, 1792–1824* (Detroit: Wayne State University Press, 1992)

John Strachan, 'Poetry of the Anti-Jacobin', *A Companion to Romanticism*, ed. Duncan Wu (Oxford: Blackwell, 1998), pp. 191–8.

From *Woolton Green* (1825)

To My Mare Gip

'Tis not that horse by Homer sung,
Which from the streaming blood had sprung,
That blood which Perseus caus'd to flow—
Medusa's head receiv'd the blow,
The purple stream from earth it springs,   5
And soars aloft—a horse with wings—
'Tis nam'd, or nick-nam'd Pegasus,
And gallops through the brain of us,
That claims alliance with the Muses,
Who, oft, alas! their aid refuses!   10
Then restive Pegasus gets master,
The poet's dubb'd—'The poetaster'.
Nor is't that horse (that's told to us)
Th' Athenians call'd Bucephalus,
Which Alexander rode and had,   15
Till pride and glory drove him mad!

Nor yet that lean and high-bon'd beast
By Quixotte rode—though last, not least
Of knight-errants, who fought and bled!
For lovely woman 'twas he shed   20
That vital stream—till grown scanty,
Left him as lean as Rosinante.
I love the objects that he fought for,
And nought's so worthy to be sought for:
But still his plan seems heterogeneal,   25
My own to me, seems more congenial,
To love the darlings, take their part,
But still at home to keep your heart,
This observation's only carry'd
To those, who, like myself, are marry'd.   30

There is a horse, (I'd near forgot)
That carry'd Syntax—'twas his lot,
Ere that adventurer made a stir,
To carry Brass, the Trumpeter.
But that is not the horse I mean   35

To make the subject of this theme,
And lest you think I act unfair,
My horse, I'll tell you, is a mare!
And as she's gray, you'll say, of course,
'The gray mare is the better horse',   40
When you shall hear this story's sequel,
For my eyes never saw her equal.
She's Gipsy call'd, (although of late,
We're oft oblig'd t' abbreviate,)
And if the tongue don't make a slip,   45
She gets no more of name, than—GIP.

A milkman call'd her his erewhile,
He kept her in the roughest style;
She never fail'd to do his bidding,
At night, she slept upon his midding: 50
A curry-comb, or whisp of straw,
Her speckl'd carcase never saw:
The only good he did for thee,
Was when he sold thee unto me.
Thou well deserv'st the home thou'st got,   55
For thine was sure a bitter lot,
To serve a man who work'd thee hard,
Who neither whip, or whip-cord spar'd,
And when, alas! thou didst thy best,
No food was thine, nor proper rest.   60

Come, prick thy ears, and lash thy tail:
If this, thy home, should ever fail,
Thy lot may be to serve again,
Some more of flinty-natur'd men:
But whilst I live, 'tis my behest,   65
That thou shouldst stay at Throstle-Nest.
The brick that forms my brewery wall,
The stable that contains thy stall,
The mortar, slate, and timber, too,
It was thyself alone, that drew,   70
Then surely it were hard, if thou,
Shouldst have to seek a master now.
Thou never shalt whilst I'm alive!
If it's reserved for me to thrive,
Thou ne'er shalt want a stall, my mare!   75

Come, prick thy ears, and lash thy tail,
This home, I trust, will never fail.

Thou'st all the tail that nature gave,
And thou shalt wear it to the grave,
'Tis cruel man that cuts the rump,   80
And leaves the beast a nine-inch stump;
If I'd my will, and nature's shears,
He'd walk around without his ears!
Presumptuous fool! and worse than Turk,
Who thinks he'll mend great nature's work,   85
Disgraces manhood to the grave—
He takes, what e'en the Turk would leave.

Short'ning rumps was first invented
By farriers, who, not contented
With curing evils incidental;   90
To make these sores are instrumental,
In order to enhance their bills,
By searing-iron, knife, and pills;
They've never had one inch of thine,
Nor any other horse of mine,   95
Nor ever shall, whilst I am able
To rear a colt within my stable:
Though some, I do regret to say,
Past through my hands, bred far away,
With scarce more tail than Shanter's Meg,   100
When past the 'Key-stane o' the brig',
When 'Cutty Sark', that Highland strump,
Bore all away, except the rump;
'Tis gone! 'tis gone! away Meg flies,—
No weapon's left to scare the flies!   105
Beneath their sting, she now must groan,
For all—except the stump, is gone.

I've heard a fox, (they're cunning devils)
That had befall'n the worst of evils:
He was entrapp'd, did much bewail,   110
And paid a ransom with his tail!
He careless, met his old acquaintance,
Said, 'A tail was quite a nuisance,
In town he'd been, and all the fashion
Was stumps, and tails were out of fashion.'   115

But Reynard met with scorn and laughter,
And never herded with them after.

And horses, were it left to them,
(Instead of knives, and cruel men,)
Would wear their tails, as nature gave them,   120
And kick the hounds that dar'd to shave them;
Come, lash thy tail, and set thy head,
If such a humble bard gets read,
As he who now thy praise indites,
Thou wilt be known, when he who writes   125
Is moulder'd into dust again,
Nought left of what now guides the pen,
When all those steeds by poets fam'd,
Which far exceed all I have nam'd,
Shall dwell upon the classic's lip,   130
Perhaps he'll find a place for Gip,
A humble steed that fill'd a dray
Of his, who wrote this humbler lay.

Thou'st shafted many a load of malt,
And never yet was seen at fault: 135
For when the word to thee was given,
The load must come, or stones were riven
From out the rooted pavement strong;
I've seen thy belly stretch'd along
The causeway, blazing still the while,—   140
Thou never flinch'dst, though 'twere a mile.
And though so well thou draw'st my malt,
Thou know'st, old Gip, thou hast a fault.
The other day, thou took the road,
Contemptuous of a lightish load,   145
A horse that travell'd on before,
Too slow for thee, which made thee sore,
Thou bolted by, upon the gallop,
Which made my empty barrels fly up;
The noise thou madest, 'twas plain to see,   150
Made him to gallop fast as thee,—
You had not gallop'd far, before
You met a justice—and what's more,
A certain clerk, with courts connected,
And in a fine were both detected;   155

'Twas fair that thou shouldst pay thy part,
Thou shouldst pay both, with all my heart,
If thou hadst money of thy own,
For he no galloping had shown,
But quietly pursued his way,   160
And would have walk'd the summer's day,
But thou for galloping was willing,
And got him fin'd full fifteen shilling;
Thy driver, Harry, paid the same,
And, though innocent, bore the blame.   165
I can reproach with other matter,
Thou'rt not esteem'd so good a backer,
Thou'lt forward pull, as I have told,
At backing thou art rather cold,
And that's a fault, Gip, now-a-days,—   170
Backers are useful many ways!
E'en prize-fighters are little thought,
Unless they're back'd, and science-taught,—
They're 'Fancy' call'd, in prose and rhyme,
It may be so,—they're none of mine.   175

When two or three months bills get out,
Drawn on whom?—you ask about
Th' accepter, drawer, have their station,
Both are rogues, in coalition;
You find out one! he's call'd Delirious;   180
The other's worse,—he's Facinereous;
Tis now for backers that you look!
If they stand good, the bill is took,
Good backers, Gip, have now no equal,
As I will prove thee, in the sequel.   185
Delirious never meets the bill,
And Facinereous never will;
A refluent course it now must take,
And each endorser now does quake:
For if a post he lets pass by,   190
The game is up!—'tis all my eye!

To seek the drawer, or his matus,
He might as well seek ignis fatuus;
The account from off his book may wipe,
And with the bill may light his pipe,—   195
Pity, that trade should be thus curs'd,

'Twas only fit for that at first!
O! that men, in this emporium,
Would use such bills, to light stramonium,
And smoke it in their cheerful pipes,   200
And hang the rogues that fly such kites;
Old Gip, thou'st not this sin to answer,
Though in thy day thou'st been a prancer;
Thou'st drawn me hops and malt in plenty;
Thou'st drawn what drowns the poor man's ills,   205
But none can say, thou drew bad bills.
Thy driver, in his cups, one night,
Was bragging of thy pow'r and might,
A curious wag, not wanting sense,
Said, 'thou could'st not draw an inference',   210
This imputation rous'd his blood,
He jump'd, and swore out-right, thou could,
He'd risk his wages, that thou'd won,
If th' inference wasn't 'bove four ton.

I've told thy faults—thy virtues, too!   215
And as no price will part us two:
If I should live to see thee dead,
Within my land thou'st lay thy head—
The hungry dog may stand aloof;
Thy flesh shall never feel his tooth,   220
Thy mottl'd hide shall ne'er be stripp'd,
Or, may I through the world be whipp'd:
Nor from thy hoof blacksmith pilfer
One nail, or shoe, although 'twere silver,
But shoes and hide shall with thee lay,   225
And some few tears will wet thy clay,
For thou'rt a favorite with my wife,
And (those, who, dear to me as life)
My prattlers—see them round thee skip,
And clap thy sides, and call thee Gip,   230
And though with lusty load thou'rt tir'd,
Thou seem'st quite pleas'd to be admir'd,
And if the maid neglect her trust,
For Gip, the rogues will steal a crust;
And should they round thy grave assemble,   235
Their tears will flow, they'll not dissemble,
Their little hearts will swell with sorrow,

They'll say, 'we'st have no Gip, to-morrow.'
Should I, before them, Gip, be call'd,
Thou'lt follow me, and be empall'd,   240
And if my wardrobe, boots don't lack,
Thou'lt bear them slung across thy back!
Perhaps thou'lt feel thou know'st my end,
Perhaps thou'lt feel thou'st lost a friend,
But should things prosper well at home,   245
To find a friend thou need'st not roam,
My son still lives—the lad's my own!

The Bard's Plaint

I'm the exile of hope and of home,
I'm a stranger to all that is dear,
I languish for days that may come,
Alas! will they never appear!
No menial that eats of my bread,   5
But is happy, far happier than I,
The pillow that's prest by this head,
Absorbs what will flow from the eye.

When I visit the bower I love,
My babes, as they stretch out their arms,   10
With smiles, their affection to prove,
Reproach me, for leaving such charms!
Ah! little they know what I feel,
When I kiss them, and bid them 'good bye',
And out of their presence I steal,   15
Lest the tear-drop should flow from their eye.
When they miss me, and cry out their dole,
Can a father's fond bosom withstand?
No:—it penetrates deep to my soul,
And with terms I am quickly unmann'd!   20
Is it wise to return and to soothe?
Ah! no: 'twill but add to their grief!

Fresh tears in their eyes will but prove
'Tis my presence alone gives relief.

Then why should I add to distress,   25
By repeating their sorrows again?
Had my lambkins but clung to me less,
I had left them the happiest of men;
But their cries still remain on my mind,
And their tear-drops are froze at my heart,   30
It reproaches a father unkind,
From such innocent love thus to part.

I'm a stranger to them and my love,
I am strange to the bow'r I have made,
E'en my dog will fidelity prove,   35
By growling, and bark at my shade!
Ah! when will those moments arrive,
That will make the sweet bower my home?
To attain that dear object I strive,
Yet I fear that it will never come!   40
For my days have both blossom'd and bloom'd,
And scatter'd their leaves in the wind!
Their fragrance the desert perfum'd,
But their fruit I never could yet find;
The yellow leaf waves o'er my brow,   45
And reveals to me wisdom and truth!
Green foliage! ah, where are thou now?
Thou perish'd unknown, in my youth!

Obscurity shelter'd the plant,
And the barren rock canker'd its root: 50
It the moisture of science did want,
And the winter's blast blighted the fruit!
Too late was it brought to the sun,
Too early its barrenness found—
The praise that its fruit might have won,   55
Has perish'd, and sunk to the ground.

In its youth, had some fostering hand,
With kindness, remov'd from the wild,
It had not encumber'd the land,
But repaid the soft hand that had toil'd!—   60
Tis past—the sweet moment has flown,

Its branch is with barrenness riven,
Its numbers on earth are unknown,
But its strain shall re-echo in heaven.
My true love, ah! little she dreams, 65
How seldom this trunk has to bloom,
Though florid and healthy it seems,
There's decline that she'll find out too soon,
For the axe now is laid to the root,
And will prove at its core there's decay! 70
The pleasure in absence she took,
Will be sorrow, when I'm in the clay!

Then she'll mourn over moments that's fled,
She'll regret the sweet hours that were lost!
In absence they past o'er her head, 75
And her sighs, and her tears are the cost;
My sweet bow'r, will it bloom as before?
Shall its beauty a stranger's eye see?
Shall its sweetness my Betsey deplore?
Alas! it has ne'er bloom'd for me. 80

But in absence and exile I mourn,
Till thy voice it grows strange to mine ear,
And the smiles of the infant thou'st borne,
Is wasted on forms that's less dear!
Do I tax thee with scorn or neglect? 85
O! perish the thought, evermore!
For thy heart, should the skillful dissect,
Would find me engrav'd on its core!
Thou'st been tender and loving to me,
And without thee, my soul would expire! 90
And the world were its grave, but for thee!
Thou'rt its God!—its Promethean fire!
Is it sin thus to love and adore!
Is it madness, to cherish the flame?
If it be—I have much to deplore, 95
For I still must adore thee the same.

I have much in myself, love, to mourn,
But I ne'er was inconstant to thee;
With patience, my temper thou'st borne,
The reflection is hateful to me! 100
Had I lov'd thee with ardour less pure,

Hadst thou known the true source of thy woe,
Thy heart had prescrib'd its own cure,
And thy tears they had ceas'd for to flow.

Though my temper's the ocean's wild surf,   105
Still my heart's like the Halcyon wave—
One will rage till I'm cover'd with turf,
One will love till I'm cold in the grave!
I've a smile for the cheerful and gay,
I've a tear for the sorrow not mine!   110
That bosom, where love hath full sway,
I will cherish, and pledge in my wine.
I covet nor riches nor fame,
I envy not Croesus his wealth,
Let dishonour, my mind never stain,   115
I'm in poverty bless'd, if I've health;
O'er my tomb let my friends heave the sigh,
Let them say, 'He's in memory, dear',
'Tis the heart I would touch, not the eye!
I ask not, I crave not the tear.   120

Will those joys, alas! never be mine?
To inhale the sweet breeze of the eve,
To partake of those blessings divine,
Which, possessing, I shortly must leave;
Will my bow'r never own me its lord?   125
Shall I visit,—as stranger, or guest?
I'm estrang'd from the form that's ador'd,—
Had I these, I'd be happy and blest.

I love to arise with the sun,
And to brush the fresh dew of the morn;   130
I could toil till his splendour is done,
And my music should flow from the thorn.
Be my mirror, thou pure glassy stream;
Be my altar, thou shady sweet grove;
If delusion like this, be a dream,   135
I'd ne'er wake, 'tis the dream that I love.
I'm the exile of hope and of home,
I'm a stranger to all that is dear,
I languish for days that may come,
Alas! will they never appear?   140
No menial that eats of my bread,

But is happy, far happier than I,
The pillow that's prest by this head,
Absorbs what will flow from the eye.

Lucubratory Lines,
Addressed to the Portrait of
The Rt. Hon. George Canning,
Which hangs over the Author's Mantle Piece

Hail to thee, CANNING, England's truest friend!
Puissant Minister, whose powers shall lend
To thy contemporaries, wit and skill,
To make their subjects boast—their Sovereign's will.
No turgid line of verse shall fill my lays,   5
For tumid numbers ne'er could sound thy praise,
Thy matchless praise! thy policy profound!
As dew spreads farther nearest the ground,
So will thy virtues spread if unconfin'd,
By metric cannons, and by strains refin'd—   10
Therefore, my Lucubrations shall be plain—
Thy praise, their glory—and its truth, their fame!
Thy sapience, honor, and thy private worth,
Some abler pen than mine should blazon forth;
But, as it is, they all decried thy name,   15
Thy clustering honors and thy rising fame,
And now, (apostate like) they blush for shame.

Thy 'Lisbon Job'—'twas thus the cant began,
Stamp'd thee a knave, and supercilious man;
And when thou dids't preside at th' 'Board Controul',   20
They spatter'd thee with lies and filth most foul—
The Spa Field rabble, worse than volcanic scum,
Their leader, one whom honest men would shun,
Bore in the air great Faction's charioteer,
His waving flags proclaim 'there's nothing to fear',   25
In cap of liberty his lies he tells:

(I would that to his cap he'd added bells)
'The nation's ruin'd—sunk beyond relief,
And every minister's a rogue and thief—
Look to your interest, then—the bank we'll seize—   30
The spoil that's left is ours—do as you please—
A Government Provisional shall be form'd:
The Bank once ours—the Tower easily storm'd—
We'll live and thrive when Parliament's reform'd.
Fear not the consequences—I have men   35
Respectable and honest, who will, when
Time shall serve, strip the Ministers their coats,
Shall send them packing, or shall cut their throats—
Watson, Waddington, Thistlewood, are all
Men that can nobly dare, or bravely fall,   40
Their truth and honor, none of you can doubt,
You'll know them better when you've found them out—
And then for active ministers, I've men,
Can wield their swords as easy as their pen,
For Generalissimo, we've Major Cartwright,   45
And Cobbett, Financier, will keep us all right;
Wooler shall lay his Black Dwarfs aside,
The Premier he shall be, he's proved and tried—
With men like these, your days will pass away,
And as for taxes—you'll have none to pay.'   50

This was the cant that fill'd the rabble's ears—
The slave yet lives that spread those idle fears,
That utter'd libels 'gainst thy hallow'd name,
And waddl'd in his filth, like ducks in rain—
I'll recommend a restrospective glance,   55
To these said Radicals, and trust to chance
Whether it mends them, or reforms their course—
One consolation's left—they can't be worse.

Hunt dated England's ruin 'one little year',
As time roll'd on it still was drawing near,   60
But when he lost his parli'ment'ry seat,
He spurious coffee made, from England's wheat,
And call'd them 'Breakfast Powders, pure and wholesome',
I drank them once—they made me sick and dolesome,
Perhaps my stomach had not been prepar'd   65
With Spa Field's tonics which the rest had shar'd—

He's chang'd his course I hear—his brain's been tacking,
Instead of stoving corn, he now boils blacking.
He now opposes Turner, Day and Martin,
And Warren wonders what he'll next be starting,   70
'Tis fitting he that nation now should polish,
Whose laws and sacred rights he'd fain demolish,
Tried to disturb the peaceful and the free—
Farewell, dear Hunt, I've had enough of thee!

Hail, Corporal Cobbett, with thy Register,   75
By bullying, here thou thought'st to make a stir,
But when thy stern pugnacity fell through,
Thy Trans-Atlantic trip thou thought'st would do,
That land thou hads't so lauded 'Great and Free',
Would not be dup'd or humbugg'd long by thee,   80
So back thou turn'dst thy course, for England roams,
And didst import to us great Tom Payne's bones—
Grand patriot, who to favor this emporium,
Has rifled Hell, and plunder'd Pandemonium.
Pity that Lucifer had spar'd such cargo,   85
What not on both have laid a strict embargo?
But had thy prophecy been put in force,
Thou here hads't had a frizzling of course,
For with thy tongue and pen thou spokest out bold,
'If e'er the Bank of England paid in gold,   90
In Smithfield they might quickly get a fire on,
And frizzle Cobbett on a huge grid-iron.'
The time is come, the grid-iron must defeat thee,
And Radicals, in wrath, they swear they'll eat thee!
They'll send about the country various messengers,   95
And keep the fire up with thy factious Registers.

Wooler, thy Dwarf is blacker than thyself—
They lay at large, unread, on every shelf—
Take to thy types, thy cases and thy press,
Reform thy morbid stuff, and publish less—   100
Let the last Dwarf, that ever sees the light,
Review my volume, and what's wrong set right,
Say what thou lik'st I glory in a rumpus,
I'll meet thee, Dwarf, at any point o' th' compass—
I'm but a bumpkin, and 'tis fit thou know it,   105
A sort of driveling, whining, small beer poet,
Who tells thee as a friend, thy Dwarf's not read,

The Whigs are turn'd—the Radicals are dead,
Smile, smile! great Minister, the work is thine—
Thy power to party thou dids't ne'er confine,   110
But Catholic, Churchman, Tory, Whig, Dissenter,
Thou heardst them all, and serv'dst them at a venture
Thou thus disarm'dst their malice, wonst their hearts—
We've not a Radical in all these parts,
Each to a man will toast the Constitution,   115
Will damn the Radicals and Revolution—
E'en Colonel Starvegut, Little Woolton's dread,
Seeks refuge for his basilistian head,
Forbears to teaze the Mercury with letters,
Learns to be humble, and respect his betters,   120
Devotes his services among his neighbours,
Their fines remunerate his ardent labours,
Instead of preaching politics profound,
His farming yard he's made the parish pound;
Instead of charging foes, this man of metal   125
Levys contributions on the cattle
Which stray along the lane without a guard,
The fines he levys are his sweet reward.
When cattle see him now, they'll fly like Tartars,
Which gives him leisure to attend the carters;   130
Blame not his taste, or blush, or frown, or scoff it,
He makes their fines produce an equal profit,
He's much belov'd—his neighbours are so civil,
They think no sin to wish him at the devil.

Some time ago, I think 'twas in September,   135
He offer'd to become a county member,
The country round was all in arms to send him,
With ev'ry pow'r and influence they could lend him,
Swore they'd return him, or they'd never rest—
This feeling breath'd and glow'd in ev'ry breast,   140
I thought it paradoxical and strange,
Or 'mongst his neighbours there was wrought a change,
And ask'd a man more eager than the rest,
'Why all this ardour?' when he thus confess'd:
We, therefore, wish him up in Parli'ment,   145
Our reasons for it, sir, are plain and clear,
When he's in Parli'ment, he'll not be here!'

This said, with loud huzza he join'd the throng,
And Colonel Starvegut dwelt on ev'ry tongue.

He searches Pedlars for their hawking license—   150
The females say, of honor he's a nice sense,
For when to filiate brats it is their lot,
He claims the time, the place, and how begot;
E'en plural lovers add not to their sins,
He'll summon both, for fear she should have twins—   155
To Publicans he proves a sore tormentor,
He'll list to Scandal's vile and base inventor:
One case remains still freshly on my mind,
'Twill show in Honor's cause he's just and kind:—
A road-side house an aged couple kept,   160
Their ale was good, their hearth was neatly swept;
They toil'd to rear their children, various ways,
And here in peace they hop'd to end their days;
Their boys were growing up and gone to trade,
They'd but one daughter—she, a lovely maid,   165
Kept clean the house and waited on each guest—
Her parents saw her charms, and felt most blest
To see their girl, without a blot or stain,
Supply each want—the village rang her fame.
One day, a blackguard blacksmith enter'd, drunk,   170
For fraud or dissipation, none was sunk
So deep, so infamous—the country knew
His fraud and knavery, and his friends were few;
Thus, drunk and money-less, he ask'd for drink—
It was refus'd, as any one may think,   175
He tried to gain his point by threats of force,
By oaths, abuse, and most obscene discourse;
The old man, lame, and tottering under years,
Could not endure to have his daughter's ears
Polluted by such language as he us'd,   180
Himself insulted, and his wife abus'd,
The old man's blood, it rush'd into his veins,
He makes an effort, and his right maintains;
To see his house from such a ruffian freed,
They struggle hard,—at length he did succeed   185
To push the ruffian from his peaceful door,
Then sank exhausted—strength could yield no more!
The trap was set, the bait it had been taken,

He goes to Colonel Starvegut,—peace was shaken!
He was the justice, he must judge the case;   190
Now, on the road, he'd much abus'd his face,
And said Old Richard thus had us'd him ill,
'Twas all believ'd, and Starvegut took his fill
Of vengeance—for he had the nicest sense
Of granting *justice!*—hearing no defence!   195
He stopp'd the licence, and he stopp'd their trade—
(Thank God, there now a better law is made,
No justice can, without good reasons giving,
Withold a licence, and deprive our living.)

Here is a guardian of our country's rights,   200
Its favors, with ingratitude requites!
He prates to Canning, with his vile effront'ry,
Who is himself the pest and scourge o' th' country!
Thou askst Reform, too,—thou! thou silly elf,
Learn to be honest, and reform thyself!   205
Thou'lt be respected then, where now, thou'rt hated,
As sure as this is truth, which I've related!
I've much more matter, be it understood,
Which ne'er shall see the light, if thou'lt be good.
O! George, thy ministry's put all to rights!   210
Thy speaking portrait now my eye delights!
'Tis treasur'd by me, dearly as my kin—
We'll never part, (I'd think it were a sin)
Whilst I've a house or room to hang it in,
But with thy friends, I'll laugh, I'll drink, I'll sing,   215
Toast George, our Minister—and George, our King!

Extemporary Epitaph
for the
Unfortunate Mr. Sadler

Who was killed from his Balloon, in endeavouring to descend near Black-
burn, by striking against a chimney, on the 29th of September, 1824; he had

made a grand ascent from Bolton, being his thirty-first aerial voyage. The weather was too boisterous—but he had such an aversion to the disappointing a public assemblage, that he could not be dissuaded from making the attempt;—he was a worthy character—the Author knew him well, and did not recover the shock his feelings sustained, at hearing of his unfortunate catastrophe, for many days. He has left one child, and an amiable wife far advanced in pregnancy, to lament his loss.

> Farewell! dear Youth! thou'st made thy last ascent!
> Thy mind, for loftier realms, display'd its bent;
> Thy spirit's purified, thy fault's forgiven,
> Thy soul's inflated with the dew of heav'n;
> Angels and Archangels welcome thee above,   5
> A Saviour crowns thee with celestial love,
> Bids thee rejoice, nor e'er regret the change,
> That gives thee through the realms of bliss to range
> With Saints and Blessed Spirits—joy is thine,
> And earthly friends are all that's left to pine,   10
> To weep thy sad disaster, mourn thy fate—
> Regret thy daring heart—alas, too late;—
> Thy Weeping Consort, and thy Sireless Babe,
> Are left to mourn that such machine was made—
> And one, just asking of its mother birth,   15
> Shall weep to learn, 'A parent's left the earth.'
> They well may weep thy loss, thou best of men—
> They'll soar to thee—thou'lt ne'er descend to them.

JAMES BIRD (1788–1839)

A failed miller turned bookseller and the father of sixteen children, James Bird was one of the more accomplished labouring-class writers of the Romantic period, publishing eight volumes of verse and two dramas over the last twenty years of his life. Bird was brought up in Earl Stonham, near Stowmarket in Suffolk, where his father was a farmer. He was educated at two local schools before being apprenticed to a miller, and finally went into the business himself. After several years of difficulty, however, most notably at a mill in the town of Yoxford, he abandoned the trade under a substantial burden of debt. He was married in 1816 to Emma Hardacre, whose father was a bookseller in Hadleigh, another Suffolk village, and it was almost certainly through this family connection that he was able to acquire his own bookselling concern in Yoxford about 1820.

Though Bird had begun composing poetry in his early years, none of his material was brought before the public until Thomas Harral, editor of the *Suffolk Chronicle* and subsequently his intimate friend, was shown Bird's narrative poem *The Vale of Slaughden* (1819) and helped arrange for its publication. Harral later said that Bird's poems 'may without impropriety be termed historical novels, or historical pictures in verse; embracing plot, character, and incident', and his summary of *The Vale of Slaughden* offers a snapshot of a typical Bird poetic narrative: 'The historical incidents [...] arise out of the Danish invasions with which England was harassed in the reign of Alfred; but the leading interest is found in a domestic tale of the loves of Edwin and Gonilda, interwoven with these incidents' (p. xiii). The majority of Bird's succeeding works, including *Machin, or the Discovery of Madeira* (1821), *Dunwich, a Tale of the Splendid City* (1828), and *Framlingham, a Narrative of the Castle* (1831) reveal a continuing interest in historical romance and epic.

There is, however, another significant strain in Bird's work, one that may be of more interest to the modern reader: *ottava rima* satires and social observations in the manner of Byron. Bird's *Poetical Memoirs* (1823) adopts the Byronic form of *Don Juan* for a leisurely telling of his life story—so leisurely, in fact, that the poem's two cantos do not bring us anywhere near to the period of Bird's public career. Even so, Bird is quite successful in exploiting the knowing, mock humility of the Byronic voice to comment on his own status: 'What! write my Life?—my Life!—and can this be / From such a Bard—a modest Bard—like me?', he asks with exaggerated horror. 'And no Apology?—no Preface here? / No page inscribed to Commoner, or Peer?' (ll. 1–2, 4–5). This opening announcement signals in clear terms Bird's awareness of the conventions governing the presentation of labouring-class poetry, and our understanding of his place within the tradition must take into account the fact that he was—in relative terms—a learned, successful, and worldly figure, one who had not internalized a view of himself as a groveling literary pretender or bounder. Indeed, Bird seems to have known that, however circumstances may have contributed to his popularity, he was a highly competent poetic craftsman, well schooled in the traditions of English poetry. The many reviews of his work tended to affirm such a view; even as important early accounts focused on his humble beginnings (Nathan Drake's discussion in *Winter Nights,* 1820, compared him to Robert Bloomfield) later reviews dwelt increasingly on his literary talents.

Bird also used *ottava rima* in his 'Metropolitan Sketches', a vigorous series of occasional poems included in the 1837 volume, *Francis Abbott, the Recluse of Niagara.* Though frequently humorous and digressive, these poems have definite thematic continuities. Everywhere Bird looks in London, he sees evidence of money, or its lack—of the things it can, and cannot, do. He is attracted to institutions like the Corn Exchange and the Excise Office where money changes hands, or, as with the Royal Academy, where it exists in a tangled relationship to beauty and art. Even as the poems reveal Bird's fascination with institutional traditions and practices, they are also openly skeptical of entrenched interests, and the Byronic form seems to encourage Bird's natural iconoclasm and independence. His paean to Thomas Guy and Guy's Hospital, for example, turns with such gusto into a satire of medical 'professionalism' that Guy's good works are almost totally forgotten. Bird's political commentary is similarly independent. While his early poem 'The White Hat' (1819)—a reference to the familiar attire of the agitator Henry Hunt—satirized the radical reform movement, his poems refer more frequently to the evils of greed and acquisitiveness. And while he repeatedly condemns excessive taxation, it is perhaps most accurate to say that it is partisanship itself that Bird most rues.

FURTHER READING

Aldine Magazine of Biography, Bibliography, Criticism, and the Arts (June 1839)

DNB

Nathan Drake, *Winter Nights; or Fire-side lucubrations,* Vol. 2 (London: Longman, 1820), pp. 184–244

Thomas Harral, *Selections from the Poems of the late James Bird; with a brief memoir of his life* (London: Simpkin, Marshall, 1840).

From *Poetical Memoirs; The Exile, a Tale* (1823)

Poetical Memoirs
Introduction

What! write my Life?—my Life!—and can this be
From such a Bard—a modest Bard—like me?
To write, regardless of the wreaths of fame,
MY OWN MEMOIRS, and print them with my *Name!*
And no Apology?—no Preface here?   5
No page inscribed to Commoner, or Peer?
'Tis even so!—Ye critics! spare your Rods;
Ye more than Men—ye less than Demi-gods!
On your goose-quills the public feeling rides,
Ye Thunderbolts—ye cruel Vaticides!   10
I own your power, I know ye are the Lords
Of Poets, armed with Tomohawks and Swords,
With which—O, barbarous!—ye, furious, fall
On rhyming heads—may Heaven forgive ye all!
Well—if ye flog me—when your rage is o'er,   15
I'll kiss the Rod, and write—two Cantos more!

                                        APRIL, 1823

Poetical Memoirs
[From *Canto First*]

I

My own Memoirs!—a most egregious theme!
    I wonder how I came to think of this,
Perhaps no more than a delirious dream,

With much of sorrow, and with some of bliss;
So, gentle Reader! sure thou wilt not deem   5
    The Bard presumptuous!—Did not Jacques the Swiss
Write his 'CONFESSIONS'—Did not Bishop Burnet
Write his 'OWN TIMES'—and so, if I can turn it

               II
To my advantage, surely there's no sin
    In penning this, MY HISTORY?—Now I,   10
A rambling, rhyming egotist, begin
    To sketch the Poet, or to paint the fly,
Which long hath fluttered 'mid the ceaseless din
    Of busy mortals! Fiction! now good bye!
And Truth! thy faultless mirror here display,   15
To shew my Muse thy image in her lay.

             III
Some Poets write long PREFACES, to keep
    Their anxious readers from their melting story,
Till, o'er the INTRODUCTION fast asleep,
    They quite forget the Muse, her shame, or glory;   20
Some cautious Poets to their subject creep
    Like bloated leeches, when their mouths are gory!
Feeling their way, like some dull Lexicographer;—
It is not thus with me—my own Biographer!

             IV
Born in a dear, delightful, rustic spot,   25
    'Mid nature's sweetest, though secluded bowers,
I drew my first breath in no lowly cot;
    My 'father's hall', though destitute of towers,
Rose high o'er stately oaks, and hill, and grot,
    And rich domains, and verdant meads, and flowers,   30
To Heaven aspiring, in its 'pride of place':
But *now,* 'tis changed—and there remains no trace

             V
Of flowery paths, o'er which my childhood strayed
    In joy, unmindful of the ills of life;
The lordly oaks low with the earth are laid;   35
    The woodman's prowess, and the axe's strife,
Have robbed the hill, the vale, the lawn, the glade,

And desolation and decay are rife;
All, all are changed—and I am changing now,
For care hath stamped her signet on my brow!   40

VI

How changed!—how fallen!—since that happy time,
   When care, nor grief, nor feat, was aught to me!
Ere my heart fixed on love—my head on rhyme—
   When fondly nursed upon my Mother's knee,
Unchanged by sorrow, and unstained by crime,   45
   I learned to lisp 'THE LITTLE BUSY BEE';
Oh! then each flower of life could yield me honey!
But since, I've wanted joy—and hope—and money!

VII

'*Money's the root of every evil*—sure!
   If so, I almost wish I were a sinner!   50
The poison that will kill, will sometimes cure—
   If money sells our peace, it buys our dinner;
Oh! gold will oft the hungry Bard allure,
   And make him sing as sweetly as Corinna!
As to myself—the fact is not atrocious—   55
I never wear my purse *pecuniosus*!

VIII

Thou potent, magic, bright, accursed gold!
   Whom the world worships!—At thy splendid shrine
Man's virtue, honour, conscience—all are sold!
   The monarch's love, the peasant's prayer, is thine,   60
Thou lead'st astray the timid and the bold,
   All, all are groveling at thy dirty mine,
Thou glittering master-key of hearts!—Thy sway
Rules universal like the God of day!

IX

I've heard our neighbours say, that, when a boy,   65
   My hair was flaxen, and my face was pale,
Expressing more of thoughtfulness than joy,
   And, like a fragile lily of the vale,
Which ruffling storm and tempest may destroy,
   Which e'en must bend beneath the gentlest gale,   70

I grew but weakly; now, my riper years
Have brought more strength—more sorrows—and more fears!

X

My Father sent me to the village school,
    But there, I fancy, that I did not shine, or,
At least, not love to sit and plod by rule—   75
    And I was self-opinioned, though a minor.
In early life we often play the fool,
    As Morland did, when over-powered with wine; or
Mad Napoleon, when he marched to Russia;
Or Voltaire, when he robbed the King of Prussia!   80

XI

Our village 'TUTOR' was a long, thin man;
    He wore a pig-tail—tails are out of fashion—
He taught his pupils on a novel plan,
    To raise up virtue, and to keep down passion;
His greatest fault, at least I thought so then,   85
    Was, that he sometimes laid the birch too rash on,
Long did I bear the memorials of his rage,
Stripes!—stripes!—the wages of my pupilage!

XII

The lily's hue soon left me, and the sun
    Embrowned my face, whose masculine contour   90
Began to say—'dame nature's work is done';
    In sooth, methought I was a boy no more,
And deemed my *own* importance just begun;
    And then I felt my young beard o'er and o'er,
And eke my whiskers, and I found the girls   95
Began to gaze upon me—through their curls.

[From *Canto Second*]

VIII

My Father told me that, to pen a Sonnet
    Or so, was well enough; but, if my brain
Spun out long Odes, whate'er I said upon it,
    (He hoped his strictures would not give me pain,)
I tell you boy, said he, the more you con it,   5
    You'll find but little pleasure, and less gain:
An over dose of verse, quite sets *me* loathing,
And will not bring *you* meat, nor drink, nor clothing!

IX

Now, though my Father was no Poet, still,
    I've often thought he was a Prophet.—Yes!   10
Though long I've laboured on the Phocian hill,
    Long written tinkling verses, numberless—
Led by the fickle Muses at their will,
    Through all the mazes of their wilderness,
And toiled as hard as Pindar, Pope, or Pliny,   15
The cheating jades have never paid one guinea!

X

But when I publish these, 'MY OWN MEMOIRS',
    I think the public, if they do their duty,
To whom I've often tendered my devoirs,
    Will see, at once, their value and their beauty,   20
And buy them rapidly—by tens—by scores—
    Else, from my rhyming cranium to my shoe-tie,
I soon shall be (I could not stoop to beg)
Nudior Ovo—like a Scotsman's leg!

XI

My Father's lecture laid my lyre asleep,   25
    It rested tranquil and unstrung awhile,
And I began to fear that it would keep
    Eternal silence, had not Nancy's smile
Awaked its strings, and made my young heart leap
    Into my mouth, (I then was free from bile)   30
But for this blessed chance, my lyre had slumbered
Till the full portion of my days were numbered!

XII

I first met Nancy by the heaving sea,
   (A very likely place to lose one's heart in)
Where every rolling billow seems to be   35
   A type of our emotion, to take part in
Our passions, foes to our tranquillity,
   While to our souls Love steers without a chart in,
And if he gets moored there, we are not able
To weigh his anchor, or to cut his cable!   40

XIII

I gazed intensely upon Nancy's face;—
   I did not think it quite polite to do it,
But there was so much beauty—so much grace—
   It could not fail to charm a youthful Poet;
Besides, I felt I could not leave the place,   45
   And that my soul clung like a bur-dock to it!
And so I lingered on the spot awhile,
And once, or twice, methought I saw her smile.

XIV

To ascertain this fact, I just glanced under
   Her parasol,—(she held it somewhat slanting)   50
Oh! then I saw more cause for joy and wonder,
   Such sweetly blushing flowers of nature's planting;
I dared not trust my tongue, for that might blunder,
   And she seemed conscious too, that she was granting
An unbecoming favour—so, she tripped off:—   55
I stood—like Cupid, with his two wings clipped off!

From *Francis Abbott, the Recluse of Niagra; Metropolitan Sketches* (1837)

From *Metropolitan Sketches*

The Royal Academy
Somerset House

I

Painters and Poets, 'Tis averred, are brothers—
   This may be true for aught that I can tell;
If so, one would imagine that their mothers
   Had all drunk deeply at the *Phocian* well;
Some have deemed Poets madmen—haply, others   5
   Have thought that Painters ought with these to dwell
In the same bedlam, where their eyes may roll
In a 'fine frenzy', flaming from the soul!

II

When spring comes laughing o'er our bonny land,
   When blithe the thrush sings on the blossomed spray, 10
When the pied meadows and the breezes bland,
   Proclaim aloud the merry month of May,
Haste from the fields, and, in the crowded 'Strand',
   Seek the far-famed 'ACADEMY'—Away!
Leave Nature's smiling scenes, and, as a foil,   15
Behold her *there* blush modestly in oil!

III

How have I longed to see the 'EXHIBITION',
   That pleasing, puzzling paradise of paint!
And, having bought my ticket, *sans* remission,
   I've sprung of the stairs, despite of those who faint— 20
Sundry fair ladies, in a fair condition,
   O'ercome by heat:—and, not without restraint,
Have I squeezed through the *posse*, like a weasel,
To view the magic wonder of the easel!

IV

Well, having gained the first embellished room,   25
    We there may gaze around with wondering eyes,
On fairy scenes, on beauty, and on bloom,
    On light and shade, and all their mysteries,
Wrought from the world of radiance and of gloom,
    Till, to find rest, the wandering vision tries   30
To fix upon some masterpiece of art,
From which the eye feels sorry to depart.

V

Perchance it rests upon some scene by *Hilton*,
    Or leans to *Landseer*'s long-ear'd lively spaniel,
Or *Etty*'s canvas with a touch of *Milton*,   35
    Or huge dead elephant, as drawn by *Daniell*.
Oh! *Constable!*—thy paint looks as though *spilt* on
    Thy rigid canvass, and rubbed down with flannel!
Thou *once* sweet painter of the winding Stour,
What made thee change thy style in evil hour?   40

VI

And thou, great *Pickersgill*, a word with thee—
    Why wilt thou draw the dandies of the age,
Whom 'tis not worth a lobster's claw to see?
    Why dost thou not search History's stirring page,
Or roam the blooming fields of Poesy,   45
    And let her scenes thy master-hand engage;
That hand woos nature—throws new beauties o'er her;
Witness thine own sweet, lovely, chaste *Medora*!

VII

The *truth* is, *Pickersgill*, that thou must sleep,
    And eat, and drink, and wear a decent coat;   50
Thou *must* paint *Portraits*, Sir, if thou wouldst keep
    Thy soul and body on life's sea afloat;
So, ply thy graphic fingers, and soon reap
    A golden harvest from rich folk of note!
Take off their heads to charm all nice beholders;   55
They seldom charm while on the wearer's shoulders!

VIII

Our Painters are as numerous as the things
   That crept, of old, into Noah's spacious ark!
Let critics point their tantalizing stings,
   Or, cur-like, bite at some, at others bark;   60
For me, a *dauber* in the art which brings
   Beauty and light, as 'twere, from chaos dark,
Shall have my sympathy, though one might blush
To see the wild vagaries of his brush!

IX

Enchanting Art!—opposer of stern death!   65
   Time's silent enemy!—the grave's deceiver
Thou keep'st alive our friends, though fled their breath;
   So true thy portrait, that the fond believer
Looks, till he fancies that the earth beneath
   Restores the dead to thee, thou kind retriever!   70
Thy power reclaims the past of life, supplies
What absence steals, and what, without thee, dies!

X

Thou call'st on beauty, and her countless forms,
   Arise, to wait upon thy magic hand;
Beneath thy touch the glowing canvass warms,   75
   And scenes come forth as though from fairy-land;
Or, more sublime, thou wak'st the fiend of storms,
   And the red lightning glares at thy command,
While the deep passions of the human soul
Await thy beck, and move at thy controul!   80

XI

'Tis thine to raise our laughter and our tears,
   Thou canst create anew the vanished scene,
Recall the memory of forgotten years,
   And show us what the state of man has been;
Raise but thy subtle wand, and quick appears   85
   The sterile hill, or smiling valley green:
Enchanting Art! to study thee aright
Attunes the soul to virtue and delight.

The House of Commons

I

Babel! in which there has been much confusion
   Of tongues!—Thee, HOUSE OF COMMONS! I would greet.
Thou great *vox populi!* thou *dear* delusion
   To some who strive to gain in thee a seat!
Thou hive, from which proceeds the full diffusion   5
   Of honied speeches, yet more long than sweet!
Hail to thee, Freedom's hot-bed! England's glory!
Den of grim Radical, sly Whig, bold Tory!

II

How shall I speak of thee, thou strange anomaly!
   Wherein so many jarring minds have met!   10
From Pitt and Fox adown to Peel and Romilly,
   Cobbett and Hume, and Wetherell the pet,
And Dan O'Connell, with his daily homily,
   That made some fall asleep, and others fret!
And many worthies, patriots of their time,   15
A list too long to classify in rhyme.

III

Oft have I sate within the 'Commons' House',
   Yet felt not proud of all I witnessed there—
As rival Statesmen would some cause espouse,
   Members were lolling with a listless air,   20
Or squinting through a glass, to look for *nous*
   And some loud snored behind the Speaker's chair:—
What! *this* a picture of the British Senate?
It *is*—my ink turns scarlet while I pen it!

IV

But *now* we have a 'House' they call—*Reformed*—   25
   I see few symptoms of the reformation;
When last I saw it, a pure Member stormed,
   And stamped, and groaned, because a sinful nation
Presumed to eat when hungry!—to be warmed
   When cold!—and, fevered by his hot oration,   30
He fiercely foamed, and, frantic, fussed and fumed,
Till, at the sight, e'en *Hume* became *unhumed!*

V

House of the People! yet a loftier strain
   Is due to thee for what thou wast, and art;
When Freedom's Sons were hunted to be slain,   35
   When feudal tyranny had thrown her dart,
When serfs stood trembling on the hill and plain,
   Then rose thy power to shield them, and impart
Just rights and equal laws to rich and poor,
To guard the Palace and the Cottage door.   40

VI

Oh! mighty minds within thy walls have shone,
   And streams of eloquence have issued there,
Whose swelling torrents shook the tyrant's throne,
   Laid the deep core of treachery's cold heart bare,
Warmed every breast that was not chilled to stone,   45
   And raised the patriot's soul to nobly dare
To burst oppression's galling yoke, and be
The bold, the brave, the fetterless, the free!

VII

The *Patriot's* meed is fame that never dies,
   He needs no bard to strike the quivering string,   50
To sound his praises to the answering skies;
   His glory, riding on time's ceaseless wing,
Soars far above oblivion's stream, that lies
   Where the dull weeds of life are withering.—
Yes! he, who seeks his country's good, will shine   55
A sun that sets not, dimless, and divine!

VIII

And now, ye Members of the 'House', give ear!
   Tories, and Whigs, and Radicals, and others!
Oh! let it quickly by your 'Acts' appear
   That ye are of the people, and their brothers;   60
Let your free votes for every coming year
   Please England's sons and daughters, sires and mothers:
Annul the taxes, if ye *can*—if not,
Make us contented with our present lot!

IX

What a most potent secret must that be,   65
    To make mankind contented!—He who sought
So many years in doubt, and grief, and glee,
    To find the *Philosophic Stone*, and caught
His death in searching:—he who eagerly
    Seeks for life's *Grand Elixir*, and finds naught   70
But bitter dregs:—Oh! these are not more blind,
Than he who thinks he can content mankind!

X

Good night, good HOUSE OF COMMONS! though thy name
    Is somewhat apt to dwindle into prose;
And thou thy Members, if awake to fame,   75
    Are somewhat apt to make their hearers doze;
Long may we know thee, unassailed by shame,
    Unscathed by foreign or domestic foes,
Still mayst thou guide the vessel of our State,
With LAW her captain, FREEDOM her chief-mate!   80

Guy's Hospital

I

For *once*, a London *Bookseller* be lauded!
    Old THOMAS GUY! immortal be thy name!
Thy soul was full of charity—not sordid—
    Here stands the monument that speaks thy fame;
Long will thy deeds be hallowed and applauded,   5
    Blessed by the sick, the helpless blind, the lame!
For this, thy HOSPITAL imparts relief,
To hearts o'er spent with agony and grief!

II

So, THOMAS GUY! I feel extremely glad
    Thou dids't not marry thy enchanting 'Maid',   10
Who would have been thy Spouse, and, if she had,

This pile had ne'er been founded, I'm afraid!
No! *then* thy children might have plagued their *Dad*,
   And by the time their lengthy bills were paid,
Thy purse, good man, might thus have lost its gilding,   15
And thou hadst lost thy virtuous rage for building!

III

But thou hast built, endowed, and freely brought
   The means to lessen human woe and pain;
Blest be thy spirit for the good it wrought;
   Bright shall thy fame upon the earth remain;   20
He who, in singleness of heart, hath sought
   To lessen woe, has more than earthly gain!
Yes! god-like charity and love will give
That peace, for which 'tis worth a heaven to live!

IV

Alas! old HOSPITAL! in thee are given   25
   Long, lingering lectures on the healing art!
Young hair-brained students in thy walls have striven
   To learn the structure of the human heart;
And, having guessed that vital blood is driven
   Through veins and arteries to every part,   30
They rush into the world, and make a bustle
Of vessel, fibre, membrane, nerve, and muscle!

V

And, oh! to hear them name their nauseous physic!
   Cathartic, sudorific, alterative,
Tonic, expectorant (this cures the phthisic),   35
   Emenagogue, refrigerent, sedative,
Demulcient (given when the patient *is* sick!)
   Astringent, lithontriptic, lubricative,
And more:—to tell you *all*, I must be able
To speak the thousand languages of Babel!   40

VI

And then, to view their odious drugs!—their manna,
   Rhubarb, magnesia, antimonial wine,
Jalap, calumba, ipecacuanha,
   Bark, gentian, calomel, salts, iodine,
Copaida, soda, gamboges, opium, senna,   45

Ammonia, arsenic, colocynth, quinine!
Valerian, aloes,—hold! As I'm a sinner,
Another word of this would spoil my dinner!

VII

What power the young Apothecary gains
    When he has passed the 'Hall'!—Ah! then, indeed,   50
Although he must not knock out people's brains,
    Yet, he may cup, and salivate, and bleed,
And give us drugs till little life remains!
    And, if he kills a few, he does not heed
The case a straw, because his *license* freely   55
Allows the man to slaughter us genteelly!

VIII

Yet thou, famed HOSPITAL of THOMAS GUY!
    We must not part with thee, and not award
The praise thy founder merits.—Bright on high
    He sits enthroned; and many a golden chord   60
Of harps angelic, with their minstrelsy,
    Will tremble softly as they throw abroad,
In tuneful melody, his deathless name—
A sound allied to virtue and to fame!

The Corn Exchange
Mark Lane

I

Mark Lane!—resort of Factors and of Millars!
    Merchants and Bakers, thrifty sons of gain,
Contractors, Farmers, Mealmen, and Distillers;
    Dealers they are, although not *rogues*, in grain:
Here smile hale faces, for your true care-killers   5
    Are they who follow in fair *Ceres'* train;
E'en *here*, though smoke surrounds us, there seems born
A rustic sunshine from the yellow corn!

II

Here stand Flour-Factors, *laughing in their souls*,
 Because, perchance, they've 'caught' the wily Bakers, 10
While *they* are planning how their next new Rolls
 May make more business for the Undertakers!
Astringent alum in its grasp controuls
 The little puffy loaf—the cheerful makers
See round them rise high pyramids of wealth, 15
And gain their bread, while others lose their health.

III

I love to see a *Miller* in MARK LANE!
 To hear him slily ask a Factor's 'price';
And, while he handles the plump rattling grain,
 Declares it *pingled*, only fit for mice! 20
Then will he turn, yet soon *re*-turn again,
 Pronounce it 'dear', yet buy it in a trice;
While, though his honest brow is somewhat lowery,
His eye is sparkling, and his speech is *flowery*!

IV

Did not fair *Ceres* make a slight mistake 25
 When she first patronized a mart like this?
Do they who sell, and buy, and grind, and bake,
 Ne'er vex the goddess when they act amiss?
And does she not, poor *Ceres*, ofttimes quake
 When rapid keels, in mingling discord hiss 30
In ocean's tide? While, on the billows borne,
The very ship-holds groan forth—'*Foreign Corn*'!

V

It comes—is sold, or placed 'in durance vile',
 In bond—while here the farmer's teeming land
Rewards him not for tillage and for toil, 35
 Nor throws its wonted profit in his hand;
He grows dis-spirited, neglects the soil,
 While hapless peasants mournful round him stand,
And, murmuring, feel a strange foreboding dread—
Though corn be cheap they cannot purchase bread! 40

VI

Not that we deem 'cheap bread' an evil.—No!
  But, when through long and heavy-burthened years
A man has tilled the earth, and tilled it too
  And sown in joy—yet often reaped in tears,
With much to bear, and something to forego,   45
  Ere a bright speck upon his fate appears—
Say, is it justice thus, that alien lands
Should snatch the profit from his toiling hands!

VII

Why is earth's produce in Britannia's isle
  Not raised as cheaply as in foreign climes?   50
What cloud has dimmed prosperity's sweet smile?
  Whence gloomed the darkness that enwraps our times?
I dare not hint that Statesmen might beguile
  Wrong by their errors,—ruin by their crimes,—
I tax no mortal—am no vain alarmer,   55
I only guess they've crushed the British Farmer!

VIII

Yet the bold Farmers bear the evil well!—
  I love to see them, and their rosy daughters,
Who, while their fathers of their losses tell,
  Shoot from the eyes a hundred thousand slaughters;   60
Ye rustic swains! how many a country belle
  With her own sweet simplicity has caught us!
When once a youth is *caught*, 'tis vain to strive
To get from love's drag-net again alive!

IX

Sweet is the fragrance of the fertile farm,   65
  When Spring comes sporting in her garb of green,
Oh hill, in vale, in budding woods, a charm
  Is felt in all that there is heard and seen,
And summer glides upon us soft as balm,
  And Autumn marches with her solemn mien,   70
And waving corn-fields bid the heart aspire
To social joys around the Winter fire!

X

MARK LANE!—MARK LANE! farewell to thee and thine!
   Dispense thy favours to the cits of London,
Indeed 'tis true (as is this lay of mine)   75
    That, without thee, the Cockneys might be undone!
Soon might they waste, for wheaten bread repine,
   Hot Rolls! fat Aldermen! there might be none done!
And therefore, all who would not life's thread sever,
Shout long and loud—'Hurrah! MARK LANE for ever'!   80

The Excise Office

I

Just on the spot where this huge building stand,
   The house of Charity was raised of yore
By one benevolent and pious hand,
   To clothe the naked and to feed the poor;
But *now!*—nine (not the tuneful nine) demand   5
   Enormous *duties!* and their cry is 'More'!
'More'!—'More'!—while gathering round them rise
The legal spoils, collected by EXCISE!

II

Strange, that we cannot eat, nor drink, nor sleep,
   Nor ride, nor walk, nor wear a decent dress,   10
Nor do scarce any other thing (but weep)
   Without a *tax* our pleasures to repress;
Things on the earth, and on the billowy deep,
   All are *exciseable*, or more or less,
And spies are sent into our very houses   15
To pry and search, in spite of scolding spouses!

III

Ye women, scrubbing at your frothy tubs!
   How have your stout hearts failed, devoid of hope;
How has the hand, the tender hand that rubs,
   Instinctive grasped and found a lack of *soap!*   20

While ye, like she-bears, growling o'er their cubs,
    Or silent, sulky, like grave owls that mope,
Have, not withstanding that it mars your beauty,
    In secret curst the soap—the suds—the *duty!*

IV

Ye yeoman! ye who love a cheerful glass   25
    Of the old English nut-brown, home-brew'd beer!
When ye would kindly toast some favorite lass,
    How have ye sighed to find the malt so dear!
And, while you let the foaming bumper pass,
    There seemed a kind of night-mare on the cheer,   30
Till, from your hearts ye hoped, like loyal wisemen,
    The *Deil* would fly away with *all* EXCISEMEN!

V

And ye who love the sweet cigar! and all
    Who court the pipe, and whiff the 'Indian weed',
How have ye felt your saddened spirits fall,   35
    Your porous hearts at every short puff bleed,
Your very palates only tasting fall
    In the bland vapour from its parent freed,
Because the tax upon the darling leaf
Abridged your puffs—expensive—burthened—brief!   40

VI

And oh, ye ladies, sippers of Souchong!
    Ye worshippers of tea-urns, hotly hissing,
Ye flirters with 'Young Hyson'! how ye long
    To catch his fragrant breath, and to be kissing
His disembodied spirit!—Then the wrong   45
    Your souls have felt, when these was, haply, missing
The *quantum suff* of your beloved Bohea:—
The *duty* stints your scandal and your tea!

VII

Office! how many searching sons hast thou
    Sent forth amongst us, with their dip-sticks clever?   50
'Tis hard before these prying ones to bow,
    Who hover round us with their books for ever;
And we must beg them to '*permit*' us now
    To add unto our 'stores', or they may sever

The dealer and his wares, and only laugh   55
To think he loses *all*, and they take *half!*

VIII

But there was *one* Exciseman, rest his soul!
   He was the grandest gauger of them all,
And, for his sake, my anger I controul
   Against the brotherhood, both great and small: 60
Yes! for while o'er us countless ages roll,
   Man succeeds man upon our earthly ball,
That with its millions ever-changing turns,
So long will beam the star of bonnie BURNS!

IX

Poor BURNS! he never gauged a butt of wine,   65
   He never placed a dip-stick in the whiskey,
But that he felt a longing to define
   The feelings of a *spirit* wild and frisky,
Nor left it till he felt his legs decline;
   Then, like a frigate in the Bay of Biscay,   70
He rolled, despite of all his neighbours' banter
Most 'glorious', like his own daft *Tam O'Shanter*!

X

One word, huge OFFICE! ere I take my leave:
   May the good time arrive, when thou and thine
Will hold no more dominion to bereave   75
   The folk of brandy, whiskey, rosy wine!
Of tea, tobacco, snuff, for which they grieve!
   Then your *Commissioners*, the noble nine,
May sit and twirl their useless thumbs alone,
Their places, profits, and their *duties* gone!   80

XI

One *final* word to ye, who love too well
   The tempting things now burthened by *Excise*;
Court smiling *Temperance*, and ne'er rebel
   Against your pulses, for it is not wise;
This truth, not we alone, but time will tell,   85
   And snatch, at last, the *blinkers* from your eyes!
Our verse records not *when* this good will be—
'None are so blind as they who will not see'!

THOMAS WILSON (1773–1858)

'Newcastle owes every thing to her coal-mines' (p. v), wrote Thomas Wilson in 1843, and the 'customs and manners' of the miner (or 'pitman') were his main poetic subjects. Raised in the Low Fell area of Gateshead, just south of Newcastle and the river Tyne, Wilson followed his father into the mines, entering as a 'trapper-boy' at the age of eight. The working conditions of boys like him, which initially involved the operation of the underground trap doors, were those of 'the most galling slavery—eighteen or nineteen hours a day, for weeks together […] in almost insupportable drudgery' (p. x). These long hours would be the pitman's lot until the age of twenty, when he would take on the role of 'hewer', 'his drudgery reduced to eight or ten' hours, and he 'got time to look around him in daylight' (p. xi). Wilson, however, had apparently learned to read and write in his early youth, and upon reaching the age of nineteen himself, he left the mines, first taking on the position of schoolmaster in the nearby village of Galloping Green and then working as a clerk for a succession of businesses, finally becoming a partner in the New-castle engineering firm of Losh, Wilson, and Bell. The steady rise of Wilson's fortunes contributed to his belief in the improving power of literacy, espe-cially as it was being encouraged by the Sunday School movement. Looking back to the period of his youth in the middle of the nineteenth century, he wrote, 'The progressive intellectual improvement of all classes of society has had its due effect upon [the pitman]. He is no longer the same ignorant, degraded being that his forefathers were—a victim to the worst prejudices and passions of our nature' (pp. vi-vii). Late in his life, having raised a family and achieved financial prosperity, Wilson was instrumental in building a school, reading room and lecture centre in Low Fell. The building opened in 1841, and was used as the local school until 1878.

Wilson began to write poetry in the 1820s, and his highly topical verse was published in local newspapers and periodicals. His major poem, *The Pit-man's Pay*, first appeared in installments in *Mitchell's Newcastle Magazine* in 1826, 1828, and 1830; it was published *in toto* and with Wilson's corrections to the text in *The Pitman's Pay and Other Poems* (1843). The poem is a kind of miniature epic of pay night at the local pub. Pictures of the work of the mine and the social behaviour of the miners are interwoven with semi-comic narratives of flirtations, wooings, and the vagaries of wedded life. Many of the characters are based on people Wilson had known. Written in three books totaling about 1,700 lines, the poem is too long for reprinting in its entirety, but all of the second book appears here. This section is the most closely focused on the actual work of the mine, and it provides a clear sense of Wilson's style without worrying about the resolution of his narrator's romantic quest (which does, indeed, end happily). Like Wilson's other poems, *The Pitman's Pay* is written in Tyneside dialect, and while dozens of its words and terms are defined below, most using Wilson's own glossary, some interpretive work on the part of the reader is still required. Several of Wilson's copious footnotes have been included as well, both for their information and to provide a sense of how carefully he contextualized the historical and factual aspects of his poetry. Specific events and individuals are the focus of many of the volume's other poems, including 'The Opening of the Newcastle and Carlisle Railway', 'The Oiling of Dicky's Wig', and 'Stanzas on the Intended New Line of Road from Potticar Lane to Leyburn Hole'; space constraints do not allow for the reprinting of these poems here, but a detailed account of the latter work in relation to local history is available online through the Gateshead website listed under 'Further Reading'.

References to the poetry of Robert Burns are scattered throughout Wilson's verse, and the comparison is salutary. Wilson is remarkably successful in evoking the social amiability and joyfulness with which Burns is associated, but underlying his apparently non-judgemental playfulness is an earnest, indeed moralistic streak that is decidedly not reminiscent of Burns. To be sure, this earnestness is most clearly visible in Wilson's 'Preface' (where, for example, he discusses the virtues of savings banks and Methodist chapels), but it is also visible in his 'On Seeing a Mouse Run Across the Road in January', a rewriting of Burns's 'To A Mouse'. Even as Wilson's poem is a spirited homage, it concludes with an advocacy of prudence that illuminates the essential sobriety of his character.

FURTHER READING

DNB

Gentleman's Magazine (1858) part i, 667–9

H. Gustav Klaus, *The Literature of Labour: Two Hundred Years of Working-Class Writing* (Brighton: Harvester Press, 1985), pp. 62–88

Richard Welford, *Men of Mark 'Twixt Tyne and Tweed*. 3 vols. (London: W. Scott, 1895)

Thomas Wilson, *The Pitman's Pay and Other Poems* (Gateshead: William Douglas, 1843). 2nd Edn. (Newcastle upon Tyne: Thomas Fordyce, 1872)

Gateshead Local Studies On-Line: <http://www.gateshead.gov.uk/ls/lowfell/1.htm>

Durham and Tyneside Dialect Group Webpage:
    <http://www.indigogroup.co.uk/durhamdialect/wilson2.html>

From *The Pitman's Pay and Other Poems* (1843)

The Pitman's Pay
Part Second

We'll now return, a peep to take
    At what JOHN BARLEYCORN had done:
Attempt a faint outline to make
    Of all his feats and all his fun.

The remnant left's a motley crew—   5
    The din they make a perfect Babel—
Contending who the most can hew,
    With thump for thump upon the table.

The unsnuff'd lights are now burnt low,
    And dimly in their sockets sweeling;   10
Whilst pots and glasses, at each blow,
    Are quickly off the table reeling.

There's drouthy TOMMY in the nook,
    For suction hard his elbow shaking;
And PHILIP, up from Derwent Crook,   15
    Remarks the very drollest making.

There's DICK that married BARBARA BLAND,
    More famous far for drink than hewing;
And PEEL, as drunk as he can stand,
    Reeling and dancing like a new un.   20

He barely can his balance keep,
    Yet still he's 'Play up, fiddler!' roaring;
But TOMMY having dropt asleep,
    JACK foots away to TOMMY'S snoring.

Some wicked wag his scraper greas'd,   25
    And stole his rosin, (ill betide him!)
But what his arm completely seiz'd,
    Was just the *empty pot* beside him.

Here lay a stool, and *there* a chair,
    With pots o'erturn'd, and glasses broken: 30
Half-chew'd quids strew'd here and there,
    And pipes no longer fit for smoking.

And though the yel's resistless power
    Had silenc'd many a noisy tongue,
Two vet'rans still, 'midst dust and stour,   35
    Conn'd o'er the days when they were young.

Eh, JACK! what years ha'e passed away
    Sin we were trapper-lads tegither!
What endless toil, byeth neet and day,
    Eneugh yen's varry pith te wither.   40

Aw put the bait-poke on at eight,
    Wi' sark and hoggers, like maw brothers;
Maw faither thinkin' aw meet steit
    Ha'e day about alang wi' others.

The neet afore aw went te wark,   45
    A warld o' wonders cross'd maw brain,
Through which they did se skelp and yark,
    As if maw wits had run amain.

Aw thowt the time wad ne'er be gyen,
    That *callin'-course* wad niver come;   50
And when the caller call'd at yen,
    Aw'd getten nowther sleep nor slum.

Aw lap up, nimmel as a flea
    Or lop, amang wor blankets spangin';
And i' the twinklin' of an e'e,   55
    Was fairly ower the bedstock bangin'.

Wor lads, poor things, were not se gleg,
    It tuik some time te fettle them:
Se stiff, they scarce could move a peg,
    And fitter far te stay at hyem.   60

It was, ne doubt, a cooen seet,
    To see them hirplin' cross the floor,
Wi anklets shaw'd, and scather'd feet,
    Wi' salve and ointment plaister'd o'er.

The duds thrawn on, the breakfast tyen,   65
    They're ready for another start,
Te slave for eighteen hours agyen,
    Eneugh to rive atwee the heart.

Wor low rope let, a-field we set,
 The *trappin' trade* quite crouse te lairn; 70
Poor mother, pairtin' wi' her pet,
 Cried, 'Hinnies, mind maw canny bairn'.

'Tis mair than forty years sin syne,
 Yet this upon maw mem'ry hings,
We met awd NELL, and CUDDY's *swine*, 75
 Twee varry far fra sonsy things.

This boded ill tiv iv'ry skin,
 And fix'd us a' like barber's blocks;
Yet faither nobbut brack his shin,
 And lost his bran-new backy-box. 80

The men were puttin' in their picks
 When we gat there; and just about
The time we gat maw faither's six
 Put in, the first were luikin' out.

Aw star'd at iv'ry thing aw saw, 85
 For iv'ry thing was new te me;
And when wor turn te gan belaw
 Was come, aw went on DEDDY's knee.

They popp'd us iv a jiffy down,
 Through smoke, and styth, and swelt'rin' heat; 90
And often spinnin' roun' and roun',
 Just like a geuss upon a speet.

We're gaun te get a geuss te morn,
 There's nowse aw get aw like se weel,
Efter they're grown, wi' stubble corn, 95
 As fat and plump as ony seal.

Aw like her stuff'd wi' onions best,
 And roasted tiv a single roun',
A' nicely scrimpt frae back te breast—
 Not burnt, but beautifully brown. 100

Of a' the kinds o' hollow meats
 That greasy cuicks se oft are speetin',
There's nyen aw tyest that iver beats
 A geuss, the yess o' trumps o' eatin'.

She myecks a real royal dish,   105
    On which a king meet myek a myel:
Aw wadn't for a better wish,
    Were aw te morn a king mysel'.

The oddments, tee, beat boil or fry,
    Provided geussy be a good un—   110
Eat famous in a giblet pie,
    Cribb'd roun' wi' coils o' savoury puddin'.

But stop! where was aw, thinks te, JACK,
    When aw began this wild-geuss chase?
It surely was a good way back: 115
    Let's try te recollect the place.

We'd pass'd the meetin's, aw've ne doubt:
    Indeed, aw think we'd reach'd the bottom,
Efter they'd bumm'd us roun' about,
    For a' the warld like a teetotum.   120

Wor nose within the barn-styen set,
    We stevell'd te the cabin, where
The men and lads their cannels get,
    The seat o' power and pitmen's lare.

The durdum now there's nowse can beat: 125
    'Haud, DICKY, till aw get a chow!'
'Here, aw say, WILLY, gie's a leet!'
    'DICK, damn ye, ha'd aboot a low!'

'Come, hinny, BARTY, len's a hand
    On wi' maw corf!' 'Ye snotty dog,   130
Put in yor tram, and dinnet stand
    There, squeekin' like a half-ring'd hog!'

The lads are huntin' for their trams—
    The hewers for their picks and clay—
The heedsman little DICKY damns   135
    And blasts, for gettin' off the way.

In bye they bumm'd me in a crack,
    And left me i' maw faither's board,
Where he was buffin' at a back
    As hard as whinstone, by the Lord.   140

He bray'd away byeth lang and sair,
    Before the stannin' corf was hew'd:
Was droppin' sweet frae iv'ry hair,
    And hidden iv a reeky cloud.

For what he gat was varry sma',   145
    Frae out the kirvens and the nickens;
The myest of which was left belaw,
    The rest like crums for feedin' chickens.

When DICKY's corf was fill'd wi' sic,
    He let his low, and stuck 't agyend—   150
Ax'd DEDDY te lay down his pick,
    And help him te the heedwis end.

Suin efter he gat crept outbye,
    And me set down ahint maw door,
JOE had the wark a' cut and dry,   155
    And ettled reet for iv'ry hewer.

This was not a'ways eas'ly duin,
    As oft they turn'd out kittle maiters,
Myest like an eclipse o' the muin
    Te wor poor cabin calculators.   160

Aw think aw see poor PETER now
    Bamboozlin' on for hours tegither,
Cursin' a roun' him black and blue,
    And fit te fight wiv ony feather.

There could not be a richer treat   165
    Than seein' PETER at a pinch;
For as he blurr'd his wooden sheet,
    His temper left him inch by inch.

Off went his specks—the sweet ran down
    A fyece wi' botheration curst—   170
His wig gawn like a pointer roun',
    Now quite awry, then backside furst.

The baitin', tee, was deev'lish gallin'—
    Rogues axin' if he'd hev a clerk;
Or in his lug for iver bawlin',   175
    'Man, will ye niver place the wark?'

Aw've seen him i' this muddled mess,
    Click up his chalk and wooden buick,
Hissell, the pictur o' distress,
    Hidden ahint some awd wa' nuik—   180

Where like a cunjurur he'd sit,
    His black airt at some cantrips tryin',
Till he gat iv'ry pairt te fit,
    Then sally forth the dogs defyin'.

The wark now placed, and pit hung on,   185
    The heedsmen, whether duin or nut,
Mun iv'ry man and mother's son
    Lay doon the pick and start te put.

Now then the bitter strife begins,
    All pullin', hawlin', pushin', drivin',   190
'Mang blood and dirt and broken shins,
    The waik uns wi' the strang uns strivin'.

Aw mind a tram byeth waik and slaw,
    Just streen'd te rags te keep her gannin'
Frae hingin'-on till howdy-maw,   195
    Ye hardly knew if gawn or stannin'.

Just pinch'd te deeth, they're tarn and snarly,
    A' yammerin' on frae morn till neet—
JACK off the way, blackgairdin' CHARLEY,
    For at the corf nut lyin' reet.   200

While CHARLEY damns JACK's hoolet e'en,
    His hick'ry fyece and endless growl;
And sweers, if he agyen compleen,
    He'll splet his nell-kneed, wall-eyed soul.

A shower o' coals wi' vengence hurl'd,   205
    Suin rattl'd roun' the lugs o' JACK,
Wi threets he'd te the tother world
    Dispatch him sprawlin' iv a crack.

JACK didn't like the journey then,
    And tried te shun the deedly blast   210
By joukin' down—nor show'd agyen
    His fyece till a' was ower and past.

The bits o' lads are badly us'd—
    The heedsmen often run them blind—
They're kick'd and cuff'd, and beat and bruis'd,   215
    And sometimes drop for want o' wind.

Sic, *then*, was the poor putter's fate,
    Wi' now and then a stannin' fray,
Frae yokens, cawd pies, stowen bait,
    Or cowp'd corves i' the barrow way.   220

Aw tuik for some time day about,
    And when aw wrought, myed fippence sure;
Besides full mony a curse and cloot
    Aw gat for sleepin' at the door.

A better berth turn'd up at last—   225
    Tho wages still but varry sma'—
For sixpence did not seem a vast
    For carryin' LUKEY's aix and saw.

But, then, at half-wark aw was duin,
    And niver hardly gat maw thumps;   230
Yet he was hettle—out o' tuin—
    And often gar'd me stur maw stumps.

Wi' grease-horn ower maw shouthers slung,
    And pockets stuff'd wi' waxy clay,
Wi' half-shoon at may bait-poke hung,   235
    Just fit me for the barrow-way.

Aw neist tuik DUMMY by the lug,
    The putter's purgatory here,
At which they daily toil and tug,
    Blackgairded by some growlin' bear.   240

Whene'er aw DAN THE DEEVIL had—
    Or some sic hell-hound—for a marrow,
Maw life, aw's sure, was full as bad
    As ony tyed's belaw a harrow.

The slav'ry borne by Blackymoors   245
    They've lang been ringin' i' wor ears;
But let them tyek a luik at wors,
    And tell us which the warst appears.

If ony, then, o' Blacky's race
    Ha'e harder cairds than wors te play,   250
Wey, then, poor dogs, ower hard's their case,
    And truth's in what wor preachers say.

Thou knaws for weeks aw've gyen away
    At twee o'clock o' Monday mornin',
And niver seen the leet o' day   255
    Until the Sabbath day's returnin'.

But then, thou knaws, JACK, we are *free*;
    And though we work as nyek'd as them,
We're not sell'd inte slavery,
    Far, far away frae frinds and hyem!   260

Yet was aw at the point o' deein',
    And meet maw life leeve ower agyen,
Aw wadn't, JACK, aw think, be 'greein',
    Unless *this* pairt was out on't tyen.

For what 's in sic a life worth hevin',   265
    Still toilin', moilin', niver duin,
Where the bit good weighs not a shavin',
    The load of bad a thousand ton.

But heavy puttin' 's now forgetten,
    Sic as we had i' former days,   270
Ower holey thill and dyels a' splettin':—
    Trams now a' run on metal ways.

This was the wark for tryin' mettle—
    Here ivry tuil his level fand:
Sic tussels nobbut pluck could settle,   275
    For nowse less could the racket stand.

And had wor bits o' yammerin' yeps,
    That wowl about wor barrow-way,
Te slave and drudge like langsyne cheps,
    They wadn't worsel out a day.   280

God bliss the man wi' peace and plenty,
    That furst invented metal plates!
Draw out his years te five times twenty,
    Then slide him through the heevenly gates.

For if the human frame te spare   285
    Frae toil and pain ayont conceivin',
Ha'e ought te de wi' getting' there,
    Aw think he mun gan strite te heeven.

Aw neist te half a tram was bun,
    But gat a marrow gruff and sour.   290
A heedsman, then, they myed me, suin;
    And efter that, a puttin'-hewer.

Another lang and slavish year
    At last aw fairly struggled through:
Gat fettled up a set o' geer—   295
    Was thowt a man, and bun te hew.

This myed me maister for mysel',
    Wi' shorter wark and better pays;
And at maw awn hand didn't fyel
    Te suin get bits o' canny claes.   300

Here, agyen, had aw'd langsyners
    Mony a weary, warkin' byen,
Now unknawn te coaly-Tyners,
    A' bein' mell-and-wedge wark then.

Aw've bray'd for hours at woody coal,   305
    Wi' airms myest droppin' frae the shouther;
But now they just pop in a hole,
    And flap her doun at yence wi' pouther.

A 'back' or 'knowe' sometimes, 'tis true,
    Set doon maw top wi' ease enough;   310
But oftener far we had te tew
    On wi' a nasty, scabby reuf.

Here's just a swatch of pitmen's life,
    Frae bein' breek'd till fit te marry:
A scene o' ceaseless pain and strife,   315
    Hatch'd by wor deedly foe, AWD HARRY:

For there's ne imp iv a' his hell
    That could sic tortur heve invented:
It mun ha'e been AWD NICKY'S sel—
    He likes te see us se tormented.   320

Then ye that sleep on beds o' doon,
    An' niver JACK THE CALLER dreedin'—
Gan finely clad the hyell year roun',
    And a'ways upon dainties feedin'—

Think on us, hinnies, if ye please,   325
    An it were but te show yor pity:
For a' the toils and tears it gi'es,
    Te warm the shins o' Lunnun city.

The fiery 'blast' cuts short wor lives,
    And steeps wor hyems in deep distress;   330
Myeks widows o' wor canny wives,
    And a' wor bairns leaves faitherless.

The wait'ry 'wyest', mair dreadful still,
    Alive oft barriers huz belaw:
O dear! it myeks yen's blood run chill!   335
    May we sic mis'ry niver knaw!

Te be cut off frae kith and kin,
    The leet o' day te see ne mair,
And left frae help and hope shut in,
    Te pine and parish in despair!   340

If ye could on'y tyek a view,
    And see the sweet frae off us poorin'—
The daily dangers we gan through,
    The daily hardships we're endurin'—

Ye wad send doon, aw ha'e ne doubt,   345
    Some cheps on what they call a 'mission',
Te try if they could ferret out
    Somethin' te better wor condition.

They wad, wi' layin' their brains asteep,
    Suin hit upon some happy scheme,   350
(Which meet be duin, aw think, quite cheap,)
    Te myek us kirve and nick by steam.

Wor factories now gan a' by steamin',
    Steam gars wor boats and packets sail;
And now, they say, they're busy schemin'   355
    Te myek *him* run the Lunnun mail!

How nice and funny it wad be,
    Te sit and see yen's jud myed riddy;
For then we'd ha'e nowt else te de
    But get *his* geer sharp'd at the smiddy.   360

He grunds the corn te myek wor breed,
    He boils wor soup (yence thought a dream):
Begock! aw's often flay'd te deed
    They'll myek us eat and sleep by steam!

A' this *he* diz wi' parfet ease,   365
    (The sting o' gallin' labour pouin'):
Then, hinny maisters, if ye please,
    Just let *him* try his hand at hewin'.

Eh, man! aw's dry: hand here the pot:
    Aw's just wi' talkin' fit te gyzen;   370
Nor will maw tongue move on a jot—
    It's dry wark, varry, moralizin'.

Then reach thy hand, awd honest truth,
    An' let me gied a hearty shakin';
An' may the frindship o' wor youth   375
    Be ne'er in hirplin' age forsaken.

And may the bairns o' byeth wor hyems
    Prove 'honest men and bonny lasses':
The former handin' doon wor nyems,
    As patterns te the workin' classes: 380

The lasses choosin' sober men,
    But seldom seen the worse o' nappy:
Blythe, kind, and good tiv ivry yen,
    And myekin' a' about them happy.

It is nut geer that makes the man,   385
    Nor fine broad claith the cliver fellow:
A fuil's a fuil, however gran'—
    The pouther'd pyte is often shallow.

For happiness is not confin'd
    Te folks in halls or cassels leevin';   390
And if wor lives be good, ye'll mind
    There'll nyen ax how we gat te heeven.

We labour hard te myek ends meet,
    Which baffles oft the gentry's schemin';
And though wor sleep be short, it's sweet,   395
    Whilst they're on bums and bailies dreamin'.

There is a charm aw cannot nyem,
    That's little knawn te quality:
Ye'll find it in the happy hyem
    Of honest-hearted poverty.   400

Yor high-flown cheps oft fyel and brick,
    But we hev a'ways yet been yable
To keep the wheelband i' the nick,
    Though oft wi' but a barish tyeble.

O dear! but they lead wicked lives,   405
    If a' be true that's i' the papers:
Oft kissin' yen another's wives,
    And cuttin' other idle capers.

They run up debts they cannot pay—
    Whiles pay off PAUL wi' robbin' PETER;   410
But, thank God, JACK, there's nyen can say
    We iver wrang'd a leevin' creatur.

Aw dinnet mean te brag o' this—
    It's but the way we a' should treed;
But where the greet se often miss,   415
    We may luick up when we succeed.

For, rather sic disgrace te share,
    An' bring a stain upon wor friends,
We'd work, on breed-an'-waiter fare,
    Till blood drops frae wor finger ends.   420

Besides, when a' is fadin' fast
    That cheer'd the droopin' spirits here—
When we luick backwards at the past,
    Te see how we'll at last appear—

'Twill form a breet and sunny place   425
    On which the mind may rest wi' pleasur;
An' *then* de mair te help wor case,
    Than hoarded heaps o' yearthly treasur.

The Washing-Day

Of a' the plagues a poor man meets,
    Alang life's weary way,
There's nyen amang them a' that beats
    A rainy weshin' day.
And let that day come when it may,   5
    It a'ways is maw care,
Before aw break maw fast, te prey
    It may be fine and fair.
        For it's thump! thump! souse! souse!
            Scrub! scrub away!   10
        There's nowt but glumpin' i' the hoose,
            Upon a weshin' day.

For sud the morn, when SALL torns out,
    Be rainy, dark, or dull,
She cloots the bits o' bairns aboot,   15
    And packs them off te skuil.
In iv'ry day throughout the week,
    The Goodman hez his say,
But this; when if he chance te speak,
    It's 'Get out o' maw way!'   20
        For it's thump, thump, &c.

Her step hez starn defiance in't,
    She luiks a' fire and tow:
A single word, like spark frae flint,
    Wad set her iv a low.   25
The varry claes upon her back,
    Se pinn'd and tuck'd up are,
As if they'd say, te bairns and JACK,
    'Come near me if ye dar'.
        For it's thump, thump, &c.   30

The cat's the pictur o' distress—
    The kittlens dar nut play:
Poor PINCHER niver shows his fyece
    Upon this dreary day.
The burd sits mopin' o' the balk,   35
    Like somethin' iv a flay:
The pig's as hungry as a hawk:

The hens lay all away.
    For it's thump, thump, &c.

The hearth is a' wi' cinders strewn,   40
    The floor wi' durty duds:
The hoose is a' torn'd upside doon
    When SALL is i' the suds.
But when the fray's a' ower and duin,
    And a's hung up te dry,   45
A cup, and blast o' backy, suin
    Blaws a' bad temper by.
        Then the thump! thump! souse! souse!
          Scrub! scrub away!
        Myek no mair glumpin' i' the hoose—   50
         Until neist weshin' day.

On Seeing a Mouse Run Across the Road in January

Stay, little, tim'rous beastie, stay,
Nor bicker wi' sic speed away;
For I, like some relentless fae,
    Seek not thy life,
To scatter want, distress, and wae,   5
    'Mang weans and wife.

At this bleak season o' the year,
When snaws are deep and frost severe,
Does hunger force thee out, to speer
    Thy scanty fare?   10
Or is't the folks at hame to cheer,
    That's now thy care?

It may be in some cosie biel,
They're waitin' for their stinted meal,
Which aiblins ye'll be forced to steal   15
    Frae barn or byre;
And, i' the act, Death's tortures feel,
    Frae cats or wire.

When Farenheit's sixteen degrees
Belaw the point where fluids freeze   20
Ye should na hae sic tow te tease,
    Sae far from hame,
Where may be sits, but ill at ease,
    Your sullen dame.

If sic be your untoward fate,   25
I wot ye'll nae be lag nor blate,
For nature's laws just operate
    On mice like men:
Besides it's now becomin' late—
    The clock's struck ten.   30

Come, then, ye daft and thriftless crew,
And in this mousely mirror, view
Yourselves display'd in colours true,
    With a' your pride:
With boasted human reason, too,   35
    Your steps to guide.

O, man! to many ills a prey—
With tott'ring steps and haffits grey,
To close in want life's chequer'd day,
    Is sad indeed;   40
For age alone soon wears away
    The brittle thread.

Then learn, ere hirplin' age appears,
When friendship oft a cauldness wears,
Which fills the aged een wi' tears,   45
    The heart wi' grief,
To live so, that the closing years
    Mayn't need relief.

JOHN NICHOLSON (1790–1843)

The career of the 'Airedale Poet' John Nicholson follows a proto-romantic narrative encompassing genius, prolixity, addiction, and tragic death. Raised in the then small village of Bingley in West Yorkshire, Nicholson received some education first from a local schoolmaster and broom-maker at Romalds Moor (whose pupils were part of the workforce), and then from Revd. Dr Hartley at Bingley Free Grammar School. Nicholson's father Thomas was a manufacturer of the fine wool fabric worsted, but though Nicholson was trained in the family business, his labouring life was spent in the more basic work of wool sorting and combing. At an early age he developed a passion for poetry and music, evidently to the detriment of other responsibilities. His early biographer and editor John James credits Nicholson's facility on the reed instrument the hautboy with bringing him into contact with his first wife, but also 'sometimes […] into riotous company, and awkward scrapes' (1844, p. viii). James's chronicle emphasizes Nicholson's dramatic swings between sober industriousness and wretched dissolution, as when, upon the death of his wife when he was still only about twenty years old, Nicholson threw himself with fervour into the local Wesleyan society: 'He now became religious even to austerity, and as an earnest of his intention to cast away the vanities of the world, buried on Romalds Moor the hautboy, where it remains' (p. viii). He remarried in 1813 and began a new family.

Nicholson's public literary endeavours began through his association with a theatre company in the local population centre of Bradford, for whom he produced the dramatic poem *The Siege of Bradford*, which in 1821 became his first publication. Shortly thereafter Nicholson made the acquaintance of J. G. Horsfall, a member of an extended Yorkshire family, who was so impressed with Nicholson's ability at impromptu composition that he instantly became his patron. Thence followed the poem that made Nicholson famous, at least locally. 'Airedale in Ancient Times' is a narrative survey of the region that traces the course of the River Aire, beginning with the formidable limestone massif of Goredale Scar in North Yorkshire, and running east and south to Leeds. The full volume *Airedale in Ancient Times* appeared in 1825, but along with this success 'commenced the unfortunate portion of

[Nicholson's] life', since he was induced 'to quit his employment, and roam about the country with the volume, to supply those who had subscribed to it, and to obtain other purchasers' (p. xiv). As Nicholson described this dilemma in the prose account *The Yorkshire Poet's Journey To London* (1828), even as his potential purchasers and patrons were advising him not to drink, 'the next sentence is—come take a single glass with me, a single glass cannot hurt you. The poet refuses—again is pressed; he knows it hurts him, but he is afraid to disoblige his friend—he is a subscriber;—points out the beauties, the defects, &c., of the work. The next gentleman he meets with does the same: perhaps another enters—another glass is consequence; the poet's heart warms—forgets his constitution—till in a few years, like lime with water, he falls away and drops into the earth' (quoted in James pp. xx–xxi). In these remarks, Nicholson anticipated his own demise: one night in April 1843, returning home late and intoxicated, he slipped on stepping-stones crossing the Aire; he pulled himself to the bank but died the next day from exposure.

In the roughly two decades between his first publications and his death, Nicholson's life fluctuated between periods of relative stability with his growing family and periods of ill-health, poverty, and drunkenness. A second volume of poetry appeared, *The Lyre of Ebor* (1827), as did a series of occasional poems, including 'Lines on the present state of the country' (1826), 'Low-Moor Iron-Works' (1829), 'The Factory Child' (1831), and 'The Factory Child's Mother' (1832). These latter were prompted by the patronage of the child-labour reformer Richard Oastler. Nicholson received grants from the Royal Literary Fund in 1828 and 1837, and had the support of a series of influential benefactors, including George Lane Fox, the poet James Montgomery, E. C. Lester, W. O. Geller, the Earl of Harewood, and Lord Ribblesdale. Beginning in 1833, and continuing for nearly a decade, he was employed as a wool-comber by Sir Titus Salt in Bradford (who would later commission the model industrial workers' village of 'Saltaire'). Yet throughout these years Nicholson's alcoholism was a source of embarrassment and woe. One particular incident produced for him unwanted national notoriety. During a stay in London in late 1827, where he had gone to sell copies of *The Lyre of Ebor*, he engaged in a day-long debauch at the Drury Lane Theatre, and was eventually brought to the criminal court at Bow Street. The event was given extended coverage in the newspapers; the *Times*'s comic account, which called him 'George Nicholson, alias the Yorkshire poet', reveled in the details of his provincial dress and manners—'the strange cut coat, corduroy breeches, unshorn chin, and yarn stockings'—and mocked his literary pretensions, quoting the presiding magistrate, Sir Richard Bernie, as releasing him with the words, 'as it seems you are a man of genius, a poet and so forth, I cannot think of detaining you' (17 Nov 1827; p. 3). One of the other episodes from this stay in London, Nicholson's encounter with the sculptor Sir Francis Chantrey, has recently been fashioned into an organizing incident in a play about Nicholson's life, *Poetry or Bust*, by Tony Harrison.

The most distinctive aspect of Nicholson's verse is his avowed, recurring interest in Melpomene, the Tragic Muse, whom he views as 'Majestically great above the rest'. Retrospectively, though, his skills appear better adapted to lyrics and songs than to the long, ringing tones of 'Airedale in Ancient Times'. Several of his poems address the subject of his alcoholism, including 'The Drunkard's Retribution', which, in its compressed evocations of guilt, recalls Coleridge's opium-withdrawal narrative 'The Pains of Sleep'. (Another important poem in this vein, 'Genius and Intemperance', is too long for reprinting here.) Such poems make especially interesting reading when placed alongside celebrations of conviviality like 'The Malt-Kiln Fire' and 'Lines on Long Tom'. Another poem of note is 'On the Ascent of a Balloon', one of the more interesting labouring-class commentaries on the status of the unlettered author. Though the poem initially seems full of unintentional humour ('The humble poet, oft, alas! / Fills his balloon with fancy's gas'), it is an original account of the disappointments and disasters awaiting poets, tyrants, and others who attempt unwisely to 'rise'.

FURTHER READING

Tony Harrison, *Plays Three: Poetry or Bust, The Kaisers of Carnuntum, The Labourers of Herakles* (London: Faber and Faber, 1996)

W. G. Hird (ed.), *The Poetical Works of John Nicholson* (London: Simpkin and Marshall, 1876)

John James (ed.), *Poems by John Nicholson, The Airedale Poet* (London: Longman, Brown, Green, 1844)

James Ogden, 'John Nicholson: Unpublished Poems', *The Bradford Antiquary: the Journal of the Bradford Historical and Antiquarian Society* n.s. XLVI(Oct 1976), 37–44. <http://www.bradfordhistorical.fsnet.co.uk/antiquary/second/vol09/nicholson.html>

<http://members.lycos.co.uk/saltaire/john.htm>.

From *Poems by John Nicholson* (1844)

On Visiting a Workhouse

Allow'd to walk into the sad retreat
Where tott'ring age and foolish fair ones meet,
I heard deep sighs from those bent down with years,
Whose cheeks were deeply furrow'd o'er with cares.
To see their locks, by ruthless Time turn'd grey,   5
Melted my heart, and took my pride away:
For who was seated in the corner chair,
But one who in my youth I held most dear.
Oft had his hand, when I was but a boy,
Handled the knife, and made me many a toy;   10
For me he caught the sparrows on the snow,
And made my youthful heart with raptures glow!
Oft had I danc'd around him with delight,
While he had balanc'd well my little kite;
But now, my aged friend, when he should eat,   15
His palsied hands can scarcely bear his meat,—
His pleasures lost, to life he's but a slave,
And only waits his passport to the grave.
Here I beheld how mortals waste away,
Shoot up to manhood, blossom, and decay!   20
In wolsey gown, close seated by his side,
His sister Ann, of Harewood once the pride,
Beauteous and fair,—upon her bridal day
The wealthy countess scarce appear'd more gay;
But the fine brow that bore the glossy hair,   25
Which once she dress'd with such assiduous care,
Was furrow'd o'er by Time's all-changing plough,
And her few locks were nearly white as snow.
When I had stood awhile, and dried the tear,
I spoke, but John my words could scarcely hear;   30
At length he cried, in exclamation strong,
'Ah! is that thee?' for still he knew my tongue.
His age-dimm'd eyes then brighten'd with a ray,
Which, like a wasted taper, died away.
Dotage had seiz'd upon his feeble brain,   35
As he revolv'd to infancy again.

Awhile he spoke of heav'n and things divine,
Then laugh'd—and stopp'd a moment to repine;
Wish'd for the grave,—next talk'd of things to come,
Then wept—and thought of his once happy home.   40
But his poor heart was most of all subdued
With daughters' pride, and sons' ingratitude.
'Alas!' said he, 'that those who owe me all,
Should know me thus, and yet refuse to call
To spend one hour, to mitigate my grief,   45
To bring one cordial, or afford relief.
Tho' they neglect a father, old and poor,
They yet may have to enter at this door;
Yet O, avert it heav'n! bless'd may they live!
O teach an injur'd father to forgive!'   50
Touch'd with the scene, I turn'd aside to weep,
And like a child he calmly fell asleep!

January

Now bleak winter on the mountains
    Whirls on heaps the dusty snow,
Seals with ice the sandy fountains,
    While the streams can scarcely flow.

Starving grouse forsake the rushes,   5
    Cover'd is their winter store,
Seek for shelter in the bushes,
    While the heath is drifted o'er.

Trees beneath their loads are bending;
    Firs like ostrich plumes appear;   10
Partridge tame the barn attending,
    Picking up the grain with fear.

Hares the snow-drifts wander over,
    Forc'd the hawthorn buds to eat;
Lost in snow the sprigs of clover,   15
    Cover'd are the blades of wheat.

Now the thrasher, old and weary,
    Stops the northern door with straw;
But the tempest, wild and dreary,
    Finds a way thro' ev'ry flaw.   20

Starv'd from woods, the beauteous pheasant
    Leaves the icy boughs and mourns,
Haunts the cottage of the peasant,—
    Snows may melt, it ne'er returns.

Thus the maids, their parents leaving,   25
    Wanton to the city fly,
Soon with woes their breasts are heaving,—
    Virtue, honour, beauty, die!

The Muse

What means it tho' the poet's cot
Be plac'd in some sequester'd spot?
Where oaks, and elms, and beeches grow,
Or on the heath, where rushes bow;
In vales, where peaceful graze the flocks,   5
Or near the mossy-vestur'd rocks.
Romantic scenes can ne'er indite,
Nor situations make him write.
'Tis genius must his breast inspire,
And light the true poetic fire.   10
Without it he may read and pore
Ancient and modern classics o'er;
May walk in ruins late or soon,
While thro' the arches shines the moon,
Where sleeps the abbot, monk, or friar,   15
But if he has not Nature's lyre,
Nor ancient ruins, nor the woods,
The rippling rills, the foaming floods,
Embattled fields, nor ancient hall,
Romantic scenes, where cataracts fall,   20

Nor works of other authors' pens,
Nor Cumbria's lakes, nor Highland glens,
Nor all the scenes which ever grac'd
The paintings of a man of taste,
Not all the arts the scribblers use, 25
Can make a bard without the Muse.

On the Ascent of a Balloon

The air balloon a picture is
Of man's most elevated bliss.
As on the wings of hope he hastes,
He finds all earthly pleasure wastes.
The sweetest bliss that man enjoys 5
In its possession only cloys;
Tho' with good fortune for his gas
He o'er the clouds of want may pass,
Yet come a storm, the weaken'd air
May drop him on a sea of care. 10

    Th' enthusiasts who soar on high,
And seem as if they'd grasp'd the sky,
With reason weak, and fancy strong,
Think all the sects but theirs are wrong;
Condemn all creeds, and think that they 15
Alone are heirs of endless day.
They cling around their car of hopes,
Till demon Nature cuts the ropes,
As thro' this evil world they pass,
And fierce temptations waste their gas, 20
They downward fall—the phantom vain
Comes rapid to the earth again;
And when they gather breath to speak,
They own they are but mortals weak.

    The playful boy, when young his hope, 25
First forms his weak balloon with soap;

With joy bright glitt'ring in his eyes,
He views it from the tube arise,
Dances and laughs to see it soar
With Nature's colours painted o'er: 30
Thus miniature balloons of boys
Are emblems true of riper joys.

   The gay coquette, whose thoughts despise
The sober youth, tho' e'er so wise,
Becomes a spendthrift's mistress soon,   35
And soars aloft in love's balloon.
Thro' all the gayest scenes they pass,—
Her marriage portion is the gas
That bears them in the circle gay,
And turns the midnight into day.   40
But after all these golden hours,
They find the air-borne chariot low'rs;
Their lofty flight they then repent,
For friends all fly from their descent,
And those who envied them before,   45
Rejoice to see their flying o'er.

   The dashing youth, who sports along,
Amid the wine, the dance, the song,
The opera, the park, the ball,
At Covent-Garden and Vauxhall,   50
Upon the turf, or at the ring,
With gold enough, is just the thing.
High in the atmosphere of pride
In his balloon he loves to ride;
While round his car the nymphs attend,   55
His ample fortune help to spend.
For ballast he no reason takes,
Till debts increas'd the phantom shakes;
He falls, amid the gloomy cloud
Of creditors, and cries aloud,—   60
'Could I but live past moments o'er,
Folly's balloon I'd mount no more!'

   The tyrant, in his horrid car,
Hung round with implements of war,
While on its edge sits rage and death,   65
And murder'd myriads are beneath,

Elatedly rides,—his flags unfurl'd,
And waving o'er a prostrate world.
The ruin'd empires see him pass,
Pride and ambition for his gas;   70
Despair below looks wildly up,
And frantic drinks the pois'nous cup;
Orphans and widows curse his flight,
And Mercy, weeping, shuns the sight!
When he to loftier heights would soar,   75
His ballast is the warrior's gore,
Which from his care the monster throws,
And sprinkles on the field of woes.
But He who rules above, looks down,—
His lightnings blaze—the tyrant's crown   80
Drops from his head,—his mighty car
Is broke upon the field of war!
The wounded warriors join with all
In joy to shout the tyrant's fall.

   The humble poet, oft, alas!   85
Fills his balloon with fancy's gas;
To see him launch it few attend,
He just is aided by one friend,
Who finds him ballast, silk, and ropes,
And keeps alive his trembling hopes;   90
Then loos'd from earth and anxious care,
Aloft he springs upon the air;
With lofty themes his passions glow,
The sordid world he views below;
The heav'nly chorus of the spheres.   95
He looks behind,—his fancy views
Close to his car, the Tragic Muse;
And, as in air he rides along
She charms him with her solemn song.
Her car's adorn'd with sword and spear,   100
The dagger and the scimitar;
The pois'nous goblet,—broken crown,
And palaces half tumbled down.—
The bloody vest, the murder'd maid,
Are on the Muse's car pourtray'd.   105
The wide-stretch'd scene is spread below,
Where rich meand'ring rivers flow;

The flow'ry fields, the foaming seas,
The mountains topp'd with waving trees;
The dancing nymphs, the sportive swains,   110
And crippled age, oppress'd with pains.—
Time present, past, and future, lies
All spread before his fancy's eyes;
While his enraptur'd passions glow,
His lines in easy accents flow: 115
But humble bards must soon descend,
And in the shades their raptures end.

Sports of the Field

When oaks are brown and birches bare,
    And not a bird is singing,
The sportsman drives away his care,
    The speckled woodcocks springing.

True joy he in the country knows,   5
    His faithful springers ranging
Among the hazel's yellow boughs,
    Or holly, never changing.

When the long-bill'd woodcock springs,
    Mark!—the sportsman calling,   10
The blue smoke curls,—its useless wings
    Through the trees are falling.

There's many a man at this would sigh,
    As sore against religion;
But at a feast just let him try   15
    At woodcock, grouse, or widgeon.

The Malt-Kiln Fire

When friends who lov'd from infant years,
   Whose friendships ne'er went wrong,
Are met to tell their joys and cares,
   Or join the cheerful song,

What bard but to the utmost height   5
   Would string the rustic lyre,
When friends and home-brew'd drink are met
   Around the Malt-kiln fire?

Sometimes we're faring low at home,
   Then feasting with a squire;   10
But we've as much as we can wish
   Around the Malt-kiln fire.

From this warm, happy, cheerful place,
   Old Sorrow must retire,
And nought but joy dare shew her face   15
   Around the Malt-kiln fire.

We talk of friends we long have known,
   Some fall'n, and some ris'n higher;
Happy as monarchs on the throne,
   Around the Malt-kiln fire.   20

What means our food? we pass away—
   Of life begin to tire;
But never was a mournful day
   Around the Malt-kiln fire.

With snuff, tobacco, and a pipe,   25
   And all we can desire,
Old Care's forgot, and pleasure shines
   Around the Malt-kiln fire.

Let blackguards swear, and rage, and fight,
   And scuffle in the mire;   30
No angry word, for all is right,
   Around the Malt-kiln fire.

Had we but spent more evenings there,
   Our spirits had been higher,
And drunk less brandy, and more beer   35
   Around the Malt-kiln fire.

The Drunkard's Retribution

Where is the ink so sable in its hue,
That can pourtray the picture dark and true;
The horrid state which language fails to tell,
The dark confusion, and the earthly hell!
In such sad state how often have I thought—   5
O! that I could sink backward into nought;
Reason subverted, anguish took its place,
I thought myself below the reach of grace.
Despair o'erwhelm'd my soul, and keen remorse;
To know I liv'd, became my bitterest curse;   10
My sorrowing friends appear'd my greatest foes,
And cheerful songs but added to my woes.
The phantom trumpets, the imagin'd band,
Methought I heard, which summon'd me to stand
High in the pillory—to meet disgrace;—   15
My trembling heart shrunk back from every face.
Thus swiftly did imagination rove,
Confusion from her throne my reason drove.
Afraid of poison from my mother's hand,
I durst not drink, suspicion fill'd my mind.   20
Each trembling leaf, if shaken by the blast,
Struck me with terror as I hurried past.
Myself the cause, I thought, of all the guilt
That fills the earth—of all the blood that's spilt,—
That purest heaven would deign on earth to dwell,   25
Were I but hurried to the deepest hell.

Lines on 'Long Tom,'
Bramham Park

O Great Long Tom! when thou with foam art crown'd,
Thou stretchest care and anguish on the ground;
Despair thou buriest deep within the grave;—

Thy contents sure would make the coward brave.
When gloomy Winter, with her roaring floods,   5
Sends her fierce tempests through the leafless woods,
When sleet falls cold and when the night is dark,
Fill me *Long Tom* with ale from Bramham Park.
Across the moors I then could cheerly go,
Though the cold sleet should change to whirling snow,   10
In sharpest frost I yet should take no harm—
In spite of all, *Tom's soul* would keep me warm.
When verdant Spring first dons her virgin shift,
And ploughmen hear the skylark in the lift,
Send them *Long Tom*, and they would sing so loud,   15
The larks would stop to listen in the cloud.
If from its verge could sip the mellow thrush,
How strong his notes upon the topmost bush;
All nature's songsters, could they drink from thee,
Would cheer the groves with louder harmony.   20
When Summer comes with all her scorching fires,
And on his way the thirsty traveller tires,
Tho' sweat fall from his locks like drops of rain,
Thy soul would cheer him till he walk'd again.
In Autumn, when the sportsman hastes away   25
With dogs and gun to spend a cheerful day,
When weary, he would better hit his mark,
Had he thy contents brought from Bramham Park.
In Winter thou art good to kill the frost,
Through circling years thy merits never lost;   30
If war should ever rage, or Britons fight
For Albion's monarch, or their country's right,
That ancient British courage may not fail,
Fill them such horns, with such as Fox's ale:
Then would their bosoms need no more t' inspire   35
Their souls to fight with true heroic fire,
Rapid as whirlwinds they would sweep along,
Vanquish the weak—and terrify the strong.
May British tars for ever have such ale,
While e'er a breeze can bend each noble sail;   40
Then would the cannons roar till every wave
Curl'd back and own'd itself Britannia's slave:
May none disloyal, no dishonest hand,
Touch thee, O *Tom!* while here thou hast thy stand.
But shouldst thou ever any soul inspire,   45

Just cheer'd, not drunk, but warm'd with honest fire,
With grateful bosom may he walk along,
And never be too drunk to give a song.

   How I could write, wert thou but hither borne,
Full as I saw thee on the opening morn,   50
When slow thy contents lessen'd every draught,
And those who knew thy pow'r stood by and laugh'd!
Then Freedom brought the tear to either eye,
And fill'd the humble Bard with ecstacy.
For generations, firm as Eldwick rocks,   55
Be thou the far-fam'd mighty horn of Fox.

Melpomene

The Tragic Muse, in sable mantle dress'd,
Majestically great above the rest,
With thoughtful look, and tears, and pallid cheek,
A comic line is scarcely heard to speak;
For higher themes her feeling breast inspire   5
Than lyric measures or the keen satire.
The widow's woes,—the virgin's love, she sings,
The fate of heroes, and the fall of kings;
On palaces in ruins, where the throne
Which now is broke, with regal grandeur shone;   10
Where once the beauteous chequer'd marble floor
With blood of kings was deeply crimson'd o'er;
There like a widow on her husband's tomb,
She sits enshrine'd amid the tragic gloom,—
Paints ev'ry scene of ancient tyrants' deeds,   15
Then gazes on the ruins cloth'd in weeds,
Till her rich mind replaces ev'ry stone,
And seats the murder'd monarch on the throne.
Musters his guards—which long in dust have been,
Beholds his knights, his heroes, and his queen;   20
Sees the vile traitor, with his murd'ring train,
Act all of his deeds of darkness o'er again;

The courtiers lov'd to-day, and rais'd on high,
Frown'd on to-morrow, and their glories die;
The dauntless heroes, mark'd with many a scar,   25
Rush on in search of glory to the war,
And on their arms the dread suspended fates
Of empires, kingdoms, or contending states;—
Shrouded in terrors, while around her plays,
In ev'ry form, the lightning's vivid blaze.   30
Wading in blood, she marks the hero's fall,
While with her crimson pen she minutes all.
When to the charge the furious steeds advance,
And red with noble blood the glitt'ring lance—
The drums, the trumpets, and the clang of arms,   35
The rattling mail, and war's most dread alarms;
The banners waving over either host,
The day hung doubtful—neither won nor lost;
The smoking tow'rs, the city wrapp'd in fire,—
With loftier themes, the Tragic Muse inspire—   40
With noise of battle plumes her tow'ring wings,
And gives terrific grandeur while she sings!

ROBERT FRANKLIN (*fl.* 1809–1851)

Robert Franklin's 1824 volume *The Miller's Muse* is not, despite its title, a chronicle of his working life in Barrow upon Humber and South Ferriby, Lincolnshire, on the banks of the River Humber. To the limited extent that the poems reflect the author's vocational experience, they are oriented more toward his time spent in domestic service, a disjunction he addresses in the volume's preface: 'Should any objection be made to the title of the book, (several of the poems having been written during my state of servitude) I can assure the reader, if I may be thus allowed to express myself, that I have been a miller at heart all my life,—that my forefathers were millers for ages past,—and I was brought up at the post mill at Barrow, till the age of fourteen, where I acquired a knowledge of the business, which, perhaps, in more mature years, I might never have so effectually obtained' (p. iv). It is believed that Franklin's parents were killed in a boating accident on the Humber when he was just two years old, and though the family's financial exigencies would eventually force him to leave the mill for service, in later years he was able to return and, in effect, resume his former life. 'I have since frequently pondered over what may justly seem to have been the work of an overruling Providence—the chain of events, by which I [...] became possessor of that very place, which, when a boy, I was unwillingly compelled to leave in tears' (p. v).

Franklin's first composition, 'The Native Village', written in 1809, was inspired by reflections of home while hearing the church-bells of Hamburg, Germany, a circumstance that may remind us, at least faintly, of Wordsworth's first sketching of childhood memories while enduring a long winter in the German town of Goslar. One of the poems included here, 'Poor William', does have some Wordsworthian echoes, though Franklin names Robert Bloomfield as his most direct source of inspiration. After returning to England, Franklin published a few scattered poems in his local newspapers, before finally deciding to gather them for publication, for which he was able to secure well over 500 subscribers. The poems are for the most part set in a few square miles on the south banks of the Humber, bounded by Barrow, Barton, and Ferriby Sluice, and the volume was published across the river in Hull. In it Franklin visits a conventional range of rustic subjects, from landscape scenes and seasonal meditations to moral tales and narratives of local legend. Though detailed accounts of labour are not in evidence, labour itself is consistently presented as the highest of virtues, while the disinclination to work is viewed as threatening the basic structure of 'social feeling' ('Poor William', l. 17). Of the twenty-three poems, three are on Napoleon and Waterloo, and it is clear that for Franklin, as for many of his contemporaries, Napoleon represented a profound, fearful disruption of the natural order—not only a physical threat, but also a kind of pathology. Though the moralistic bent of the volume is not at all unusual, Franklin is at his most idiosyncratic in his tendency to meditate at length on the mental anguish of guilty parties. In 'The Convict', printed below, the first-person narrator laments the permanent severing of his ties to England, family, home, and happiness. Even as the elaboration of the speaker's suffering serves as a cautionary tale, it also provides a kind of satisfaction-in-retribution for Franklin, a retribution he seems to desire even when, as in this case, the crime is in some sense understandable (the convict has stolen to feed his family). Similar psychic dynamics are presented in 'The Poacher', who is said to be 'Fraught with the terrors of a guilty mind' (l. 35), and 'Reflections on Napoleon', in which the disgraced aggressor is said to 'wear in thought the captive's chain' (l. 49). When Franklin transfers a sense of psychic unease to himself, he produces the most interesting poem printed here, 'A Visit from Bridlington to Flambro' Head', a gothic-tinged travel narrative which conveys genuine awe at the rugged Yorkshire coastline.

Franklin continued intermittently to produce verse in the decades following 1824. As with 'The Banks of the Humber', the closing poem in *The Miller's Muse,* this later verse reflects Franklin's admiration for the charitable paternalism of the landed classes. The title poem of *The House of Brocklesby* (1844) praises the stewardship of the Brocklesby estate, and Franklin dedicates the volume to the Earl of Yarborough. The volume has a diminished lyric emphasis, with no short poems or effusions, and Franklin seems increasingly to view his role as that of historian and custodian of local memory. A representative poem from this volume, 'The Village Clerk', is presented below. Franklin's long final poem, 'Wanderings in the Crystal Palace' (1851), fails to produce any of the surprises suggested by its title. Its essential tenor is made clear in its opening lines: 'Say not such springs from vanity and pride; / There's nothing here but leans to virtue's side'.

FURTHER READING

Sketches of Obscure Poets (London: Cochrane and McCrone, 1833), pp. 142–50

Rosemary F. Doria, 'Robert Franklin, Miller Poet of Barrow on Humber', *Lincolnshire Life* 21.4 (July 1981), 22–3.

From *The Miller's Muse* (1824)

Poor William

However long we pass life's fleeting hours
Remote from relatives and native bow'rs,
At our return, some secret thoughts unfold
Some nameless feelings, never to be told.
And much I love to tread yon well-known lane,   5
Where *William* dwelt, alas! poor hapless swain!
Ah! see that cottage, with its roof of thatch,
Whose door still opens with a wooden latch;
There was he once beheld a lovely boy,
A father's blessing, and a mother's joy;   10
Nor was aught noted, in his rising years,
To grieve or steep a parent's couch with tears;
For tho' a swain, he, in his native place,
Was deem'd superior to the rustic's race,
Till to that state, O! mournful state! consign'd,   15
Bereft of all the faculties of mind;
While ev'ry social feeling ceas'd to flow,
He fail'd to labour, and forsook his plough.
And now th' afflicted youth would ceaseless roam,
Regardless of his friends and peaceful home,   20
In lonely solitude, through wood and wild,
With solitary scenes alone beguil'd.
But whence the change? his own, or from above—
Whether distractive care or hopeless love—
The woeful cause why reason thus withdrew,   25
The wisest of the village never knew.
In a remote, sequester'd, dreary vale,
Where human footsteps seldom did prevail—
Save when some shepherd wistful took his round,
Led by the wand'ring sheep-bells' tinkling sound,   30
Thro' furze and briar, that cloth'd the niggard soil,
And mock'd the ploughshare and the ploughman's toil—
There would he dwell whole days in wretched plight,
And there would pass the darksome moonless night.
Yet strange, for hours awake, and those he slept,   35
Two sep'rate haunts, two drear abodes he kept;

Within a turf-built shed, of shapeless form,
Where shepherds shelter'd from the beating storm,
Here he would nightly lay his shiv'ring head,
The cold unfriendly earth his joyless bed;   40
And when the gloomy shades of night gave way
To the bright beams of all reviving day,
Crept to a neighb'ring brake, (mysterious plan),
And shunn'd, for ever shunn'd, the face of man.
E'en cold and hunger, ever-powerful foes   45
To human nature, and to man's repose,
He there sustain'd, and mark'd with listless eye,
The raging tempest and the wintry sky.
Yet times there were, when he, in sullen mood,
From thence would wander in the quest of food;   50
With stockings loose, a waistcoat unconfin'd,
And tatter'd coat that flutter'd in the wind,
Within the village seen; but even then,
For if at home awhile constrain'd to stay,
When unobserv'd he always stole away—   55
And, tho' on pity's bounty chiefly fed,
He never crav'd, he never begg'd his bread;
But when the gen'rous hand his wants reliev'd,
He ever cold and thanklessly receiv'd.
His senseless breast was never made rejoice,—   60
Dead to the sound of soft compassion's voice;
But when his hands of food a portion bore,
And stinging hunger broke his rest no more,
He, with unweary'd step, retrac'd the road,
To reach his lonesome, comfortless abode.
Thus pass'd his cheerless days in youthful prime,   65
Whose fancy travers'd nature's coldest clime;
Nor friends, nor parents, could his course restrain,
They strove and wept—but wept and strove in vain.
Oft have my childish steps been led astray,
Fearful to meet him on the public way;   70
But false my fear, and causeless my alarm,
His bosom never meditated harm.
And could I *now* his wonted form review,
My rising soul might render pity due.
For oh! if soothing sympathy would find   75
Her greatest object in distress'd mankind,

If there be one supreme, 'tis surely he,
The hapless victim of insanity,
Whom no sound joy or ray of hope can cheer,
Upon this chequer'd, sublunary sphere.   80
Such William was;—for lo! arriv'd the hour,
When frenzy fir'd each intellectual power.
No more the abject wanderer trac'd, forlorn,
Those barren fields, ne'er clad with waving corn;
Freedom, alas! he might no longer share,   85
Nor breathe his mental woes in ambient air;
But, sad to tell, close bound, he rav'd and sigh'd,
And, in yon poor-house walls, in chains, he died.

A Visit from Bridlington to Flambro' Head

'Twas summer; and the morning gay
Bespoke a clear, a beauteous day;
The sea, with sun-beams dimpled o'er;
The billow lightly touch'd the shore;
When safe on board, a cheerful band   5
Proclaim'd adieu to those on land;
The breeze was fresh, the tide ran strong;
Quick o'er the deep we dash'd along,
Some little to the right inclin'd,
And left the sandy shores behind.   10
    Due left the northern hills were seen,
Corn fields, and woods, a pleasing green;
But to the right, 'twas to the eye
One blue expanse of sea and sky.
Who, while the world lies hush'd in sleep,   15
Launch out upon the foaming deep,
Extend the sail or ply the oar,
And quit their friends and native shore,
And, dashing o'er the ocean's spray,
Far on the billows bound away;   20
Thus days, and months, and years are past,

Till age or sickness close the last.
Whilst others sweep the neighb'ring strand,
And drag the scaly tribe to land,
Climb the lone cliffs, or cavern's glen,   25
Far from the busy haunts of men;
And, plac'd where waves and tempests frown,
Live, to the world how little known!
   As up the winding hill we drew,
The tow'ring light-house rose to view;   30
A comely structure, form'd to please,
And ever faithful to the seas;
With changing shades of red and white,
That variegate the gloom of night;
Here, ranging round, and round, and round,   35
Until the topmost step was found,
Plac'd high in air 'twixt earth and sky,
Say what engag'd the wond'ring eye!
   'Tis true no waveless lake was seen,
Skirted with woods of beauteous green;   40
'Tis true, no mountain's tow'ring height,
Arose to strike the eager sight;
Tho' certainly the eye was borne
O'er many a field of rip'ning corn,
And straggling trees, and hamlets brown,   45
And reach'd indeed was ancient town;
Tho' dimly seen, the view was our's,
Of Filey rocks and Scarbro' tow'rs.
   But chiefly Neptune's realms convey'd
A changing view of light and shade;   50
Beyond the bosom of the cliff
Appear'd a little neighb'ring skiff,
And many a boat, with vig'rous oar,
Ply'd round the solitary shore;
And from that very shore upright,   ·   55
(Good Heavens! it seem'd a dreadful height)
We gaz'd, till gazing cherish'd pain,
For leagues across the dark blue main,
And noted many a distant sail,
That sought in vain the friendly gale;   60
For not a breath was felt to blow,
The ocean's flood lay calm below.

Young men and maids, a cheerful few,
In bloom of health, compos'd our crew.
   Now each had left their rocky seat, 65
To view the cavern—lone retreat—
Which few approach without some dread;
The mighty cliff o'ertops your head;
'Tis darkness on your entrance here,
Through one rude passage damp and drear— 70
When, all at once, a sudden light
Bursts forth on the astonish'd sight;
And some were here would scarce agree,
Such place could have been form'd by sea,
Or that the archways here display'd, 75
The ruthless winds and waves had made;
Through which the ocean was descry'd,—
And one proclaim'd return of tide,
And begg'd there might be no delay,
And loudly talk'd of parting day. 80
'Twas kind—for night was drawing near:
And now for home—the boat was here—
When each and all with help of hand,
Embark'd, and left the lonely strand;
No fav'ring breeze, no friendly gale, 85
In kindness fill'd our parting sail;
To force our little vessel through,
The busy oars had all to do.
Here many a gloomy rock was past,
And pointed crag beheld the last, 90
And jutting cliffs were left behind,
Food for the philosophic mind,—
Till Flambro', fading from the view,
Obtain'd our very last adieu!
   Once more we skimm'd along the main, 95
Our friends, our home, our port to gain;
Beyond the hills, to us unknown,
We mark'd the glorious sun go down—
The cloudless skies from east to west,
And the smooth ocean's peaceful breast. 100
The earth in summer's bloom and pride,
While we were borne along the tide,
Display'd a most imposing scene,
Mild, beauteous, soothing, and serene.

At length, our pleasing voyage o'er,   105
We trod the welcome friendly shore;
And altho' strangers, led to roam,
Each found a hospitable home,
With plenty and attention blest,
Till night brought on the hours of rest.   110
Remembrance wakes the feeble lay
That tells the pleasures of a day;
But those who form'd our humble train,
On Flambro' cliffs, and on the main,
Cannot deny, till life shall fail,   115
That truth alone inspires my tale.

The Poacher

Behold that broken window! shatter'd sight!
With patch and board that half exclude the light:
Observe that roof, with ev'ry tempest shook;
That door as wretched, on a crazy hook;
Where ruin and distress, alike combin'd,   5
Pourtray an emblem of its owner's mind.
He, far remov'd from nature's gen'ral plan,
O'er looks the brute, but scarce arrives at man.
In ignorance and vice matur'd and bred—
Rude as the storms which howl above his head: 10
Oft on his filthy bed he may be found,
When Sunday's sacred bells chime sweetly round;
Or vilely plac'd amid a chosen few,
That form, at best, a most unhallow'd crew.
Of late a dark and dreadful howling squall,   15
Threw down his long-neglected garden wall;
Fast fell the rain, the wind from westward blew,
Which laid a wretched rood of land to view,
O'ergrown with weeds, with briars compass'd round
Where various lumber interspers'd the ground;   20
Where many a bone and many a wing was laid,

To prove and testify his pilf'ring trade.
His trade consists of death in various shapes;
Fish, flesh, nor fowl, his murderous hands escapes!
At dead of night, when weary eye-lids close,   25
When the wild world is hush'd in soft repose;
When sorrow, on her couch, gives way to sleep,
And wretchedness awhile forgets to weep;
When not a star illumes the aerial doom,
He stalks abroad, regardless of the gloom,   30
Through many a secret haunt and winding way,
A nightly robber, in the quest of prey!
A sneaking cur attendant, in the dark,
Receives his curses, if he chance to bark:
Fraught with the terrors of a guilty mind,   35
He dreads a foe in ev'ry breath of wind;
There plies the meshy net and treach'rous snare,
Death to the rabbit and the tim'rous hare;—
And when the business of the night is done—
Business that honesty will ever shun—   40
Ere dawn of day disperse the clouds of night,
Slinks to his hut, and sleeps away the light.
'Tis strange! that man should e'er, on British soil,
Prefer such life to that of honest toil!
And pass his fleeting days in acts of shame,   45
The great and good will never cease to blame.

Reflections on Napoleon

The sword is sheath'd, the battle's o'er,
The sounds of war are heard no more;
No more the beacon's blazing light
Sheds terror through the silent night;
No more are dreadful feats perform'd,   5
Or towns defac'd, or cities storm'd
By hostile armies, crowd on crowd;—
The *War Chief* slumbers in his shroud!

On St. Helena's lonely isle,
Where Hope disdain'd to wear a smile—   10
Midst gloomy rocks and seas of foam,
Far, far from country and from home—
And far from scenes of glory past,
'Twas here *Napoleon* breath'd his last!
Ah! what avail'd *Marengo's* fight?   15
The battle won, the foemen's flight!
When *Gallia's* eagles dash'd along,
Victorious o'er the perish'd throng!
Or *Austerlitz* dread field of fame,
That gilded o'er the victor's name;   20
Till vanquish'd chiefs his feats allow'd,
And warriors cring'd, and monarchs bow'd.
Ah! what avail'd, in evil hour,
That thirst of conquest and of power?
Regardless of the dying groan,   25
The *Widow's* grief, the *Orphan's* moan;
Regardless of the *Mother* wild,
Who frantic mourns her slaughter'd child;
Regardless of the drooping *Maid*,
The *Lover*, and the peaceful shade,   30
He sever'd in the battle's strife,
The nearest, dearest ties of life;
A host of foes in arms withstood,
And grasp'd a throne through seas of blood!
But short his triumphs, short his sway—   35
Behold the *mighty* and the *gay*,
From that proud throne, so late attain'd,
And from that height so hardly gain'd,
Now falls—his dream of glory o'er—
And in that fall to rise no more!   40
Now plac'd beneath misfortune's frown,
And doom'd to quit his kingly crown;
To other chiefs, more favour'd, yield
The scepter, senate, and the field—
His former pomp and power forego,   45
And plead the mercy of his foe;
Compell'd to pass his lonely time
In distant land, in foreign clime;
And wear in thought the captive's chain,

Amid the vast Atlantic main.   50
No child, no *bosom friend* was there,
His heart to cheer, his griefs to share;
To check the lone, dejected sigh,
And dash the tear from sorrow's eye.
And did he pass his days so drear,   55
Unaided, hopeless, *friendless*, here?
Were none found faithful to the end?
O, yes! indeed he had a friend;—
Nor scarcely lives, howe'er distress'd,
The man who finds no feeling breast,   60
To kindly act some tender part,
And soothe an almost broken heart;—
But without one more near allied,
While here, he liv'd;—and when he died,
No pitying mother mark'd or took   65
His last *farewell*, his *dying look*;
No faithful *wife*, at latest breath,
Hung fondly round the couch of death;
No brother's sigh—no sister's tear,
Was heav'd or wept beside his bier!—   70
Nor was his latest earthly doom
A pompous grave, a princely tomb;
Beside the *spring* and *willow's* shade—
To which, in life, he visits made—
And sat beneath the noon-tide ray,   75
Or pass'd in thought the close of day—
(Where no fair, hallow'd temples rise)
'Tis here the mighty victor lies!
And what! no monumental stone,
To mark the warrior's mould'ring bone?   80
'Tis said, no statue hangs its head,
In mournful silence o'er the dead!
Then let the weeping *willow* wave,
That skirts his deep, his lonely grave,
A drooping emblem of his fate,   85
Memento of his last estate;
And St. Helena's sea-girt isle
Record the name of *him* the while,
Who shews the world, whate'er betide,
The vanity of human pride!   90

The Convict

And is this the lone region, assign'd
   For the hopeless to heave the deep sigh,
Where guilt breathes her woes to the wind,
   And the wretched are banish'd to die?
Yes! here I must languish forlorn!   5
   It is here I am doom'd to deplore
A country from which I am torn,
   And friends I may visit no more!

Tho' so healthful the clime, and around
   While nature in grandeur is drest,   10
Not a charm in this land have I found
   To soothe my sad bosom to rest;—
Still Britain! dear land of my birth!
   Tho' thy frowns and thy tortures are felt,
Still how fondly I cling to the earth   15
   Where my forefathers happily dwelt!

Thy hills and thy vallies so fair,
   In my youth so engaging to me,
With countless endearments ensnare,
   And chain my affections to thee.   20
Never more at the close of the day,
   From my cottage, so near to the brook,
Shall I mark the bright sun's setting ray,
   O'er the wood that embosom'd the rook!

Never more shall the smiles of that home,   25
   On me their kind influence bestow;
Tho' a grief to my friends I must roam,
   It is pleasure to think, and to know
I shall not rob a father of joy;
   For his griefs and his sufferings are past;   30
I receiv'd his kind look when a boy,
   And remember that look was his last!

But, ah! where's the mother so kind,
   And kindred that press'd the same knee?
Do they still live to bear me in mind?   35
   Peradventure they still think of me.
Yet my child, and my own bosom friend,

From whom I was hastily torn,
Who shall kindly protect, and defend
   From distress and the world's bitter scorn?   40

But name not my faults to my child,
   Nor her to my mind ever dear—
No guilt has their bosoms defil'd;
   And for me, O! suppress the sad tear.
Unconscious were they to the last;   45
   Tho' the deed I was tempted to try,
Was to screen them from poverty's blast,
   And shield them from misery's sigh.

Heav'ns! had I but reason obey'd,
   To virtue's firm dictates prov'd true,   50
In chains I had ne'er been array'd,
   Nor banish'd from love and from you!
But, 'tis done! and 'tis here I must dwell—
   None, through life can my freedom renew!
Kind friends and relations farewell!   55
   O, England! for ever adieu!

The Banks of the Humber

See yon mansion so fair, where the woodbine and rose
Unite on its walls, and together repose;—
See yon mansion, by nature so favour'd and blest,
With its back to the hills and its front to the west;
Where summer sheds beauties that no one can number;—   5
Yon lovely abode on the *Banks of the Humber!*

How fresh blows the air, and how fair are the flowers
That bloom all around and enliven its bowers;
Here the heart is made glad, and delights to declare
How fruitful the prospect around, and how fair!   10
And peace, and content, and the sweetest of slumber,
Are nightly enjoy'd on the *Banks of the Humber!*

At the silence of eve, when the leaves are all still,
When the air is scarce felt on the verge of the hill,
How delightful to wander along the green way,   15
Ere the moon gilds the dew-drop that hangs on the spray;
When is heard, smoothly dashing, the skiff's gentle oar,
And the billow as gentle that dies on the shore!

In that lone little wood where no footsteps intrude,
To mar the enjoyment of calm solitude,   20
I have sat—and so free was my bosom from pain,
I'm resolv'd to be found there again and again.
O, 'tis pleasing to quit the rude world and its noise,
To cherish that quiet my spirit enjoys!

On yon banks, now so gay, doom'd to flourish and fade,   25
By summer and winter that vary their shade,
It might please you to witness each near-passing sail,
With their oars in the calm, and a reef in the gale;
As o'er the dread depth of the water they glide,
Borne along by the ebb or the flowing of tide.   30

All health to the owners who claim this abode!
And joy to their bosoms on life's chequer'd road!
Long, long may they live to inhabit the place!—
The same to their offspring who keep up their race;
Who may traverse these walks, and may visit yon shore,   35
When the *poet* and *parents* can view them no more!

I love the fair spot, all embosom'd in wood,
From whence you may gaze on the high-swelling flood.
And O! when my days have arriv'd at their bourn—
Since whatever is earthly to earth must return;—   40
When the cares of this life can no longer encumber,
May *this* form rest in peace on the *Banks of the Humber!*

From *The House of Brocklesby* (1844)

The Village Clerk

Remov'd from this world's joys, its cares, and woes,
Where does our humble MADDISON repose?
'Tis here he lies amongst the silent dead.
Had education of the higher kind
Beam'd on his quick and comprehensive mind,   5
And smiling plenty gratified his need,—
No doubt but this man had been great indeed!
And great he was!—though not enroll'd by fame,
Or tomb to bear the record of his name.
A stone o'ergrown with moss, memento here,   10
Carv'd by himself, he *left with* friend sincere,
Requesting him, at death, to kindly show
The month and year he left his father's cot,
To till the soil and bear the peasant's lot,
And braved, unmurm'ring, winter's snow and sleet,   15
The chilling blasts of spring, and summer's heat;
Seed-time and harvest—and the various cares,
All that the hale and hardy ploughman shares.
In after years he changed from what he'd been,
To different service, and a different scene;   20
Time in his mind this new resolve display'd,
He rais'd a loom, and next assumed a trade!
And many a well-wrought web from him was found,
When bleach'd, that pleased and clothed the neighbours round.
Still farther name the gifts to him assign'd,   25
For sure he was a wonder of his kind!
Old clocks he clean'd, and practis'd small repairs,
Form'd the best bee-hives and re-seated chairs;
A wheelwright!—and his wheels were better made
Than some by those who really learnt the trade;   30
Cages for birds he framed—made children's toys;
In each employ he had his harmless joys.
A mimic ship of war his table graced,
Rigg'd by himself, with scarce a rope misplaced.
The ancient abbey and the church in frame   35
Proclaim'd him artist—he deserv'd the name!

He faithful sketch'd each tower and turret grey,
And snatch'd their beauties pleasing in decay;
In short, whate'er his vigorous mind pourtray'd,
His hands the fancied picture soon display'd.   40
A poet, too—he tuned, if not sublime,
'The life of Joseph' into each rhyme.
Great were his toils, for he had much to do;
Was singer, ringer, clerk, and sexton too.
Three priests he serv'd, who singly, one by one,   45
Have each departed, now are dead and gone;
Or 'twould have been their very pride to tell
How faithfully he serv'd them, and how well!
On his first clerkship tithes were ta'en in kind,
Hence some declared he had a barb'rous mind,—   50
Who took not truth and reason for their guide,
Nor knew how firm he stood on duty's side;
Yet what found those in him a failing part
Was error of their heads, and not his heart:—
'Twas not in him to take by force or storm;   55
Yet could not swerve from what he must perform;
But future years, to him, brought better days,
And some who slander'd, liv'd at last to praise;
And some who rail'd, at length made open vow,
They miss'd the good wide common and the cow;   60
And own'd those trifles lightly press'd before,
Since fields enclosed had made them very poor.
Music from bells, he lov'd their merry round,
His ear was good and chaste,—his judgment sound;
And seldom first to pause—or grudge the time,   65
In lively peal, or sweetly plaintive chime.
No drunkard he, found staggering o'er the bowl,
And yet he had a cheerfulness of soul,
A lively spirit—aye! and one of use—
More lasting than the grape's refreshing juice!   70
True as the new-year came, with calm delight
He made a feast, and saw his friends at night—
His ringing friends;—and proved to all who came,
That friendship lay in deed as well as name.
At others' good he welcome joy exprest,   75
And shared his cup and blessings with the rest.
A thousand hearts have mov'd before him gay,

Pleas'd with his presence on their wedding day:
Thousands have shared his serious look or smile,
Whole years of Sabbaths in that sacred pile:—   80
Yet one sad thought befits the cypress shade—
Alas! how many in their graves he laid;
And weary toil'd in cold and sultry day,
To form their humble tenements of clay,
'Midst moul'dring bones, to him in life well known—   85
A true prophetic emblem of his own!
Though some might dread to lead the life he led
In toils and walks around the silent dead;
In night's thick gloom, he sought that lonely tower,
Gay and serene, at e'en the latest hour;   90
For passing bell, or aught that claim'd his care,
No coward he!—or he had not been there!
No fancied spectre broke his quiet rest,
A peaceful conscience fortified his breast.
In books he took delight;—and what he read   95
A faithful memory treasured in his head.
Deeds on the ocean, fights or wrecks forlorn,—
He told, with joy, where lay the point Cape Horn;
Show'd science taught the first advent'rous band,
To brave the billows and forsake the land;   100
At times he dwelt with somewhat mournful look,
On the sad fate of much-lamented Cook:—
In lighter mood would tell with half a smile,
How gallant Bruce explored the source of Nile;
And not unconscious of his mortal state,   105
Prepared for death ere it was deem'd too late.
Pond'ring the scripture o'er, with pious care,
He found a lasting consolation there.
Except when sleep or sickness chain'd his powers,
'Tis truly said he spent few idle hours;   110
And deem'd by some so strictly just and true,
He made their wills, and kept them secret too!
'Twas thus he lived; and mark the course he ran,—
An active, useful, honest, good old man;
Beloved by most, and firm on virtue's side,   115
Crown'd with long life, and hoary locks he died;
And, taking all his little works combin'd,
Scarce left his equal in the place behind!

NOTES

Abbreviations

DNB   *Dictionary of National Biography*, ed. Sir Leslie Stephen and Sir Sidney Lee, 22 vols. (London: Oxford University Press, [1921–22])

OED   *Oxford English Dictionary*, compact edition, 2 vols. (Oxford: Clarendon Press, 1982).

ANN[E] CANDLER

From *Poetical Attempts by Ann Candler* (1803)

Text   *Poetical Attempts by Ann Candler, A Suffolk Cottager; With a Short Narrative of Her Life* (Ipswich: John Raw, 1803). The volume lists more than 250 subscribers, including fifteen different members of the Cobbold family.

From 'Memoirs of the Life of Ann Candler'

I hastened to the town Depending on her route, a distance of three or four miles.

My friend advised me…to let my husband enter into the Militia This plan was based on the distinction between the Guards (domestic units of the British Army) and the Militia (units drawn from the civilian population which, apart from the sort of regular training periods Candler describes, would be activated for service only in an emergency).

disembodied Disbanded; not active.

Madam Probably Elizaberth Cobbold, one of Candler's patrons; the *Memoirs* are written in the form of a letter addressed to two unnamed patrons.

Rev. Dr. J—n The Revd. Dr Thomas Jackson; c. f. 'To the Rev. Dr. J—n'.

cockade A colorful ribbon or insignia, denoting affiliation with a military unit, political party, etc.

Mr. W—, at the Hall Mr. Woodward, the owner and farmer of the lands associated with Sproughton Chantry Hall, a building which still stands.

this house 'Tattingstone House of Industry' (author's note). Built in 1766 by the Samford Union Corporation, this imposing, U-shaped structure still stands, though it has been remodeled and added to several times since Candler's day. For much of the twentieth century it was used as a hospital.

hoys Small sailing vessels, often used for transporting goods, as in Charles Lamb's reminiscence, 'The Old Margate Hoy'.

the late I. C—n, esq … my ever lamented friend, dear Miss F—n … the late M-e R-ss-ll, esq.
Local gentry. Collinson's first name is unknown; the others are Mary
Firmin and Metcalfe Russell.

On the second day of June, the dreadful riots in London broke out The Gordon Riots of sum-
mer 1780, violent anti-Catholic demonstrations that began after Lord
George Gordon presented a petition to Parliament attempting to overturn
the 1778 Catholic Relief Act. For ten days mobs in the streets attacked
Catholic churches, homes, and individuals; several hundred people died in
the violence.

the Chauntry Sproughton Chantry Hall and/or its farmlands.

J. C—n, Esq. Probably the son of I. Collinson.

On the Birth of Twin Sons in 1781

Text   These are the sons the *Memoirs* describes as later dying, aged fourteen and
            eighteen weeks.

Addressed to the Inhabitants of Yoxford, in 1787

Text   'These lines were occasioned by reading a Paragraph in the Ipswich Jour-
            nal, that the inhabitants of Yoxford intended to petition Parliament for a
            charter to hold a weekly Market, whether such a petition were presented or
            not I know not' (author's note).

7   *maugre* In spite of.

24   *Ceres* Roman Goddess of agriculture and fertility.

26   *elate* Rejoice.

To the Rev. Dr. J—n

Title   The addressee is the Revd. Dr Thomas Jackson; Majesty's chaplains were
            appointed by the monarch, or by a high-ranking member of the court or
            aristocracy. In Candler's time there would have been over fifty such posi-
            tions, with varying jurisdictions.

23   *boxes…pit* The most and least expensive seats in the theatre.

Reflections on My Own Situation

24   *a friend indeed* Elizabeth Cobbold.

49–73   *strange fairy…these eastern writers* Almost certainly a reference to one of the
            Arabian Nights tales, perhaps either 'The Adventures of Prince Camaralza-
            man and the Princess Badoura' or 'The Story of the Second Calender',
            though in neither case is the correspondence exact. The tales were first
            made available in English in the so-called 'Grub Street version' (1708).

On Perusing the History of Jacob

4   *The laws were rig'rous, ev'ry task seem'd cross* Here and in the lines that follow,
            Candler is referring to the harsh regimen of the workhouse, in which resi-
            dents would typically be required to work around ten hours a day. Work
            would involve basic maintenance activities of the institution itself: for

women, laundry, cooking, sewing, and washing; and for men, chopping wood, breaking stones, and grinding corn.

10   *Like me … did Jacob find* In the account from Genesis 31, Jacob works for Laban for twenty years, increasing his stores and flocks by hard work and meticulous planning, and adapting to constantly changing circumstances. Candler pursues the analogy between herself and Jacob for the duration of the poem; her interest in the analogy speaks at once to her powerful sense of religious devotion; to the exhaustion she feels after so many years of labour in the workhouse; and, perhaps, to a certain level of righteous indignation at how she has been treated.

20   *Ten times his wages chang'd, his hire detain'd* Genesis 31: 38–42.

22   *a strange return did Laban make* Though not prosperous himself, Laban accrues some wealth indirectly, from his long but conflicted association with Jacob.

25   *so her pangs encrease* I.e., envy's pangs.

44   *Departs in silence* In Genesis 31: 13–22, Jacob is ordered by God to return to the land of his fathers, and to take with him certain of the livestock and belongings. Candler's version de-emphasizes the fact of the divine command, instead focusing on Jacob's unhappiness and sense of longing.

45   *e'er Laban mist his son* Despite Candler's phrasing, Jacob is Laban's nephew; he is the son of Rebekah, Laban's brother.

54   *The Syrian, though a heathen, told his dream* See Genesis 31: 22–30. After Laban discovers the departure of Jacob and his daughters and begins to pursue them, God comes to Laban in a dream and tells him to maintain a sense of neutrality when speaking to Jacob. Laban, however, fails to heed his instruction and criticizes Jacob harshly. Candler's emphasis here is not so much on Laban's disobedience, but on Laban's acknowledgement of the reality of the Hebrew God.

59–71   *While Jacob urges how he oft was wrong'd…deserve reproof* In the Genesis passage, Jacob is aggressive in defending himself against the charges of theft and dishonesty leveled by Laban. Yet Jacob's sense of certainty is partly based on his continuing ignorance of Rachel's theft of Laban's pagan idols.

78   *They both a pious sacrifice ordain* In the closing verses of Genesis 31, the two men make a covenant and are reconciled.

92–4   *But Jacob yet was not exempt from fear…Esau* That is, Jacob worries still about his relationship with his brother Esau, since he had earlier stolen Esau's birthright (Genesis 25) as well as the blessing of their father Isaac (Genesis 27). Candler's decision to continue her poem at this point, going beyond the natural break offered by the resolution of Laban's story, does not suggest her own need to resolve a past transgression. Rather the Esau portion of Jacob's narrative simply allows her to express a desire for a future that is more 'tranquil than the former part' (l. 115).

100   *Esau's martial host* In Genesis 32, Esau is described as heading a company of 400 men.

106   *his brother's kind embrace* Jacob follows God's plan for approaching Esau, and
        the two are successfully reunited; see Genesis 32–33.

WILLIAM HOLLOWAY

From *The Peasant's Fate* (1802)

Text   *The Peasant's Fate: A Rural Poem. With Miscellaneous Poems.* The copy text is
         the 1803 American edition, printed in Wilmington, Delaware. The volume's
         epigraph is drawn from Dryden's translation of Virgil's *Georgics*, IV:

> The time is come I never thought to see;
> Strange revolution for my farm and me!...
> Farewell to my pastures,...my more fruitful flock,...
> No more my sheep shall sip the morning dew,
> No more my song shall please the rural crew!

The volume was reviewed in the *Monthly Mirror, Critical Review,* and *Monthly
Review,* among others; the *British Critic* offered the thoughtful comment that
Holloway was 'full of particular discontent and universal benevolence: he
disapproves of everything that is, yet flatters himself that his mind is replete
with kind feelings' (quoted in Adams 1982, p. 171).

From Preface

The changes in rural life and manners... The entire excerpt is redolent of Wordsworth's
'Preface to Lyrical Ballads' (1802).
the system of engrossing small farms An enclosure-related process by which the separate
small holdings of numerous farmers would be amalgamated under the con-
trol of a single interest. These large plots were often given over to
pasturage.
'passages that lead to nothing' Thomas Gray, 'A Long Story', line 8.

From The Peasant's Fate

Text   The original poem is divided into two books, totaling 1052 lines. Excerpted
         here are Book I, lines 25–48 ('Former division of Downs') and 387–548
         (beginning with 'The ancient Pastor'). The sub-headings employed here are
         those printed in the text, and have been retained in order to capture the
         character of the original, not to denote any editorial deletions or breaks.
         Because the block of text beginning with 'The ancient Pastor' is consecu-
         tive, the line numbers do not re-start with the appearance of each sub-
         heading. For the sake of clarity, however, a number of ellipses that appear in
         the original text have been removed.

['Former division of Downs...Modern changes']

4   *To fence the hovel, or recruit the flames* That is, the 'well-dried stores' of line 2 are
      used by families in winter either for home maintenance or as fuel for fires.

8   *Keeper* 'His Dog' (author's note).

14–17   *the military bands…martial strains* An extended metaphor in which Holloway compares the bands of enclosers to invading armies.

['The ancient Pastor']

4   *'His life adorn'd the doctrines which he taught'* The exact reference here is uncertain, but the language echoes Goldsmith's 'Deserted Village', which Holloway often cited approvingly.

['Modern Rector and Curate']

21   *cure* Parish.

22   *to an ill-paid stranger leaves his cares* I.e., he sub-contracts the basic work of the church so that he may be absent.

23   *hies* Runs.

25   *the needful visit* The annual visit to the village he is required to make under the terms of his contract.

28   *Somnific* Sleep-inducing.

31–8   *Fain would she plead the worthy Curate's cause* The implication of these lines is that the absent Rector's badly-paid deputy is, though worthy, both overworked and not sanctioned by the Church to fully minister to the congregation. Further, he is painfully aware of his inability to meet the congregation's various needs.

['Village Smith']

49–50   *proffer'd toil repaid…to the mind convey'd* The implication is that the local boys receive the 'payment' of the smith's worldly wisdom in return for the small chores they perform for him.

52   *since royal Anne was queen* Anne reigned from 1702 until her death in 1714.

54   *Scythian* Pertaining to a wide geographic area of Asiatic Russia, but especially here its vast plains or steppes.

60   *traces* Straps connecting a horse to a vehicle or load.

61   *Ball* A generic name for a plough-horse.

63   *idly-pamper'd steeds* In a note to this line, Holloway offers the following citation from 'Mortimer's Lectures', presumably the *Lectures on the elements of commerce, politics, and finances* (1801) by Thomas Mortimer: 'It has been fully proved, that more than one half of the produce of all our lands is now consumed by horses. Does not true political economy require, in this case, the exportation, or other means of getting rid of 50,000 horses, kept for parade or pleasure, independent of those which are usefully employed, and which consume annually 3,245,000 quarters of oats?'

68   *petty farmer's early wain* The term 'petty farmer' is an alternative to 'husbandman', denoting a farmer of relatively small holdings. His 'early wain' (or wagon) may be taken as a figure for his industriousness.

72   *The toil-contending reapers to regale* I.e., the petty farmer keeps the reapers regularly supplied with ale.

73   *Now into one a hundred fields are thrown* A reference to the process of 'engrossing' fields, referenced above in the note to Holloway's Preface.

['Poor-House']

81   *an unhappy remnant still remains* 'The author does not here pass a general censure on poor-houses, but condemns the policy that, from a state of comfort and independence, subjects the labouring class of people to those mansions of misery, by incapacitating them from supporting themselves; and pays too little attention to the regulation of such institutions, the management of which is frequently left to the most careless, negligent, and unfeeling members of the community' (author's note).

82   *grudging Pride with scantly dole sustains* That is, the well-to-do provide a minimal level of charitable support.

108   *'the catalogue of human woes'* See 'I hate that drum's discordant sound', by the Quaker poet John Scott of Amwell (1731–83), line 16.

['England compared with the most fruitful Countries']

125–30   *Rhine…Arno…Hesperian…Ganges* This geographical list, focused mainly on famed rivers, proceeds generally from north to south. 'Hesperia' was a term used at different times to denote either Italy or Spain. More broadly, it simply means 'western land'.

132   *laves* Laps up against; washes.

135   *Pan* Greek god of plains, pastures, forests, and flocks, associated with natural vitality and bounty.

136   *Pomona* Roman goddess of fruit and fruit-bearing trees.

137   *ALBION* England.

139   *a venal band* Those engaged in enclosure or other commercial activities.

144   *Timur-like* 'Timur, notwithstanding the blandishments of poetry, was undoubtedly a tyrant, only in a degree less than Bajazet, on whom he is said to have inflicted the punishment intended for himself, had he been defeated in his engagement with that monarch' (author's note). In Elizabethan drama, Timur was called Tamburlaine or Tamerlane; he defeated the Turkish sultan Bajazet at Ankara in 1402, and was said to have carried him in a portable iron cage.

From *The Minor Minstrel* (1808)

Text   *The Minor Minstrel; Or, Poetical Pieces, Chiefly Familiar and Descriptive* (London: Printed for W. Suttaby; and Darton and Harvey: Sold by Vernor, Hood, & Sharpe, Poultry; and L.B. Seely, Fleet Street.)

To Robert Bloomfield, on the Abolition of the Slave Trade

Title   In 1807 the British Parliament voted to abolish British involvement in the trade in slaves.

9   *Olney's Poet* William Cowper (1731–1800), a vocal abolitionist.

The Common; Or, The Soil of Liberty

Title   In its endorsement of material simplicity, communal holism, and quiet isolation in nature, this poem is perhaps the most Wordsworthian of the Holloway selections here.

7   *Circassian* Referring to the Caucasus, a 'mountainous region between the Black and Caspian Seas' (*OED*).

19   *hies* Runs.

55   *Hampstead* A village north of London famous for its large, undeveloped heath.

Sam Sear's Three Tokens; Or, John Hurdler's Tale

Title   'The drift of this tale, and its moral tendency, will not be mistaken; it having been allowed by the best and wisest of men, that the weapons of ridicule are never better employed, than in attacking the strong holds of superstition' (author's note). It is not clear why the poem is subtitled 'John Hurdler's Tale', since the other character who appears is named John Woodrow. Perhaps Holloway heard the story from a John Hurdler.

1   *wear* 'Or dam' (author's note).

32   *lug* Ear.

69   *ween* Suppose; believe.

73   *Jack o' Lantern* A will of the wisp; the combusting gas around marshy ground.

85   *Fegs!* An expression of strong conviction.

Roke Down

3   *Kine* Cows.

23   *barrow* 'One of those Barrows, or round hillocks, so common in the west of England, was opened some years since on this down, and in it were found human bones, fragments of urns, &c' (author's note). The barrow in question is probably located in southern England, in the area of Roke Manor, fifteen miles north of the port city of Southampton.

Charity

Title   The scene described in this poem, in which the children of London's charity schools are brought to Saint Paul's for their annual service of praise and thanksgiving, is now well known to literary history through William Blake's 'Holy Thursday' from *Songs of Innocence*.

31   *Xerces-like* 'It is recorded of Xerces, that when he reviewed his mighty army, he melted into tears, at the consideration, that not one of that immense multitude, would be living at the end of a hundred years!' (author's note). Xerces I, king of Persia between 485 and 465 B.C., is referred to as Ahasuerus in the Bible.

NATHANIEL BLOOMFIELD

From *An Essay on War* (1803)

Text   *An Essay On War, In Blank Verse; Honington Green, A Ballad; The Culprit, An Elegy; And Other Poems, On Various Subjects: By Nathaniel Bloomfield.* (London: Thomas Hurst, and Vernor and Hood, 1803). The mixed nature of the volume's reviews can be quickly illustrated. The *Critical Review* said that 'the poems, in general, are not without merit', but it protested against the vision of reproductive nature in the 'Essay', calling it 'an opinion so mischievous and so absurd: it is the corner-stone of atheism, and of atheistic morals; for it denies the existence of an over-ruling Intelligence; and asserts, that man must, like the beasts, blindly indulge his sexual appetite, however deplorable and ruinous the consequences. Such an assertion may be credited by the inhabitants and by the visitants of the brothel; but they must be lamentably ignorant of history and of metaphysics, who are the dupes of such a system. Mr. N. Bloomfield has hastily assented to a doctrine which he has but half examined' (p. 410). The *Poetical Register* also acknowledged the volume in general terms, saying that the poems 'certainly do credit to Mr. Bloomfield [and] shew that the author has a reflecting and an amiable mind', but, as with most of the periodical reviews, expressed annoyance with Lofft's puffery: 'Had Mr. Lofft contented himself with claiming a large share of praise for the man who in such a station [...] could write such poems, his claim would have been readily allowed; but when he compares him to Lucretius, and asserts that few men have ever reached before to such a height on Parnassus, it is impossible to repress a smile, of something like contempt, at his utter want of taste and judgement' (pp. 428–9). The *British Critic* admitted 'It must be confessed, that both [the 'Essay'] and the smaller poems show a command of language, that would formerly have been thought extraordinary in a man of low origin; but the diffusion of small knowledge has destroyed the wonder of these things [...] We shall only add, that what is very extraordinary for an uneducated man to write, may be very unedifying for persons of education to read' (p. 82).

An Essay On War

Text   All of the ellipses printed here reproduce the typography of the first edition.

2   *surplus* Though Lofft asserts that Bloomfield 'never saw' (p. xxii) Thomas Malthus's *Essay on the Principle of Population* (1798), much of the poem seems to follow from that work. 'Through the animal and vegetable kingdoms', Malthus writes, 'nature has scattered the seeds of life abroad with the most profuse and liberal hand. She has been comparatively sparing in the room, and the nourishment necessary to rear them [...] The race of plants, and race of animals shrink under this great restrictive law. And the race of man cannot, by any efforts of reason, escape from it'. (eds E. A. Wrangley and David Souden [London: William Pickering, 1986], p. 9). But while the natu-

ral inclination of both human and animal populations is to expand geometrically (rather than arithmetrically), Malthus identifies several natural checks on the human population: crime, disease, war, and vice.

14   *Assays* Makes an attempt; ventures.

39   *glebe* Land, soil.

66   *Immanity* 'Monstrous cruelty' (*OED*).

104   *parley* An 'informal conference with an enemy' (*OED*).

119   *Covert* Privacy. The sense is that, initially, such conflicts do not involve women because of a certain pervasive ideal of male honour.

148   *mound*s Dams.

244   *Pean* Paean; song of praise.

247   *adventitious* Having a distant or external origin.

286–97 *Age of Chivalry…Danes…Roman Tyranny* In this passage the poet is moving backward in time, from the Middle Ages to the Anglo-Saxon period to a more ancient era of Roman occupation.

289   *perfidious* Treacherous.

298   *Tweed* The chief river of the border region between Scotland and England.

328   *Greeks…and long-exil'd Jew* A reference to cultures and nations, not particular individuals.

332   *memento mori* A reminder or memorial of death; here perhaps prayers commemorating the dead or pleas of the dead themselves to be remembered.

347   *Let not mistaken fondness dote on Peace* Bloomfield here argues that a condition in which free societies practice war is actually superior to one in which a false peace is enforced by tyranny and slavery.

364   *smacks the ichor* Savours the blood of an animal.

390   *Human Wit* Ingenuity.

396   *Shambles* Meat markets were cattle are slaughtered; the evocation of human's superiority here is possibly meant to be ironic.

Elegy on the Enclosure of Honington Green

Title   In the volume's preface, Lofft notes, 'The Spot which is the subject of the Ballad is less, I believe, than Half an Acre. It did certainly ornament the Village; independent of a just and laudable partiality in the Author. Thus it would have seem'd to the casual glance of a stranger. To the BLOOMFIELDS every circumstance gave it peculiar endearment. There the Author of 'THE FARMER'S BOY,' and of these POEMS, first drew breath. There grew the first Daisies which their feet press'd in childhood. On this little Green their Parents look'd with delight: and the Children caught the affection; and learn'd to love it as soon as they lov'd any thing. By its smallness and its situation it was no object: and could have been left out of Enclosure without detriment to the General Plan, or to any individual Interest' (pp. xviii–xix).

3   *Coulter* The cutting blade of a plow.

7   *Ceres* The Roman goddess of agriculture.

20   *cinctur'd* Encompassed; encircled.

21   *causeways* Raised pathways.

40   *unportion'd* Literally, having no portion; i.e., without money or property.

50   *the matron* Apparently, his mother.

66   *Who died when I was but a Child* According to Lofft's Preface, Nat's father George Bloomfield died of smallpox when Nat was eight years old (p. vii).

73   *pelf* Riches.

87–8   *In no Tale of Mark Sargent he fail'd, / Nor in all Robin Hood's Derry-downs* The implication is that he was well-versed in popular stories and ballads.

90   *Her father* Identified by Lofft as 'Mr. Robin Manby' (p. vii).

92   *six Children so small* Nat and his siblings.

131   *lucre* Money.

        he That is, the personification of Avarice.

134   *As a Shark may disport with the Fry* In the manner of a predator playing with its helpless victim, probably adapted from John Dryden's long poem *Annus Mirabilis* (1667), lines 809–12:

> So, close behind some promontory lie
> The huge leviathans t' attend their prey,
> And give no chase, but swallow in the fry,
> Which through their gaping jaws mistake the way.

138   *halcyon* Peaceful.

139   *infantine Peasantry* An elaborate term for local poor children.

More Bread and Cheese

12   *the news from Versailles or the Hague* Though serving generically as shorthand for the endless cycles of international strife, this reference suggests several major events involving France dating from late 1792 and early 1793, including its official abolition of the monarchy (Sept 1792), the start of the trial of King Louis XVI (Dec 1792), the execution of Louis (January 1793), and France's declaration of war on England and the Netherlands (February 1793).

42   *incor'gible* Incapable of being corrected.

Lyric Address to Dr Jenner

Title   In the Preface, Lofft quotes from George regarding Nat's terrible experience with the smallpox: 'He lost two sweet Boys: who both died within a few days of each-other, by that dreadful disease' (p. x). Further, reports Lofft, 'while this Preface was in the Press', the disease 'has been fatal to another promising Child, THOMAS; born *Aug.* 1799. The Father, oppress'd with grief, reproaches himself for not having inoculated this Child with the Small-Pox. But when it is consider'd how formidable, after two such Losses, the SMALL-POX in any form must appear to affectionate Parents, I think it will be evident that he is too severe to himself in this reproach. The inoculated SMALL-POX is sometimes fatal: had he inoculated the Child he would have reproach'd himself, and still with more feeling than justice, for so doing' (pp. x–xi). For more on the Bloomfield family in relation to the disease, see Tim Fulford and Debbie Lee, 'The Jenneration of Disease: Vaccination, Romanticism, and Revolution', *Studies in Romanticism* 39 (2000), 139–63.

5   *Meed* Reward or recompense.

THOMAS BA(T)CHELOR

From *Village Scenes* (1804)

Text   T. Bachelor, *Village scenes: The progress of agriculture, and other poems* (London: Vernor and Hood, 1804).

From The Progress of Agriculture; Or, The Rural Survey

Text   The full text of the poem is 609 lines long; its epigraph is from James Thomson's *The Castle of Indolence* (1748), Canto II, 238–43:

> New scenes arise, new landscapes strike the eye,
> And all th' enliven'd country beautify;
> Gay plains extend where marshes slept before;
> O'er recent meads th' exulting streamlets fly;
> Dark-frowning heaths grow bright with Ceres' store
> And woods embrown the steep, or wave along the shore.

7   *Phoebus* The sun.

8   *Refulgent* Brilliant; dazzling.

28   *Ceres* The Roman goddess of agriculture.

32   *O *****!* The location is uncertain, probably referring to some portion of the lands belonging to the Duke of Bedford.

37   *Mantuan lyre* I.e., that which inspired the poet Virgil.

39   *Georgic* Related to rural life, especially agriculture and animal husbandry.

57   *rushy slips contiguous roods divide* A description of a poorly cultivated, poorly drained field, into which patches of marsh plants have spread; a rood is a parcel of one-quarter acre.

58   *worthless commons* Disorganized and inefficiently-used land, of the kind that Batchelor would like to see enclosed.

67   *downy nuisance* The floating seeds of thistles.

70   *a tenth he must not call his own* An apparently unapproving reference to the ten-percent tithe that the farmer is effectively forced to render to the Church.

78   *ling* Plants growing on the heath; heather.

84   *boreal* Northern.

85   *Arabia!* The comparison of climates – and by extension, cultures – is a kind of rhetorical set-piece of much georgic and pastoral poetry, following from Virgil. For another version in this volume, see William Hollway's *The Peasant's Fate*, ll. 121–52.

88   *imbrue* Stain; defile.

90   *banditti* Bandits.

93   *the timorous, light-heel'd race* Probably rabbits.

96   *Cynthia's* The moon's.

99–104   *chace...Scythian...shiv'ring native knows* These lines, possibly following from
          Dyer's *The Fleece* IV.138–52, describe the hunting practices of nomads
          native to Asiatic Russia. Ermines are creatures of the weasel family that live
          in northern climes; their fur is white in winter and highly prized.

113   *mephitic* Foul-smelling; noxious.

117   *Delusive lights* The fiery, dancing phosphorescence caused by combustible
          marsh gases, commonly called the will-o-the-wisp.

119   *irriguous* 'Supplying water or moisture' (*OED*).

120   *Ouse* The Great Ouse, the river on which Bedford stands, flows into the
          North Sea at King's Lynn.

120   *Naiad* A nymph or female spirit of lakes or rivers.

133   *Cam* The river on which the city of Cambridge sits, and a tributary of the
          Great Ouse.

145   *Batavia* The Netherlands.

159   *Pomona* Roman goddess of fruit and fruit trees.

160   *gold and rubies* Yellow and red apples.

174   *furry people* Rabbits.

181   *argil* Clay.

189   *Caledonia* Scotland.

204   *cyper* Though 'cyper' can denote a sedge or marsh-plant such as galingale, it
          seems possible that this is a misprint for 'cypher', and that the speaker is
          actually viewing an engraved figure of some sort. In either case, the object
          summons to the speaker's mind the subject of fen-drainage and the person
          of Russell (see next note).

206   *gen'rous Russel's name* Francis Russell, Fourth Earl of Bedford (1593–1641),
          who was instrumental in organizing the region's first major fen drainage
          program, begun in 1634 under the supervision of the Dutch engineer Sir
          Cornelius Vermuyden. Batchelor's praise of Russell follows that of John
          Dyer in Book II of *The Fleece* (1757), who celebrates the 'Bedford Level', a
          substanial area of peat that the Earl succeeded in having drained:

> Bedford Level, erst
> A dreary pathless waste, the coughing flock
> Was wont with hairy fleeces to deform;
> And, smiling with her lure of summer flow'rs,
> The heavy ox, vain-struggling, to ingulph;
> Till one, of that high-honour'd patriot name,
> Russel, arose, who drain'd the rushy fen,
> Confin'd the waves, bid groves and gardens bloom,
> And through his new creation led the Ouze,
> And gentle Camus, silver-winding streams:
> Godlike beneficence: from chaos drear
> To raise the garden and the shady grove. (ll. 165–76)

It should also be noted that Batchelor was a tenant on the estate of the Earl's namesake and descendant, Francis Russell, Fifth Duke of Bedford (1765–1802), who was himself greatly interested in agricultural policy and the functioning of the rural economy.

265   *champaign* Level, open country.

266   *Reynard* Fox.

266   *sward* Grass; greenery.

268   *Promiscuous* Mixed together.

290   *Gallic* French.

291   *anana* Pineapple.

293   *sweet cane* Sugar. With this reference Batchelor is implicitly condemning the slave trade.

333   *colewort* Cabbage.

402–23   *Fled is your long-accumulating store…their sighs with mine* This passage captures the sense of conflict and indeed defensiveness Batchelor feels in his multiple perspectives as poet, farmer, agricultural theorist, and local historian. Though generally an advocate of enclosure insofar as it 'scientifically' promotes efficiency, order, and productivity, he is troubled by its excesses, especially monopolistic practices that lead to the engrossment – and permanent erasure – of traditionally autonomous parcels.

409   *still* Always.

CHARLOTTE RICHARDSON

From *Poems Written on Different Occasions* (1806)

Text   *Poems Written on Different Occasions, By Charlotte Richardson. To which is prefixed Some Account of the Author.* (York, T. Wilson and R. Spence, 1806). The charitable aim behind the volume's production is everywhere in evidence, perhaps most clearly in the list of subscribers, which includes a separate list of those 'who have contributed more than Five Shillings per copy'. This format is continued in the 1809 volume.

    The volume contains thirty-six poems, but we can infer from Cappe's Preface that this did not constitute the totality of Richardson's output at the time; Cappe notes that Richardson 'brought me a whole book of manuscript poems, from which the following selection is taken' (p. xvii).

Written Under Great Doubt, and Anxiety of Mind

Title   The anxiety to which Richardson refers involves her having to decide between two suitors; the issue was resolved within a few months of the writing of this poem with her marriage to Robert Richardson in 1802. The successive family health crises the couple would face makes the poem appear sadly prophetic. Several other poems in the volume allude to the importance of a careful decision in marriage.

5   *Wisely to choose is my desire* 'If young ladies who move in a sphere however different from that of a simple cook-maid, would in this instance follow her

example, and entreat of God to direct and bless their matrimonial connections, should we hear so frequently of their uniting themselves with men of the most unprincipled and libertine character – Would our Newspapers be filled with so many unhappy cases in Doctors Commons, and would the manners of too many among the great, continue to be, as they are at present, a disgrace and a reproach to their country?' (Cappe's note).

8   *false pretender* The suitor who should be refused.

He Sleeps

Title   This 1805 poem on the death of Richardson's husband is the one Cappe describes as her introduction to the aspiring poet: 'By what is usually called an accident, but in stricter language [...] will afterwards be found by a careful observer, to be a sort of master key fitted to unlock the future current of events, the little piece, entitled, "He Sleeps," was put into my hands. Struck with the piety of the sentiments, and the pathos with which they were expressed, and utterly astonished at the neatness, not to say elegance of the composition, it excited in my mind a new interest for the writer: I made further inquiry, and found, to my no small surprise, that she had long been in the habit of putting down in measure the genuine effusions of a very feeling heart' (p. xvi–xvii).

20   *I own the stroke divine* That is, I will try to accept and embrace the fact that this apparent calamity was at God's bidding.

27–8   *Since pain and sorrow are the lot, / Of all of woman born* See Genesis 3:16.

35   *Calumny* Slander.

49   *when th' Archangel's voice is heard* See 1 Thessalonians 4:14–16: 'For if we believe that Jesus died and rose again, even so them also which sleep in Jesus will God bring with him. For this we say unto you by the word of the Lord, that we which are alive and remain unto the coming of the Lord shall not prevent them which are asleep. For the Lord himself shall descend from heaven with a shout, with the voice of the archangel, and with the trump of God: and the dead in Christ shall rise first'.

From *Poems, Chiefly Composed During the Pressure of Severe Illness* (1809)

Text   *Poems, Chiefly Composed During the Pressure of Severe Illness. By Charlotte Richardson. Published by Subscription for the Benefit of the Author, By the Editor of her former Publication.* (York: Thomas Wilson and Son, 1809). The title-page reads 'Volume II', indicating not that this 1809 publication was issued in two volumes, but rather identifying it as a second collection of Richardson's writings. The subscriber list numbers well over 600.

After Reading Clarkson's Narrative

Title   The title employed here is that of the volume's table of contents; the full title (as it appears internally) is, 'After Reading Clarkson on the Abolition of the Slave Trade, August 1808'. Richardson includes four other poems on slavery and abolition in the volume: 'The Negro', 'Address to the Freeholders of Yorkshire', 'Ode on the abolition of the slave trade', and 'Address to Mr Clarkson on the Slave Trade'.

Thomas Clarkson (1760–1846) had been a leading proponent of abolition since the late 1780s, though for a period around the turn of the century health and financial concerns led him to withdraw from active public agitation. Over the years he produced a series of letters, books, and pamphlets on the issue, but the poem's date and triumphant tone suggest that Richardson is referring to his *History of the Rise, Progress and Accomplishment of the Abolition of the African Slave Trade* (1808), published the year following Parliament's vote to abolish the trade. Richardson's poem also reflects the fact that Clarkson believed himself to have been chosen by God to pursue the abolitionist cause.

7   *Freely devoted talents, fortune, time* Clarkson was from a fairly prosperous family, and nearly spent himself into poverty in pursuit of the cause, though he was later accused of self-glorification in his accounts of these activities.

21   *Interest* Financial self-interest.

23   *At length the glorious victory is yours* A reference to the long battle Clarkson and others had fought since they formed the Committee for Abolition of the African Slave Trade in 1787. The Abolition Bill was introduced to Parliament several times in the early nineteenth century before finally passing in 1807.

The Washerwoman's Reply to E. Waring

Title   The poem is a reply to E. Waring's 'The Washing-day' (printed below), apparently a periodical poem. Waring's identity is unknown; he is possibly the Elijah Waring who was the close friend of the Welsh poet Edward Williams ('Iolo Morganwg'), but this is by no means certain. Indeed, it is possible the name is a pseudonymic pun on 'wearing'. (For Williams and Elijah Waring, see Tim Burke, ed. *English Labouring-Class Poetry 1780–1800* (London: Pickering and Chatto, 2003, pp. 275–7).

Richardson reprints the entirety of Waring's poem alongside hers, presumably to emphasize the close and clever inversions she performs. The tone and decisiveness of her poem also suggest an increase in Richardson's artistic confidence. Her poem is reminiscent – though in greatly diminished form – of what is perhaps the most famous intertextual exchange in the labouring-class tradition: Mary Collier's reply, in 'The Woman's Labour' (1739), to Stephen Duck's 'The Thresher's Labour' (1730). See William Christmas, ed. *English Labouring-Class Poetry 1700–1740* (London: Pickering and Chatto, 2003). E. Waring's 'The Washing-day' also has strong thematic continuities with another poem printed in this volume, 'The Washing-Day' by Thomas Wilson (q.v.).

'The Washing-day. By E. Waring. July 1808'

Hark! 'tis the important day of washing;
Discord, clack, incessant splashing;

Soap-suds all around are dashing,
       Unceasing.

The rooms all tumbled inside out;   5
Linen in heaps is thrown about;
And all is racket, noise, and rout,
       Displeasing.

See, close around the fire-side
Wet garments hanging to be dried;   10
Hose, and a hundred things beside,
       Wet dropping!

O! wretched day beyond expressing;
To me a day, the most distressing;
Though 'tis our women's greatest blessing,   15
       This slopping.

In vain we seek for comfort round;
Comfort is nowhere to be found;
On washing days 'tis forbidden ground
       To any.   20

And when one washing day is o'er,
Our pleasure's damp'd by dread of more:
O! joy to come, but sorrow sore
       To many.

GEORGE BLOOMFIELD

The Poets at Odds

Text   George Bloomfield to Thomas Hill. fMS Eng 391. *By permission of the Houghton Library, Harvard University.*

The poem is contained in a letter dated 11 June 1809. Though Bloomfield addresses William Holloway (q.v.) throughout most of the letter, it appears the intended recipient of this copy was in fact Hill, proprietor of the *Mirror Monthly* Magazine; internal evidence suggests that Bloomfield was sending virtually identical letters to both men at the same time.

The transcription of the poem is a joint effort of myself and George Collins. Provisional readings are contained in brackets; the words appearing in italics are underlined (in several cases double-underlined) in the manuscript. Bloomfield is especially inconsistent in his use of possessives and upper- and lower-case initial letters. Possessives have been added where they are clearly implied; cases of letters have been changed only infrequently, though in several cases it was difficult to discern the original form.

18   *arch-fiend* Milton's name for Satan. See *Paradise Lost* I, lines 156 and 209.

24   *clime* Climb in manuscript.

39   *Sophist* Philosophers who manipulate or distort truth.

40   *Sin and Death* See Milton, *Paradise Lost,* II.1024.

44   *Resist not* 'Matthew 5:39' (author's note). Matthew 5 begins with Christ's
        reciting of the beatitudes to the disciples, concluding, 'Think not that I am
        come to destroy the law, or the prophets: I am not come to destroy, but to
        fulfill' (17). The specific verse referenced by Bloomfield's note is part of the
        familiar sequence of verses 38 and 39: 'Ye have heard that it hath been said,
        An eye for an eye, and a tooth for a tooth: But I say unto you, That ye resist
        not evil: but whosoever shall smite thee on thy right cheek, turn to him the
        other also'.

46   *defensive war* Pursuant to lines 44–5, a defensive war would be one of 'self-
        defense', in which a decision was made not to turn the other cheek.

55   *scanted* Left in short supply.

59   *laurels* Garlands of triumph.

74   *Commissioned War* That is, a war of commission or choice.

78   *warft* Possibly 'wafts', though 'warft' seems a viable colloquialism.

80   *white* A misspelling of 'wight', meaning a living being or mortal.

MARY BRYAN

From *Sonnets and Metrical Tales* (1815)

Text   *Sonnets and Metrical Tales by Mrs. Bryan.* (Bristol: Printed and Sold at the City
        Printing Office, 1815). The epigraph is from Robert Burns's 'A Vision':

> [A]ll beneath th' unrivall'd rose,
> The lowly daisy sweetly blows;
> Tho' large the forest monarch throws
>   His army shade,
> Yet green the juicy hawthorn grows,
>   Adown the glade.

To William W—h, Esq.

Title   In a note to the poem, Bryan alludes to the publication of Wordsworth's
        Excursion (1814) (which she has not seen), declaring that whatever its vir-
        tues or defects Wordsworth can never 'impair the strength or beauty of that
        everlasting monument of argumentative truth – his Preface to his Lyrical
        Pieces' (p. 137). This citation of the *Lyrical Ballads* Preface as the primary
        document through which to read Wordsworth stands as a remarkably early
        and acute historical judgment. As with her successful imitations of the Lucy
        poems, it is evidence that Bryan was exceptionally attuned to the nature
        and character of his power. Though there is no decisive evidence that
        Wordsworth ever corresponded with Bryan, it seems possible that he did
        so, based on one of her remarks to Scott: she acknowledges that 'neither
        your generous example nor Mr Wordsworth's will avail me any thing here,
        and that I must effect all by personal application' (NLS MS 3905, ff. 187–

8). Quoted by permission of the Trustees of the National Library of Scotland.

When Bryan's note to this poem is considered in conjunction with the volume's many other echoes of Wordsworth, we can deduce that her exposure to his work ran from the 1800 *Lyrical Ballads* through *Poems in Two Volumes* (1807). Jonathan Wordsworth hears echoes of 'The Mad Mother', 'The Idiot Boy', and 'Michael'; Stuart Curran's discussion of Wordsworth's 'The Two April Mornings' as the precursor text for Bryan's 'Anna' provides us our best critical discussion of any single Bryan poem. For 'To William W—h' itself, I would suggest that we can also hear soundings of 'Ode: Intimations of Immortality' and 'Elegiac Stanzas…Peele Castle', both first published in *PTV*.

3   *ungenial* Inimical to creativity.

32   *Too pure to be refin'd* The poem's concluding quotation is from Wordsworth's 'To the Spade of a Friend (An Agriculturist)', which appeared in *PTV*; the friend was Thomas Wilkinson, the Cumberland poet. Bryan's decision to focus her admiration of Wordsworth through the spade poem – a piece that has frequently been ridiculed for its bathos – may be viewed as evidence of the totality with which she embraced his program of simplicity.

Anna

Title   For discussion of this poem, see Curran, p. 117.

15   *playful prattler's suit* Evidently, a smooth-talking suitor who successfully wooed Anna but then abandoned her.

24   *L***'s* One would assume that this word is 'Love', yet the poem's final line mysteriously declares that it is not so. Possibly it is a place-name, like the village of Lillesdon, near North Curry, where Bryan evidently lived for a time.

On Reading Lines to Tranquility

Title   Bryan would seem to be citing Charlotte Smith's sonnet 'To Tranquillity', though another of Smith's sonnets, 'Should the lone Wanderer, fainting on his way', seems more appropriate to the dialogue Bryan's poem imagines. After describing how 'Poesy' had temporarily stayed her 'sense of sorrow' (ll. 7, 6), Smith concludes the latter poem wearily: '…Hope reclines upon the tomb; / And points my wishes to that tranquil shore, / Where the pale spectre Care pursues no more' (ll. 12–4). Bryan may actually have had in mind yet a third Smith sonnet, 'Far on the sands, the low, retiring tide', where Smith laments, 'Alas! can tranquil nature give me rest' (l. 7). (*The Poems of Charlotte Smith*. ed. Stuart Curran [New York: Oxford University Press, 1993]). Though none of these three sonnets contains Bryan's closing phrase 'boundless love', the ending of 'Far on the sands' is lexically the closest match.

Bryan's poem is confusing in other ways as well. Where all three of Smith's sonnets offer a forthright contrast between earthly distress and heavenly rest, Bryan seems to resist this easy distinction, even as the allegory potentially includes Smith herself. Whatever Smith poem or amalgam of poems Bryan had in mind, she describes her regard for Smith in a lengthy passage from the preface to *Sonnets and Metrical Tales*: 'Dreadful and accumulated must be the evils that can crush the independent mind. – Alas! it is a pitiable struggle; few are its resources: opposed by insult, injustice, and treachery; cruelly wounded, yet unyielding, its efforts sometimes cease only in that fate which they accelerate: and the case becomes affectingly heightened when the welfare of those helpless objects of tenderest interest depends on the exertions to which they stimulate. Mrs. CHARLOTTE SMITH, under the latter circumstance, became a successful candidate for public support; but Mrs. S. required no indulgence: on the contrary, her genius arose another "star in the literary hemisphere of her country", contributing to its glory; untarnished by that dark cloud of affliction from whence it burst pure brilliant, and over which it shed rays of beauty. Admired Woman! blessed Mother! under all thy cares, blessed in that independence which thy talents secured to thy children!' (pp. ix–x).

To — — [;] Sonnet

Title   Though called a sonnet, the meter here is highly irregular, with lines of mostly iambic tetrameter and trimeter. The rhyme scheme is similarly idiosyncratic.

13   *a bitter throe* A feeling of pain or misery.

The Spinning-Wheel

Title   Given the volume's other echoes, it seems natural to seek some relationship between this poem and Wordsworth's 'Song for the Spinning Wheel'. But since Wordsworth's 1812 poem was not published until 1820, Bryan would have had to see his poem while it was in manuscript, and there is nothing in the record to suggest this level of intimacy between them – even assuming they had any personal contact at all. Wordsworth's short poem focuses on the local belief that while the sheep are sleeping, the spindle that weaves their wool 'Runs with speed more smooth and fine, / Gathering up a trustier line' (ll. 11–2).

Julia

Title   In the Table of Contents, this poem is titled 'Julia's Grave'.

From Unpublished Manuscripts

The Village Maid

Text   National Library of Scotland MS 3889, ff. 187–8. Reprinted by permission of the Trustees of the National Library of Scotland. This poem was enclosed in a letter from Bryan to Walter Scott of 16 September 1818. (Ragaz dates the letter 16 August 1818.) The transcription is my own;

where Bryan's writing is unclear, provisional readings are enclosed in brackets. There are transcription difficulties throughout, but especially in lines 77–80, where sealing wax used on the letter has rendered several words almost totally illegible.

20   *roundelay* A dance in a circle, though the word can also denote a song with a repeated tune or refrain.

30   *umbrage* Thick foliage that creates shade.

39   *naiad* A nymph who inhabits fountains and streams.

42   *fillets* Decorative ribbons.

46   *rest* Both here and in line 48, the reading of 'rest' is provisional, with 'nest' a possible alternative in both cases. Neither seems perfectly appropriate, though the apparent repetition is not in itself problematic since Bryan frequently repeats words.

61   'The fate of Chatterton was the occasional source of deep regret' (author's note). Bryan clearly identified herself with Chatterton, writing on 5 Sept. 1827 to Scott, 'Surely Sir Walter Scott is above the world's dread laugh – I am aware that much ridicule has occasionally been cast on that literary patronage which was once probably too hasty and indiscriminating – perhaps the fate of Chatterton and the feelings which it awakened occasioned this flow of benevolence towards obscure and unfortunate genius; and surely it was peevish and ungenerous in men of sense to be so sarcastic on a harmless folly (if folly it were) which in some cases, gave a brief importance to inferior talent: but this will not affect my purpose' (NLS MS 3905, fols. 7–10).

99   *cote* A small enclosure for a bird.

Stanzas

Text   National Library of Scotland MS 3905, ff. 7–10. Reprinted by permission of the Trustees of the National Library of Scotland. This poem was enclosed in a letter from Bryan to Walter Scott, dated 5 September 1827. The verses are simply titled 'Stanzas'. The transcription is my own.

8   *long unbroken night* A reference to her severely impaired vision.

25   *sear* Withered.

39   *thrall* Bondage.

JOHN MITFORD

From *Poems of a British Sailor* (1818)

Text   *Poems of a British Sailor. By John Mitford* (London: Printed for the author by W. Flint, 1818).

Mary; or The Suicide

1   *Wansbeck* 'A romantic stream, flowing through Mitford vale, and washing the base of Mitford castle' (author's note).

3   *Mitford's mouldering towers* The castle, located outside of Morpeth in North-
       umberland, is now a ruin.

6   *Alde church* Possibly Mitford Church, St Mary Magdalene in Morpeth, but
       the reference is confusing since the Alde river and the Aldeburgh church
       are located in Suffolk, not Northumberland.

19   *long live* '"May he outlive his relations and friends", was the heaviest curse a
       Roman could bestow upon his most bitter enemy' (author's note).

The Maniac's Song; or The Coat of Blue

2   *coat of blue* The standard uniform of British sailors.

7   *Egypt's shore* A reference to the bloody Battle of the Nile, 1–2 August 1798,
       in which the British under Nelson defeated the French. It is estimated that
       over 200 British and 600 French sailors died in the confrontation.

Elegiac Stanzas, To the Memory of Robert Burns

Epigraph 'The traveler shall come, he that saw me in youth and beauty shall come;
       his eyes will search the field, but they shall not find me'. A slight misquota-
       tion from the opening of James MacPherson's 'Berrathon', *The Poems of
       Ossian* (London, 1796), p. 173.

5   *native wood-notes wild* John Milton, 'L'Allegro' (1645), l. 134.

7–8   *Scotia's darling child…Ayr's green bank* Burns, born in Alloway, Ayrshire, on
       the west coast of Scotland.

22   *her eyes* That is, the eyes of Burns's widow.

27   *'voice of COILA'* The poem 'The Vision' tells the story of Burns's meeting
       with his muse, who tells him, 'Coila my name; and this district as mine I
       claim' (ll. 151–2).

Sorrow; to Bertha

11   *Mecklinn stream* The location is uncertain, but probably near Mecklin Park in
       Cumbria.

12   *jessmine* The jessamine tree.

15   *mantling* Blushing.

Death of the Sailor-Boy

Text   The *Zealous*, cited at the close of the poem, is the ship on which Mitford
       was stationed at the Battle of the Nile, which had occurred in August 1798,
       only two months before the putative date of this poem. The 74-gun *Zealous*,
       staffed by almost six hundred men, was captained by Samuel Hood. Mit-
       ford's account of his activities during this famous engagement is a central
       focus of his entry in the *Dictionary of National Biography*. C.f. the note to line
       7 of 'The Maniac's Song'.

1   *scud* Low, ragged clouds.

4   *boatswain* The ship's officer responsible for the deck crew.

9   *boatswain's pipe* A special shrill whistle whose sound could be heard above
       that of the ocean, used to communicate basic orders to the sailors.

11–12   *run…clew* Various navigational and mechanical operations, all except 'steer-ing' done with the sails. To trim is to adjust the sails, with the intent of achieving the best balance between wind direction and the ship's desired course; to reef is to bring in some portion of a sail, in order to limit its use; to furl is to wrap a sail against the yard to which it is attached; to clew is to raise or lower the corners of sails with ropes called clew-lines.

19   *messmate* Mealtime companion.

The Island Fiend

Title   *Island Fiend* Napoleon (1769–1821).

1   *Elba* The island off the coast of Italy to which Napoleon was exiled in 1814, and from which he escaped the following year.

4   *manes…quarries* Elba's famous iron mines and granite quarries; the mines had been in operation at least as early as the 8th century B.C.

7   *diadem* Crown. Though exiled, Napoleon was granted the title 'Emperor of Elba'; he had an entourage of 1000 and had full sovereignty over the island for the ten months he was there.

18–20   *dog…dove…fly* References to Napoleon's reputation for wanton cruelty, a trait associated with the Roman Emperor Domitian (51–96 A.D.), of whom Suetonius wrote in *The Lives of the Twelve Ceasars,* 'At the beginning of his reign he used to spend hours in seclusion every day, doing nothing but catch flies and stab them with a keenly-sharpened stylus'.

23   *PICHEGRU, PALM, D'ENGHEIN, WRIGHT* The French General Jean-Charles Pichegru (1761–1804) and Louis Antoine Henri de Bourbon-Condé, Duc d'Enghien (1772–1804) were suspected of being part of a conspiracy to overthrow Napoleon and restore the French monarchy. Pichegru was strangled in his cell before his trial. D'Enghien, who was not actually part of the conspiracy, was kidnapped from his residence, court-martialed, and shot. The British naval captain John Wesley Wright (1769–1805) secretly brought Pichegru and other conspirators associated with Georges Cadou-dal to France on the HMS *Vencejo.* His throat was cut while he was imprisoned at the Temple Prison, Paris, though the officials reported it as a suicide. Johann Philipp Palm (1766–1806), a Nuremberg bookseller, was executed by firing squad for publishing pamphlets critical of Napoleon and urging German resistance.

29–30   *venomous heads…reptiles* The Tuscan archipelago, of which Elba is a part, was known for exotic plant and animal life, including poisonous vipers and a wide variety of lizards.

31   *the final decree* Death.

Donald and Mary, A Tale of the Isle

Title   The Isle of Arran is located off the west coast of Scotland, and provides the western boundary of the Firth of Clyde, the estuary of the river Clyde. The estuary technically encompasses the tidal portion of the river all the way to the city of Glasgow, as well as numerous towns and islands of the west coast.

Mitford writes, 'The above ballad was written to commemorate an event which happened in the summer of 1808 – A man, belonging to the Isle of Arran, situated near the entrance of the Firth of Clyde, had, with the savings of many a laborious year, purchased a small open boat, with which he went to Ireland, went fishing, &c. It was returning from thence one day, after disposing of his little cargo of fish, that he was ordered alongside of a tender, near the shores of his own island. Being a young and healthy fellow, they wished to impress him, and finding a *few pounds of soap* in his boat, it furnished them with an excuse for their barbarity. They seized him as a *smuggler*, hurried him into the receiving ship at Greenoch, and burnt his boat (the sole support of a wife and infant child, together with a lame and helpless parent)[...] A twelvemonth after the impressed man had sailed for the West Indies, his wife received the terrible news that he had fallen a victim to that dreadful scourge of the human race – that avenger of African misery – the yellow fever.

A year of bodily, as well as mental affliction, passed in poverty, and aggravated by "hope deferred", which the psalmist truly says, "maketh the heart sick", had not left the poor forlorn MARY strength to bear up against this last final blow to all her peace in the world; she, *also*, died, and left a helpless orphan to execrate that free and *happy* constitution, which cannot subsist without being defended by a portion of its subjects dragged into slavery.[...]

Captain TATHAM, of the royal navy, then regulating captain at the port of Greenoch, addressed two letters to the author in the Greenoch Advertiser, which were replied to by him: – Captain TATHAM is not one of the number who could perpetrate such an act of wanton cruelty. Humanity shudders at the contemplation of horrors, inflicted by petty tyranny and merciless oppression; but a day of awful retribution will most certainly arrive, in a place where favour can be of no avail – where power and distinction have no place.

It remains only for me to say, that this ballad was written at the request of Captain JOHN FULLERTON, proprietor of an estate in the Isle of Arran, who furnished the author with the particulars [...] (author's note).

3   *Goat-fells* 'A lofty mountain on the Isle of Arran' (author's note).

3   *lou'r* Lower.

9   *the western flood* That is, the ocean at the base of the cliffs.

15 *transports* Powerfully elevated feelings.

16 *Erin's green isle* Ireland.

17 *bark* Boat.

21 *Ten guineas* A sum of money perhaps representing several months' wages for someone of Donald's means.

28 *didst never see more* I.e., at the moment of arrival Donald meets with disaster, as described in l. 29 and following.

30–1   *tender…hulk* The tender is a small ship operating in the service of the larger naval vessel (the hulk).

34   *He pleaded his wife* That is, he pleaded with the men who have impressed him, on the basis of his having a wife. At the time of the Napoleonic wars, there was a general increase in Britain in the practice of impressment.

37–48   *White…expir'd* These lines describe Donald's aged father, who 'in a few weeks died of a broken heart' (author's note).

49   *fell India* In this case, the West Indies.

50   *pestilence* The yellow fever.

53   *Ruthless Destroyer* That is, the unnamed agent of this crime.

60   *horrent* Standing erect, or bristling.

War Song

11   *prostrate Helvetia* Switzerland, which the French had invaded in 1798. Napoleon later attempted to institute a central governmental authority that would dissolve the traditional Swiss cantons; local resistance forced him to withdraw briefly from the country in 1802, and a civil war followed.

14   *Conscription the son* The modern practice of conscription, in which large segments of the male population were legally forced to join the military, was begun by the French in the Napoleonic period.

18   *undone* Raped.

25   *murderer of Jaffa* A reference to Napoleon; after his 1799 attack on the Mediterranean port city of Jaffa (now part of Tel Aviv), he had several thousand of the city's defenders executed rather than taken prisoner, and the event became synonymous with his ruthlessness.

The Glories of Britannia; or The Records of Fame

7   *laurels* A wreath of laurels used as a victory crown.

11   *NEPTUNE…trident resigning* The God of the Sea; his three-pronged spear, the emblem of his sovereignty, was also used as a symbol of British naval supremacy.

14   *WELLINGTON* Arthur Wellesley, 1st Duke of Wellington (1769–1852), British army commander who defeated Napoleon at the Battle of Waterloo (1815).

21   *NELSON* Horatio Nelson, 1st Viscount Nelson (1758–1805), Britain's most revered naval commander in the era of the Napoleonic Wars. In the Preface to *Poems of a British Sailor*, Mitford writes that 'beneath the protecting eye of the soul-inspiring Nelson' he acquired a 'general affection for the human race', and that that affection, in turn, 'will insure him the attention of those, who, overlooking trifling critical errors, can be pleased with natural pictures, drawn without embellishment, directly from the heart of a BRITISH sailor' (p. vii). Laughton in his *DNB* entry discusses Mitford's dubious claims about relaying a message to Nelson at the Battle of the Nile.

JAMES CHAMBERS

From *The Poetical Works of James Chambers* (1820)

Text There is uncertainty over the editorship of the volume and the authorship of the biographical sketch that introduces it. The edition cited here, and by Johnson, reads 'Printed for and sold by the Editor, C. Ragan'. There is, however, another 1820 imprint of the same volume extant, which reads, 'Printed for and sold by the editor, J. Gissing'. Both editions list Ipswich as the place of publication. The opening biographical sketch of Chambers only adds to this confusion. After a discussion of Chambers's early life, a series of contemporary accounts are cited and quoted, but the typography is such that it is impossible to say with certainty where these embedded sources begin and end – and, indeed, if the unidentified writer himself ever resumes the narrative.

 The volume does not present a complete list of subscribers, but does name a few individuals as having 'in the greatest degree befriended the author'. One of these, 'J. Cobbold, Esq., of Holywells', is most probably John Cobbold, a prosperous brewer with large extended family in Suffolk. Cobbold's second wife, Elizabeth (1767–1824), was the 'Mrs. Cobbold' who was instrumental in arranging for the publication of Anne Candler's *Poetical Attempts* (q.v.). She was also the author of several volumes of her own verse.

Morning Winter Piece

3 *Verd'rous* Lushly green.

10 *Cut out paths for public good* Clear the snow to prevent accidents.

22 *with trials quite replete* Faced with many difficulties.

31 *carpet* That is, a ground covering of plants and grasses.

38 *exigence* A situation requiring immediate action, here describing birds whose attention must be focused on finding shelter rather than singing.

40 *matins* Morning song.

44 *flatuous* Windy.

45 *gelid* Extremely cold.

48 *terrene* Earthly.

53 *Boreal* Northern.

73 *Fulgent luster Sol displaying* I.e., the sun shines brilliantly.

81 *Fain* Happily.

86 *Some for drink and some to smoke* Plants usable for brewing and for smoking.

89 *Urania* The muse of astronomy. Milton famously summons Urania at the opening *Paradise Lost* VII, and it is probable that Chambers was consciously evoking Milton here since elsewhere he uses the word 'omnifick' ('Acrostic…to Robert Roe', l. 3), a word attributed to Milton that also appears in *PL* VII.

94 *Highest Friend* God.

98 *Ether* The upper atmosphere.

99   *terrene* Earth-bound.

102   *fiat* Command.

114   *orient* Two usages of 'orient' are possible here, either 'shining' or 'eastern'.

119   *parterres* Formal flowerbeds.

123   *supernal* Celestial.

141   *There* Heaven.

            gelid thrillings Cold winds.

147   *Vital coronets unfading, / Flourish in eternal bloom* That is, the saints' crowns ('coronets') shine for eternity, as if flowers whose blooms will never fade.

Lines on a Little Black Dog Stealing the Author's Meat

26   *med'cine* Herbs used for medicinal purposes.

29   *sanguinest* Most optimistic.

            below On earth, as opposed to heaven.

35   *dear* Costly.

44   *regeneration* Spiritual rebirth.

57   *suet* The 'lard' of line 56.

60   *poor patient Joe* In Hannah More's didactic poem 'Patient Joe, or the Newcastle Collier', a similar event was made to save the life of the title character, who believes that through God all things 'work together for good' (l. 8). When Patient Joe's dinner is stolen by a dog, he sets off in an unsuccessful pursuit; meanwhile, his fellow miner Tim Jenkins, who earlier has ridiculed Joe's unswerving faith, dies in a mine collapse. The poem ends with Joe asking, 'How could it appear to a short-sighted sinner, / That my life would be saved by the loss of my dinner?' (ll. 71–2).

On a Brindled Greyhound, Carrying a Piece of Meat to the Author

Title   *brindled* Having dark flecks or streaks.

5   *the Buck's Horns* Presumably the Inn mentioned in line 31 of 'Lines on a Little Black Dog' (q.v.).

11   *An excellent Prophet* Elijah; see 1 Kings 17:1–6.

The Author's Second Day At Helmingham

Title   In the 1820 volume, this poem follows one titled, 'On the Opening of a New Peal of Eight Bells, the Gift of the Right Honorable Earl of Dysart', in which Chambers ventures to Helmingham and describes the festival atmosphere surrounding the bells' dedication. It was probably Wilbraham Tollemache, 6th Earl of Dysart, who provided the bells. This poem picks up the narrative on the next day and, as with the earlier poem, shows Chambers using his rhyming skills to win favor from the gentry in attendance.

3–8   *as I'd success last night … oblige them all* I.e., Chambers decides to avoid the booths where games and contests are being held, in order to market more of his rhymes. The Hall is Helmingham Hall, in Suffolk, which was completed in the early sixteenth century.

12   *kine* Cows

17   *spacious park* The Deer Park at Helmingham is 400 acres; John Constable (1776–1837) painted a wooded part of the property in his 'A Dell at Helmingham Park'.

24   *capacious moat* Helmingham Hall is surrounded by a moat and still has two operating drawbridges.

Verses on Grundisburgh Fair

6   *Whitsuntide* The weekend or week including Whit Sunday, the seventh Sunday after Easter.

15–16   *at the Dog…The reck'ning pay in ready chink* I.e., they drink at one of the local taverns, and use coins to pay the bill.

17   *Yeoman* A farmer.

21   *fairling* A trinket or treat.

23   *beaux* Foppish, wealthy men.

26   *treacled* Sweetened with molasses.

27   *Jingling Match* '[A] game in which one player keeps ringing a bell while the others, all blindfolded, try to catch him or her' (*OED*).

34   *lowns* Low or mean people.

50   *fleering* Gibing, jeering.

56   *enerves* Enervates.

68   *Ebriety.* Drunkenness.

The Poor Poetaster

Title   'Poetaster' is a term of derision, denoting a poetic dabbler or hack.

21   *whin-shed* Possibly a dwelling made of grasses or gorse.

33   *gelid* Freezing.

       does Probably an alternative spelling of 'doze', rhyming with repose in the previous line.

35   *morts* A crowd or gang.

36   *cote* Pen; enclosure.

66   *a weekly collection* Money.

70   *noding choice twine* Making nets.

82   *ringles* Metal rings, frequently of iron, used to attach ropes or harnesses.

84–6   *commence spinner…flogged* Chambers is tasked with working a spinning wheel, and must complete a certain lot, by the rules of the workhouse; failure means hunger and perhaps a whipping. Compare this description of life in the workhouse with that of Candler in 'Reflections on My Own Situation' (q.v.).

105   *prison* The workhouse.

130   *fulgid* Dazzling.

148   *That I, like John Bunyan, experience may write* Bunyan (1628–88) wrote many of his works, including the beginning of *The Pilgrim's Progress,* while he was imprisoned for unlawful preaching.

153   *one in Newgate* Possibly the Quaker William Penn (1644–1718), the founder of Pennsylvania.

159   *Soham mansions of industry* The workhouse in Soham, Cambridgeshire, the town in which Chambers was born.

160   *Belial's sons* Sons of the devil; more generally, lawless and reckless individuals. See, for example, Judges 19:22, and 1 Samuel 2:12.

165   *Grub-street* The London residence of many poor and struggling writers, connoting literary hack-work.

Treble Acrostic—James Chambers, Itinerent Poet

Title   Though the title page of the volume spells 'Itinerant' conventionally, this acrostic relies on an alternate spelling.

Treble Acrostic…for Robert Roe

3   *Omnifick* All-creating. John Milton is usually credited with coining this word; see *Paradise Lost* VII.217: 'Said then, th' Omnific word, your discord end'.

ROBERT MILLHOUSE

From *Blossoms* (1823)

Text   *Blossoms: By Robert Millhouse. Being a Selection of Sonnets from his Various Manuscripts* (London: Printed for the Author by J. Nichols and Son, 1823). The volume received several favourable reviews, including that in *Monthly Magazine* 55 (April 1823): 'The sonnets are written with much simplicity and pathos, and bear the impression of a sensitive, honourable, and virtuous mind. A sufficient passport to public approbation will be found in the intrinsic merit of these little compositions' (p. 252). This echoed the response accorded his first volume, *Vicissitude,* of which *Monthly Review* 96 (Sept 1821) said, 'With many disadvantages and defects, we think that this humble aspirant is still a poet; – uncultivated, deficient, and with all the poetic sins that belong to inexperience and youthful enthusiasm, but redeeming them by the presence of a rich and overflowing spirit; which, though it sometimes betrays him never forsakes him […] He seems to write from the heart; as if he really rejoiced in the creations of his fancy, and in giving language to his thoughts' (pp. 98–9).

To Gold

Title   According to the *Eclectic Review* n.s. 19 (March 1823), this poem 'would have done no discredit to John Clare, or even to Wordsworth' (p. 259).

The Proud Man's Contumely

Title   'Contumely' means scorn. The title specifically alludes to *Hamlet*'s 'To be, or not to be' soliloquy:

> For who would bear the whips and scorns of time,
> The oppressor's wrong, the proud man's contumely,
> The pangs of despised love, the law's delay,
> The insolence of office and the spurns
> That patient merit of the unworthy takes,
> When he himself might his quietus make
> With a bare bodkin? (*Hamlet* III.i.78–84)

Written in the Country

6   *raging main* The ocean.
8   *'pertain* Belong.

To Antiquity

14   *the last Trumpet summon to the Doom* The Christian Day of Judgment; see 1 Corinthians 15:52, 'In a moment, in the twinkling of an eye, at the last trump: for the trumpet shall sound, and the dead shall be raised incorruptible, and we shall be changed'.

The Bard

6   *Rill* Stream.

From *Sherwood Forest and Other Poems* (1827)

Text   *Sherwood Forest and Other Poems* (London: Printed for the Author, 1827). The front-matter includes excerpts from six reviews of earlier Millhouse volumes, and a list of ninety subscribers, most of them living in and around Nottingham.

The Lot of Genius

4   *Oppression's tools* Powerful people who are instruments of oppression.
13   *base piles* Meaningless monuments.

To the Herb Chickweed

3   *fallows* Ploughed land left to lie fallow.
      sward A covering of greenery.
12   *to cool the anguished wound* An extremely common weed with many varieties, chickweed was and is favoured by herbalists as a soothing skin treatment.

Address for a Society of Odd Fellows

Title   According to *Brewer's Dictionary of Phrase and Fable* (8th edition, 1963), the Odd Fellows were a 'secret society with benevolent aims and of uncertain antiquity. Records go back to 1745, and in the following years it flourished despite considerable persecution on account of its alleged "seditiousness." In 1813 it awakened to new vigour as the Independent Order of Odd Fellows, in Manchester; it has since then become the greatest of such beneficent orders, spreading into most of the countries of North Europe and into North America' (p. 655).

10   *front* Brow or forehead, continuing the metaphor of the face.

17   *benignant* Kind.

30   *Benevolence…the receiver and the giver blest.* See Portia's speech in *The Merchant of Venice* IV.i.186–9:

> The quality of mercy is not strain'd
> It droppeth as the gentle rain from heaven
> Upon the place beneath. It is twice blest:
> It blesseth him that gives, and him that takes.

36–7   Cf. 'Autumn' l. 169 and 'Spring' ll. 230–1 in James Thomson's *The Seasons*.

WILLIAM SMITH

Verses…[on]…Raising and Selling the Newly Buried Dead

Text   1819. Sold as a broadsheet, price one penny. An introductory note to the poem reads, 'WILLIAM SMITH, the Author of the following Verses, being of a weakly constitution, and unable for work, he hopes the PUBLIC will accept this as a proper Apology for offering them for Sale. At the same time he would humbly hope that they will meet the Approbation, and rouse the Feelings, of most of his readers'. It provoked several broadsheet poems in response, including 'The Haddington Cobbler Defended, Or The Doctors Dissected. By an East Linton Gravedigger' (1829?). For discussion of several poems by familiar writers touching on the subjects of grave-robbing and medical dissection, see Marshall, *Murdering to Dissect*, esp. pp. 175–218 (Further Reading).

The era's most famous case was that of William Burke and William Hare, who provided corpses for Robert Knox, the famed anatomist and director of the Edinburgh Medical School. In fact, Burke and Hare were not actually grave robbers: they murdered prostitutes and transients whose absence might well evade the attention of the police. They were brought to trial in December 1828, with Hare testifying against Burke. Burke was convicted and hanged in Edinburgh on 28 January 1829, in front of a crowd in excess of 20,000. His body was then dissected by Knox's professional rival, Alexander Monro, and his skeleton is still on display at the Medical School's Anatomy Museum. Hare was released from prison shortly after Burke's execution.

13   *Love of money – root of evil* 'For the love of money is the root of all evil: which while some coveted after, they have erred from the faith, and pierced themselves through with many sorrows' (1 Timothy 6:10).

24   *When the last trump the dead shall call* 'In a moment, in the twinkling of an eye, at the last trump: for the trumpet shall sound, and the dead shall be raised incorruptible, and we shall be changed' (1 Corinthians 15:52).

47   *A better mansion is provided* 'In my Father's house are many mansions: if it were not so, I would have told you. I go to prepare a place for you' (John 14:2).

63   *Dust to dust is then consigned* See the burial service in the *Book of Common Prayer* (1662): 'we therefore commit his body to the ground; earth to earth, ashes to ashes, dust to dust'.

From *A Collection of Original Poems* (1821)

Text   *A Collection of Original Poems, Moral, Instructive, and Entertaining* (Edinburgh: Printed for and sold by the Author, 1821). The frontispiece indicates that Smith had previously published at least one poem in addition to 'Verses on Raising the Dead', called 'A Few Thoughts on Creation'. *A Collection of Original Poems* contains thirty-three poems by Smith, and one by a subscriber to the volume, the Revd. Dr Sibbald of Haddington. This is probably William Sibbald (1760–1833); there is nothing else in the volume to suggest that Sibbald was an especially significant patron.

The volume's epigraph, from William Cowper's 'Table Talk' (1782), reads in full:

> The Nightingale may claim the topmost bough,
> While the poor Grasshopper must chirp below:
> Like him, unnotic'd, I, and such as I,
> Spread little wings, and rather skip than fly
> Perch'd on the meagre produce of the land,
> An ell or two of prospect we command,
> But never peep beyond the thorny bound,
> Or oaken fence that hems the paddock round.

The Mansions of the Dead, or The Grave Watcher's Soliloquy

Text   The poem is dated 5 August 1819. In a newspaper item recounting the career of Smith, the Haddington churchyard is described as being 'lonely on two sides' and thus vulnerable to grave-robbers. (J.G. Wallace-James, 'A Forgotten Haddington Poet', *The Haddingtonshire Advertiser* [4 March 1910]).

31   *Love strong as death* 'Set me as a seal upon thine heart, as a seal upon thine arm: for love is strong as death; jealousy is cruel as the grave: the coals thereof are coals of fire, which hath a most vehement flame' (Song of Solomon 8:6).

A Call to the Watchmen

Text   The poem has the following epigraph, a slight misquotation of lines 23–8 from 'A Night-piece on Death' (1722), by Thomas Parnell:

> I pass with melancholy state
> By all these solemn heaps of fate;
> And think, as soft and sad I tread
> Above the venerable dead,
> 'Time was, like me, they life possess'd,
> And time will be when I shall rest.'

The Poet's Plea

10   *rude Boreas* The north wind.

40   *To strew wild tares* A reference to the Biblical parable of the wheat and the tares (*Matthew* 13:24–30), in which a farmer's enemy secretly mixes undesirable seeds of tares with good wheat seeds.

68   *awl* A pointed leatherworking tool. The implication of these lines is that if Smith does sometimes compose while on the job and in good health, the speed and efficiency of his shoemaking is not harmed.

84   *Let independence blush to scornful seem* I.e., any economically independent person who would condemn Smith should be embarrassed at making such a judgement.

The Effects of Nature and Cultivation Contrasted

2   *sanguine* Optimistic.

13–14   *Full many spots...nicest plan* Possibly an allusion to Thomas Gray's 'Elegy Written in a Country Churchyard' (1751), ll. 55–6: 'Full many a flow'r is born to blush unseen, / And waste its sweetness on the desert air'.

51   *wight* Man.

55   *lear* Learning or instruction.

68   *mite* A 'modest contribution to a cause, charity, etc., *esp.* the most the giver can manage' (*OED*).

The Country Wright

Title   In the 1821 volume, this narrative is followed by another comic tale of disappointed aspiration, again with clear implications for the apprentice poet. 'The Painter; or the Fruitless Attempt' concludes, 'They who attempt all men to please, / Their labour lose, and brains do teaze; / All critics' favour for to gain, / Th' attempt both fruitless is and vain'.

1   *wright* A mechanic or craftsman, esp. one who works with wood.

From A Summer Evening Walk Improved

15   *bukes* Books.
    lear Learning.

16   *sair* Suffice.

19   *unco* Uncommon(ly).

21   *henna health* Have no(t) health.

22–4   *To screen themsel's on bo'rd they bring…their bukes to sell* Apparently a description of one of the money-making schemes mentioned in line 18, whereby lazy workers leave their village with a cargo of books to sell or barter. They are thus 'screening themselves' in several ways: escaping from domestic criticism; pretending to be infirm, and, possibly, feigning authorship of the volumes they have 'on board'.

24   *gear* Goods, esp. food.

27   *gang* Go; walk.

31   *his braw poem, Man's fa' and a'* I.e., his fine poem concerning the Fall of Man. This is presumably a reference to Smith's earlier 'A Few Thoughts on Creation'.

32   *claw* (To) scratch. In this case, the implication is that Smith's earlier poem criticized his fellows behind their backs.

33   *bairns* Children.

35–6   *If samples ay are like the stocks, / His weans will be like ither fo'ks'* Weans are children; the man is suggesting that Smith's children (the 'samples' deriving from his 'stock') will be just as flawed and sinful as those Smith criticizes in his earlier poem.

40   *ken* Know.

44   *auld lang syne* Days gone by.

45   *wiss* Wish.

48   *parritche pan* Porridge pot.

51–2   *to bed he's no confin'd / Yet gaen trouble's lang unkind* I.e, though Smith is no longer confined to bed, the effects of his ill-health are sure to linger.

54   *stealth* Deceit.

55   *mense* Honour; dignity.

64   *poortith mean* Low poverty.

68   *claith* Cloth.
        hale Whole.

From The House of Mourning

79   *mite* Any small unit or currency.

88   *Pinch'd Independence blushes to complain* That is, the mourner avoids complaint even in his state of terrible distress. Compare with line 84 of 'The Poet's Plea'.

Ye are Idle – Exod. v.17

Title   In *Exodus* 5, Moses and Aaron follow God's command and ask Pharaoh if the Hebrews may be given three days to go into the desert and sacrifice to their Lord. Pharaoh, asserting that this request is evidence of the slaves' idleness, increases their workload.

4–8   *no straw for you to-day…your tale of bricks shall finish* In the earlier verses of the chapter, Pharaoh's taskmasters increase the Hebrews' labour by insisting that they gather their own straw while also continuing to produce the requisite daily output of bricks. Twice the Hebrews are told they must finish the 'tale of [the] bricks' (KJV), a phrase Smith seizes upon since it implicitly strengthens the poem's suggestion that writers, like cobblers and slaves, are habitually scorned and condemned as lazy.

The Biblical episode has given rise to a popular phrase, 'to make bricks without straw', meaning the attempt to accomplish a task without the proper materials. But arguably the episode itself is focused on difficult and punishing work, rather than on work that is literally impossible.

The Turbot's Head Dissected

Title   The turbot is a large and much prized flat deepwater fish, also known as a Greenland halibut; the reference to dissection suggests some self-referential playfulness on Smith's part. Here 'dissection' stands for his own analysis of the possible implications of accepting the gift. Even as Smith makes full use of the fish, still its head remains – and so does the memory of the favour. This residue from the transaction worries him as he imagines his friend 'turn[ing] politician' and wanting the favour returned.

Though this poem differs in subject and tone from the others printed here, it is similar in argumentative perspective. Just as Smith's other poems describe him condemning laziness, and then worrying that he might himself be described as lazy, here he begins by roundly condemning the accepting of bribes and then wondering if he is 'catch'd in the snare' himself.

3   *aiblins…pricks* I.e., perhaps have some experience with bribery's dangers.

8   *glibery* Manipulation; smooth talk.

18   *mak' a stand* Present an appearance of resistance, perhaps in order to inflate the amount of the bribe.

23–4   *Syne in her cheek Squire slips the bliss…guineas* I.e., pays for sexual favours, though 'the bliss' also refers to the kiss itself; the phrasing suggests that the squire lewdly kisses her and then gives her a gift of money.

29   *head a'* Behead all.

32   *cutty stool* In the Calvinist Church, the low stool on which fornicators were forced to sit during services in order to be publicly rebuked.

39   *rin* Run.
      jink Turn quickly; dodge.

48   *banes* Bones.

50   *callan* Boy.

51   *John B------n* Evidently, simply the name of the friend who gives him the fish, and not a reference to John Barleycorn

53   *aff or on the fang* The meaning is uncertain. As a term in Scots law, a fang is a thief apprehended with his loot. Used here, it signals the uncertain nature of the gift, including the possibility that the fish was stolen.

54   *atween* Between.

54   *by my sang* A solemn oath or asseveration, meaning 'by my word'.

56   *The Nor'-East Port* The section of Haddington in which Smith lives.

60   *gin ye're mista'en* I.e., if you are mistaken.

62   *The law ca's gifts as free's fok's ain* I.e, the speaker is worried that the law (police) might still declare this fish to be someone else's.

63   *Sae I'se no break it* A pun; he'll neither break the law or break (into) the fish.

69   *Rob M------y's oven* A local establishment with proper cooking facilities.
       Syne Then.

70   *the birkie stoven* A birkie is a proud fellow; Smith presumably means the fish itself has been well cooked or stewed.

71   *crump* Crispy.

72   *mess* Meal.

74   *ilka bane* Every bone.

76   *weans* Children

89   *I tak' a smoke* I.e., he will return the favour by buying tobacco at Johnny's shop.

96   *chiel* Fellow; man.

103   *put on your hat* I.e., declare your party allegiance.

105   *gin* If.

110–11   *never sham'd the breed / O' turn-coat glory* That is, never been politically compromised by taking a bribe.

113   *saishin'* Possibly an ornamental ribbon or sash.

JOHN SHAW

From *Woolton Green* (1825)

Text   Printed by Perry and Metcalfe, Liverpool, *Woolton Green: A Domestic Tale; with Other Miscellaneous Poems* is a substantial volume of fifteen poems; the title piece runs to over 4,000 lines, representing about forty percent of the whole. Given Shaw's loquacity, it is not surprising that he envisions further publication, specifically a second volume of poetry and a work 'whose hero is theatrical' (p. xi). Though there is no evidence that either of these particular projects ever appeared in print, Shaw is almost certainly the author of several separately published poems, including 'Don Juan, Canto XVII' (Liverpool, 1824), 'Don Juan, Canto XVIII' (Liverpool, 1825), 'Ten days in Ireland by the poet laureate to the Liverpool Agricultural Association' (Liverpool, 1835), and 'The Borough Laureatship, not a sinecure office, a splendid epic poem in one book' (Liverpool, 1836). It is possible he published others in the 1830s.

To My Mare Gip

14–16   *Bucephalus* The favoured horse of Alexander the Great, which he reputedly tamed while an adolescent.

18   *Quixotte* Don Quixote, knight-errant, the protagonist in Cervantes' *Don Quixote* (1605, 1615), who is delusionally attached to stories of chivalric adventure.

20   *lovely woman* Dulcinea, the country girl whom Quixote mistakenly identifies as the most beautiful of all women.

22   *as lean as Rosinante* Quixote's Rocinante is a bedraggled old drudge horse; Quixote himself is thin, worn, and weak.

25   *heterogeneal* Varied; diverse. In comparing their 'plans', Shaw says that while he shares Quixote's chivalric ideals and love for romantic adventure, he cannot, as a married man, actually engage in questing.

32   *That carry'd Syntax* Dr Syntax was the protagonist in a popular series of verse satires by William Combe, featuring illustrations by Thomas Rowlandson; Syntax's old horse was named Grizzle. The first volume, *Dr. Syntax in Search of the Picturesque*, appeared in 1809, and three later installments appeared between 1819 and 1822.

40   *The gray mare is the better horse* A familiar proverb, referring to a woman who dominates her husband.

50   *midding* Probably a variant of 'midden', a scrap heap or manure pile.

51   *curry-comb* A brush used in horse-grooming.

61   *Prick thy ears, and lash thy tail* I.e., show me you're listening.

66   *Throstle-Nest* Shaw's home, the Inn at 168 Scotland Road, Liverpool, which still stands.

80–1   *cuts the rump* The rump in this case is not the body itself, but the tail. Nine inches would be a typical length after docking.

86   *Disgraces manhood to the grave* A reference suggesting an analogue between tail-docking and the practice of male circumcision, which Shaw evidently deplores.

87   *Turk* Proverbially, a Turk is a person of particular cruelty, but Shaw's evident linkage of Turks and circumcision is probably a reference to Othello's final speech before committing suicide (*Othello* V.ii):

> in Aleppo once,
> Where a malignant and a turban'd Turk
> Beat a Venetian and traduced the state,
> I took by the throat the circumcised dog,
> And smote him, thus.   (361–65)

89   *farriers* Smiths or others who shoe and care for horses. In the lines that follow, Shaw attributes the practice to greed and misguided fashion, rather than medical necessity.

100–4   *Shanter's Meg* In Burns's poem *Tam O'Shanter*, the drunken Tam and his horse Meg are chased by the witch Cutty Sark; they must pass the central point in the bridge over the River Doon (the 'Key-stane o' the brig') in order to reach safety. They do so, but not before the witch pulls off Meg's tail.

109   *the worst of evils* An iron animal trap.

132   *dray* 'A low cart without sides used esp. by brewers for carrying heavy loads' (*OED*).

134   *shafted* Pulled.

139–40   *thy belly stretch'd along* I.e., Gip strains mightily to pull the load, even in hot and difficult conditions.

173   *Unless they're back'd, and science-taught* In the original volume, these lines appear under the running header 'Reflections on Backers'. Having criticized Gip for not 'backing well' with his load, Shaw turns to wordplay involving backers of other kinds, referring first to fighters who have financial backers and who are 'science-taught' to back (retreat) in the ring.

176   *When two or three months bills get out* This passage, which describes Shaw's customers attempting to avoid payment, involves some elaborate punning around 'backing' and 'drawing'. Two customers, given the horses' names of Delirious and Facinereous (wicked), concoct a scheme to back out of payment by drawing on funds that are fraudulently backed. In the concluding lines of the passage, the 'endorsers' of these bad instruments must take a 'refluent' course – that is, a route that is backwards-running – to avoid post-offices, where the scam might be revealed.

191   *'tis all my eye!* A proverbial expression indicating the speaker's belief that something is nonsense, or surpasses belief.

192–3   *matus…ignis fatuus* I.e., trying to catch either of the conspirators is like trying to catch swamp gas. The Latin is intentionally fractured.

199   *stramonium* The thorn-apple tree, or a substance derived from it.

201   *such kites* Fraudulent monetary documents, as in 'check-kiting'.

210   *thou could'st not draw an inference* Another pun; Gip's doubter says she has so little strength (as a dray horse) that she couldn't 'draw an inference'.

240   *empall'd* Covered in black for his funeral procession.

The Bard's Plaint

9   *bower* 'Throstle Nest' (author's note), Shaw's home.

17   *dole* Sorrow.

106   *like the Halcyon wave* I.e., one that is calm and peaceful.

114   *Croesus* Ancient king of Lydia, possessor of legendary wealth.

Lucubratory Lines, Addressed to … Canning

Title   An early friend of William Pitt the younger in the early 1790s and a former editor of the *Anti-Jacobin Review*, a Tory-affiliated publication that attacked Wordsworth, Coleridge, Southey, and Lamb, George Canning had risen to the heights of political power by the time of this poem; he would go on briefly to become Prime Minister before his death in 1827. Canning held various Parliamentary seats, including the Liverpool seat from 1812–23, and he also served as Treasurer of the Navy, Foreign Secretary, Ambassdor to Lisbon, and Governor-General of India. Canning was a close friend of Sir Walter Scott, and may have been involved with Scott in founding the conservative *Quarterly Review*.

1   *England's truest friend* It is impossible to know whether or not Shaw is referring to a particular policy here, but Canning was deeply involved with

British military and foreign policy for a number of years; he was also an abolitionist.

6   *tumid* Bloated; bombastic.

8–10   *As dew spreads farther nearest the ground* I.e., it will be most efficacious to praise Canning in simple language.

15   *they all decried thy name* Because of Canning's fierce anti-Jacobinism and his support for Catholic emancipation, he was a controversial figure and the subject of many printed attacks between 1815 and 1830, including the anonymous 'Suppressed Letter to the Right Hon. George Canning' (1818).

18   *Lisbon Job* Canning was ambassador to Portugal from 1814–15, while holding his Liverpool parliamentary seat. His holding of this post was criticized as a matter of insider favouritism. For more on this reference see Hinde, *George Canning*, pp. 268–76.

20   *Board Controul* A reference to Canning's tenure as President of the Board of Control for India, which ran from 1816–20.

22   *Spa Field rabble* Referring to a series of three political rallies in 1816 and 1817, but particularly the 'Spa Field riot' of 2 December 1816, in which a pro-reform crowd attempted to take control of the Tower of London and the Bank of England, with the hope that mass insurrection would follow.

23   *Their leader* Though Henry 'Orator' Hunt was perceived as having been the leader of the Spa Field uprising, his emphasis on universal suffrage and constitutional reform put him at odds with the 'Spencean Philanthropists' who organized the meeting; they had a specific policy agenda advocating national communal land-holding. See Malcolm Chase, *'The People's Farm': English Radical Agrarianism 1775–1840* (Oxford: Clarendon Press, 1988); see also note to line 39. Shaw's broadsides at various reformers and revolutionaries in this poem collapse the frequently strong internal disagreements within the radical community; see Belchem, *'Orator' Hunt, passim.*

25   *His waving flags* Hunt spoke before a tricolour flag, meant to suggest sympathy with the French Revolution.

26   *cap of liberty* A reference to an extreme radical journal of that name, which, like *The Black Dwarf*, was priced cheaply in order to make wide dissemination possible.

27   *to his cap he'd added bells* I.e., worn the garb of the fool or jester.

30   *the bank we'll seize* See note to lines 22–3 and 39.

39   *Watson, Waddington, Thistlewood* James Watson (1766–1838) and Arthur Thistlewood (1770–1820) were at the center of the 'Spencean Philanthropists', the radical reform group which organized the Spa Field rally. Both men were charged with treason, but Watson was not convicted, and the charge against Thistlewood was dropped. Thistlewood was subsequently involved in the infamous 'Cato Street Conspiracy', a plot to murder the entire cabinet after the death of George III in 1820, thus bringing about a revolution. Many of the details of the plot were suggested by George Edwards, a government agent who had infiltrated the Spenceans. Thistlewood was one of five men excuted for his part in the conspiracy. For information on Tho-

mas Spence's literary activities, see Tim Burke (ed.), *Eighteenth-Century English Labouring-Class Poets,* Vol. 3, 1780–1800 (London: Pickering and Chatto, 2003). 'Waddington' is probably the radical activist Samuel Waddington, called 'Little Waddy' because of his short stature.

45–7   *Cartwright…Cobbett…Wooler* John Cartwright (1740–1824) came from a well-to-do family and eventually joined the British navy, where he supported the cause of the American colonists and began developing a series of ideas about parliamentary and electoral reform. After leaving the navy he was made a major in the newly formed Nottinghamshire Militia, where he served for many years despite his political opinions. William Hazlitt used Cartwright's obsession with parliamentary reform as the focus for his essay 'On People with One Idea'. William Cobbett (1762–1835), editor of the *Political Register* and author of *Rural Rides,* is perhaps the best known of all the era's reformist writers. For information on the *Register,* see note to line 98 below. For Wooler, see Scrivener, *Poetry and Reform,* pp. 249–81, and the note to line 98 below.

52   *The slave yet lives* Henry Hunt lived from 1773–1835.

59   *Hunt dated England's ruin 'one little year'* Perhaps a reference to a prediction by Hunt that revolution was only a year away.

61   *lost his parli'ment'ry seat* A reference to Hunt's failed attempt to win the seat for Westminster in 1818. He would eventually serve as an M.P. from 1831–3.

62–3   *He spurious coffee made…Breakfast Powders* 'Hunt started manufacturing [his "Breakfast Powder"], a cheap substitute for highly-taxed imported coffee, based on a special method of preparing and roasting English rye, towards the end of 1819 as part of his policy of abstinence from excisable goods. The Excise soon intervened however, and took possession of his manufactory together with half a ton of the stock. Hunt decided to try the question in the courts' (Belchem, p. 139). For further discussion, see Belchem, pp. 139–40 and 167–8.

67   *He's chang'd his course I hear* Shaw here implies that Hunt's business ventures, and perhaps his political commitments, were impulsive. In fact Hunt had a surprisingly long career as a manufacturer of the Breakfast Powder, an herbal tea, a shoe-blacking, a composite coal substitute, and a waterproofing agent for shoes. See Belchem, pp. 167–72.

68   *he now boils blacking* 'From the Post Office and trade directories it would seem that Hunt started manufacturing shoe-blacking in 1825. It was an immediate success, enjoying much free publicity from satirists, cartoonists, playwrights, hecklers, and political opponents, none of whom could resist cheap jokes and jibes about Hunt "the Blacking Man"' (Belchem, p. 168). See also note to lines 69–70. From the dates of Shaw's poem and the Horace Smith poem quoted below, we can assume that Hunt was actually in the blacking business before 1825.

69–70   *Turner, Day and Martin…Warren* Prominent makers of shoe-blacking. Hunt is mentioned in conjunction with these figures in Horace Smith's satire,

'Laus Atramenti, or the Praise of Blacking. A New Song', *New Monthly Magazine* (November 1824), 416:

> Day and Martin now laugh as they ride in their coach,
> Till they're black in the face as their customers' boots;
> Warren swears that his blacking's beyond all approach,
> Which Turner's advertisement plumply refutes;
> They hector and huff, print, publish, and puff,
> And write in the papers ridiculous stuff,
> While Hunt, who was blacken'd by all, and run down,
> Takes a thriving revenge as he blackens the town.
> Their labels belibel each other – each wall
> With the feuds of these rivals in blacking is white;
> But the high polished town seems to patronise all,
> And the parties get rich in each other's despite;
> For my own part I think, I shall mix up my ink,
> In a bottle with lamp-black and beer to the brink,
> And set up at once for a shiner of shoes,
> Since I never shall shine by the aid of the Muse.

The ubiquity of the advertising for Warren's product gave rise to the remarkable *Warreniana* (1824) of William Frederick Deacon, which features a series of parodies of the era's leading writers – with the twist that each of the 'contributions' is a puff for Warren's blacking agent. See *Parodies of the Romantic Age*, vol. 2, eds Graeme Stones and John Strachan, 5 vols. (London: Pickering and Chatto, 1999).

71   *now should polish* Another reference to Hunt's blacking business.

75   *Register* Cobbett's *Weekly Political Register*; see note to line 98.

78–9   *Trans-Atlantic trip…That land* Cobbett spent most of the 1790s in America, writing under the pseudonym 'Peter Porcupine'.

82   *didst import to us great Tom Payne's bones* The radical Thomas Paine (1737–1809) was born in England but lived much of his life in America, where he died. Cobbett was convinced Paine needed to be returned to his homeland and given a proper memorial, and in 1819 he exhumed the body from its burial place in New York and, with some difficulty, arranged for its return to England. (The ship carrying Cobbett and Paine's bones docked in Liverpool, so for Shaw the event had local significance.) The passage thus implies that Cobbett imported both Paine and his ideas, and it also emphasizes the peripatetic ways of both men.

83   *emporium* A market or commercial site, especially one offering specialty items.

87   *thy prophecy* As partly elaborated in the lines that follow, this refers to Cobbett's belief that England must abandon its use of paper money and return to a metal standard. See note to lines 90–2.

88   *frizzling* An uncomfortable encounter with a sizzling fire.

90–2   *Bank of England...grid-iron* Cobbett had argued strongly that the system of paper money was a vast fraud, enriching currency speculators, banks, and financial insiders while burdening the country's citizens with massive tax liability to finance the ever-increasing debt. These lines also assume knowledge of Cobbett's flight to America in 1817 to avoid arrest on charges of sedition. The sense of the whole passage is that if his 'prophecy' came true – if a proper (metallic) bounty were placed on his head – he might well be caught and executed. Smithfield is the London locale where traitors, murderers, and religious dissenters were burned at the stake.

98   *They lay at large, unread* 'Unlike the market in fine books, the periodical market in the Romantic period was characterized by low prices and by very high numbers of copies. By 1810, major periodicals like the staunchly Tory *Quarterly Review* often printed as many as 5,000 copies....[O]ne of the most famous radical journals of the Regency, Thomas Wooler's *Black Dwarf*, appeared in some 12,000 copies in 1819' (Stephen Behrendt, 'The Romantic Reader', *A Companion to Romanticism* ed. Duncan Wu (Oxford: Blackwell, 1998), p. 94. However, this wide distribution was severely limited by taxes, and Shaw's focus on the distribution of these papers is important. A tax of 4d. had been established for all newspapers in 1815, making them prohibitively expensive for most people. After Cobbett began selling his *Weekly Political Register* as a pamphlet at 2d. per copy, a series of laws known as the Six Acts of 1819 extended this duty to virtually all cheap periodicals. This ushered in the period of the Stamped Press. Though many unauthorized papers and periodicals were issued in the coming years, the onerous obligations required of publishers put great stresses upon them. The newspaper duty was not totally eliminated until 1855.

112   *Thou heardst them all* Perhaps a reference to Canning's reputation for being at least somewhat freethinking within an intensely partisan environment.

117–209 *Colonel Starvegut, Little Woolton's dread* This long passage on the person Shaw calls 'Colonel Starvegut' is meant to express both the dire social effect of having a reform-minded bureaucrat in office – Starvegut is apparently a judge – and to contrast his position with Canning's. Starvegut's actual name is unknown; 'Little Woolton' is an area to the south-east of Liverpool proper.

118   *basilistian* Royal; kingly.

119   *Mercury* The *Liverpool Mercury* newspaper.

124   *His farming yard he's made the parish pound* That is, Starvegut has impounded many animals for violating local ordinances.

125   *this man of metal* A sarcastic pun. While Starvegut sees himself as a man of unyielding judicial principle, he is for Shaw merely an obsessive imposer of fines.

129   *Tartars* Wild, violent individuals.

130   *the carters* A carter is a person who draws a cart; the term is suggestive of low birth. As with the rest of the passage, the implication is that though

Starvegut is supposedly a reformer, his policies and behaviour make life miserable for the ordinary person.

132   *their fines produce an equal profit* The implication is that he is pocketing the money himself.

136   *a county member* Member of Parliament.

137   *all in arms to send him* I.e., working hard to get him elected.

194   *nicest* Most scrupulous (used ironically).

Extemporary Epitaph for the Unfortunate Mr. Sadler

Title   William Windham Sadler had become famous seven years earlier, in July 1817, when he had made the first successful crossing by balloon from Ireland to England, crossing the St. George's Channel in a flight from Dublin to Holyhead. Windham's crossing followed several unsuccessful attempts, including one by his father James, the pioneering English balloonist. In his classic early book on the history of aeronautics, *The Dominion of the Air* (1902), J. M. Bacon offers an account of the father's failed attempt of 1812, and follows it with this description of Windham's triumph: 'This aspiring aeronaut, emulating his father's enterprising spirit, chose the same starting ground at Dublin, and on the longest day of 1817, when winds seemed favourable, left the Porto Bello barracks at 1.20 p.m. His endeavour was to 'tack' his course by such currents as he should find, in the manner attempted by his father, and at starting the ground current blew favourably from the W.S.W. He, however, allowed his balloon to rise to too high an altitude, where he must have been taken aback by a contrary drift; for, on descending again through a shower of snow, he found himself no further than Ben Howth, as yet only ten miles on his long journey. Profiting by his mistake, he thenceforward, by skilful regulation, kept his balloon within due limits, and successfully maintained a direct course across the sea, reaching a spot in Wales not far from Holyhead an hour and a half before sundown. The course taken was absolutely the shortest possible, being little more than seventy miles, which he traversed in five hours'.

JAMES BIRD

From *Poetical Memoirs; The Exile, a Tale* (1823)

Text   Originally published in 1823, the copy text here is the (apparently identical) second edition (London: Baldwin and Cradock, 1824). The volume lists the publication date as 1833, but this is a misprint. Bird's friend and editor Thomas Harral had only limited appreciation for the 'Poetical Memoirs', calling it 'extremely amusing' but cautioning that 'the work is not of a character upon which its author must be allowed to rest any portion of his fame' (p. xv).

In the end pages of the volume, Bird included a single additional stanza of *ottava rima*, under the title 'Poetical Memoirs', which hinted at the possibility of future cantos:

> I wrote the 'EXILE' in my teens – but stay,
> > Ye tireless Muses! let me rest awhile,
> And brush the dust of memory away,
> > Polish my thought, and brighten up my style; –
> Yes, I must think, for I have much to say
> > To those who love to weep, or love to smile,
> I'll give a long Tale in my next long Canto,
> Romantic – like 'THE CASTLE OF OTRANTO'.

Poetical Memoirs. Introduction

10	*Vaticides* A latinate neologism, suggesting the killing of that which is prophetic or inspired.
12	*Tomohawk* A short axe. Because of its association with the North American 'savages', this image is meant to turn the tables on critics' claims to sophistication and elevation.
16	*kiss the Rod* A gesture of subservience to authority.

Poetical Memoirs. *From* Canto First

1	*egregious* Extraordinary.
6–8	*Jacques the Swiss...Bishop Burnet* Jean-Jacques Rousseau, *Confessions* (1782–88) and Gilbert Burnet, *The History of My Own Times* (1724–34).
23	*Lexicographer* One who edits or writes a dictionary.
40	*signet* An impression made by an official seal.
46	*'THE LITTLE BUSY BEE'* One of the *Divine Songs for Children* by Isaac Watts (1674–1748).
49	*'Money's the root of every evil'* 'For the love of money is the root of all evil: which while some coveted after, they have erred from the faith, and pierced themselves through with many sorrows' (1 Timothy 6:10).
54	*Corinna* An early Greek poetess, said to have taught Pindar.
56	*pecuniosus* Wealthy; i.e., he is rarely brimming with money.
78	*Morland* 'Poor [George] Morland! What a lack of worldly wisdom he had! Many of the best pictures of this incomparable artist were painted in ale-houses, to discharge his reckoning; and it not unfrequently happened, that interested persons, by the temptation of a "cup of sack", became possessed of pieces of inestimable value' (author's note). Morland (1763–1804) was a well-known painter of rustic and sentimental subjects; he was known for reckless behaviour in his last years. For more on Morland in a literary context, see John Barrell, *The Dark Side of the Landscape: The Rural Poor in English Painting 1730–1840* (Cambridge: Cambridge University Press, 1983).
79	*Napoleon...Russia* Napoleon's long, doomed march to Moscow began in June of 1812 and ended in retreat in October of the same year.

80   *Voltaire…King of Prussia* Voltaire was a guest at the court of Frederick the Great for a period of several years, where he was paid a pension. He left in 1753 after several years of increasing personal conflict. Their relationship is discussed in an essay by Lytton Strachey, 'Voltaire and Frederick the Great' (1915).

95   *eke* Also.

Poetical Memoirs. *From* Canto Second

11   *Phocian* Of Greece and the Muses.

15   *Pindar, Pope, or Pliny* 'Should it be affirmed that *Pliny* was not a Poet, I must beg to observe that he would, perhaps, have been more fortunate, had he attempted to explore Parnassus rather than Vesuvius! His unfortunate death was occasioned by the sulpherous exhalation, from the burning lava of this mountain, in the year 79' (author's note).

Bird's friend and editor Thomas Harral favored the Popean aspects of his verse: 'Mr. Bird was one of the few writers of the present day who have the honour of sustaining the credit of the old English heroic verse – the verse of Dryden and of Pope – the verse which will live and triumph again in renovated vigour and beauty, when much of the modern measureless measure shall have been consigned to deserved oblivion' (pp. xvi–xvii).

16   *jades* Disreputable women

19   *tendered my devoirs* Paid my respects.

24   *Nudior Ovo – like a Scotsman's leg* Naked and white; exposed; unclothed.

46   *bur-dock* A plant with prickly fruit.

From *Francis Abbott, the Recluse of Niagara;* *Metropolitan Sketches* (1837)

Text   The title-page of this volume uses the sub-heading 'Second Series', apparently in reference to the 'Metropolitan Sketches'. In his earlier volume *The Emigrant's Tale* (1833) Bird had included some sketches of London life under the rubric of 'Miscellaneous Poems'. Here he offers poems on twenty-one London sites, including Waterloo Bridge, Vauxhall Gardens, the Antiquarian Society, and the Two-Penny Post Office. Still, what is most striking about Bird's selections is less their variety than their insistently mercantile focus.

The title character in the poem 'Francis Abbott' is based upon an historical figure described in Captain James Edward Alexander's *Transatlantic Sketches* (1833). Abbott was apparently an English officer who became entranced, to the point of insanity, with Niagara Falls, and finally died there in an accident.

The Royal Academy

4   *Phocian* Of Greece and the Muses.

8   *'fine frenzy'* Shakespeare, *A Midsummer Night's Dream* V. i. 12.

13   *Haste from the fields…Strand* The Royal Academy buildings at Somerset House are on the south side of the Strand, a well-known avenue just north of the Thames. For a full discussion of this milieu, see David H. Solkin, *Art on the Line: The Royal Academy Exhibitions at Somerset House 1780–1836* (New Haven: Yale University Press, 2001).

19   *sans remission* Without reduction; i.e. he has paid full price.

23   *posse* A crowd or assemblage.

33–6 *Hilton…Daniell* William Hilton (1786–1839) produced, among other work, the best known portraits of John Clare (q.v.) and John Keats. Edwin Landseer (1802–73) was well known for his animal paintings, such as 'The Monarch of the Glen' (1851). William Daniell (1769–1837) and his uncle Thomas (1749–1840) spent seven years in India in the late eighteenth century, and were renowned as artists of exotic Asian scenery. The reference to William Etty (1787–1849), famous for his female nudes, may be to his 1828 painting 'The Dawn of Love', which takes its title from Milton's 'Comus'.

37–40 *Constable…evil hour* John Constable (1776–1837) produced many large, finely detailed paintings of the Stour river and environs in Suffolk, including his family's mill, but in the years after 1820, and especially after his wife's death in 1828, his style became more slashing and impressionistic, and his depictions of the natural world darker and more violent.

41   *Pickersgill* Henry William Pickersgill (1782–1875), an accomplished portrait painter whose many subjects included Robert Peel, Richard Owen, William Godwin, Jeremy Bentham, and William Wordsworth.

49   *Medora* Presumably a painting by Pickersgill, though perhaps not its standard title.

61   *dauber* A crude or amateurish painter.

The House of Commons

3   *vox populi* Voice of the people

4   *dear delusion* The delusion is that Parliamentary elections are fair and open.

11–13 *Pitt…Dan O'Connell* A list meant to convey sharply contrasting political convictions and personalities. William Pitt and Robert Peel were prominent Tories; Charles James Fox and Samuel Romilly prominent Whigs. William Cobbett and Joseph Hume were Radicals, as was Daniel O'Connell, who was heavily involved in Irish issues. (Peel and O'Connell nearly fought a duel in 1815.) Charles Wetherell was an aggressive opponent of the reform movement.

21   *nous* Common-sense.

25   *Reformed* Elected after the passage of the First Reform Bill (1832), which had expanded the parliamentary franchise.

27   *a pure Member stormed* 'The fastidious oration of Mr Percival will, perhaps, occur to the Reader's recollection' (author's note). This is probably a reference to Spencer Perceval (1795–1859), M.P. and Teller of the Exchequer, and not the more famous Spencer Perceval, (1762–1812), known as the only British Prime Minister to be assassinated while in office.

32   *Hume* Joseph Hume (1777–1855), a prominent Radical voice in Parliament, was particularly known for his resistance to high governmental salaries and sinecures. The reference to him becoming 'unhumed' is perhaps Bird's way of describing a plea for reform that was so passionate that even Hume's rhetoric seemed pale by comparison.

68–70   *Philosophic Stone…Grand Elixir* Mythical alchemical substances imagined, respectively, as allowing the transmutation of base metals into gold, and imparting eternal youth and health.

Guy's Hospital

1   *Bookseller* 'Mr. Guy was a Bookseller, and, for the application of his Hospital to charitable purposes, the public are indebted to a singular and trifling circumstance. Guy employed a female servant, whom he had agreed to marry; some days previous to the intended ceremony, he had ordered that the pavement before his door should be mended up to a particular stone, which he marked, and then left his house on business. The servant, in his absence, saw a broken stone beyond the mark, which the workmen has not repaired, and, on pointing to it, they acquainted her that Mr. Guy had not ordered them to go so far; she, however, directed it to be done, and remarked, "Tell him I bade you, and he will not be angry." When Guy returned he was enraged to find they had exceeded his orders, renounced his engagement to his servant, and devoted his ample fortune to public charity' (author's note).

Thomas Guy, M.P. (1644–1724) made his fortune primarily through the printing and selling of Bibles, and also through investments in the South Sea Bubble. The hospital was founded in 1721; John Keats later pursued his medical studies there.

10   *thy enchanting 'Maid'* See note to line 1.

27   *hair-brained* Variant of hare-brained; foolish, mentally scattered.

33   *physic* A general term for medicine, but in the list that follows Bird mentions several agents that are purgative. A cathartic is a laxative; a sudorific generates sweat; an emenagogue promotes menstrual flow. A demulcient (or demulcent) is an oily substance meant to soothe irritated membranes, as is aloe; Bird suggests that its use might be required because of the action of the other, unnecessarily applied, physics.

35   *phthisic* Not to be confused with 'physic', this term denotes a condition, specifically a cough.

41   *drugs* Many of the items in this list, including jalap, ipecacuanha, colocynth, gamboges, senna, and gentian, also have strong cathartic properties, hence Bird's comment that 'Another word of this would spoil my dinner!' (l. 48).

50   *passed the 'Hall'* A colloquialism for gaining one's licence. The Apothecaries' Hall itself, which still stands in Blackfriars Lane, was an early site of drug manufacturing, and included (at the time of Bird's poem) a retail pharmacy.

51–6   *must not knock out people's brains…slaughter us genteely* Throughout this stanza, Bird is arguing that apothecaries administering drugs actually inflict as much damage to the body as doctors performing surgeries. 'Cup' in line 52 refers to a procedure by which heated glass cups were placed against the skin in order to draw out blood or other fluids.

The Corn Exchange

Title The Mark Lane Corn Exchange, fronted by Greek columns, dated from the middle of the eighteenth century, but a substantial addition had been built in 1827. Mark Lane is near the Tower of London.

1 *Factors and…Millars* Mercantile agents and millers.

3 *Mealmen* Those who sell grain meal.

6 *Ceres' train* Ceres is the goddess of agriculture; Bird seems to be referring to all people who are interested in agriculture's various workings and branches.

10–11 *'caught' the wily Bakers…new Rolls* Bird suggests that both the flour factors and the bakers are secretly adulterating their products and attempting to cheat one another. 'They' in line 11 refers to the bakers.

13–16 *Astringent Alum…lose their health* Alum, a binding agent, was used as an additive in flour because it made the finished bread seem whiter, softer, and moister. Its chemical properties, however, actually made the bread difficult to digest and stripped it of much of its nutritional value. In the novel *Humphry Clinker* (1771), Tobias Smollett writes, 'The bread I eat in London is a deleterious paste, mixed up with chalk, alum and bone-ashes; insipid to the taste and destructive to the constitution. The good people are not ignorant of this adulteration; but they prefer it to wholesome bread, because it is whiter than the meal of corn: thus they sacrifice their taste and their health, and the lives of their tender infants, to a most absurd gratification of a misjudging eye; and the miller, or the baker, is obliged to poison them and their families in order to live by his profession'. Ed. Angus Ross (New York: Penguin, 1967), p. 152.

20–2 *Declares it pingled…yet buy it in a trice* A depiction of bargaining tactics; the miller first rejects the grain as spoiled, then declares it too expensive, then hastily buys it.

23 *lowery* Gloomy, threatening. When read with the following line, the implication is that although the miller pretends to be troubled by the transaction, he is actually enjoying himself.

32 *Foreign Corn* The larger context here is that of the Corn Laws, which had been introduced in 1815 to prevent the importation of foreign grain unless and until domestic grain prices reached a certain level. This artificial price floor resulted in generally high prices for bread. The price level was slightly reduced in 1828, prompting increased imports of foreign corn and, in Bird's view, hurting the domestic farmer. For further discussion, see the entry on Ebenezer Elliott, the 'Corn-Law Rhymer'.

33 *in durance vile* In prison or storage.

34–41 *here the farmer's teeming land…'cheap bread'* The reduction or elimination of the price thresholds on foreign grain was supposed to have the effect of mak-

ing bread cheaper, a central issue in the campaign for the total repeal of the
Corn Laws, which eventually was enacted in 1846.

44   *sown in joy – yet often reaped in tears* An inversion of Psalm 126:5.

74–6   *cits…Cockneys* In this context, both of these terms seem to imply Londoners generally.

The Excise Office

4   *clothe the naked…feed the poor* Matthew 25:34–6.

5   *nine* 'The Excise Office was erected in 1763, on the site of the Alms' Houses founded by Sir Thomas Gresham. The business is managed by *nine* Commissioners, who receive the duty on all exciseable commodities' (author's note). Bird makes punning reference here to the Muses ('the tuneful nine'), and the pun resounds further because the Excise Office on Old Broad Street was located near to the building called the Temple of the Muses in Finsbury Square.

15   *spies* Since local constables were paid a percentage of the penalties levied for excise offenses, they had an incentive to seek out even small violations.

20   *soap* According to Peter Cunningham, *Hand-Book of London: Past and Present* (London: John Murray, 1850), the items generating the most revenue for the Excise were malt, spirits, and soap. The tax on soap, which had been in place since the early eighteenth century, was repealed in 1853.

24   *curst the soap – the suds – the duty* Bird's pun has mothers doubly frustrated by the duty (task) of bathing their children, and the duty (tax) that prevents them from purchasing an adequate quantity of soap.

32   *Deil* Scots for devil. Bird is anticipating his citation of Burns.

34   *Indian weed* Tobacco.

41   *Souchong* A black tea from the south of China.

43   *Young Hyson* A Chinese green tea, prepared from young leaves; the name, Anglicised, means 'before the rains'.

47   *quantum suff* A sufficient amount.
   Bohea A black tea. Though the name has come to be a blanket term for common or inferior black tea, for a period it was used to signify a superior blend, which Bird seems to mean here.

50   *dip-sticks* Specialized rulers, sometimes with logarithmic functions, used especially for measuring liquid in a cask.

56   *half* '"Half to the Informer, and half to the King", this is the "custom of the *Customs*"; and, we might add –

     Ditto, or *like* WISE,
     The same of the *Excise*!' (author's note).

58   *gauger* Excise officer.

64   BURNS For more on excise practices as they relate to Burns, see Graham Smith, *Robert Burns the Exciseman* (Ayr: Alloway Publishing, 1989).

65   *butt of wine* 126 gallons.

68   *The feelings of a spirit wild and frisky* Bird here is repeating the widespread belief that Burns drank himself to death.

70   *Bay of Biscay* A large region of the Atlantic bounded on two sides by the coasts of France and Spain, notorious for its dangerous currents.

72   *Most 'glorious', like his own daft Tam O'Shanter* The title character of Burns's comic poem who, upon becoming delightfully drunk, is described in these famous lines: 'Kings may be blest, but Tam was glorious, / O'er a' the ills o' life victorious!' (ll. 57–8).

88   *'None are so blind as they who will not see'* A proverbial English expression, versions of which date from at least the sixteenth century.

THOMAS WILSON

From *The Pitman's Pay and Other Poems* (1843)

The Pitman's Pay. Part Second

Text   *The Pitman's Pay and Other Poems* (Gateshead: William Douglas, 1843) contained thirty poems altogether. 'Stanzas on the Intended New Line of Road', 'The Oiling of Dicky's Wig', and '[s]everal of the smaller pieces' (p. xv) originally appeared in the *Tyne Mercury* newspaper in the mid-1820s. Most of the definitions of dialect words below are taken from Wilson's own glossary. A second edition of the volume, published by Thomas Fordyce (Newcastle Upon Tyne, 1872), includes a memoir of the author.

Describing his attempt to provide 'a faithful picture' of the life of the pitman in the title poem, Wilson comments that '[n]othing on this subject, to my knowledge, has appeared, since CHICKEN'S "COLLIER'S WEDDING", upwards of a century ago' (pp. vi–vii). For the text and a discussion of Edward Chicken's 700-line poem, perhaps the first printed work incorporating some Geordie dialect, see William Christmas, ed., *English Labouring-Class Poetry 1700–1740* (London: Pickering and Chatto, 2003), pp. 53–71. Christmas notes that '[o]nly one first edition copy [of Chicken's poem] appears to have survived' and he quotes William Cail, the editor of an 1829 edition of 'The Collier's Wedding', as saying that this copy was 'in the possession of Mr. John Bell' (quoted in Christmas p. 53). Since Wilson thanks both John Bell and Thomas Bell 'for much valuable information in connection with Gateshead Fell' (p. xv), a possible narrative suggests itself: Wilson may have been inspired to compose *The Pitman's Pay* after seeing this same surviving copy of 'The Collier's Wedding', and the appearance of the first two installments of *The Pitman's Pay* in 1826 and 1828 may in turn have inspired Cail to produce his new edition of Chicken's poem. That Wilson was inspired by 'The Collier's Wedding' seems clear enough, since his opening line, 'I sing not here of warriors bold' (*The Pitman's Pay, Part First,* line 1), is a purposeful echo of the first line of Chicken's poem: 'I sing not of great Caesar's Might'.

Wilson would later say of Cail's 1829 volume, 'It is accompanied by many interesting facts of [Chicken] and his family, as well as several notes explanatory of the text, and is neatly got up, but, unfortunately, has never come fully before the public' (*The Pitman's Pay,* p. vii). At the very least, we can infer that Wilson, Cail, and the Bells were friends with a shared interest in books. Thomas Bell was not only Wilson's business partner, but a bibliophile in his own right, while John Bell was well known for his volume *Rhymes of Northern Bards* (Newcastle upon Tyne: M. Angus, 1812) and was one of the founders of the Newcastle Society of Antiquaries.

I am indebted to Professor Katie Wales of the University of Leeds for help on Wilson's dialect.

Title Wilson comments that the action described in *The Pitman's Pay* refers to the period around 1800 and that, since then, 'important changes have taken place in the pitman's labour, tending to limit the duration as well as lessen the severity of his toil' (p. vi). Prior to 1800, Wilson notes elsewhere, 'it was customary to send girls down the coal-pits; but that disgraceful practice ceased in this neighbourhood nearly sixty years ago. The custom was more prevalent on the Wear than on the Tyne' (p. xii).

2 *JOHN BARLEYCORN* Alcohol drink made from barley malt, especially malt liquor, whisky, or ale.

7 *hew* Work coal.

10 *sweeling* Melting; wasting away.

12 *off the table reeling* The 'thumps' of l. 8 are jostling the crockery.

13 *drouthy* Thirsty.

13 *TOMMY* 'TOMMY COULSON, a stone-mason, and performer on the violin, who lived at Cow Close, and attended on all occasions of merry-making....If he attended a merry night at a public house on the Saturday evening, he was sure to be found there on the Monday morning, and perhaps longer. There are several anecdotes told of him, arising out of his love of "suction". Amongst others is the following: – He had either been balloted for the Militia, or entered as a substitute, in one of his drunken frolics. The regiment had been some time at a distance; and TOMMY, having a wish to see his wife MALLY, obtained, on some pretext or other, a furlough, and wrote MALLY, that about such a time she might expect him. The time appointed passed over, but TOMMY never appeared....At length she received a message, saying that he was at a public house, at about a half a mile distance, and that if she wanted to see her husband, she must come soon to *him,* as his furlough was now up, and he had not time to come to *her*' (author's note).

13 *nook* Corner.

14 *suction* Ale or beer.

15 *PHILIP...Derwent Crook* 'PHILIP SHORT was a pitman, and died an old man, in Gateshead poor-house, in the summer of 1834 ...' (author's note). Derwent Crook was a colliery (coal mine) in the Low Fell area.

17 *DICK* 'DICK TAYLOR, a pitman, was only famous as having married BARBARA BLAND, the daughter of old NELL BLAND, the only *real* witch we had on the Low Fell. NELL was one of the party that was watching the corpse of

TOM FORESTER the *first* time he died, and had her arm broken by being tumbled heels over head down stairs at his resurrection; for, be it known, contrary to established usage, poor TOM died twice. After he made his exit the first time, and was laid out a decent corpse, the neighbours, as is customary on such occasions, were sitting up in the same room with the body, and holding what they call a "Lake Wake"; when, to their utter astonishment, they perceived the corpse gradually raising its head, until it sat upright. In the moment the room was cleared, and the whole company, that had been the instant before enjoying themselves and telling stories, were tumbling one over the other down-stairs; and more, it is said, than poor NELL came off with broken bones...' (author's note).

19 *PEEL* 'JACK PEEL was a pitman, and a "theaker", a business of some note when the cottages on the Fell were all covered with "divots", but now extinct, since the common was enclosed' (author's note). That is, he thatched houses with turf or sod.

20 *un* One.

25 *scraper* Bow.

26 *rosin* Resin.

31 *quids* Chews of tobacco.

33 *yel's* Ale's.

35 *stour* Dust floating in the air.

36 *Conn'd* Recounted; reminisced.

39 *byeth neet and day* Both night and day.

40 *Eneugh yen's varry pith te wither* That is, to such a degree as to wither one's body to the very core.

41 *Aw* I.

 bait-poke A 'bag in which a pit-lad carries his provisions' (author's note).

42 *sark and hoggers* 'Shirts, and stockings with the feet cut off' (author's note).
 maw My.

43 *meet steit* Might as well.

45 *wark* Work.

47 *skelp and yark* Move rapidly.

48 *amain* Out of control.

49 *Aw thowt the time wad ne'er be gyen* I thought the time would never be gone.

50–1 *callin'-course...caller* The 'time at which pitmen are called to work' (author's note), and the person who does the summoning.

51 *yen* One.

52 *nowther sleep nor slum.* Neither sleep nor rest.

53 *Aw lap up...spangin'* I.e., I jumped up, nimble as a flea leaping among our blankets. 'Lop' is another word for flea.

54 *wor* Our.

56 *bangin'* Moving quickly.

57 *gleg* Quick, clever.

58 *fettle* Order, get ready.

59 *a peg* A step.

60   *hyem* Home.

61   *cooen seet* Disheartening sight.

62   *hirplin'* Walking lamely.

63   *anklets shaw'd…scather'd feet* Ankles 'injured by friction' and 'feet injured from water and small coals, in the shoes' (author's notes).

65   *duds* Working clothes.

           tyen Taken.

68   *rive atwee* Break in two.

69   *low rope* A 'piece of rope lighted at one end' (author's note).

70   *trappin' trade* The 'business of a trapper' (author's note).

           crouse Brisk, lively.

72   *Hinnies* Friends.

           canny bairn A good, mild, affectionate child.

73   *syne* Since.

74   *hings* Hangs.

75   *awd NELL, and CUDDY's swine* 'Pitmen consider it unlucky to meet a *oman* or a *pig* on their way to work: of course they are on the look-out through the day for some untoward event, when that has been the case …' (author's note).

76   *Twee* Two.

           sonsy Lucky, pleasant, agreeable.

77   *tiv iv'ry skin* To everyone.

78   *barber's blocks* Blocks for holding wigs.

79   *nobbut brack* Only broke.

80   *backy-box* Tobacco box.

84   *luikin'* Looking.

87   *gan* Go.

88   *DEDDY's* Daddy's.

89   *iv* In.

90   *styth* Foul air.

92   *a geuss upon a speet* A goose upon a spit.

93   *gaun* Going.

94   *nowse* Nothing.

98   *tiv a single roun'* To a uniform texture.

99   *scrimpt* Crispy.

101   *hollow meats* Presumably, fowl that can readily be gutted and cooked on a spit.

102   *speetin'* Cooking on a spit.

103   *nyen aw tyest* None I taste.

104   *yess o' trumps* Ace of trumps.

106   *meet myek a myel* Might make a meal.

108   *te morn* Tomorrow.

109   *oddments, tee* Giblets, too.

117   *meetin's* Midway down the pit, or where the full and empty corves or baskets pass each other.

118   *bottom* That is, the bottom of the mine shaft.

119   *bumm'd* Hurried.

120   *teetotum* Spinning top.

121   *barn-styen* The 'roof of the mine at the entrance of the workings' (author's note).

122   *stevell'd te the cabin* I.e., staggered to the central gathering area near the bottom of the main shaft, from which the individual miners will be dispersed to the various workings.

123   *cannels* Candles.

124   *The seat o' power and pitmen's lare* The reference is evidently to the 'cabin' of l. 122; since individual work-orders are issued from this location at the start of the day, it is a 'seat of power' and 'pitmen's lare' (learning).

125   *durdum* Noise.

126   *Haud* Stop.

126   *chow* A quid of tobacco.

127   *gie's a leet!* Give us a light.

128   *ha'd aboot a low!* Hold a light around.

129   *hinny* A favourite term of endearment.

130   *corf* A basket for bringing coals out of the pit.

131   *tram* A 'small carriage upon which a corf or basket is placed; or it sometimes means two boys who have the charge of this carriage, the one drawing and the other pushing it' (author's note).

132   *half-ring'd hog* One in the process of having a ring put through its snout.

135   *heedsman* 'Headsman' (author's note), presumably positioned at the front of the tram. *Greenwell's Glossary of Terms Used in the Coal Trade of Northumberland and Durham* (Newcastle-upon-Tyne, 1849) defines headsman as a boy not strong enough to 'put' (move the coal tram) alone.

136   *off the way* That is, off track.

137   *In bye* Underground, towards the coal face.
       crack A short space of time.

138   *board* The space allotted to one man to work in, in a colliery.

139   *buffin' at a back* Labouring at a parting in the coal.

140   *whinstone* An especially hard basaltic rock.

141   *bray'd* Hit.
       byeth lang and sair Both long and sore.

142   *stannin'* Standing.

146   *kirvens and the nickens* 'The preparatory operations for bringing down the jud or top, and which produce only small coal' (author's note).

147   *myest* Most.

149   *sic* Such.

150   *agyend* Against.

152   *heeedwis end* Headway, or passages that lead to the crane or shaft.

153   *outbye* Towards the shaft or bottom of the pit.

154   *ahint* Behind.

155   *a' cut and dry* Sorted out and arranged.

156   *ettled reet* Arranged or contrived properly

158   *kittle maiters* Ticklish or difficult matters.

160   *poor cabin calculators* I.e., those who aren't gifted at logic or mathematics.

162   *Bamboozlin'* Puzzling.

164   *wiv ony feather* At the slightest provocation.

166   *pinch* Difficult situation.

167   *blurr'd his wooden sheet* Smudged his writing tablet.

          pointer roun' Spinning dial.

173   *baitin'* Teasing.

176   *place the wark* Arrange the labour for the day, directing each man or crew to
          a different location within the mine.

178   *his chalk and wooden buick* I.e., the writing implements he is using to do calcu-
          lations and make organizational plans

180   *Hidden ahint some awd wa' nuik* Hiding behind a nook in the wall in an effort
          to finish the calculations necessary to 'place the wark'. 'Such cases were not
          uncommon formerly, and this is true to the letter; but since the schoolmas-
          ter came aboard, they have no doubt been less frequent' (author's note).

182   *cantrips* A charm or incantation.

186   *duin* Done.

          heedsman See note to line 135.

193   *tram* A 'small carriage upon which a corf or basket is placed; or it some-
          times means two boys who have the charge of the carriage, the one drawing
          and the other pushing it' (author's note).

          Aw mind…slaw I remember a tram both weak and slow.

194   *Just streen'd te rags te keep her gannin'* Strained to pieces to keep her running.

195   *Frae hingin'-on till howdy-maw* From the start of the work day to its conclu-
          sion; 'howdy-maw' is the day's last basket or corf.

197   *tarn* Fierce.

200   *For at the corf nut lyin' reet* Because the basket isn't lying properly.

201   *hoolet e'en* Owlish eyes.

202   *hick'ry fyece* Ill-tempered face.

203   *compleen* Complain.

204   *nell-kneed, wall-eyed* Wilson defines these terms as 'in-kneed' and 'white-
          eyed'; the implication is that Jack is weak and fearful. He also makes clear in
          another note that Jack and Charley are brothers, and both are weak, facts
          that increase their mutual rancour.

206   *lugs* Ears.

208   *Dispatch him sprawlin' iv a crack* Throw him down in an instant.

211   *joukin'* '[S]toop[ing] down to avoid a blow' (author's note).

213   *bits o' lads* Smaller boys.

217   *putter* The boy who works the tram, and conveys the coal from the working
          face.

218   *stannin' fray* A stand-up fight.

219–20   *Frae yokens, cawd pies, stowen bait…cowp'd corves i' the barrow way* A series of
          problems said to be the sad lot of the putter; respectively, collisions

between trams; cold or stolen food; coal baskets overturned in the tram-way.

222   *fippence* Fivepence.

223–4   *cloot…door* A punch or cuff in punishment for falling asleep near the ventilation door.

225   *berth* Job; situation.

229   *half-wark* The time 'when the day's work is half over' (author's note).

230   *thumps* Probably blows of punishment.

231   *hettle* Hasty.

232   *gar'd me stur maw stumps* That is, Lukey forced the speaker to get up and walk around, presumably to do some small job.

233   *grease-horn* Probably a device for oiling the trams, or possibly for use with the candles.

234   *waxy clay* Candle tallow.

235   *half-shoon* Old shoes with the toes cut off.

235   *bait-poke* A 'bag in which a pit-lad carries his provisions' (author's note).

237   *DUMMY* A particular tram.

240–1   *Blackgairded…DAN THE DEEVIL* That is, cursed at or criticized by a brutish worker like 'Dan the Devil'.

242   *marrow* A working partner or companion.

244   *As ony tyed's belaw a harrow* As that of a toad caught beneath the blades of a sharp plow.

245   *Blackymoors* Black slaves from Africa.

247   *wors* Ours.

250   *Ha'e harder cairds than wors te play* Had harder cards than us to play; i.e., had a more difficult situation.

252   *And truth's in what wor preachers say* The abolitionist movement was largely based in churches.

258   *nyek'd* Naked.

271   *holey thill and dyels a' splettin'* The broken surface of holes and split planks on which the coal trams formerly ran.

272   *metal ways* 'Previous to this, bringing out the coals to the crane or shaft, or what is called "putting", was the most distressing slavery. It was generally performed by boys, in nine cases out of ten too weak for the purpose – if even the materials had been better than they were, over which the trams then passed. What, then, must it have been, when a beech board was a god-send? And, more frequently, they had to drag their load over a fir deal or the bare "thill", the former too often split from constant wear, and the latter too soft to bear the load passing over it. Now, the whole way is laid with metal plates, even up to the face of the workings, so that a man or lad may run the tram before him both out and in, the plates being so formed as to keep the tram in a right direction…' (author's note).

276   *nowse* Nothing.

277   *yeps* Apes.

278   *wowl* Cry or howl.

279   *langsyne cheps* Chaps who lived long ago.

280   *worsel out* Outlast.

282   *metal plates* Metal rails; see note to l. 272.

286   *ayont* Beyond.

289   *neist* Next.

       half a tram 'One of two that manage a tram' (author's note).

       bun Bound.

290   *marrow* Partner; companion.

291   *myed me, suin* Made me soon.

292   *puttin'-hewer* A 'young man bound either to put or hew' (author's note); that is, he frequently had to work the tram, which was considered a boy's job, though sometimes he worked at the adult job of hewing (working the coal).

295   *fettled* Made ready.

296   *bun* Obligated; contracted.

299   *fyel* Fail.

300   *canny claes* Fine clothes. 'When a young man commences hewing, it is no uncommon thing for him to take his earnings into his own management, giving his parents a certain weekly sum for his board; or, if the parties cannot agree on this point, he takes lodgings at some neighbour's, where he finds his own victuals, and pays so much a week for lodging and attendance. This is called "picklin' in his awn poke neuck". It does not infrequently happen that he pitches his tent where the daughter of the house ultimately becomes his wife. This is too often the real attraction that draws him from home, though a very different one may be pretended' (author's note).

302   *byen* Bone.

304   *A' bein' mell-and-wedge wark* 'This alludes to the present practice of shooting down the "jud" or "top" with powder, instead of bringing it down with the "wedges", as formerly. In drifting in stone, powder was always used, but in coal only in late years. In hewing, this is as great as improvement and saving of labour, as metal plates are in putting' (author's note).

305   *woody coal* 'Tough, and difficult to separate' (author's note).

308   *yence* Once.

       pouther Powder.

309   *A 'back' or 'knowe'* 'Partings in the coal, which set the "jud" down with little trouble, after the "kirving" and "nicking" are completed – sometimes even before' (author's note).

311   *tew* Struggle, toil.

312   *scabby reuf* '"Scabby roof" is where the coal does not part freely from the stone at the top' (author's note).

313   *swatch* A 'pattern or sample'.

314   *breek'd till fit to marry* That is, from the time one is first put into breeches as a youngster until one is old enough to marry.

316   *AWD HARRY* The Devil.

321   *doon* Down feathers.

322   *JACK THE CALLER* A reference to the man who summons the labourers from their beds; cf. ll. 50–1.

323   *hyell* Whole.

329   *fiery 'blast'* A powder explosion used to bring down coal.

333   *wait'ry 'wyest'* Watery waste; specifically, water that may flood the workings and trap the miners. In a note, Wilson refers to the 'Heaton catastrophe of the 3rd of May, 1815, [in which] 75 persons (41 men, and 34 boys, lost their lives, together with the whole stock of horse which were in the pit at the time. For the details, see *Sykes's Local Records*'. More details on this disaster are available through the web page of the Durham Mining Museum, <http://www.dmm.org.uk>.

334   *huz* Us.

340   *parish* Perish.

346   *what they call a 'mission'* An improvement scheme.

349   *asteep* Literally, to soak; by extension, to ponder or mull over.

352   *kirve and nick by steam* Carve and cut out the coal using steam.

354   *gars* Makes.

356   *run the Lunnun mail* Power the London mail. In a note Wilson adds, 'This has already been effected'.

358   *jud myed riddy* The coal face made ready.

360–1   *He* In these lines, 'He' refers to steam, following from l. 356.

363   *Begock!* A term of exclamation.

        aw's often flay'd te deed I'm often scared to death.

366   *pouin'* Pulling.

370   *te gyzen* To crack, as a result of being dry from insufficient drink.

376   *hirplin' age* Old age, when one limps.

377   *bairns* Children.

378   *'honest men and bonny lasses'* A quotation from Robert Burns's 'Tam O'Shanter' (l. 16). This section of *The Pitman's Pay* also features several echoes of Burns's 'A Man's a Man for A' That', a poem which celebrates 'honest poverty' (l. 1) and ridicules the 'tinsel show' (l. 6) of wealth and social rank. See especially ll. 385–88, and indeed the entire passage concluding with Wilson's phrase 'honest-hearted poverty' (l. 400).

382   *nappy* Ale.

388   *pouther'd pyte* Powdered pate, suggestive of a pun: just as some coal faces opened with gunpowder are shown to contain only small amounts of usable coal, so do the cosmetic powders used on human faces sometimes hide the shallow character of a fop or dandy.

396   *bums and bailies dreamin'* Bumbailiffs; i.e., fretful dreams of bankruptcy. The implication is that the debt-ridden gentry are haunted by perpetual anxiety, while the sleep of the pitman, however short, is blissfully free from such concerns.

401   *fyel and brick* Fail and break.

403   *keep the wheelband i' the nick* Literally, keep the tire in the groove; metaphorically, maintain a working household.

408	*cuttin' other idle capers* Engaging in other dishonest activities as a way of passing the time.
415	*greet* Great.
425	*breet* Bright.

The Washing-Day

Title	This remains a famous song in Tyneside down to the present day. It has an interesting thematic continuities with 'The Washing-day', by E. Waring, reprinted in the notes to the entry on Charlotte Richardson (q.v.).
Text	The different spellings of 'Washing' (title) and 'weshin' (text) follow from the original.
9	*souse! souse!* Soak, soak.
11	*glumpin' i' the hoose* Sulking in the house.
13	*Sud* Should.
	torns out Turns out (to do the washing).
15	*cloots the bits o' bairns aboot* Strikes the children about with her hands.
18	*Goodman* Husband.
23	*a' fire and tow* That is, all full of fire and leaving a wake of anger.
25	*iv a low* Into a flame.
26	*claes* Clothes.
33	PINCHER Wilson's dog, whom he elegizes in the poem, 'The Author's Favourite Dog, Pincher' (not included here).
35	*balk* A main beam or rafter.
36	*iv a flay* In a fright.
46	*A cup, and blast o' backy* A drink and some tobacco.
51	*neist* Next.

On Seeing a Mouse Run Across the Road in January

Title	The allusions to Burns's poem 'To a Mouse', which this poem imitates and rewrites, are so numerous that the two works should be read alongside one another. Another poem in Wilson's volume 'On Parting with a Favourite Mare', opens with the wistful plea, 'had I the muse of Burns…' (l. 1); here he employs some dialect words that are Scots rather than Geordie (e.g. 'weans').
2	*bicker* Hasten.
3	*fae* Foe.
5	*wae* Woe.
6	*weans* Children.
9	*speer* Seek, inquire.
13	*cosie biel* A snug place of shelter.
14	*stinted* Small, scanty.
15	*aiblins* Perhaps.
16	*byre* A cowhouse.
17–8	*Death's tortures…cats or wire* Mortal dangers the mouse faces in trying to gather food.

21   *Ye should na hae sic tow te tease* I.e., you shouldn't have such a load to worry about.

26   *I wot ye'll nae be lag nor blate* I.e., I know you'll be neither slow nor shy.

31   *ye daft and thriftless crew* That is, the improvident readers of this poem; Wilson hopes they will see in the mouse's story a reflection of their own imprudent ways: they will 'view' themselves 'in colours true' (ll. 31–2) when they see their own behaviour through this 'mousely mirror' (l. 32).

38   *haffits grey* Gray hair on the sides of the head.

42   *brittle thread* The fragile forces of health and strength.

43   *hirplin' age* Old age.

44   *cauldness* Coldness.

JOHN NICHOLSON

From *Poems by John Nicholson* (1844)

Text   The selections here are drawn from the volume edited by John James, F. S. A., author of *The History of Bradford* (1841). It includes a useful biographical sketch, a list of approximately 700 subscribers, and a selection of three memorial poems to Nicholson written by Robert Story, Thomas Crossley, and Edward Collinson. The 1876 volume, *The Poetical Works of John Nicholson* (London: Simpkin and Marshall), edited by W. G. Hird, is also recommended.

Some discussion of Nicholson's unpublished work, including transcriptions of three short poems, appears in the essay in the *Bradford Antiquary* by James Ogden listed in the 'Further Reading' section above.

On Visiting a Workhouse

Title   The workhouse described here may have been in Bradford; in Nicholson's time there were over thirty operating workhouses in West Yorkshire.

21   *woolsey* Woollen.

22   *Harewood.* A small village, five miles north of Leeds.

24   *countess* Specifically, the Countess of Harewood; Nicholson is saying that Ann could be mistaken for her. Harewood Hall continues to this day to be the seat of the Earl of Harewood, and the village remains within the fiefdom.

46   *cordial* A medicine or tonic, especially a liqueur.

January

17   *thrasher* Thresher.

The Muse

2   *some sequester'd spot* An allusion to Thomas Gray's 'Elegy Written in a Country Churchyard' (1751), lines 45–6 ('Perhaps in this neglected spot is laid / Some heart once pregnant with celestial fire') and 75–6 ('Along the cool

sequester'd vale of life / They kept the noiseless tenor of their way'). The title of Nicholson's poem, though generic, also echoes Gray's lines 'the Muse's flame' (l. 71) and 'th' unletter'd muse' (l. 81).

6 *vestur'd* Clothed with.

7 *Romantic scenes can ne'er indite* The scenes themselves cannot do the poet's writing for him.

22 *Cumbria's lakes...Highland glens* Presumably a reference to the haunts of Wordsworth and Burns, although Burns was not from the Highlands and his work evokes them only occasionally, e.g., 'My Heart's in the Highlands'.

On the Ascent of a Balloon

11 *enthusiasts* Members of various non-conformist religious groups, especially those believing they receive divine visions.

16 *heirs of endless day* I.e., those chosen for eternal life.

18 *demon Nature cuts the ropes* In context, this reference appears to be to human nature or inherent sinfulness, and not to external agency.

38 *marriage portion* Dowry.

39 *the circle gay* The social circle of the idle rich.

50–1 *Covent-Garden...Vauxhall...the turf...the ring* Respectively, the famous London theatre and environs; the popular London gardens; the horse track; and the boxing ring, all synonymous with pleasure and dissipation.

88 *one friend* A patron. In making this remark, Nicholson may have been thinking of John Clare (q.v.), of whom he said, 'What have I had to suffer, compared to what he had? 'Tis true my family have been more numerous; but then I have had more friends. When he, poor man, had worked hard for his twenty shillings to pay for three hundred copies of a very humble prospectus, and when they were all distributed, what was the number of subscribers? Seven!!! Only seven. Oh what must he have felt! He had no one to whom he could unbosom his mind, at least who had any influence. I sadly want to know my fate; but if my works should clear me forty or fifty pounds, I would be well dressed, take a day when I thought, and scribble over another poem. You will say, What, not tired yet! No, sir, I know I can leave my children no other legacy than a volume of trifles, if they can find a real friend to publish them. I will tell you what I am afraid of – many will compare my works with those who have had far greater privileges, and then they will be found wanting' (quoted in James, p. xxii).

101 *scimitar* A sword with a curved blade.

Sports of the Field

6 *springers* A breed of spaniel especially favoured as hunting dogs.

The Malt-Kiln Fire

Title The fire used to dry soaked and germinated malt; this particular kiln was probably located in the village of Harden, two miles west of Bingley.

35   *And drunk less brandy, and more beer* As with other parts of the poem, this reference indicates a preference for the true joys of 'low' company.

The Drunkard's Retribution

15   *pillory* A wooden frame, with holes for the head and hands, into which criminals were placed for public humiliation.

Lines on 'Long Tom'

Title   'Whilst on a visit to the Lakes of Cumberland, [Nicholson] became acquainted with the steward of George Lane Fox, Esq., of Bramham, who recommended Nicholson to the notice of that gentleman, who, being pleased with the perusal of Nicholson's poems, and hearing of his distress, with characteristic generosity gave the poet twenty pounds; and ever afterwards he was welcome to the hospitalities at Bramham Park. There he often quaffed the contents in strong beer of a horn, holding about three pints, called "Long Tom". The clever lines to "Long Tom" were written while under the inspiration of this bacchanalian horn' (James, p. xvii).

The house of Bramham Park, seven miles north-east of Leeds, was severely damaged by fire in 1828, and was not thoroughly repaired until the twentieth century.

38   *tars* Sailors.

55   *Eldwick rocks* The area around Eldwick, near Bingley, features great varieties of topography, including various rocky outcrops. Nicholson may have in mind here a particular 'huge flat rock which overlooks the pleasant valley at Harden Beck'; James reports that in summertime Nicholson 'generally rose at four o'clock, and strayed to [this] accustomed post for poetic contemplation and expression' (p. xii).

Melpomene

Title   Regarding Nicholson's attraction to tragic and dramatic forms, James notes that '[h]is favourite authors were Pope's Homer, Shakespeare, and Young's Night Thoughts. The former he incessantly read, and had a considerable portion of it by memory. To this love of Homer may be imputed the partiality he evinced […] to battle scenes' (p. vi).

ROBERT FRANKLIN

From *The Miller's Muse* (1824)

Text   *The Miller's Muse: Rural Poems* (Hull: Printed and Sold by I. Wilson, Lowgate, 1824). The list of subscribers is headed by 'The Right Hon. Lord Yarborough', 'Sir Henry Nelthorpe', and 'Lady Nelthorpe', and its considerable length suggests that Franklin was able to move with some facility amongst the professional classes and the gentry. The copy held by the New York Public Library, evidently purchased by one of the original subscribers,

Thomas Westaby, contains fragmentary handwritten notes which testify to Franklin's knowledge of the Humberside region.

Poor William

Title   As Wordsworth does in many of his rustic poems, Franklin testifies to the truth of this tale: 'Poor William, though a singular character, is a copy from real life, – his name was William Gawthorpe, a native of Barrow' (p. vi).

31   *furze* A thorny, dense evergreen shrub.
      niggard Stingy; miserly.

37   *turf-built shed* A structure made from cut pieces of earth or sod.

43   *brake* Thicket.

56   *on pity's bounty chiefly fed* His food came primarily from charitable neighbours.

80   *sublunary* Earthly.

88   *yon poor-house* Possibly a workhouse believed to have been functioning at Grimsby in the early nineteenth century.

A Visit from Bridlington to Flambro' Head

Title   This section of the Yorkshire coast, north of Kingston-upon-Hull, is particularly treacherous, and features Flamborough Head, a chalk promontory that juts dramatically out to sea just five miles north of Bridlington. One infers from the poem that Franklin had visited the area with a boating party, and it is perhaps because participation in such an adventure would have been a singular event for someone of Franklin's class that he concludes the poem with an impassioned testimonial to its veracity, promising, 'till life shall fail, / That truth alone inspires my tale'.

In the poem, the greatest danger the party faces is being stranded on the rocks during a rising tide, and the subsequent becalming of the wind forces them to row in order to gain needed distance from the shore. As residents of this coast they would have been familiar with any number of catastrophic wrecks in its waters, one of which is described in a passage from an early work on nautical navigation, Henry Taylor's *Instructions for Mariners* (1792):

> In the winter of 1767, [Taylor] sailed from Shields in company with fifteen sail; only six survived a dreadful storm [...] They could not conceive the reason why the ship would not steer, but in the morning they found that the tiller was broke in the rudder-head [...] [T]he gale was excessive, and the wind had veered during the night to N.E. and N.E. by E. [and] they found themselves in the morning abreast of Flambro' Head, distant six miles.
>
> During the night the boats and every thing on the deck were washed overboard. The foresail, which had stood fast, now gave way [...] With some difficulty they got the broken tiller out, and another put in, and then attempted to get the ship before the wind, to try for Bridlington Bay, in hopes that their anchors would hold, but to no purpose; she would not move off from the wind[...] They had now

little hope of keeping off the land until morning. A dark night was approaching, the wind at N.E. and the storm unabated; however, they did not abandon themselves to despair, but succeeded in getting the mainsail tolerably well set, and by lying in the hollow of the sea, the ship got head-way. At daylight in the morning, they were abreast of Dimlington, and about three miles off. The Humber was now their only hope, which if they missed, they must (as the wind was) in a few hours have inevitably perished [...] [T]hey let go their anchor a little above Spurn Point; then letting go the main geers, the main yard came down, for they were so exhausted by hunger and fatigue they could not haul the mainsail up. Henry Taylor, *Instructions for Mariners Respecting the Management of Ships at Single Anchor ... to which is prefixed a memoir of the author's life*. 1792. 7th Edn. (London: James Imray, 1861).

30   *The tow'ring light-house* The lighthouse, built in 1806 by John Matson of Bridlington, was a relatively new structure in Franklin's time, and is still in use today. Standing nearly 90 feet tall, it was perched on a chalk cliff of at least 150 feet. Set further back on the same stretch of coast is a seventeenth-century structure known as the Beacon light tower, which was designed as an elevated platform atop which a fire could be lit during a storm. It is the only known example of such a structure in England and was restored in the 1990s.

48   *Filey rocks* A natural breakwater, made up of large boulders, extending out of the bay where is situated the town of Filey, a few miles south of Scarborough. The rocks were called the 'Bridge' or 'Filey Brigg'; Bulmer's *History and Directory of East Yorkshire* (1892) said they provided 'the finest sea walk in England'.

The Poacher

Title   Though the poem describes the poacher's depravity and mental anguish – rather than the legal punishment for his crime – legal sanctions for poaching in the nineteenth century were wide-ranging and sometimes extraordinarily severe, including transportation and even death.

7   *nature's gen'ral plan* The influence of Pope, especially the *Essay on Man* (1733–34), is strongly felt in these opening heroic couplets. Franklin, however, is more inclined to conceptualise order and disorder at the level of local social behaviour.

18   *rood* A quarter-acre.

20   *various lumber* Assorted trash.

Reflections on Napoleon

Title   Franklin notes in the volume's preface: 'Having read the newspapers during the peninsular campaigns, and reflected on the dreadful accounts of war and bloodshed, at the time of Bonaparte's first overthrow, and subsequent to his banishment to the island of Elba, I felt truly rejoiced at the cessation of hostilities' (pp. vi–vii). Though Franklin does not mention Elba in the poem, it may be assumed that Napoleon's escape from that Italian island in early 1815, and his further attempt at military domination of Europe, is part of what fuels the poem's ire.

9   *St. Helena's lonely isle* The small, remote island in the South Atlantic where Napoleon was exiled after his final defeat at Waterloo. He died there in 1821, having had bitter conflicts with the British Governor, Sir Hudson Lowe. His body was returned to France in 1840.

15–8   *Marengo's fight* A reference to the bloody Battle of Marengo (Italy), fought 14 June 1800, in which Napoleon was able to overcome a series of difficulties and defeat the Austrian army. The victory allowed France to negotiate a favorable settlement with Austria in the months that followed.

17   *Gallia's* France's.

19   *Austerlitz' dread field of fame.* The Battle of Austerlitz (Austria) was widely viewed as Napoleon's greatest victory, and assured his reputation as a brilliant tactician. On 2 December 1805 he split and defeated combined forces of Austria and Russia.

67   *No faithful wife, at latest breath* Napoleon's marriage to Josephine had been annulled in 1809, and he then married Archduchess Marie-Louise of Austria. Romantic legend has it that his dying words on St. Helena were 'France, the army, Josephine'.

The Convict

9–11   The prisoner has been transported from England, possibly to the Caribbean, but 'lone region' (l. 1) is more suggestive of Australia.

34   *kindred* Siblings.

The Banks of the Humber

1   *mansion* 'The seat of John Nelthorpe, Esq. at South Ferriby, forms the subject of the verses entitled The Banks of the Humber; the introduction to them is descriptive of the front of his house, which, at the period of their composition, was covered with woodbine and roses, the tendrils of the woodbine extending up to the slates; and at the spring time of the year, it was one of unvaried bloom. Although my stay with the above gentleman was not very long, and immediately previous to my becoming a miller, yet I can justly observe, that I never felt the shackles of servitude press lighter, than while in his service. But to say the least, it never was my misfortune to meet with *hard masters*, – I have reason to respect them all' (pp. vii–viii). The mansion Franklin describes is in all likelihood South Ferriby Hall. Scawby Hall, where George Stubbs dissected horses as part of his anatomy research, is another Lincolnshire home that was owned by the Nelthorpe family.

39   *bourn* Boundary; limit.

From *The House of Brocklesby* (1844)

Text   Published two decades years after *The Miller's Muse, The House of Brocklesby* (Hull, 1844) extends some of the features of the earlier volume, while doing away with other features altogether. Six poems comprise the entire work: the title piece (which runs to over forty pages); 'Lines on Visiting Thornton Abbey'; 'The Justice of the Peace'; 'The Village Churchyard'; 'The Village Clerk'; and 'Coronation Ode'. These poems continue to display pious moralism and aggressive rectitude, but Franklin gives himself over even more fully to a nostalgic, Burkean conservatism. Only the Thornton Abbey poem makes any gesture toward lyric spontaneity.

The Village Clerk

2   *Maddison* 'Thomas Maddison, thirty-six years clerk of Barrow Church' (author's note).

11   *Carv'd by himself, he left with friend sincere* 'John Bell, still living' (author's note).

35   *The ancient abbey and the church in frame* 'Thornton Abbey, and Barrow Church' (author's note).

42   *'The life of Joseph' into each rhyme* Probably a reference to the unswerving sense of Christian duty and responsibility advocated in Maddison's poems, with particular reference to the nature of Maddison's stewardship. As lines 49–62 of the poem suggest, Maddison's actions as clerk of the church for nearly four decades were not always respected by the citizenry; in *Genesis* 49: 22–26, when Jacob blesses his sons as the heads of the twelve tribes of Israel, Joseph is singled out for his stewardship, even though separated from, and persecuted by, his brethren:

> Joseph is a fruitful bough, even a fruitful bough by a well; whose branches run over the wall. The archers have sorely grieved him, and shot at him, and hated him. But his bow abode in strength, and the arms of his hands were made strong by the hands of the mighty God of Jacob; (from thence is the shepherd, the stone of Israel). Even by the God of thy father, who shall help thee; and by the Almighty, who shall bless thee with blessings of heaven above, blessings of the deep that lieth under, blessings of the breasts, and of the womb. The blessings of thy father have prevailed above the blessings of my progenitors unto the utmost bound of the everlasting hills: they shall be on the head of Joseph, and on the crown of the head of him that was separate from his brethren. (*KJV*)

44   *singer, ringer, clerk, and sexton too* A series of church duties, respectively: chorister, bell-ringer, record-keeper, grave-digger.

49   *On his first clerkship tithes were ta'en in kind* Accepted in some form other than money, e.g. hay or livestock.

59–62   *And some who rail'd, at length made open vow* The connection between enclosure and the townsfolk's gradually improving view of Maddison is unclear here. It is possible that he spoke out against enclosure, and that the passage describes the later, public acknowledgement of his prescience on this issue. Yet the passage may be saying simply that, as the residents of Barrow confronted the real poverty that came with the loss of 'the good wide common and the cow', they came to realize that Maddison's demands for tithes had been fair and comparatively mild.

97   *Deeds on the ocean* These passages describing Maddison's reading may well reflect interests he shared with Franklin, especially as the latter was actually related to Sir John Franklin (1786–1847), the Arctic explorer who famously sought the Northwest Passage and who was also a native of Lincolnshire. However, Rosemary Doria's assertion that the poet was a 'descendant' (p. 22) of the explorer is clearly incorrect: for although we do not know the poet's date of birth with certainty, we do know that he was a contemporary of the explorer, and in all likelihood was actually born before him.

98   *Cape Horn* The southernmost tip of South America.

102   *the sad fate of much-lamented Cook* Captain James Cook was killed in Hawaii in 1779, apparently after a dispute with native islanders about items that may have been stolen from his ship. Cook's death was widely recounted in verse and prose narratives.

104   *gallant Bruce* James Bruce (1730–1794), whose journeys in Ethiopia were described in *Travels to Discover the Source of the Nile* (1790).

THEMATIC INDEX

NARRATIVE VERSE/ORAL TRADITION

PATRONS AND PATRONAGE

SELF-REPRESENTATION AND CREATIVITY

LABOUR AND THE WORKPLACE

LOCAL AND TOPOGRAPHICAL VERSE; NATURAL DESCRIPTION

DIALECT VERSE

POLITICAL POETRY

INTERTEXTUAL VERSE

RELIGIOUS, PHILOSOPHICAL AND MEDITATIVE VERSE

SATIRE, PARODY, HUMOUR, IRONY

LOVE AND SEXUALITY

MORAL AND DIDACTIVE VERSE

INDEX OF FIRST LINES

INDEX OF TITLES